TIME LONGER THAN ROPE

The West Indian slave, anticipating Einstein's transfusion of the categories, made a proverb: "Time longer dan Rope." That might well be taken as the motto of Africanism.

Lord Olivier, in THE ANATOMY OF AFRICAN MISERY

TIME LONGER THAN ROPE

*A History of the Black Man's
Struggle for Freedom in South Africa*

EDWARD ROUX

THE UNIVERSITY OF WISCONSIN PRESS

Published 1948, 1964

The University of Wisconsin Press
Box 1379, Madison, Wisconsin 53701
The University of Wisconsin Press, Ltd.
70 Great Russell Street, London

Second edition printings 1964, 1967, 1972, 1978
(First edition 1948 by Gollancz)

Printed in the United States of America

ISBN 0-299-03204-3; LC 64-12728

FOREWORD

THERE CAN BE FEW historians of Africa or friends of the South African people who will not welcome the reappearance of Professor Edward Roux's *Time Longer Than Rope*. It deserves its place in the historiography of South Africa as a pioneer history of non-white political activity, and it was first written in an era when South African history was still universally understood to be the history of the white minority. But Roux's account is less than a balanced history of South Africa in the twentieth century, and more than a political memoir, though it covers the period of the author's own political activity.

As a work of history it is *sui generis*. The middle section of the work is partly a political memoir, even though the author often refers to himself in the third person and tries to subordinate his own role to the central theme. There is, indeed, a double thread. One strand is the account of the rise and fall of Clements Kadilie and the Industrial and Commercial Workers' Union, the most significant non-white protest movement until the re-emergence of the African National Congress after the Second World War. The second strand is the personal account of an individual white South African who participated in a succession of political movements.

His personal course of action is one example of the political alternatives open to these members of the inter-war generation with a sense of the injustice around them. No one set of responses could be called typical, and Roux's was certainly not. He began atypically as the son of a "mixed" marriage between an Afrikaner and an English nurse at the time of the Anglo-Boer War, when such marriages were rare. In the course of his political career he marched with the Citizens' Comandos in the "Rand Revolution" of 1922, passed on into active participation in the Communist Party of South Africa, then to adult education, and finally, disillusioned both with the Communists and with some African political leaders, back to his early interest in science. (He has recently been appointed Professor of Botany at the University of the Witwatersrand.)

The core of the book is thus a detailed, and often first-hand, account of the inter-war generation in African politics.

The remainder is a document of quite a different kind. It is, in fact, two historical essays—one on the period before Roux's active participation and one on the years that followed his withdrawal in the later 1930's. These sections derive their continuing interest from the point of view of the author. They do not claim to represent new historical research, but they are full of judgments about Roux's predecessors and successors. These judgments are sometimes harsh, often original, and always enlightening. In one sense, they are the judgments of a man who tried and failed in his own generation to deflect South Africa from its obvious course toward social fragmentation. As he examines those who came before and those who followed, he may not find human failure in precisely those quarters the historians of the future will choose; but future historians will want to take advantage of his insights. These insights are not those of an impartial historian, standing on the sidelines. They are, rather, those of a man who was himself a player during an important part of the game. We are thus given the views of the once-committed man, who can see history from an unusual perspective.

PHILIP D. CURTIN

PREFACE TO
THE SECOND EDITION

THE WRITING OF THIS book was begun in 1935 and the first edition was published in 1948. At that time there were a number of standard books on the history of South Africa but no single work dealing with the political history of the indigenous peoples, the organisations they had built and the individuals who had led them. Much of this history was in fact very recent and its significance was not generally appreciated. A new school of South African historians, led by W. M. Macmillan (*The Cape Colour Question*, 1927; *Bantu, Boer and Britain*, 1929), had in fact begun a reinvestigation of the historic background of the country's racial problems, but these writers were more concerned to correct the distortions of the past, particularly those of the early nineteenth century, than to write in any detail about more recent events. J. S. Marais, in *The Cape Coloured People, 1652–1937* (1939) had included a chapter on "Latter-day Phases," but his book dealt only with a minority group of South Africa's non-Europeans.

I therefore felt the urge to write a book, a book which in the first place was needed by the Africans themselves. In 1935 I was engaged, as a full-time "activist" in the Communist Party, in propaganda work among Africans. I was concerned, among other things, in teaching and in the organisation of night-schools, where we tried to make African workers literate and provide them at the same time with the elements of political education. Essential background would be some knowledge of their own history. My first essays in this direction were a number of lessons in simple language, often mimeographed and sometimes published as articles in the communist newspaper I was then editing. These elementary "lessons" were subsequently elaborated into more sophisticated articles which were published in the magazine *Trek* in the early 1940's, and these in turn, with additional material, finally formed the basis of the first edition of *Time Longer Than Rope*.

The volume necessarily contained materials derived from many different sources and having very different values as historical writing. Parts I would describe as history at third-hand. This comprised material lifted 'bodily or condensed from the writings of South African historians. Most of the first six chapters, for instance, were based on the standard histories of Theal and Cory.

Second-hand history I regard as writings based on "original sources," such as files of old newspapers, letters, reports and other documents. History of this type involves research and is the proper field of the academic historian. Parts of this book embody material of this sort. I give some examples. For the chapter on "Jabavu and the Cape Liberals" I spent many hours working through the file of *Imvo Zabantsundu*, the only extant copy of which is to be found in the South African Public Library at Cape Town. For the chapter on "The Black Joan of Arc" I found interesting material in the *Grahamstown Journal* and *The King Williams Town Gazette* for the years 1856–57. Some significant facts about Makana, the prophet, were found in Kropf's *Kafir-English Dictionary*.

Most of the later chapters however, were based on my own first-hand experience of the events described, and this has given a personal and perhaps not altogether unprejudiced flavour to certain sections. It has also introduced a rather disconcerting element from the point of view of the academic historian, who is quite prepared to consult a written history or a historical autobiography but not something which is a mixture of the two. For one thing he would like to know at any particular point in the story whether the writer is record-ing straight history or personal reminiscence. It has therefore been suggested that in my introduction to this second edition I should supply some autobiographical details with this end in view.

I was born in the Transvaal in 1903. My father belonged to the group of South African colonials descended from the original Dutch and French-Huguenot settlers and known to-day as Afrikaners. He was educated in English at a Cape provincial school and served an apprenticeship under a Scottish apothecary in a small village in the Eastern Province. He became a free-thinker and subsequently married an army nurse who had come to South Africa from England. He was thus an atypical Afrikaner, differing markedly in outlook from other members of his family. Round about 1910 he was converted to Marxist socialism (of the Daniel de Leon school) by some Australian immigrants who opened a cobbler's shop next to his pharmacy in a Johannesburg suburb.

To these fortuitous circumstances I owe my early interest in the socialist movement and the fact that I was one of a group of young people who founded a communist youth organisation in 1921. In the decade 1912–1922 the Witwatersrand was a labour cockpit where white capital and white labour quarreled over the division of profits largely obtained from black labour. A series of clashes culminated in the "Red Revolt" of 1922. These events which went on in my home town and district fascinated me, as did also the great Russian Revolution of 1917, which proved to me quite clearly that communism was the hope of mankind.

In 1923 I joined the Communist Party. There I came under the influence of Sidney Bunting who at that time was trying to persuade an almost exclusively white party that its main task was to organise the non-whites for revolution. In 1924 while still a student at the university (where I was studying biology) I became honorary secretary of the Communist Party. My first contacts with Africans (on a political level) were made with Dunjwa and Letanka, of the African National Congress (A.N.C.). In 1924 I was associated with two young Africans, Thomas Mbeki and Stanley Silwana, who started a Johannesburg branch of the big African union, the I.C.U. I first met its leader, Clements Kadalie, in 1925.

During the years 1926–29 I was at Cambridge doing research in plant physiology, supported by an 1851 Exhibition Scholarship. During this period I served from time to time on the "Colonial Committee" of the British Communist Party and in the summer of 1928 attended the Sixth Congress of the Communist International in Moscow as a South African delegate. I met Kadalie at an Independent Labour Party summer school in 1927. This was subsequent to the expulsion of the communists from the I.C.U., which had occurred in December 1926.

Back in South Africa towards the end of 1929 I resumed my work in the C.P.S.A. There was some talk of my becoming paid-secretary of the newly-formed Non-European Trade Union Federation in Johannesburg, but this did not happen and I accepted employment in the Government Low Temperature Research Laboratory at Cape Town. My experience as a civil servant did not last long. After three months I was dismissed for "engaging in politics." I had been the only white man to march in an A.N.C. demonstration on the Grand Parade.

In Cape Town, facilities for printing the communist newspaper seemed better than in Johannesburg. Also I liked the place. I persuaded Bunting to allow transfer of the paper to Cape Town and for a year I published it there. I was editor, printer, cartoonist and street salesman rolled into one, and I really enjoyed myself. During this year I met Lancelot Hogben then Professor of Zoology in Cape Town, and his wife Enid, who between them provided help in more ways than one. Contacts with non-whites, both Coloured and African, were numerous. Association was particularly close with B. Ndobe and E. Tonjeni, leaders of the African National Congress in the Western Cape. I also met and got to know Dr. A. Abdurahman, founder of the Coloured organisation, the A.P.O.

In 1931 leadership of the C.P. was taken over largely by Douglas Wolton who had been to Moscow and was charged with carrying through the "new line." It was found that I had committed a number of deviations during the previous year and it was considered that the party organ should be directly under the control of the Political Bureau in Johannesburg.

My membership of the C.P. continued until 1936. Most of 1931 was spent in Durban where I had my first term of imprisonment. While in Natal I got to know A. W. Champion of the I.C.U. *yase* Natal and John Dube of the A.N.C. My relation with these two men was of interest in revealing traits not uncommon among African leaders. Champion was publicly a non-communist: it was he who had moved the resolution which had expelled the communists from the I.C.U. in 1926. Dube's section of the A.N.C. had received the Government's blessing as "not coupled with the activities of communist agitators." I was surprised therefore when Dube came to see me and asked me to coach a class of boys at his school at Inanda, who were studying for the Junior Certificate Examination. This I willingly did. I agreed also to write articles for his newspaper *Ilanga lase Natal*. These, of course, were published anonymously.

In 1935 Josiah Ngedlane and I were charged jointly with

X

the crime of *lese majeste* for publishing an article in the communist newspaper urging Africans to boycott the (segregated) celebrations of King George V's silver jubilee. The article in question, written by me, had been translated into Zulu by Champion at my request. Champion had added pepper and salt: the translation was much "hotter" than the original. Dube is now dead, Champion a very old man. I hope this revelation will not be held against him in his old age. In any case our modern Afrikaner Nationalists should not object to anti–monarchial sentiments now that we are a republic.

I left the Communist Party in 1936 for reasons which anyone who has read my book *S. P. Bunting–A Political Biography* will understand. The control exercised by the Communist International over its South African section had produced a situation which I and a number of others began to find intolerable. We had looked to Moscow for inspiration, for guidance and for material assistance. The inspiration might have stood the test of the Stalin–Trotskyist quarrel, but as the purges continued and as one admired leader after another made his confession of "anti–revolutionary activity" before being "physically liquidated," one's faith diminished. These overseas heroes, Trotsky, Bucharin, Zinoviev, Radek and the like, were not known to us personally. But when Bunting in turn was described as an "imperialist bloodsucker" and expelled from the party one gained a new idea of the meaning of the "campaign against the Right danger."

But so wedded was I to the party that even Bunting's expulsion did not cause me immediately to leave. What finally made me decide was the Seventh Congress of the Communist International which swung as far to the Right as the Sixth Congress had swung to the Left. And still they would not reinstate Bunting who, strangely enough, was still willing to come back.

I returned to Cape Town in 1936 and also to my profession as a botanist. I got work eventually at the local university doing research on fruit storage problems. When the war came I was offered a commission in a department of the army concerned with food supplies and nutrition. I had been a pacifist during the First World War and had suffered at school as a non–cadet. I could not imagine myself walking about in uniform behind the lines. I took a job in a fish oil factory in the Cape Town Docks and helped to produce vitamins which were in short supply throughout the world. I was asked by the Government, who realised that I had some influence with Africans, to help in recruiting volunteers for the army. They were to be employed as stretcher–bearers and labourers and were not to carry arms. I replied that if the Government would abolish the pass laws I would think about it.

At the end of the war Professor John Phillips asked me to come and help run a course in soil conservation for ex–servicemen which he had started at the University of the Witwatersrand. Thus I returned to my old college and have been there ever since.

Since leaving the Communist Party I have tried not to fall over backwards, as so many one–time communists have done. I have continued to be interested in Leftist movements and retained personal contact with many old friends who remained communists.

If I were asked if I were still a communist and a Marxist I would say "no." Marx, I believe, has contributed largely to our understanding of society. Marxism goes wrong, I think, when it ceases to be an empirical study and becomes a dogmatic creed. But this is not the place to elaborate these views in detail. In South Africa the communists did pioneer work in organising the oppressed people at a time when members of other creeds and parties were not interested, and history will remember them for this.

However, I have not been allowed to forget my former membership of the Communist Party. When the party was banned in 1950 I was placed on the list of "named" persons. This did not affect me at first in any practical way except that it is probably the reason why I have been consistently refused a passport to travel overseas. However in 1963 a further restriction was imposed by a ministerial edict prohibiting "named" persons from belonging to any organisation which discusses or criticises any form of state or any policy of any state. This has made it necessary for me to leave the Liberal Party which I joined in 1957. I have fortunately not been subjected to any of the other restrictions, such as house arrest, which so many ex-communists, and liberals too, must now endure. This is probably a reflection on the poor quality of any political activity which I am still able or willing to undertake.

The reader will learn from the concluding paragraph of

Chapter I that the three terms Bantu, Native and African are used in this book to refer to the same people. To-day the only term acceptable to the more sophisticated members of the group concerned is "African." However this usage developed slowly, and gradually became more common. This is indicated in this book, the writer himself gradually employing the term "African" more and more frequently. In Part II the word "African" is used exclusively except where the sense would be destroyed. The old word "Native" is retained for Native Affairs Department because that was its official title until it became the Bantu Affairs Department. Similarly "Native Reserves" is used for the areas subsequently called by the authorities the "Bantu homelands." The organisation which Africans first formed to embody their political aspirations was called by them quite innocently the "Native National Congress." Only later did they change its name to "African National Congress." Similarly the communists themselves, who to-day would never think of using any term but "African," between 1927 and 1936 advocated a "Native Republic," again without any idea that the term "Native" might prove offensive.

Finally, I insist, in spite of the criticism by African nationalists, that there are occasions when accuracy demands the use of "Bantu." This is the only available word to distinguish the Bantu-speaking group of Africans from the Negroes of West Africa and the Sudan, and from the Hottentots, Bushmen and other groups.

My first chapter, "The Coming of the Bantu" would not make sense if it were called "The Coming of the Africans," for there were Africans (Hottentots and Bushmen) in South Africa long before the Bantu arrived here.

I am most grateful to the University of Wisconsin Press, which has undertaken the publication of a second edition of this book. Thanks are due in particular to my colleague and friend, Julius Lewin, who for many years has been actively seeking a possible publisher. It was he who introduced me to Professor Philip Curtin, of the University of Wisconsin, who very kindly consented to write a foreword to this second edition. I have left it to Professor Curtin to point out why the additional chapters (XXIX to XXXVI), which have been added to bring the book up to date, lack so much that was present in the earlier chapters, and why it was nevertheless found necessary to include them. Professor Jeffrey Butler, African Studies Program, Boston University, has offered valuable criticisms and suggestions, many of which have been adopted in the second edition. His help is gladly acknowledged.

In the Preface to the First Edition I offered thanks to many unnamed friends of all races who helped me to write the book and to my wife who acted as general editor and critic. She has again proved most helpful, as has Mr. Julius Lewin, in preparing this second edition.

EDWARD ROUX

JOHANNESBURG
FEBRUARY 1963

NOTE ON THE SPELLING AND
PRONUNCIATION OF BANTU NAMES

THOUGH A STANDARD ORTHOGRAPHY covering most of the Bantu languages has been evolved in recent years, it has not yet received universal recognition. Most of the popular Bantu newspapers adhere to the old orthographies, while Bantu personal and place names tend to keep their original spelling.

In the Bantu languages plurals and most other derivatives are formed by the addition of prefixes. Thus we speak of the *Bechuana* (people), a *Mochuana* (individual), *Sechuana* (language). *Chuana* in the new orthography is written *Tswana*. French missionaries were responsible for reducing the southern Suto language to writing. They did not use the semi-vowel *w*. Northern Suto, on the other hand, uses *w*. Thus the southern Suto *oa* and *oe* are spelt *wa* and *we* in northern Suto. *Suto* itself may also be written *Sutu* or *Sotho*. The English sound *th*, as in *the* or *thing*, does not occur in Bantu languages. *Batho* (= people in Suto) is pronounced *batoo*, the *h* indicating that the preceding consonant is strongly aspirated. The ordinary *r* sound is absent in Xhosa and Zulu, the letter *r* being used instead to represent the uvular *ch*, as in the Scottish *loch*. The name *Radebe* is pronounced *cha-déh-beh*.

The click sounds which abound in Zulu and Xhosa, written as *c*, *x*, or *q*, are of three different kinds, all extremely formidable to the European. Failing the correct sounds, an approximation is achieved by rendering them all as *k*.

To discuss even broadly these problems of pronunciation and spelling would require a lengthy chapter. As a rough guide to the reader the following examples are given to show the approximate pronunciation of some Bantu names used in this book. It should be noted that the syllables are all open—that is, the consonants all occur at the beginning of the syllables and should be pronounced in that way, for example *Sandile* is pronounced *Sah-ndeé-leh:* the *a* long as in *father*, the *e* as in *met*.

ZULU-XHOSA

Msilikazi (msee-lee-káh-zee)
Dube (dóo-beh)
Seme (séh-meh)
Xhosa (kó-sah)
Thema (téh-mah)
Ngcayiya (nkah-yée-yah)
Nongqause (no-nkah-óo-seh)
Gumede (goo-méh-deh)
Cetiwe (keh-tée-weh)
Tyamzashe (Chah-mzáh-sheh)
Ndlambe (ndláh-mbeh)
Gaika (gah-ée-kah)

SUTO-CHUANA

Mote (móo-teh)
Moshoeshoe (moo-shwéh-shweh)
Thaele (tah-eé-leh)
Mochochonono (moo-shó-sho-nó-noo)
Maphutseng (mah-poo-tséng)
Moroe (móo-rweh)

CONTENTS

TIME LONGER THAN ROPE

CHAPTER I

THE COMING OF THE BANTU

When Vasco da Gama came to the Cape in 1497, he found the southern continent thinly populated by little brown-skinned peoples, the Hottentots and the Bushmen, who led a primitive, nomadic life, wandering ever to fresh hunting grounds. As the Portuguese sailed north along the coast seeking the route to India, it was not until they came to Delagoa Bay that they saw the first black men and heard from them stories of a great black kingdom in the heart of the land, the Kingdom of Monomatapa. This was the first encounter of the forerunners of the two races, European and Bantu, who were in the future to overrun the land of the little brown-skinned men.

Of this Kingdom of Monomatapa little is known. It is generally agreed that the capital was at Zimbabwe. But it was not until the nineteenth century, when Zimbabwe lay in ruins, that any white man ever set foot there. These enormous ruins of stone buildings were attributed variously to King Solomon, to the Phœnicians, or people from southern India. But the careful investigations of Miss Caton-Thompson have shown beyond all reasonable doubt that the Zimbabwe culture, which left ruins, not only at Zimbabwe, but over a wide area in what are now Southern Rhodesia and the northern Transvaal, was still extant at the beginning of the eighteenth century and that Zimbabwe itself was built not more than 800 years ago, and possibly very much later. What caused the decay of the might of Monomatapa? There are no written records and the piled stones of Zimbabwe keep their secret. For the collapse of this incipient civilisation various causes have been suggested: civil wars, trypanosomiasis (sleeping sickness, spread by the tsetse fly) and soil erosion.

The results of Miss Caton-Thompson's researches are of more than academic interest, for they show that the black men did attempt to build a civilisation in tropical Africa.

If we follow Toynbee in believing that civilisations arise in response to challenges, then the challenge in this case was provided by the tropical environment with its forests and diseases. The Zimbabwe people defeated the forest by burning or cutting it down and by building their stockades and fortifications in stone. But this destruction of the vegetation, which was perhaps the chief factor leading to the development of a grander and more permanent agriculture, and which may have helped to reduce the incidence of insect-borne diseases, was to prove in the end a curse rather than a blessing. For there is evidence that there was serious soil erosion in ancient times about the sites now marked by ruins. The potential civilisation of Zimbabwe perished in its infancy.

Whether the Bantu would have developed beyond tribalism in the healthier environment of South Africa is an interesting speculation. This change would in any event have taken hundreds of years. But the invasion of South Africa by Europeans from the south-west, coinciding as it did with the Bantu invasion from the north-east, ruled out such a development.

The Bantu came in from the north-east. Who are the Bantu and whence did they come? They form part of the great Negro or Black Race. But it is clear that they are not of pure Negro stock. Among them we see often individuals with distinctly aquiline features, the curved nose, characteristic of many of the peoples of northern Africa and southern Europe. Another non-Negro trait which is also fairly common among them is the so-called mongoloid type of features, with high cheek bones. But this latter is almost certainly the result of later admixture with the aboriginal Hottentots and Bushmen, those little brown peoples whom the Bantu conquered, absorbed or annihilated in the course of their long journey south.

Their culture, too, bears evidence of their mixed origin. Their agriculture, based on the use of the iron hoe, was probably inherited from their Negro ancestors, their cattle-herding from their Hamitic or Semitic forbears. What most probably happened was that a cattle-herding nomadic race of "dark-white" type conquered a Negro agricultural people and from the fusion of these two cultural and racial elements the Bantu race and culture were born. It is perhaps significant that Bantu tribal tradition and taboo exclude women from

4

having anything to do with cattle, while men are forbidden to take part in cultivation.*

The term Bantu (from *abantu* = the people) refers to the languages spoken, and to-day includes most of the dark-skinned peoples in Africa living south of a line drawn roughly from the Gulf of Guinea to the east coast just north of Mombasa.

From all the evidence we may conclude that the Bantu peoples and languages came into existence some thousands of years ago among peoples living in Africa north of the equator. The Bantu then are a Negroid-Hamitic race who moved gradually south, spreading southwards and eastwards, occupying the land and encountering little serious resistance from the more primitive Hottentots and Bushmen, finally halted in their conquests only by the Europeans who were moving northwards into the continent.

This great Bantu movement must have begun over a thousand years ago. But it was gradual. It was not until about 1600 that black men were reported as far south as Port Natal. The Dutch made their settlement at Cape Town in 1652. By 1750 the first outposts of white trekkers moving eastwards had come into contact with the Bantu advance guard near where Port Elizabeth now is.

Of this southward movement of the Bantu, of their gradual spread over most of the centre and south of the African continent, history can tell us little. Even at the beginning of the nineteenth century Africa was still the Dark Continent. Archæology has told us much of the Stone Age in southern Africa and new discoveries are still being reported. But these discoveries refer to the earlier inhabitants of the sub-continent, to the Bushmen and to others before them. Except for the discoveries at Zimbabwe, very little is known of the history of the Bantu prior to their first contacts with Europeans. This is not surprising. A semi-nomadic people inhabiting a tropical or sub-tropical country, who had not learned the art of writing, whose buildings were for the most part made of thatch and mud, could not be expected to leave much to interest the archæologist. It is known that the Bantu learned how to

* This prohibition applies to the main agricultural crop, millet or, latterly, maize. Men are, however, allowed to grow certain vegetables. It is likely that these less important crops were introduced later and so escaped the taboo. The introduction of the plough, pulled by oxen, has given the men a place in agriculture. A very good thing!

make iron at quite an early stage in their history. Their arms were the stabbing spear, the throwing spear, the ox-hide shield. They were organised in tribes with hereditary chiefs. Tribes tended to split up after they reached a certain size.

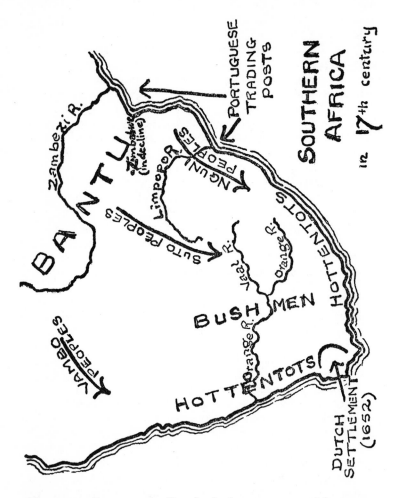

The new tribes moved off, colonised new areas and in course of time developed new languages. And so the process continued until the Bantu shields and assegais, wielded by warriors of ferocious courage, met their inevitable defeat by the guns of the white men. So to-day the grandchildren of these warriors, still of magnificent physique, are police "boys" and mine "boys," factory hands and house servants.

Of South Africa's population, now (1963) numbering 16 million people, only slightly over 3 million are white. About one million are Coloured persons of mixed blood, including the descendents of the Hottentots. There are nearly half a million Indians, mainly in Natal. Nearly 11 million are Africans (Bantu), fairly evenly distributed, except in the western part of the Cape Province, where the population is mainly Coloured people, descended from the aboriginal Hottentots and from imported Javanese (Malay) and Negro slaves, all mixed in varying degrees with European (white) blood. Having never penetrated here before the arrival of the Whites, many thousands of Africans have, since the 1920's, come to the western Cape. In recent years the government has discouraged further African immigration to this area and intends eventually to remove these people entirely from the Western Province.

From the language point of view the Bantu people of South Africa are divided into two main groups. Along the eastern coast and eastward of the main mountain ranges we have the Nguni peoples, originally perhaps a single tribe but now broken up into Swazis, Zulus, Chopis, Mpondos, Xhosas, Fingoes and others. The two main languages of this group are Zulu and Xhosa, the former spoken in Natal, the latter in the Cape Province. The two languages are very similar, Zulus and Xhosas having little difficulty in understanding each other.

The other main group of Bantu peoples is found on the inland plateau region. They too are presumably descended from a single group which differentiated from the Nguni group a long time ago, probably in Central Africa. These high-veld peoples include the Suto, Pedi, Venda and Tswana tribes. The chief languages are Southern Suto (spoken in Basutoland), Northern or Transvaal Suto (Pedi) and Tswana, the last found in and near Bechuanaland and also in certain parts of the Orange Free State. The differences between these various Suto-like languages are somewhat more marked than those between the different Nguni languages. Nevertheless, differentiation has not proceeded so far as to make it impossible for a Suto to understand a Tswana and vice versa. On the other hand, a Suto would probably find Zulu or

Xhosa as difficult as a modern Englishman finds German or Dutch.

There is as yet no very satisfactory designation for these dark-skinned, negroid, tribalistic people. The term "Negro' has seldom been used, nor would it be accurate. "Bantu" is scientifically adequate to describe the languages spoken and possibly most of the people who speak them, but the word smacks somewhat of the academic. "African" is the term preferred by the better educated of these people, especially as contrasted with "European." (Everywhere in South Africa one sees notices, "Europeans only.") But the word "African" becomes almost meaningless when translated into South African Dutch, for the Boer to-day calls himself an "Afrikaner" and his language "Afrikaans." The phrase "South African" almost always implies "white South African." "Kafir," from the Arabic, meaning "heathen" or "unbeliever," was used originally for the Xhosas, the most westerly tribe and thus the first to make contact with Europeans. To-day it is used by many Afrikaners for all negroid South Africans, who in turn regard it as a term of contempt and do not apply it to themselves. Nor do any sympathetic whites ever use it to-day. "Native" has obvious shortcomings, especially when one realises that most of the two million whites were born in the country and that the Hottentots and the Bushmen (of whom a few hundred are still living in a remote part of British Bechuanaland north of the Orange River) have an even stronger claim than the Bantu to be considered natives. In this book all three terms: Bantu, African and Native (spelt with a capital) will be used to refer to the same people.

CHAPTER II

MAKANA THE PROPHET

THE FIRST SPORADIC CONTACTS between the Bantu and the European colonists occurred about the middle of the eighteenth century in the neighbourhood of Sundays River. They were simply encounters between the advanced patrols of both sides. In 1770 the Gamtoos River had, by official proclamation of the Dutch Governor at Cape Town, been declared the eastern boundary of the Cape, and at this time there were almost certainly no permanent Bantu settlements west of the Fish River. Some of the country between the Gamtoos and the Fish Rivers was sparsely populated by Hottentots.

In 1780 Governor van Plettenberg advanced the boundary to the Fish River. Certain Bantu chiefs of the Xhosa tribes had agreed to recognise the Fish River as the boundary between the two peoples. But within the year the agreement was broken. The Xhosas raided across the river into the eastern district of the Cape, penetrating as far as the Bushman's River. They were driven back by a Boer commando led by Adriaan van Jaarsveld. Returning to the attack, the Xhosas continued to raid the white men's cattle. They infiltrated into the Suurveld, the area lying directly west of the Fish River. During the next twelve years clashes along the frontier were frequent, taking the form of raids and counter-raids. Both Xhosas and Boers were in the main semi-nomadic cattle-herders, and the chief object of the raids was the capture and recapture of cattle. It was only when raiding became general that the conflicts became known as wars.

In the Second Kafir War, in 1793, the Xhosas penetrated into the Colony as far as the Swartkops River. Commandos drove them back and followed them across the Fish River, but retired, having failed to make effective contact with the enemy. Again the Xhosas, led by their chiefs, Cungwa and Ndlambe, returned to the Suurveld. The Third Kafir War, 1803, failed to dislodge them from this position, but in 1811, in the Fourth Kafir War, they were finally driven back across the Fish River. Forts were built along the frontier, the chief of these being at Grahamstown which soon became an important white settlement.

It should be mentioned that the Cape had ceased to be a Dutch possession in 1806, when it was occupied by British forces. This made little difference to the relations between Xhosas and Boers except that to an increasing extent British regular troops came in to aid the commandos in the various frontier wars.

The Fifth Kafir War, 1818-19, is of particular interest because in this war we are able to discern issues and problems of significance for the Bantu as a whole.

In this war the leading figure was that of Makana. The story of his life provides plenty of material for the study of

9

the impact of an expanding civilisation upon the barbarian peoples on its borders. Of such impacts Arnold Toynbee, in his *Study of History*, has written, using examples from such scattered times and places as Europe during the decline of the Roman Empire, the Balkans in the Middle Ages, and the United States in the eighteenth and nineteenth centuries. He pictures two sorts of relation between a civilisation and the barbarians on its borders. In the early vital phase of a civilisation, when it is growing spiritually, it exercises an attraction for the uncivilised. Not only does it attract but also it can assimilate them, and such assimilation is not necessarily by the sword. In this way, for instance, Italy was assimilated by the Hellenic civilisation. In the decline of a civilisation, however, though it may continue to expand technically and territorially, its culture creates among the barbarians a certain feeling of repugnance. They, though they cannot help being influenced in many ways, both ideologically and materially, yet refuse to accept in unaltered form the ideas of the ruling minority in such a civilisation. Thus the Nordic barbarians beyond the Roman frontier developed their own "barbaric pantheon" of gods, in the likeness of a war-lord and his band. At the same time the internal proletariat of the Roman Empire reacted to oppression by passive resistance and by becoming converts of the new non-Hellenic universal religion of Christianity.

An external proletariat, says Toynbee, may react to the impact of a decaying civilisation in either a violent or a gentle manner. A gentle reaction is usually led by a "prophet," a violent reaction by the leader of a war-band. Sometimes a prophet throws off the robe of gentleness and takes to the sword. The North American Indians, in their reaction to the European advance, produced leaders of both gentle and violent types, and some who tried first one method and then the other. But the movement of the frontier of Western civilisation across the North American continent from Atlantic to Pacific was too rapid to provide more than a few ephemeral instances of such reactions on the part of the Red Indians.

In South Africa, too, the advancing frontier moved fast. The First Kafir War was in 1779, the last in 1879. A century after the first clash west of the Fish River the Europeans had by-passed the Transkeian frontier, conquered the Suto, Pedi and Zulu tribes, and penetrated into southern Natal. In 1894 Rhodes annexed to the Cape the last independent Native territory, Pondoland. The Bambata Rebellion* in Natal, in 1905-6, was possibly the last of the tribal wars, and as such it was an attempt to re-establish the frontier. But it could probably be more accurately described as an unsuccessful revolt by a section of an internal proletariat, though Bambata himself was more of a Vercingetorix than a Spartacus.

In this brief 100 years during which the Bantu were being driven back and overwhelmed by the Europeans, they produced in their resentment at least two movements of the kind instanced by Toynbee. The first, led by the prophet Makana, combined both gentle and violent aspects. The second, inspired by a girl, Nongqause, was gentle only.

Of Makana's birth and childhood nothing is known. It is probable that he was born in Xhosa country in the 1780's. His people, the Xhosas, called him by his nickname of Nxele, the Left-handed, which the Boers translated as "Links" and the English subsequently corrupted to "Lynx." As a young man he is said to have visited the Rev. van der Kemp's mission station at Swartkops, to have argued with him about Christianity and to have gone away unconvinced. Another story has it that he was present when van der Kemp preached a sermon on the Resurrection, and that he was so much impressed that thereafter he persuaded the Xhosas to bury their dead and not to leave their bodies to be eaten by jackals. But in A. D. Martin's biography of Johan van der Kemp there is no mention of Makana. If indeed Makana did meet the missionary, it is unlikely that it was at Swartkops, which was a mission station for Hottentots near the Port Elizabeth of to-day. Such a meeting might have occurred in Xhosa country, for van der Kemp tried first to establish a mission station among the Xhosas before, finding this too difficult, he retreated to Swartkops. According to Thomas Pringle, Makana, before 1818, frequently visited Grahamstown, where he delighted to converse with van der Lingen, the Army chaplain, about religious problems.

In any case it is clear that Makana knew of the Christian religion not merely at second hand, and that he reacted to it in his own way. Xhosa tradition still preserves the knowledge of Makana's barbaric pantheon. According to Kropf,[1] Makana's god was Dalidipu, the god of the black people, who was greatly superior to Tixo, the god of the white people.

* Bambata Rebellion. See Chapter IX.

Tixo was only an *inkosana* (small chief). Dalidipu's wife had very long, pendent breasts; she resided in the reservoir of heaven and bestowed rain at pleasure on the earth; when she turned her face away from men, no rain fell.

Nxele taught that Dalidipu did not reckon fornication and adultery as sins and that he allowed polygamy; that the Xhosas had no sins except for witchcraft, but the white men had many and great sins. Nxele taught also that Dalidipu would punish Tixo and his worshippers, and that he himself was Dalidipu's agent to destroy all Europeans, the enemies of Dalidipu, and to bring back to life all Africans who had died, as well as slaughtered cattle.

It is significant that the Bantu people in general have produced no organised pantheon such as Makana attempted to create for them. It required the impact of a civilisation across a frontier to produce a prophet and a galaxy of gods. The defeat of Makana himself and his premature death and the fact that the Xhosas were converted in so short a time from an external into an internal proletariat caused the complete eclipse of the new gods. Incidentally, we may note how much more attractive Makana's religion must have appeared to tribal Africans than the coldly puritanical Christianity of the missionaries with its virgin goddess and the missionaries' prohibition of the "sin" of buying wives.

As a prophet Makana gained great influence; but he had political as well as religious ambitions; or, rather, his general aims could not be achieved, he believed, except by political action. As a commoner he could not aspire to a chieftainship since Bantu tribal tradition insists strongly that chiefs must be of royal blood. Makana therefore sought a chief with whom he could ally himself and who would share his aims.

At this time Hintsa was the nominal paramount chief of the Xhosas. But he lived far away beyond the Kei River. He had little authority over the clans to the west, and these, under their different chiefs, were often quarrelling among themselves. The two leading figures in these disputes were Ndlambe and Gaika (Ngqika). Ndlambe had a long record as a frontier fighter and as an unyielding enemy of the white colonists.[2] His younger rival, Gaika, was what would nowadays be known as a "good boy" chief. He was prepared to ally himself with the colonists in return for favours. The historian, Theal, has a low opinion of Gaika's mentality. That chief was too much preoccupied with "drink and women" and in any case quite unfitted to appreciate or understand Makana's political ideals.

It was inevitable, therefore, that Makana should go into partnership with Ndlambe; and the two of them set out to achieve the first step in Makana's programme, the unification of the western Xhosas under the leadership of Ndlambe. This meant that they had first to defeat Gaika. Makana became a sort of prime minister, bishop and field-marshal all in one, at the same time maintaining his role as prophet of the new religion.

The different roles of prophet and leader of a war-band may be fundamentally incompatible, but Makana, like others before him, attempted to combine them. History gives us no record of his mental evolution and we do not know at what stage he finally decided to throw off the robe of gentleness and take up the sword. But the decision once taken he acted vigorously and to good purpose. At the Battle of Amalinde Gaika's forces were put to rout by the army of Ndlambe and Makana.

But Gaika, having escaped to the Winterberg Mountains, sent urgent messages to the Colony pleading for help. The question whether the whites or the blacks started a particular Kafir war is usually a moot point, but in this case, the war of 1818, there is no doubt that the whites were the aggressors. In December of that year white troops crossed the Fish River, the "legal boundary" of the Colony. They were joined by some of Gaika's followers and Makana and Ndlambe were forced to retreat to the forests. After burning down all the huts they found and capturing some 23,000 cattle, the colonists retired, though first they shared the cattle equally between themselves and Gaika.

But without continued white support Gaika could not hold his own. When Ndlambe and Makana attacked him once more, he was hopelessly defeated. "Following the tracks of their cattle," as they said, the Xhosas then crossed the Fish River and carried the war into the Colony. Makana's army advanced in the spirit of a crusade. They sang that they came:

> "To chase the white men from the earth
> And drive them to the sea.
> The sea that cast them up at first
> For AmaXhosa's curse and bane
> Howls for the progeny she nursed
> To swallow them again."[3]

In the early morning of April 23, 1819, 10,000 warriors, led by Makana, made an attack on Grahamstown. But the white troops were in a camp surrounded by a stockade, and cannon were mounted at the corners. Makana's spearmen were mown down by grapeshot and finally driven back. Thus Makana failed to take Grahamstown.

Three months later a white army crossed the Fish River and drove the Xhosas back as far as the Kei River. Many of the Africans were killed and all their remaining cattle were captured and their homes burned. But one day Makana suddenly appeared in the English camp and gave himself up. "People say that I have occasioned this war," he said. "Let me see whether delivering myself up to the conquerors will restore peace to my country."

Makana was sentenced to life imprisonment and was sent to Robben Island. Some days after his surrender a number of his *amapakati* (councillors) came to the camp of the English commander, Colonel Willshire. They came to ask that Makana should be set free and they offered themselves and other leading men as prisoners in exchange. The words of their spokesman were taken down by Captain Stockenstrom, who was present. They explain so clearly the causes of the war and the feelings of Makana's followers that they are worth recording in full.[4]

Speaking with dignity and with great feeling, the black man said: "The war, British chiefs, is an unjust one. You are striving to extirpate a people whom you forced to take up arms. When our fathers and the fathers of the Boers first settled in the Suurveld,* they dwelt together in peace. Their flocks grazed on the same hills; their herdsmen smoked together out of the same pipes; they were brothers . . . until the herds of the Xhosas increased so as to make the hearts of the Boers sore. What those covetous men could not get from our fathers for old buttons, they took by force. Our fathers were *men*; they loved their cattle; their wives and children lived upon milk; they fought for their property. They began to hate the colonists who coveted their all, and aimed at their destruction.

"Now, their kraals and our fathers' kraals were separate. The Boers made commandos on our fathers. Our fathers drove them out of the Suurveld; and we dwelt there because we had

* Suurveld—that is, west of the Fish River.

conquered it. There we were circumcised; there we married wives; and there our children were born. The white men hated us, but could not drive us away. When there was war we plundered you. When there was peace some of our bad people stole; but our chiefs forbade it. Your treacherous friend, Gaika, always had peace with you; yet, when his people stole, he shared in the plunder. Have your patrols ever found cattle taken in time of peace, runaway slaves or deserters, in the kraals of our chiefs? Have they ever gone into Gaika's country without finding such cattle, such slaves, such deserters, in Gaika's kraals? But he was your friend; and you wished to possess the Suurveld. You came at last like locusts.* We stood; we could do no more. You said, 'Go over the Fish River . . . that is all we want.' We yielded and came here.

"We lived in peace. Some of our bad people stole, perhaps; but the nation was quiet . . . the chiefs were quiet. Gaika stole . . . his chiefs stole . . . his people stole. You sent him copper; you sent him beads; you sent him horses, on which he rode to steal more. To us you sent only commandos.

"We quarrelled with Gaika about grass . . . no business of yours. You sent a commando . . . you took our last cow . . . you left only a few calves, which died for want, along with our children. You gave half of what you took to Gaika; half you kept yourselves. Without milk . . . our corn destroyed . . . we saw our wives and children perish . . . we saw that we must ourselves perish, we followed, therefore, the tracks of our cattle into the Colony. We plundered and we fought for our lives. We found you weak; we destroyed your soldiers. We saw that we were strong; we attacked your headquarters, Grahamstown: . . . and if we had succeeded, our right was good, for you began the war. We failed . . . and you are here.

"We wish for peace; we wish to rest in our huts; we wish to get milk for our children; our wives wish to till the land. But your troops cover the plains, and swarm in the thickets, where they cannot distinguish the man from the woman and shoot all.

"You want us to submit to Gaika. That man's face is fair to you, but his heart is false. Leave him to himself. Make peace with us. Let him fight for himself . . . and *we* shall not call on you for help. Set Makana at liberty; and Islambi, Dushani, Kongo and the rest will come to make peace with

* Referring to the attack in 1818.

you at any time we fix. But if you will still make war, you may indeed kill the last man of us . . . but Gaika shall not rule over the followers of those who think him a woman."

The Government, however, would not make peace, and the burning of houses and taking of cattle continued. At last the commando went back to the Colony with another 30,000 cattle taken from the starving blacks. Gaika, for whose good the war was supposed to have been fought, was forced to give up nearly 3,000 square miles of the best Xhosa land, which, a few years later, was handed over to the white farmers. He is said to have remarked to a British official, "When I look at the large piece of country which has been taken from me, I must say that, though protected, I am rather oppressed by my protectors." A missionary put it like this: "We used Gaika as long as he served us. When he failed to conquer Ndlambe we did so ourselves and then took Gaika's country."[5]

In the meantime Makana was on Robben Island. Among his fellow prisoners were a number of his own countrymen as well as slaves who had been sentenced for taking part in revolts. Among these men Makana soon became the natural leader. Within a year of his imprisonment he began to organise an escape. On Christmas Day the prisoners rose, overpowered the guards and took away their guns. Then, getting into a boat, they made for the nearest point on the coast away from Cape Town. This was Blaauwberg Beach, four miles away. They would all have escaped but for an unlucky chance. The overloaded boat, as it came into the breakers off Blaauwberg, capsized so that the men had to swim for their lives. All reached the shore except Makana, who, it was said, clung to a rock for some time, encouraging the others with his deep voice, until he was swept off and drowned.

So died one of the greatest of Bantu leaders. In Xhosaland they would not believe that he was dead. Years after his death some of his followers were still saying: "One day Makana will come back and help us again." But he did not come back and the expression "*Kukuza kukaNxele*" (It is the coming of Nxele) has now become proverbial. It means "deferred hope."

It is perhaps futile to speculate on what would have happened if Makana had not mixed soldiering with prophecy. Would he have succeeded in establishing his barbaric pantheon, thus giving the Bantu a religion of their own to oppose to Christianity? It seems extremely unlikely that the

16

Xhosa Dalidipu would have been more successful than the Nordic Wotan in opposing the advance of a religion such as Christianity. Makana's gods would probably have gone down before the shafts of the "pale Galilean" as his warriors before Colonel Willshire's grapeshot.

CHAPTER III

SLAVERY AT THE CAPE

When Jan van Riebeek and his Hollanders landed at the Cape in 1652 to form the first European settlement in South Africa, they found the country sparsely populated by a race of people who called themselves Khoi-Khoi and whom the white men called Hottentots. These people were not numerous. They led a nomadic life, wandering about in search of pasture for their flocks and herds. They knew the use of iron, though it is probable that they did not make it themselves. They lived in mud huts, were ruled by chiefs, and kept long-horned cattle and fat-tailed sheep. They did not till the ground. Their culture was higher than that of the Bushmen who still occupied some of the less hospitable regions of the interior. The Bushmen were Stone Age hunters, kept no animals except the dog and did not practise agriculture.

Both Hottentots and Bushmen had light yellow-brown or red-brown skin, also "peppercorn" hair and high cheek bones. The Bushmen were little people, even smaller than the Hottentots, the adult males averaging only five feet in height. Some authorities believe them to be a southern hybrid branch of the Congo pygmies, though the latter are black-skinned. It is believed that at one time they occupied the whole of southern Africa, and were then, during the last fifteen hundred years or so, overrun by the Hottentots in the west and by the Bantu in the centre and east.

The Hottentots offered little serious resistance to the

European invasion. Owing to their nomadic way of life, their hold on any particular piece of land was not strong. Returning to their traditional grazing grounds in due season, it would sometimes happen that they found the land had been settled by European farmers. Sometimes, however, a Hottentot chief would be given a small present in payment for the land, though it was clear that he had no manner of right to alienate the land of his people in this way. What he had consciously done, probably, was to give the white men the right to use it. That was all. Individual land tenure and the fence were new ideas to these nomadic tribesmen. Gradually the fenced-off farms spread over the country. Land of better quality was naturally the first to be taken. The Hottentots were forced either to keep their cattle on land of poor quality or to move away to places beyond the white settlements.

Though the Hottentots usually gave in without fighting, they did resist on occasion. A Hottentot War is recorded in 1657 and another in 1673. Chief Gonnema, whose people lived on the Berg River in what is now the district of Malmesbury, fought an intermittent war which lasted for ten years. It ended in the defeat of the Hottentots, who were driven into the mountains, having lost both their cattle and their land.

During the eighteenth century the Hottentots seem to have become reduced both in numbers and in wealth. Many of them had lost their cattle. They wandered about those parts of the country which were still left to them, living as best they could by collecting wild fruits and roots, and by hunting. The chief cause of their decrease in numbers was disease. The great smallpox outbreak of 1713 killed many thousands of them. Certain diseases, which in the ordinary way were not very dangerous to Europeans, became virulent when they spread among the Hottentots. Many died of measles and other such complaints.

Till the beginning of the nineteenth century there was little demand for Hottentot labour. The farmers preferred to make use of slaves from overseas. Such slaves could not run away easily because they had no knowledge of the country outside the farms on which they lived and worked. The first slaves were brought to Cape Town in 1658. These were Negroes taken from a Portuguese slave ship captured at sea. A few years later the Dutch themselves imported slaves from the coast of Guinea. Other slaves were brought from East

Africa. Malays from the Dutch East Indies were also brought in as slaves. Many of these Malays were political prisoners who had engaged in attempts to overthrow Dutch rule in the East Indies. One of the most famous of these political exiles was Sheikh Joseph, who had been a leader in the Bantamese civil war of 1682 and who was a resolute opponent of the Dutch. His tomb near the head of False Bay near Cape Town is still a place of pilgrimage for Moslems in South Africa.

Throughout the course of history it has always been difficult for chattel slaves, whether black or white, to stage a successful revolt. South African slaves were no exception in this respect. But there were a number of unsuccessful rebellions, one of which, strangely enough, was started by a white man. This was in 1808, two years after the final annexation of the Cape by Great Britain. Hooper was a young Irish labourer. At the house where he lived in Cape Town he met a man named Louis, a native of Mauritius. Louis, though a slave, was allowed to work about town, paying his master a fixed sum every month, "a custom," says Theal,[1] "not uncommon in those days." Louis was so light in colour that he was able to pass as a white man, and he was married to a free woman. Some time in 1808 Hooper and Louis made a plan for setting free the entire slave population. They planned to set up a secret organisation, get a large number of non-Europeans to join them, make themselves masters of Cape Town and declare general freedom.

The next recruit to this artless plan was a black slave named Abraham. In October, Hooper and Abraham went on horseback to a farm in the Swartland, the wheat-growing area north of Cape Town. At the farm of Pieter Louw, Hooper announced himself as a traveller and Abraham as his servant. They stayed overnight and Abraham approached the slaves, who agreed to join in the uprising.

After their return to Cape Town they were joined by another young Irishman, Michael Kelly, a sailor. On October 24 they prepared to put their plan into operation, using Louw's farm as a starting point. The four conspirators went to Louw's farm, but the two Irishmen thought better of it. They decided at the last moment to give up the idea of a rising and so they returned to Cape Town. But Louis, Abraham and a number of the slaves from the farm were resolved, in spite of the defection of the two white men, to go ahead with the plan. They took Louw's farm wagon and went on to the next farm, where they said that the chief Government officer had ordered all slaves to proceed to Cape Town to be set free, while all white men were to be made prisoners. In this way they went from farm to farm and were joined by most of the slaves. A number of white men were taken prisoner, but none was injured in any way.

Three days later they turned back towards Cape Town with a following of at most a few hundred slaves, whom they judged sufficient. The Cape Town garrison at this time numbered 5,000 soldiers! On October 27 some 326 slaves were re-captured without offering any resistance. Some of the leaders escaped, but were caught shortly afterwards, including Hooper and Kelly. Louis, Hooper, Abraham and two other leaders were hanged. Some fifty of the slaves were flogged or sentenced to imprisonment for life in chains. The others, after being forced to watch the executions, were sent back to their masters. The bodies of the hanged men were afterwards slung in chains and exposed to the public view.

There were other slave uprisings, some less bloodless from the masters' point of view than that of 1808. In 1825 slaves rose against their masters at Worcester, killed three slave-owners, and, helped by Hottentots, resisted an armed force of farmers for some days till they were forced to surrender. Two of their leaders were hanged, their heads were cut off, mounted on pikes and exhibited to the public. Others were beaten with knotted whips and then sent to prison for life.

Between 1796 and 1802, the period of the first English occupation of the Cape, more slaves were imported than ever before. In 1806, at the time of the second English occupation, there were about 30,000 slaves; the white population numbered about 26,000, and there were about 20,000 nominally free Hottentots in white employ. Besides these there were an unknown number of Hottentos and Bushmen living a free life in the wilder and more distant parts of the Colony.

After 1807, when the British Government made the slave trade illegal, any ship coming into the harbour at Cape Town with slaves on board was liable to have its slaves taken away by the ·authorities. These slaves were then supposed to be free, but, if they seemed to be unable to look after themselves or to find work, they might be indentured for not more than fourteen years to employers. In practice, those who were thus indentured were little more than slaves, and, as they could be got cheaply, there was a great demand for them among employers. The Collector of Customs was the so-called guardian of these "prize Negroes" and was responsible for giving them out to employers. This became a regular racket. The Collector of Customs, one Charles Blair, kept a large number of the Negroes for himself. The rest he turned over to a merchant, Samuel Murray, who in turn hired them out to others. Blair and Murray made a good profit out of the business. The racket was finally exposed by the action of two citizens, Launcelot Cooke and William Edwards. The occasion was as follows. One of these prize Negroes, Jean Ellé, had been hired out by Samuel Murray to Cooke, who was a good master and treated him well. But, since Ellé was a cook and thus perfectly well able to find work and to look after himself, he should never have been indentured at all. However, six months before the fourteen years' indenture was due to end, Murray died. Now the Collector of Customs decided to indenture Ellé to a friend of his who was in need of a cook. Accordingly, the Negro was ordered to leave his employment with Mr. Cooke and to report at the office of Blair. Ellé did not want to go, as he liked his master, and Cooke, who did not want to loose him, decided to take the matter to court. At this stage William Edwards, a Cape Town lawyer, comes into the story. He offered to defend the case *pro bono publico*. Feeling that they were not likely to obtain satisfaction in the local courts, Cooke and Edwards decided to appeal to the Government in London. They drew up a petition which they gave to the Governor, Lord Charles Somerset, asking him to forward it to London. But Lord Charles did not choose to send the document to London. He handed it over to the Fiscal (chief legal officer), who proceeded to prosecute Cooke and Edwards for "defaming a public servant."

The trial aroused great interest in Cape Town, as well it might. Edwards put in a list of fifty-nine witnesses to be called for the defence, but the Court refused to call them. In the course of the argument Edwards called the Fiscal a liar. He said that the Fiscal had been "guilty of a gross and detestable falsehood in not religiously adhering to the truth of the evidence before him." The trial was held up while Edwards went to prison for a month for contempt of court. When the case was resumed the irrepressible Edwards continued to conduct the defence in the same spirit. He stated that "the quiet leisure of prison, so conducive to contemplation, had enabled him to reconsider what he had stated in the court in the earlier part of the trial, and that the result of that meditation and self-communing was that he had become confirmed in the belief that the Fiscal had been guilty of a detestable falsehood; for fear of further incarceration, however, he would not pursue the exception."[2] After a long and stormy trial, the case was finally won by Cooke and Edwards on appeal to the High Court. Cory states that this "triumph of Messrs. Cooke and Edwards . . . produced the greatest joy and enthusiasm in Cape Town and undoubtedly did much to encourage the prevailing spirit of resistance against what was felt to be the injustice and tyranny of the Colonial Government at that time."

Unfortunately for Edwards, he continued to attack the Governor in further cases in which he was employed as the defending attorney. Because of two letters he sent to the Governor, he was charged with libel. Among the witnesses he wanted but was not allowed to call were the Governor himself and a number of other high officials, also a "manumitted female slave, a concubine living with Lord Charles Henry Somerset," and Dr. Barry, the famous woman doctor who passed as a man.

In the end Edwards was found guilty of libel and sentenced to New South Wales for seven years. Only after he had gone was it discovered that he was himself an escaped convict. His real name was Alexander Lockaye and he had been convicted in England of stealing a horse and cart. This was in 1818. Transported for life to the convict station in New South Wales, he escaped in 1821 and made his way to Cape Town, where he practised as a lawyer under the name of Edwards.

Sentenced for the second time to New South Wales, the indomitable Lockaye-Edwards made a last bid for freedom. This was in winter, when ships could not sail from Table Bay on account of the strength of the prevailing contrary winds. As the coach bearing him to Simonstown neared Wynberg, Edwards leapt out and plunged into the thicket. It is painful to have to record that he was recaptured and transferred to the ship. South Africa knew this lively personality no more.

Slavery was finally abolished in 1834. The freed slaves merged gradually into the general Coloured population of the Cape, to-day numbering over a million. Many strains have blended in forming the Coloured people of to-day: Negro slave, Malay, English and Dutch, Bushmen and Hottentot. The Griquas form a special group of the Coloured people. They are descended from Dutch men and the women of a tribe of Hottentots living near Piquetburg in the Western Province. Unions between white men and Hottentot women were not unpopular in the early days of the settlement.

J. S. Marais says: "The marriage in 1664 of the Hottentot woman, Eva, to van Meerhoff, the explorer, which was celebrated by a bridal feast at the Government House of the day, is a well-known incident in South African history. But Eva had few successors, since it soon came to be considered a disgrace for Christians (i.e. Europeans) to marry people of colour, even if they were free. Marriage between whites and slaves of full colour was prohibited by law in 1685. Irregular unions, however, continued."[3] Of the four major elements which went to make the Coloured people, Marais considers that the two most important were the slave and the Hottentot with the slave predominating.

Not all the descendants of the slaves and Hottentots are to-day recognised as Coloured people. Considerable numbers of them have been able to cross the colour line and escape into the white population. George Findlay[4] has pointed out that the Coloured population acts as a bridge between white and black and across this bridge intermingling of the races goes on, in spite of the fact that there are very few direct sexual unions between white and black. Findlay estimates that about one-third of the nominally white population has coloured blood in its veins and that it includes some of the most well-known South African families. Probably this is an exaggeration, but there can be no doubt of the general truth of his thesis.

CHAPTER IV

THE PHILANTHROPISTS

THE ATTITUDE KNOWN AS the Afrikaner outlook, which is characteristic to-day of both English- and Afrikaans-speaking sections of white South Africa, originated in the eighteenth century. It was a natural development in a country where all white men were either actual or potential slave-owners and where all non-whites were slaves or near-slaves. The trekking Boers who spread eastwards from the Cape took with them their slave-owner mentality. In addition to this, they acquired a typical frontiersman's outlook upon the Bantu. They regarded their chattel slaves as inferior beings but seldom feared them, for slave revolts were few and far between. In general their attitude to their slaves was paternal. Slaves were not so badly used in South Africa as in some other countries. Nearly all of them were in the category of domestic slaves: there was no planatation system at the Cape.

The Bantu, on the other hand, when the Boers first met them were a numerous, free and warlike people. The muzzle-loading musket and the horse gave the individual white man a definite superiority in war over the individual tribesman armed with shield and assegai. But this technical superiority was offset, to a large extent, by the superior numbers of the blacks. The Bantu were for generations a very serious danger to the Boers and they were accordingly both hated and feared. It became an axiom of white government, as the Afrikaner knew it, that the "black must be kept in his place," that no equality, social or political, must ever be tolerated between black and white.

The democratic revolutions in France and England, of the eighteenth and the beginning of the nineteenth centuries, caused a general revulsion against chattel slavery. The first bearers of this new liberal spirit to South Africa were the Hollanders, Jansens and de Mist. In 1795 the French revolutionaries invaded Holland. A considerable section of the Hollanders welcomed them and these were allowed to set up their own model government, known as the Republic of Batavia. An *émigré* royalist government was set up in London and it was nominally on behalf of this government that the English occupied the Cape for the first time in June, 1795. They held it until 1803, when, in accordance with the terms of the Treaty of Amiens, it was handed back to the Dutch.

The Batavian Government then sent out General Jansens as Governor, and Jacob de Mist as High Commissioner. These men held views considerably in advance of those of the average colonist. They tried to improve the conditions of service of Hottentots, and de Mist himself believed in the abolition of slavery by stages. But against a system so firmly established they could do little in the brief three years of their rule. In 1806 the British again occupied the country.

More important than the activities of the enlightened Batavian officials in establishing a nucleus of liberal thought in South Africa was the conduct of the missionaries. The first missionary to come to the Cape was George Schmidt, a member of the Moravian Church, who came out from Saxony in 1737. He established a mission for Hottentots at Genadendal, 100 miles from Cape Town. He left after six years and missionary activity lapsed until 1792, when the Moravian mission at Genadendal was revived.[1]

The Moravians at first encountered considerable hostility from the Boers, who had previously regarded Christianity as a white monopoly and who were, moreover, anxious for their labour supply. In 1795 the Moravians were forced by local "rebel" Boers to retire to Cape Town. They soon returned, however, and with added Government support. As time went on the Boers changed their opinion of Genadendal. They had discovered that Genadendal-mission-trained Hottentots made much better servants than the Hottentot in a state of nature. The Moravians, it seems, confined their work largely to the training of the Hottentots, and did not interfere in political matters or antagonise the Boers by preaching social equality. The typical Genadendal-trained Hottentot servant apparently fitted well enough into the Afrikaner picture of what a good non-European should be: industrious, obedient, respectful to the white man and willing to accept without question his inferior position in a patriarchal society. And that in fact has been the traditional characteristic of the Cape Coloured people. As we shall see later, of all the oppressed peoples of

South Africa they have been the least politically-minded, and it is only in comparatively recent times that they have begun to produce a crop of rebels and agitators.

The missionaries of the London Missionary Society, who made their first appearance at the Cape in 1799, were in sharp contrast with the unprovocative Moravians. They were propagandists of equalitarianism and they had no qualms about taking political action in support of their views. Marais, in his well-documented work on the Coloured people, points out that this difference between the Moravians and the London Missionary Society is easily explained: "The Moravians, whose traditions were shaped in the absolutist states, believed in passive obedience to the constituted authorities in secular affairs. In the Cape Colony, moreover, the Moravian missionaries were foreigners, and thus naturally felt it advisable to be particularly respectful to its Government. The L.M.S., being a British society with British Nonconformist traditions, had an entirely different attitude to the Government. Its missionaries in the Cape Colony, whether of British or of Dutch nationality, had grown up in countries where criticism of the Government was legitimate and habitual. Of the two most remarkable of these, the first, the Netherlander Dr. van der Kemp, had held decided political views while still living in his native land, and the second, the Scotsman Dr. Philip, was continually accused of being more of a politician than a missionary."

Mention has already been made of van der Kemp and his possible contact with Makana the Prophet. From 1799 to 1801, in the region that is now the Ciskei, he worked among the Xhosas. Thereafter he conducted the London Missionary Society mission station at Bethelsdorp in the Colony, where his chief concern was with the Hottentots. He went further than any other leading missionary in putting into practice the Christian belief in the brotherhood of man. It may be worth while recording an opinion of him by a modern writer whose views are fairly typical of those held by Christian missionaries in South Africa to-day. J. du Plessis* says: "It must be confessed that van der Kemp had the courage of his convictions. To the Hottentots he became as a Hottentot in the most literal sense of the words. He adopted their

* J. du Plessis was principal of the Dutch Reformed Church's theological school at the University of Stellenbosch. His revisionist views on the inspiration of the Bible led to his dismissal by the Dutch Reformed Church Synod in 1930.

dress, ate their food, lived in their huts, and finally married a 'woman of Madagascar extraction'—so he himself states in a letter to the Colonial Secretary—the seventeen-year-old daughter of a slave woman. He so impressed his own views upon his colleague Read, who seems to have been a worthy, though not very literate man, that the latter also contracted a matrimonial alliance with a Hottentot girl, who had been baptised but a few days previous to the marriage. A century of Christian missions in South Africa has since proved the fallacy of the opinions held by van der Kemp as to the superiority of the savage state and the natural equality of all men. No responsible missionary to-day would venture to preach or to practise the doctrine of social equality between the white and coloured races, or to plead for intermarriage between European and Native. But during the first quarter of the nineteenth century the doctrines of the school of English philanthropists attained their greatest vogue, and of that school van der Kemp was the South African prophet."[2]

The Rev. Dr. John Philip, who succeeded van der Kemp in 1819, soon became a power in the land. He had the ear of the Government in London and used his political influence with some effect. He was continually sending reports to London. Governors who would not take his advice and who wanted to support the interests of the farmers when these were opposed to the interests of the Native peoples were often faced with orders from the British Government which forced them to change their policy or to resign their positions.

In the meantime, the expansion of European settlement at the Cape and the growth of farming resulted in an increased demand for cheap labour. After 1807 slaves could no longer be brought into the country. The price of slaves went up. The farmers naturally began to turn their attention to the Hottentots and other Natives as a possible source of supply. Pressure was accordingly brought to bear on the authorities to introduce laws which would force the Hottentots, who still made an independent living of a kind on what poor land was left to them, into the service of the white farmer. Accordingly, in 1809, the Hottentot pass law was introduced. Note that it was an English and not a Dutch government which first introduced the pass system into South Africa.

Under the pass law all Hottentots who were not working for white masters were described as "vagrants." Any Hottentot who was a vagrant was breaking the law. Every white man, not only the police, had the right to demand of any passing Hottentot that he should show his pass. No Hottentot could carry a pass unless he had entered into a labour agreement with a white farmer. The law said nothing about how much wages were to be paid and usually the Hottentot was paid little or nothing. Those who had not made labour agreements were arrested under the pass laws and hired out among the farmers. At the same time a system of child slavery, politely termed apprenticeship, was devised for Hottentot children. This provided the farmer with a supply of labour for which he did not have to pay and at the same time tended to prevent the Hottentot parents from going away to other farms, because by so doing they would abandon their children.

After the pass laws had come into force there were at the Cape two sorts of slavery existing side by side. There was chattel slavery, the old system under which slaves could be bought and sold; and there was the new system of forced labour which resulted from the pass laws and which in practice was very little different from chattel slavery. The Hottentot could not be bought and sold, but he was tied to the land in such a way that usually he could not leave it. He was certainly not a free man. The system of forced labour slavery, or "pass law slavery," as we may call it, is the fate of the great mass of the Bantu population to this day. But the Hottentots were more fortunate, as we shall show, and escaped from it to some extent.

It was against such forms of discrimination against "free persons of colour" as well as against the more obvious chattel slavery that the Christian "philanthropists" conducted their fight.

In 1828 the British Government took steps, supported by the missionaries, to give a certain amount of freedom and political rights to the Hottentots. "Ordinance 50," which was promulgated on July 17, 1828, did away with all earlier laws made against the Hottentots. It went on to say: "As it has been the custom of this Colony for Hottentots and other free persons of colour* to be subject to certain hindrances as to their place of living, way of life and employment, and to certain forced services which do not apply to other subjects

* That is, those who were not actually slaves.

of His Majesty, be it therefore made law that from and after the passing of this Ordinance, no Hottentot or other free person of colour, lawfully living in this Colony, shall be subject to any forced service which does not apply to others of His Majesty's subjects, nor to any hindrance, interference, fine or punishment of any kind whatever, under the pretence that such person has been guilty of vagrancy or any other offence, unless after trial in due course of law, any custom or usage to the contrary notwithstanding."

Thus, in the high-sounding language of the law, it was stated that Hottentots, and all other Coloured persons who were not slaves, were not to be subject to the special colour bar laws, that no farmer might take the law into his own hands and whip his Hottentot servants, and that the pass laws were to go. The new law gave to the Hottentots the right to possess land (though nearly all of them were far too poor to buy any), and it stated that in future all labour contracts of over one month were to be in writing.

The new law did not change the position of the slaves, but six years later, in 1834, these received their freedom, while, by a further ordinance in 1842, all non-Europeans within the boundaries of the Colony were given the same rights before the law as the white people.

But, in spite of their early spectacular successes, the philanthropists fought a losing fight against the forces of colour prejudice. The interests of the overwhelming majority of the white colonists demanded the economic enslavement of the aboriginal populations. Nigrophilism remained an exotic growth in South Africa and it was only by continual reinforcement from overseas that it was able to survive. In the Colony itself the forces of liberalism were obliged by the weight of circumstances continually to give ground.

The line of retreat of the missionaries was first to deny social equality, then to introduce colour bars in their churches, finally to become subservient in almost every way to the dominant interests of the white colonists. The Dutch Reformed Church at an early date brought forward Biblical testimony to prove that it was God's will that the sons of Ham should remain hewers of wood and drawers of water. Other churches, which drew their inspiration less exclusively from the Old Testament with its patriarchal order, found it more difficult to reconcile the precepts of the Sermon on the Mount with current social practice in South Africa. But Christianity is adaptable, and most of the Churches seem to have experienced little difficulty in making the necessary adaptations. Salvationists, Seventh-Day Adventists, Baptists and other "left-wing" religious groups segregated their congregations even more rigorously than the "right-wing" Anglicans and Roman Catholics. In fact, it has been the Anglicans more than any other important body of churchmen who have most consistently opposed the prevailing colour prejudice. This has been mainly due to the fact that the leaders of the Church of the Province have been in almost all cases Englishmen from overseas who came to South Africa only after their social and religious outlook had been fully formed. Christianity has failed notoriously in influencing the attitude of the colonial white man towards the Natives.

Dr. Philip, as we have seen, was both a churchman and a politician. He was cordially hated not only by the Boers, but also by the English settlers, and he has come to be regarded as the black sheep of South African history. His good name and the soundness of his policy have been defended in two interesting books[3] on South African history by W. M. Macmillan, formerly Professor of History at the University of the Witwatersrand.

Of lay exponents of liberalism in the early days perhaps the best known was Thomas Pringle, who came out with the 1820 settlers and took up farming on the eastern frontier. In 1822 he went to Cape Town to start the first newspaper ever published in this country. It was called the *South African Magazine* and was to appear monthly. Actually it survived only two issues. An article in the second issue called forth the anger of the Governor, Lord Charles Somerset, who then tried to get Pringle to undertake not to print articles of a political nature. Pringle refused and the paper ceased publication. In 1826 Pringle left for England, where he became the Secretary of the Anti-Slavery Society. George Greig and John Fairbairn were associated with Pringle in early attempts to secure the freedom of the Press in South Africa. Their paper, the *South African Commercial Advertiser*, was at first prohibited by the Governor. After a long fight, in the course of which Fairbairn visited London, they managed to persuade the Government in England to agre hat "henceforth the Press in the Colony should be free from the control of the Governor and Council and in October, 1828, the *Advertiser* was commenced for the third time and the struggle for the freedom of the Press was at an end."

John Fairbairn got into trouble with the settlers in the eastern districts because his paper criticised the policy of the Government in the Sixth Kafir War. "The paper made unfavourable but hardly unjustified comments on the high-handed treatment the frontier tribes had received. Thereupon 479 infuriated frontiersmen (at Grahamstown) signed their names to a declaration denouncing these and former 'false statements,' alleging 'the visit of its Editor to the frontier as among the causes of a confederacy among the Caffre chiefs which threatens the total ruin of a large portion of the Colony,' and vowing a severe boycott" (Macmillan).

Another member of this early group of nigrophiles was a South African Dutchman, Andries Stockenstrom. He was a magistrate and afterwards a soldier on the eastern frontier and took part in a number of wars against the Bantu. He heard and recorded the eloquent plea of Makana's followers and came to realise that the Bantu were not being fairly treated. He did what he could in his official position to oppose the policy of the settlers. He made friends with Dr. Philip at first, but afterwards quarrelled with him (Macmillan). He came to be specially hated by the Boers because of his "extreme caution" in permitting commandos against the Bushmen and because of the heavy sentences he gave to farmers found guilty of acts of cruelty against Hottentots, Bushmen and slaves. In particular, it was held against him that he had caused the public hanging of a Boer named Smit who had murdered a Hottentot, a sentence that would, of course, be incredible in any South African Court of to-day.*

In effect, the protests of the early London missionaries, of Pringle, Stockenstrom and other obstinate and courageous individuals, availed nothing against the hot indignation of the frontier Boers and the self-interest of slave-owners and employers of Hottentot labour. Despite all their efforts, the mounting wave of colour prejudice and hatred was not stayed,

*One of the few white men to be hanged in recent times for the murder of a Native in South Africa was Stassen, who was executed on the Rand after the strike of 1922. Martial law prevailed at the time. Stassen, who had been a striker, was tried by a panel of judges and did not have the option of trial by jury.

but grew in volume and momentum until it spread over the whole of the unhappy land.

CHAPTER V

BLACK JOAN OF ARC

ONLY 100 YEARS AGO the majority of the Suto, Zulu and Xhosa tribes still ruled themselves and opposed the white man's advance across definite though rapidly shrinking frontiers. The conflicts of 1846 and 1850-3, though they were not exactly the end of the Kafir wars, were the last large-scale attempts of the Xhosas to turn the tide of white aggression which had been running strongly against them for half a century. Their ancient boundary, the Fish River, the frontier across which in 1819 a white army had come to defeat Makana and his warriors, had been restored to them by Lord Glenelg in 1835. But now, ten years later, Lord Glenelg's policy was reversed. The boundary of the Cape Colony was steadily moved eastwards from the Fish to the Kei River, thereby incorporating in the Colony the whole of the Ciskei, then known as British Kaffraria. From this time the Ciskei became increasingly the chequer-board we know to-day, where white farms occupy the river valleys and small Native reserves are perched on the hillsides or straggle across the arid patches.

The war of 1834, the Sixth Kafir War, had begun in the usual way with raids and counter-raids. On this occasion the Xhosas were pushed back as far as the Kei River and the troops even crossed that river and raided into the country of Hintsa on the eastern side. After the war the colonists, as usual, prepared to divide the conquered territory into farms. Sir Benjamin d'Urban, the Governor, had agreed that the Kei should in future be the eastern boundary of the Colony.

"But," to quote an orthodox South African school history book, "the British Government unwisely decided to interfere, acting on the advice of a well-known missionary, Dr. Philip, and a retired South African official, Captain Andries Stockenstrom. The Governor was ordered to restore to the Xhosas the country taken from them, on the ground that the war had been an unjust one. Captain Stockenstrom was sent out from England, where he had gone to make his protest, to be Lieutenant-Governor of the eastern districts of the Colony, and he was given power to make treaties of friendship with the surrounding Kafir tribes. The Secretary of State for the Colonies, Lord Glenelg, had made a serious mistake by consulting a handful of agitators rather than his own South African official advisers. Sir Benjamin d'Urban protested in vain; the only result was that he was withdrawn from his post. The seed was now sown, and the people on the spot recognised at once that the Colony would have to reap a fresh crop of Kafir wars before long. Nor was this the only evil result of Lord Glenelg's mistake. Large numbers of the Dutch burghers became convinced that British rule meant nothing but disaster to them, and made up their minds to seek their fortune in unknown lands, where they would no longer be troubled by a government which seemed to them so unjust and so grossly prejudiced in favour of the Native and against the European."[1]

So the Boers trekked away to the north, 10,000 of them, to set up governments of their own where there would be "no equality in Church or State between black and white." Of what happened to them we shall have more to say later. In the Cape Colony for a time it seemed that there would be peace between black and white and that the Bantu would be able to keep their land, the country still held by them west of the Kei.

On the frontier this uneasy peace was maintained, more or less, for some ten years, until the Seventh Kafir War, the War of the Axe, broke out in 1846. Stockenstrom, as Lieutenant-Governor of the eastern districts, made an attempt during this period to try out his plan of securing peace by a number of treaties with the Bantu chiefs. But the plan did not work. This was partly because Stockenstrom was not in command of the armed forces, which were under direct control of the Governor, partly because there was a "war party" among the colonists (perhaps it might better be described as a "more land party"), partly because the Bantu themselves did not understand the reasons for the giving back to them of the conquered land in 1835 and interpreted this as a sign of weakness on the part of the Government. Cattle-stealing on both sides continued. Stockenstrom became more and more unpopular with the colonists and with the Governor, and in 1836 the Secretary for the Colonies in London decided that he must go. He was awarded a knighthood. According to Macmillan, this was to "console him." With the departure of Stockenstrom, the way was now open for a change of policy. The stage was set for the War of the Axe.

As it happened, it was the Xhosas who provoked it. A Xhosa prisoner, accused of the theft of an axe, was handcuffed to a Hottentot and was being taken under police escort from Fort Beaufort to Grahamstown when the Xhosas attacked the little party. To free their compatriot, they cut off the hand of the Hottentot, who subsequently died. The Governor became convinced, if indeed he had needed convincing, that the time had now come when it was impossible to tolerate any longer what seemed the "systematic violation of justice and good faith on the part of the Kafirs."[2]

This Seventh Kafir War dragged on for two years. As a result of it, English rule was extended eastwards as far as the Kei River, but the Bantu were allowed to keep certain reserves of land west of the Kei, where they were to be permitted to live under the control of the Government. At the end of the war all the chiefs and headmen of the conquered territory were called together and were made to swear to keep the following agreements:

(1) To obey the laws and commands of the Governor as representing the Queen of England.

(2) To compel their people to do the same.

(3) To stop the practice of witchcraft.

(4) To prevent the attacks on women.

(5) To hate murder and to put to death every murderer.

(6) To make their people honest and peaceable and not to rob from the Colony or from one another.

(7) To acknowledge that their lands were held from the Queen of England.

(8) To acknowledge no chief but the Queen of England and her representatives.

(9) To give up the sin of buying wives.

(10) To listen to the missionaries and make their people do so.

(11) As this day comes round every year, to bring to King William's Town a fat ox, in acknowledgement of holding their lands from the Queen.[3]

It is quite clear that those who drew up this document had no real knowledge of Bantu laws or customs. Some of its preposterous clauses violate not only the principles of ethnology and psychology, which indeed had not at that date been thought of, but also the rules of ordinary common sense. The "sin of buying wives" refers to the *lobola* system, by which the husband must, according to Bantu custom, deposit with the father of his bride a number of cattle. These cattle are a guarantee for her good treatment and also a compensation to the father for the loss of a bread-winner, for Bantu women are the agriculturists of the tribe. To attack *lobola* would be to strike at a most intimate bond in Bantu tribal unity. It should have been obvious that the chiefs could not keep, and could have no intention of keeping, this and other impossible promises to which they had to swear. But they had to swear. The document is interesting also for its attempt to force Christianity upon the Natives at the muzzle of the gun.

Further wars were inevitable. In less than two years came the Eighth Kafir War, "the longest and most costly in blood and treasure that the Cape Colony had ever engaged in."[4] The chief significance of this war for the historian is the part played by the Hottentots. It had been hitherto the custom of the Government to employ them as soldiers against the Bantu.[5] But on this occasion large numbers of Hottentot soldiers mutinied and joined the Bantu. This did not affect the issue of the war. At the end of it large tracts of land previously occupied by the Tembu tribe were given to the colonists.

Not only was a considerable part of the Xhosa people now reduced to the status of an internal proletariat, but the external proletariat across the Kei River also felt the increasing pressure of the white advance. Many of them must have felt that as an independent people they were doomed and that only a miracle could save them. It was as though the Bantu, beaten by the guns, horsemen and superior organisation of the Europeans, turned to the spiritual world for help. As some thirty years earlier they had listened to the prophet Makana, so now they were willing to listen and find hope in the leadership of a new prophet, the girl Nongqause.

The story of Nongqause* and the great cattle-killing of 1856 is still the subject of controversy. In some ways this Xhosa girl of sixteen resembled the French Joan of Arc. She was the prophet of Xhosa nationalism as Joan was of French. Like Joan, she heard voices telling her to come forward and save her country. Like Joan she was called to her great mission when she was but in her teens. Unlike Joan, she was not burnt as a heretic nor did it fall to her lot to be canonised as a saint: she lived to be an old woman.

Her story begins on the morning in May, 1856, when she went to draw water at the Gxara, a small river east of the Kei. On her return she said she had met the spirits of the dead. The "eternal enemies of the white man, they announce themselves as having come from battlefields beyond the sea to aid the Xhosas with their invincible power in driving the English from the land."[6] Nongqause's uncle, Mhlakaza, took the message to the paramount chief, Kreli. The spirits had given orders that all the cattle were to be killed and eaten and no one was to cultivate the land. Then, on a certain day, millions of fat cattle would spring out of the earth and great fields of corn would appear ready for eating. At the same time the sky would fall and crush the white people and with them all the blacks who had not obeyed the commands of the spirits.

There are a number of variants of this story. One has it that Nongqause was working in the fields when she met ten young men who gave her the message. She went to fetch her uncle, who was able to communicate with the young men through her, though he could not see them.[7] Some reports said that they were Russians! This story undoubtedly owed its origin to the fact that more or less distorted accounts of the Crimean War, which ended in 1856, had penetrated to Xhosaland; to the Xhosas the Russians were the enemies of the English.

The cattle-killing was begun almost immediately. It had the full support of Kreli, who set an example by destroying his favourite horse. Mhlakaza himself destroyed all his own cattle. The people became divided into believers and non-believers, but the former steadily gained ground. Many of the Ciskeian

* Pronounce it *Non-kah-oo-seh* if you cannot achieve the click.

tribes also became infected. A traveller between Peddie and East London in December, 1856, reported that he hardly saw a single beast or a single acre under cultivation over a distance of eighty miles. "The Kafir women are, in their adherence to the Prophet (Mhlakaza), far more stubborn than the men. These have a tale among them to the effect that a Kafir man attempted, in opposition to the mandate of the Prophet, to turn up the ground, but that he had no sooner struck his hoe into the land than he became paralysed, could not move from the spot, and it was only after great difficulty that the charm was broken and the offender liberated."[8]

Another writer in a colonial newspaper said that the proceedings of the Kafirs were the most extraordinary ever known. They were perfectly reckless in making away with their cattle; a cow or a calf might be bought for a few shillings which a short time before would not be parted with at any price. The trade in hides was enormous. The notorious witch doctor had predicted that very shortly two suns would be seen at one time, that a desperate battle or collision would take place between them and that then would ensue a time of profound darkness. After that "all, whether black or white, who wore *trousers* would be swept away by a whirlwind, the lucky *sansculottes* being left in undisturbed possession of the whole country."[9]

Of the non-believers the most numerous and consistent were the Fingoes. Refugees from the wars of Dingaan and Tshaka, Zulu chiefs, they had fled to the Cape, only to come under the domination of the Xhosas. The Cape Government had made them its allies, giving them land taken from the Xhosas. They were often "trouser" people and more Westernised than the majority of the Bantu in the Eastern Cape. They steadfastly refused to kill their cattle, but were quite prepared to buy cattle from the prophet-ridden Xhosas. As one reporter put it, "the wild stories so freely circulated had no effect on them; they stood their ground, ready for bargain or battle."

The general feeling among the colonists as they witnessed this spectacle of a nation's suicide was that the cattle-killing was merely the prelude to an armed attack on the Colony. It was believed by many that behind the whole mad business was a plot on the part of the chiefs to throw the whole Xhosa people, fully armed and in a famished state, upon the Colony.[10] It was reported in a Grahamstown paper in August, 1856, that scores of farmers had abandoned their homesteads and that many missionaries had removed their furniture to King William's Town. On the other hand, it was said that adequate

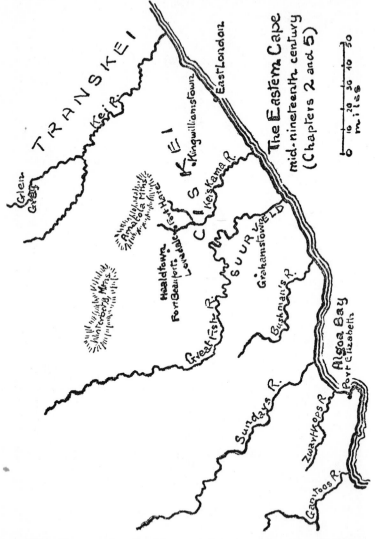

The Eastern Cape
mid-nineteenth century
(Chapters 2 and 5)

military preparations had been made to stop any armed break-through on the frontier.

Resurrection Day was originally fixed for Friday, August 15, 1856. Nothing unusual happened on that day. It was said that the date had been postponed. There was a comparative lull in the cattle-killing. It was said that Kreli had begun to get tired of the game he was playing and had ordered his people to cease from destroying their cattle. According to another story, he had asked the Prophet for three months' extension, his herds being so immense that it would be impossible to sacrifice the whole in a shorter time.

But the slaughter of the animals was soon revived. Charles Brownlee said in January, 1857: "I think not less than three or four hundred thousand cattle have been killed or wasted." It became impossible for Mhlakaza, or whoever was at the back of it all, to delay any longer. Starvation was already staring the people in the face. The day of the full moon in February, 18, was finally decided on. "At length," says Theal, "the morning dawned of the day so long and ardently looked for. All night long the Xhosa had watched, expecting to see two blood-red suns arise over the eastern hill." At length the sun rose looking much as usual and with no supernatural companion. "But perhaps after all it might be midday that was meant. And when the shadows began to lengthen towards the east, perhaps, they thought, the setting of the sun is the time. The sun went down, as it often does in that fair land, behind clouds of crimson and gold, and the Xhosas awoke to the reality of their dreadful position."

If it had been the intention of the instigators of the cattle-killing to lead a hungry army in a final assault on the Colony, they had bungled badly. The warriors had not been collected at a single point on the border ready to burst through. Now it was too late to collect them. "The only chance of life was to reach the Colony, but it was as suppliants, not as warriors, that the famished people must now go." It was estimated that between 25,000 and 50,000 people died as a result of the cattle-killing, out of a total population of possibly 150,000. Thousands managed to reach the Colony, where they were given food and work. Nongqause and Mhlakaza had indeed effectively solved the labour problems of the colonists! But the military might of the Bantu was broken and it was a generation before they were able to fight again.

It was believed that Mhlakaza died of starvation. Kreli and Nongqause fled to the Bashee. No attempt was made to arrest the paramount chief, but Nongqause, according to Cory, was sought out by a group of Africans and handed over to the authorities. She was afterwards released, changed her name to Victoria Regina, as a safeguard it is said, since many of her countrymen had threatened to kill her. She married and had children, ending her days in obscurity at Alexandria, near Port Elizabeth, in 1909. The history books are not concerned with the later days of Nongqause, but a Cape Town journalist, D. R. D'ewes, visited the scene of her death, conversed with people who had known her, and put on record the story of the last days of this black Joan whose voices so betrayed her.

As to what was behind the cattle-killing, that national suicide of the amaXhosa, as it has been called, opinions differ. Many young African students at Fort Hare to-day, arguing after the event, maintain the belief that the whole thing was started by certain astute Europeans as a clever move to solve the labour problems of the developing Colony. Undoubtedly the labour shortage at this time was acute and the cattle-killing did result in a flood of cheap labour which the colonists welcomed with open arms. Moreover, at quite an early stage in the cattle-killing, months before the final debacle, many colonists were already calculating on the supply of labour which would soon become available. It may be interesting to quote some of the published statements of that time. Thus a writer in the *King William's Town Gazette* of August 14, 1856, asks whether, if war could be averted, starvation would not compel the Natives to hire themselves as farm workers and servants. "Some may think that instead of resorting to these expediencies they will be impelled to robbery and murder, but we have ever observed, in connection with the native character, that lean and starving men are always tractable and civil, but the well-fed and sleek, impudent and easily led to mischief. And, above all, may not the advent of the Germans* have a most powerful and salutary influence in subduing the rising spirit of the various tribes?"

An anonymous writer in the same paper on December 6 expressed himself as follows: "War *may* take place. Can we prevent it? I answer most decidedly—Yes, it is possible to avert war, if we can find employment for the natives. The Galekas might be employed in repairing the Kei, or upon

* The Anglo-German Legion, ex-soldiers from the Crimean War, whom the Government proposed to settle in the East London district.

other public works. If a Register Office for servants were established in the Galeka country, hundreds would hire themselves for farm servants or labourers to the colonists, as they are already beginning to suffer from starvation."

Evidence of the labour shortage is contained in a report of the Inspector of Roads, dated Grahamstown, Novemebr 20, 1856. He apparently did not think much use could be made of "labourers found in the colony, such as Europeans, Hottentots, late apprentices and Fingoes, a few of whom might be picked up about the towns for about 2s. 6d. *per diem*, including rations. These would be the best labourers, but cannot always be depended upon, as all of those classes who would accept of employment on the roads are almost sure to be drunkards." On the other hand, "numbers of so-called Mantatees* are in the habit of entering the N.E. borders of the colony in small parties in search of employment. . . . As they are very steady men I would prefer them to any others, provided they could be obtained in sufficient numbers, which I think might be accomplished by the intercession of His Excellency the Governor with their chief Moshesh. They would not cost more than from a shilling to fifteen pence a day, including rations. . . . As the late insane proceedings of the Kafirs in killing all their cattle must of necessity lead to great distress and starvation, many of them will doubtless be happy to accept of employment in the colony at wages similar to what I have estimated for the Mantatees. They are, however, not such good workmen, being exceedingly lazy and indolent."

Finally, a leading article in the *Grahamstown Journal* of December 20, 1856, advises: "It is quite within the range of probability that the present perturbed state of Kafirland may be turned to ultimate advantage, that is as far as the Colony is concerned. Let it be seen that there is sufficient power at hand to repel and punish aggression and the Kafir will bend before the white man and be willing to earn by honest labour the food which he would much rather wrest from him by the hand of savage violence."

There is evidence enough to prove that employers in the Colony, both public and private, were quick to see and welcome an obvious consequence of the cattle-killing. That does not, however, prove that some Machiavellian white man or group of whites instigated it. If it were so it would be one

* Basuto.

of the most amazingly clever and diabolical frauds ever perpetrated by a civilised upon a savage people. Against this idea it must be noted that to conceive such a scheme would have required a degree of intimate knowledge and comprehension of the Bantu psychology such as no colonist, and above all no hostile colonist, of the day could have possessed The actual initiation of the scheme, moreover, assuming it were conceived, would present difficulties of a practical nature which would render the whole plan doubly impossible. Clearly we shall be justified in rejecting this all too facile explanation.

Whether Nongqause was genuine, as Joan of Arc appears to have been, in her belief that she heard voices and saw spirits, no one can say. Mhlakaza may have engineered the whole business and the young Nongqause may have been his conscious or unconscious instrument. On the other hand it is possible that she was the prime mover, that her dreams or visions came to her as she said they did, and acted as a spark to fire an explosive charge the ingredients of which were present in the situation in which the Xhosa people found themselves at that time. In that case, she, Mhlakaza, Kreli, the other chiefs and the whole Xhosa nation were equally the victims of their own primitive ideas as to the nature of the world in which they lived.

The Xhosa were primitive and superstitious and their superstition proved their undoing. But it is interesting to note that the Europeans who came among them both to teach and to exploit them were themselves not altogether free from superstition. By 1856 missionary influence and missionary teaching had spread far and wide in Kaffraria and beyond. Missionaries were tolerated and respected even by the heathen. (In the frontier wars missionaries, as well as white women and children, were almost always treated as non-combatants by the Bantu.) But missionary dogma, at least in its most elementary forms, which naturally were the forms most readily understood by the Bantu, was a poor weapon to use to discredit a belief in a coming day of judgment and resurrection of the dead. Cory, in recounting the reactions of certain Ciskeian chiefs who were asked to dissuade their people from killing their cattle, states that Chief Siwani was "of opinion that Mhlakaza's talk was as truthful as and more acceptable than that they heard from the missionaries and not so incredible as some parts of the Gospel."

Consider the following account of an interview between Charles Brownlee and Sandile, the Gaika chief.[5] It is recorded in a report dated August 5, 1856, and sent by Brownlee, who was Commissioner to the Gaikas, the largest Ciskeian tribe, to Colonel Maclean, Chief Commissioner. The interview took place in the presence of Sandile's councillors. Sandile opens the proceedings by giving a report on the general state of unrest among his people on account of the influence of Mhlakaza and the cattle-killing which is going on among neighbouring tribes. Brownlee tries to convince Sandile that Mhlakaza is a fraud. Not only must Sandile refuse to allow his own tribe to join in the cattle-killing, but he must visit Kreli, the paramount chief, and try to persuade him to break with Mhlakaza. Brownlee's line of argument is to show that prior to the previous war (in 1850-3) there had been another prophet among the Xhosas, one Umlanjeni, who had made all sorts of ridiculous promises which had not been fulfilled, such, for instance, as that the bullets of the English would turn to water. He, Brownlee, had told the Gaikas at the time that Umlanjeni's prophecies would not be fulfilled. Events had proved him right. Now he told them the same about Mhlakaza, and again he would be right.

Having argued at some length on lines of which any modern empirical materialist would approve, Brownlee suddenly changed over to a theological approach. "Now, as I foretold you with Umlanjeni what will take place, I will again tell you what will take place. God created the heaven and the earth and all things in six days, and on the seventh He rested His work being completed, and from God's Word we learn that there will be a resurrection of all men, who will come before Him to give account of all the deeds done in this body, when some will go to everlasting happiness and others to everlasting punishment; and that then the world will be destroyed by fire; but the time is not yet. Mhlakaza professes to have his revelations from God. God is a God of truth, and what He has once revealed to man stands as unchangeable as Himself. There will be no resurrection of men and beasts as predicted by Mhlakaza, for his resurrection is opposed to the Word of God."

In his reply, Sandile said that he did not believe in Mhlakaza. God did nothing in secret; all his works were open and manifest, and he would not so long be making secret communications to Mhlakaza without some evident manifestation of power to convince the unbelieving. He (Sandile) had already prohibited the slaughtering of cattle in his tribe, and even should his people disregard his word he would still retain his cattle. God had given corn and cattle for the support of man, and he considered that those who destroyed his gifts were more exposed to his wrath than those who preserved them, and that though darkness should cover the land, as predicted by Mhlakaza, and though Sandile's cattle should be swept off the face of the earth, he knew God was merciful and would again feed him as heretofore, because if he committed a sin in disobeying Mhlakaza it was a sin of ignorance and therefore could not be severely punished.

From all of which it should have been clear to Brownlee that he had failed to convince Sandile; and in fact Sandile and his people did subsequently join in the cattle-killing. It must have seemed to Sandile and others that the white people themselves believed in and preached a day of resurrection and judgment. Since all agreed there would be a resurrection, why the white man's resurrection in preference to their own? And if God was to punish the guilty, why should he not punish the white man who had taken the black man's land? What they failed to understand was that the whites had grown sufficiently knowledgeable and sophisticated to postpone their apocalypse to some very vague date in the future and for all practical purposes refused to call in the aid of supernatural forces. The Xhosas, on the other hand, put their trust in the spirits and the spirits failed them. There are different degrees of superstition. The difference in this case was highly significant in its effect on the history of the Bantu people.

CHAPTER VI

THE CHIEFS' LAST STAND

THOSE BOERS WHO TREKKED AWAY from the Cape to escape the interference of the British Government went first to Natal, where they encountered the military power of the Zulus. The rise of Zulu militarism was not unique in Bantu history. Powerful kingdoms had arisen from time to time in central and east Africa. But though not unique it was sufficiently striking. Born on the banks of the Umvolosi River in 1783, Tshaka, the black Napoleon, was the son of a chief of a small and unimportant tribe. When still a boy he excited the jealousy of his father and was forced to flee for his life. He was taken in by Dingiswayo, the chief of an aggressive tribe, who in his youth, it is alleged, had come into contact with the Europeans and learned something of their military system.[1] As a youth Tshaka became a soldier in one of Dingiswayo's regiments, and so distinguished himself that when Dingiswayo died he succeeded him as chief of the tribe. Tshaka started on a campaign of conquest about 1822 and soon subdued all the neighbouring tribes, thus laying the foundations of a considerable empire.

The success of the Zulus was the result of the superior organisation of their armies and the discipline of their soldiers. When they conquered new tribes, the old people of the defeated tribe were killed, but the young women, and often the young men also, were absorbed and became part of the Zulu nation. The whole of what is now Natal came under the domination of Tshaka, and his armies penetrated into what are now the Orange Free State, the Transvaal and Portuguese East Africa.

Though the Zulus were armed only with the assegai or stabbing spear, they were able to put up a considerable resistance to the white settlers who attempted to conquer Zululand. In spite of their superior equipment, their guns and their horses, the Europeans were not able to defeat the Zulu impis. They were obliged to resort to intrigue and the methods of divide-and-rule in order to get the better of the warlike Zulus.

It was 1837 when the Voortrekkers crossed the Drakensberg into Natal. By this time Tshaka was dead, killed by his two brothers, Mpande and Dingane. Dingane succeeded Tshaka as king of the Zulus. Historians report that he was as cruel as Tshaka, and cunning, but less able. At first he made overtures of peace to the Voortrekkers, craftily lured their leader, Piet Retief, to his kraal for a friendly parley, then turned on the white men who had put down their arms in token of peace, and massacred Retief and a number of his followers. Dingane's armies then fell upon some of the Boer encampments and killed men, women and children, in contrast to the Xhosas who, when they made war, regarded women and children as non-combatants and did not harm them. But at the Battle of Blood River, on December 16, 1838, Dingane's army was beaten. It was not this battle, however, but the defection of his brother Mpande, who joined forces with the Boers, that finally brought about the defeat of Dingane.

Though the Europeans occupied Natal south of the Tugela River, they were unable to conquer Zululand itself. The Zulu military system remained intact and capable of training further reserves of soldiers. "Dingaan's Day," December 16, has become for the Boers a national day of thanksgiving, a public holiday on which they celebrate the fact of their triumph over the black man. Nevertheless, the Battle at Blood River was by no means the decisive event some historians would have us believe.

The Dutch in Natal were driven out by the English, who had actually made a settlement at Durban on the coast before the Boers entered the country. The Boer "Republic of Natalia," with its capital at Pietermaritzburg, collapsed after a short war in which the Boers made unsuccessful attempts to capture Durban. The English then, in 1843, took over the country south of the Tugela.

Trouble with the Natives continued. The Zulu were continually drifting back over the Tugela and the English made spasmodic attempts to drive them back into Zululand, or to confine them to limited "reserves" within the colony, thus keeping the best land for the white colonists.

Between 1845 and 1875 Native policy in Natal was in the hands of Sir Theophilus Shepstone, the famous administrator. Shepstone's policy in Natal has been contrasted with what has been called the "Cape policy of Identity."[2] He introduced the system now known as "segregation" or "indirect rule." The Natives were to be governed as far as possible through their own chiefs. They were to be segregated in special areas. Native law was to be recognised in as far as it did not conflict with the "requirements of justice." Thus Native chiefs were to continue to act as judges in civil actions between Native and Native. All cases involving Europeans were to be dealt with by the white courts, as were also all infractions of the criminal law by Natives. Shepstone declared that his ultimate object was to raise the Natives to a state of western civilisation. In theory, his ideas were in harmony with the principles of modern anthropology. "You cannot control savages by civilised law," he said. And "Native law gives government greater power of introducing civilised ideas."

In practice the system has played into the hands of the imperialists and the white farmers. It has resulted in keeping the Natives backward, mere hewers of wood and drawers of water for their white rulers. The extreme backwardness of the majority of the Natives in Natal and the stagnation of the Native reserves has been laid at the door of the Shepstone policy; though Shepstone's admirers declare that this result may be more justly attributed to the fact that the British Government refused to give Shepstone the money he demanded for carrying out his schemes for social work among the Natives of Natal.

Writing of Shepstone, C. W. de Kiewiet[3] says that his "contributions to creative Native policy are surprisingly unimportant. . . . It is easy to recognise that he was essentially at one with the colonists. It is significant that he was never unpopular with them. It is an important explanation of his impressive reputation that he did not in the days of his greatest power seriously oppose the European demand for labour and land. He was even eager that the country should be more numerously settled by white colonists."

Though the British, when they took possession of Natal in 1843, had declared that "in the eye of the law there shall not be any distinction of qualification whatever founded on mere distinction of colour," they went back on this promise and drew up the "Natal Code," a special set of laws for the blacks. This system made the Governor-General the "Supreme Chief" of the Natives and thus gave to the Government dictatorial powers over the tribes. Thus, while in the Cape black, white, and Coloured enjoyed, at least in theory, equality in the eye of the law, this was never the case in Natal.

Maurice Evans, in *White and Black in South-East Africa,* considers that the two main principles in the early European administration of Natives in Natal were firstly the securing of peace by keeping the tribes separate so that tribal differences were perpetuated and unity of action on the part of the Bantu rendered impossible, and, secondly, the appointment of a Native Administrator who would act as a "father and protector." But at the same time the authorities were prepared to allow a small number of Natives to be exempted from the operation of the Natal Code of Native law. Elaborate provisions were drawn up for such exemptions, but no Native could claim exemption as a right, the Governor-General having the power to refuse to grant it; also the children of an exempted Native did not inherit their father's status. Natives living in polygamy were not eligible to apply for exemption.

A law of 1865 allowed Natives of Natal to apply for registration as voters. The applicant had to have been resident in the Colony for twelve years; he must own immovable property to the value of £50 or pay at least £10 a year in rent; he must have been exempted from the operation of the Natal Code for at least seven years; he must produce a certificate signed by three qualified electors of European origin and endorsed by a magistrate or justice of the peace. Having complied with these conditions, he had still no legal right to the franchise, but was then entitled to petition the Governor asking him to grant the privilege. The Governor in fact often refused such petitions. Once obtained the franchise could not be considered as a right but as a privilege. Under these prohibitive conditions the Natives were virtually disfranchised and not more than a dozen or so ever became voters.

In the meantime, on the other side of the Tugela the Zulus were still nominally an independent nation. Their military system was preserved; their chiefs ruled. In 1878, by which time Cetywayo had succeeded Mpande as their chief, war broke out once more between the Zulus and the white colonists of Natal. At Isandlwana the British forces were routed, but Cetywayo suffered a heavy defeat at Ulundi and was subsequently captured. The dynasty of Tshaka was declared abolished, and Zululand was divided into thirteen districts with a minor chief over each. These chiefs were supposed to be subservient to the British Government. Cetywayo himself was confined in Cape Town Castle and later on a farm in southern Natal.

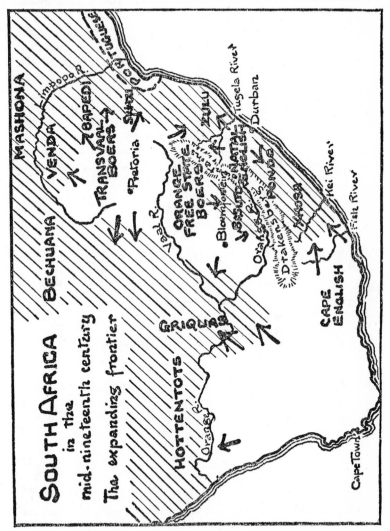

But the struggle against the English was carried on by his son, Dinizulu, who, by calling in the aid of the Transvaal Boers, defeated one of the puppet chiefs, Uzibhepu. In return

49

for their help, he was compelled to give the Boers a slice of territory, including the modern districts of Vryheid and Utrecht. In this way he was able temporarily to restore the unity and independence of Zululand. But the English again intervened and in 1887 formally annexed Zululand to the British Empire. Dinizulu was arrested for continuing his opposition, and in 1889 he was banished to St. Helena. Considerable tracts of the best land of the Zulus, particularly in the sugar country along the coast, now fell into the hands of white farmers.

During this period of conflict between the British and the Zulus, the Boers in the Orange Free State and the Transvaal were occupied in subjugating the Native populations of those provinces. The mountainous area round about the headwaters of the Orange River was the home of the Basuto people, and their lands extended westward over the central plateau. In endeavouring to displace them from these regions the Boers initiated a second series of Kafir Wars.

The first half of the nineteenth century was a period of great misery for the Bantu in South Africa. War was almost continuous. Hundreds of different tribes and factions fought with each other, and matters were made yet more complicated by the spread into the interior of the Boers, British and Griquas,* who fought amongst themselves as well as against the Bantu peoples.

The area now comprising the Orange Free State, Basutoland and the Transvaal was continually crossed and recrossed by the warring armies. Many tribes which had been defeated and driven from their homes by the Zulus moved to new parts of the country, where in turn they attacked and displaced other tribes. Over a large part of the country there was no security of life or limb. Those few people who still tilled the land had to do so with arms at hand and always on guard against the

* The Griquas, also called the Bastards by reason of their Dutch-Hottentot origin, coming from Piquetberg in the western Cape, occupied Griqualand West, near Kimberley. Here, when diamonds were discovered in 1867, on land claimed by the Dutch farmers, the Griqua chief of the time, Waterboer, also claimed the land. He protected his right by selling it to the British. The dispute ended only in 1876, when Waterboer's claim was proved invalid. The British Government accordingly paid compensation to the tune of £90,000 to the Orange Free State. Later the Griquas were moved from the diamond district and settled in Griqualand East in the northern Transkei, where Kokstad is named after Adam Kok, one of their chiefs.

attacks of enemies. People could travel about only in large armed bands. Conditions of starvation and misery prevailed. Some even took to cannibalism to appease their hunger.

It was from such conditions that the Basuto nation arose. One of the smaller chiefs of the central highland region, Moshoeshoe (Moshesh), established his people on a flat mountain top, Thaba Bosiu, which he fortified in 1824. While a good fighter, Moshesh was prepared also to make use of diplomacy to secure peace for his people. He is credited with having established peace between himself and the Matabele, a horde of Zulus who had broken away from Tshaka and swept across the Drakensberg under the leadership of Msilikazi (Moselekatse), by first defeating them in battle and then giving them food. He set himself the task of federating the various quarrelling tribes in his neighbourhood and he gathered round him people from far and wide who were looking for security in the prevailing welter of bloodshed and anarchy.

Moshesh allowed members of the French Protestant Mission to settle in his country in 1833. He did not himself become a Christian, but retained the religion of his ancestors to the end of his days.

For a long time he was successful in securing his independence by playing off the rivalry of the Boers and British. The English were prepared to utilise Basutoland as a buffer between themselves and the Dutch, and in 1843 the country was recognised as a "treaty state." In 1858 the Boers made an attack upon Thaba Bosiu, but were driven off. The Basuto had by this time learned the use of firearms and were even able to manufacture a certain amount of gunpowder. The horse had been introduced and bred into the Basuto pony, strong, sturdy and sure-footed on the mountain tracks. Thus the Basuto were able to meet the Boers on more or less equal terms and they gave a good account of themselves. Again the Boers attacked, in 1865, and again they failed to capture Moshesh's mountain stronghold. But the western section of Basutoland had been overrun by the enemy and, in order to prevent the complete carving up of Basutoland into Boer farms, Moshesh was forced in 1868 to agree to annexation by the British.

Though Basutoland thus became part of the British Empire, the Basuto retained their arms. After 1870 many Basuto went to work on the diamond mines at Kimberley and with their wages bought guns and ammunition. In 1880 the British Government attempted to disarm them. Letsea, the son of Moshesh, and the chief Jonathan were willing to submit. But other chiefs refused, among them Masupha and Lerothodi. Soldiers sent from the Cape met with fierce resistance. Mounted on their tough little ponies and armed with battle-axes as well as guns, the Basuto proved more than a match for the trained English soldiers. When this war came to an end the Basuto were allowed to keep their arms.

What the Whites failed to accomplish by direct attack, however, they have finally achieved by more subtle tactics over a period of fifty years. Though theoretically the Basuto are still entitled to possess arms, in practice the conditions under which guns are now obtainable are so difficult that only a few favoured persons have rifles.*

The former broad lands of Moshesh have been reduced to a comparatively small and mountainous area. Its population of 500,000 acts as a labour reserve, chiefly for the Rand mines. But in 1959 a limited measure of self-government was granted to Basutoland. It has become a refuge for political exiles from the Union. As a possible enclave of African self-rule within white-dominated South Africa, its future as an independent state is likely to prove hazardous and dependent on continued willingness on the part of Britain to protect it. Such protection would in fact be welcomed.

In the Transvaal the Boers set up their South African Republic—a semi-feudal state in which a few thousand whites lorded it over nearly a million Natives. The old pass laws and colour restrictions which had existed in the Cape prior to the coming of the Philanthropists were revived. The *grond-wet* (constitution) of the Transvaal declared that there should be no equality between black and white in Church and State. Natives were not permitted to walk on the sidewalks of the main streets of Pretoria. When the Boer drove by on a country road the Native stood hat in hand and made obeisance—"*Môre, baas.*"

This patriarchal rule had its redeeming features. In general the Boers were not unkindly, though the Native must "keep

* In 1930 Chief Hlajoane Seshophe was sentenced to five months' imprisonment for selling his gun to another Mosuto without permission.

Note. *Mosuto*, a Suto person; *Basuto*, the Suto people; *Lesuto*, the Suto country; *Sesuto* (Sesotho) the Suto language.

his place." The more vicious and intensive forms of exploitation were to come later, with the opening up of the mines and the growth of agriculture.

In 1877 the Transvaal was annexed by the British Government and remained part of the British Empire until after Majuba in 1881. In 1878 a combined force of English and Boers defeated Sekukuni, chief of the Bapedi, the only remaining independent Native chief in the Transvaal.

Paul Kruger, who became President of the Transvaal after its reconquest by the Boers, was not averse to missionaries working among the Natives, and the Christianising process which had begun in the Cape was extended to the north. The Wesleyans and other Protestant sects made great progress.

CHAPTER VII

JABAVU AND THE CAPE LIBERALS

THE HISTORY OF DEMOCRATIC government in the Cape begins in 1853 with the granting of a constitution by Queen Victoria. This gave to the people of the Colony representative but not responsible government. The right to vote for members of the Assembly was granted to every man over the age of twenty-one years who was a British subject and who had property in land or buildings worth £25 or who received a salary of £50 a year. There was no colour bar in this constitution. Any Malay, Coloured person or African, provided he had the necessary property or salary qualification, was entitled to the vote. This, of course, excluded the overwhelming majority of Africans. At the beginning there were very few non-European voters, but as time went on increasing numbers were able to qualify, until they formed a small but significant minority of the electorate.

In 1872 responsible government was granted and thereafter the administration of the country was in the hands of a prime minister and cabinet as we know them to-day.

The steady growth in the number of their voters naturally led Africans to take an increasing interest in politics. At election times white candidates came and asked for their votes. Many of the Bantu, though eligible as voters, were politically uneducated and quite unable to distinguish between the different candidates. Open bribery was often resorted to and presents of blankets on a wholesale scale were sometimes distributed during election campaigns. Hence the term, "blanket vote."

However, it was not long before African voters began to secure some sort of organisation and leadership and to display an increasing amount of discrimination at election times. Early in the 'eighties a young African, John Tengo Jabavu, began to contribute political articles to the *Cape Argus*. This young man was destined to play an important part in political affairs, and he founded a family which has carried on the tradition of what we might call Bantu political liberalism.

Born near Healdtown in 1859 of parents who had been converted by the missionaries, Jabavu was an example of the growing class of Westernised Africans—the "School people," as they were sometimes called to distinguish them from the "red blanket people," pagan tribalists who had not yet succumbed to Christianity and the wearing of European clothes. He attended the Wesleyan mission school at Healdtown and gained his teacher's certificate in 1875. He became a teacher at Somerset East and it was at this time that he began to contribute articles to the Press. He worked in his spare time as printer's devil in the local newspaper office.

In 1881 Jabavu was invited by Dr. James Stewart, Principal of Lovedale,* to edit the Lovedale Mission paper, *Isigidimi SamaXosa* (*Xhosa Express*). While at Lovedale he continued his studies and in 1883 was the first African to pass the matriculation examination. His interest in politics continued. "He exposed the anti-Native utterances in parliament of the very members sent thither amidst election acclamations by

* Lovedale Mission Station of the United Free Church of Scotland, founded 1820, trains Natives for the Church and as teachers, farm labourers and domestic servants, gives technical instruction in printing, weaving, etc. The Lovedale Press prints and publishes numerous books for Africans, also the *South African Outlook*, a missionary journal.

unsuspecting native voters."[1] Such activities were frowned upon by his employers and Jabavu was forced to leave Lovedale and the *Isigidimi*.

Jabavu took up politics seriously during the General Election of 1884, when he acted as the election agent of James Rose-Innes, who was contesting Victoria East. At this time there were three political parties in the Cape, or rather three main political groupings, for the lines of demarcation were not always clear. The main party of the English-speaking colonists was led by Sir Gordon Sprigg. Their chief supporters were among the frontier farmers and the inhabitants of the eastern seaports of East London and Port Elizabeth. They tended to be both anti-Native and anti-Dutch. Their chief opponents were the Afrikander Bond. This was the largest single party and it was led by the famous Jan Hendrik Hofmeyr, "Onze Jan." The great majority of the Dutch (Afrikaner) electorate voted consistently for the Bond. Its political outlook was dictated chiefly by the interests of the rich and conservative Afrikaner landlords of the Western Province. Its attitude to the Natives was in general a hostile one, though Hofmeyr had the reputation of being a liberal.

Between these two large parties was a smaller group of independents, led by three men of professedly liberal views: Rose-Innes, Sauer and Merriman. The Independents counted on the vote of the more liberal English. They had the support of the more settled and commercialised English community in Cape Town. Though they were in a minority among Europeans in the frontier towns, their candidates sometimes managed to get in with the help of the Native vote. With this group Jabavu identified himself at an early date.

The political affiliations of the Cape Coloured and Malay voters, of whom there were numbers in the Western Province and afterwards in Kimberley too, were not so definite as those of the Natives. They tended to vote for the politician who was most powerful locally. In the rural districts of the Western Province most of them appear to have voted for the Bond. It was said that the majority of Hofmeyr's constituents at Stellenbosch were Coloured. In Cape Town itself they usually gave their support to the Independents.

During 1884 more definite steps were taken by the Independents in the Eastern Province to organise the African voters for election purposes and to stabilise their influence over them. In this task the labours and the growing prestige of Jabavu proved invaluable. On November 3, 1884, the first Bantu political newspaper was launched. *Imvo Zabantsundu* (*Native Opinion*) was published weekly in Kingwilliamstown. Its Editor was John Tengo Jabavu. Financial support was provided by a group of Europeans, including Richard Rose-Innes, brother of James. At the beginning Jabavu was "placed upon a small salary," though later he became the official owner of the paper. *Imvo* contained articles and news in both English and Xhosa. Its opinions were often quoted in the South African Press.

Writing in the first issue, Jabavu stated that "the time was ripe for the establishment of a journal in English and Xhosa to give untrammelled expression to the feelings of the native population before the Government and the European public." Native views, he said, were not given sufficient prominence in the colonial Press. The paper wished to help educated Natives to establish bonds of contact among themselves and between their people and the Europeans. Regarding politics, Jabavu declared that his policy would be to support moderate men, although "measures would always be considered more important than the individuals who propose or support them." Brave words, but we shall see later how far he eventually departed from this principle.

Reading through the early volumes of *Imvo*, one is struck by the fact that the problems which agitated Bantu opinion then are still the problems of to-day. Among these subjects of perennial interest were pass laws, location regulations, liquor laws, the continual struggle (generally unsuccessful) against anti-Native legislation and the unequal administration of justice in the courts.

One of the first matters with which *Imvo* had to deal came under the last of these headings. A white farmer, William Pelzer, shot an African and killed him at Burghersdorp in January, 1885. He was allowed to go virtually unpunished by the magistrate, an event hardly more remarkable then than now. But the case had an unusual sequel. A white parson, the Rev. John Davidson Don, was prosecuted for criminal libel, for having published in the *Cape Mercury* a letter denouncing this miscarriage of justice. Don was defended by the young liberal barrister, Richard Solomon, and was acquitted. There were scenes of great rejoicing when Don returned to

Kingwilliamstown to be welcomed by crowds of Africans. Jabavu celebrated the event by naming his newly born son Davidson Don. The child grew up to become Professor Jabavu.

It may be said that the Cape Constitution of 1853 granting representative government was colour-blind. It had not been conceived by South African colonists, but was imposed on the country from England. Had the colonists had any voice in its drafting, the majority of them would certainly not have allowed Africans to share democratic rights with Europeans. However, they welcomed a Constitution which gave them for the first time some say in the management of their own affairs. After the granting of responsible government in 1872, the British Parliament retained the right, in practice seldom if ever exercised, to veto laws passed in Cape Town. It was understood that any fundamental change in the Constitution involving the introduction of a franchise based openly on colour would meet with opposition from the Imperial Government. The colonists therefore sought to limit the political power of the non-Europeans by steadily raising the qualifications upon which the franchise was based.

There commenced a long struggle on the franchise question, which was finally settled by Hertzog's Bill in 1936. The Cape African voters profited in some degree from the hostility between the Boers and British, a hostility which was by no means confined to the Cape. The Boer republics of the Transvaal and the Orange Free State stood in the way of British expansion. Rhodes schemed in the 'eighties to realise his dream "of empire to the northward, aye, one land. . . ." These clashes on the wider field of South African politics served only to intensify antagonisms at the Cape.

It happened often in the Cape that the African voters held the balance between the contending parties. Since the Cape Dutch party, the Bond, was openly hostile to the Natives, these naturally gave their votes to the English candidates. Thus many of the latter had a vested interest in preserving the Native vote. The supporters of the Bond, though they wished to abolish the Native franchise, were less enthusiastic about taking the vote away from their own Coloured supporters. At the same time both English and Dutch feared the growth of an African electorate so strong that it would begin to exercise an independent influence in Cape politics or even return black men to the House of Assembly. Hitherto no African candidate had presented himself at an election. But with a further increase in the Native vote in certain frontier constituencies that possibility became one that had to be reckoned with and both parties agreed that this had to be prevented.

A rapid growth in the Native electorate between 1882 and 1886 resulted in the first attempts to alter the Constitution of 1853. In the five frontier constituencies of Aliwal North, Kingwilliamstown, Queenstown, Victoria East and Wodehouse the total number of voters, white and black, had increased from 7,068 to 12,290. But the Native vote, which had been only 14 per cent. of the total in 1882, had risen to 47 per cent. in 1886. In two of these constituencies, Aliwal North and Wodehouse, the Natives were actually in the majority, numbering 54 per cent. and 51 per cent. respectively. These figures were quoted by the liberal Hofmeyr to show "the gravity of the position."

A measure known as the Parliamentary Registration Bill was introduced by the Sprigg Government in 1887. It proposed to strike off the roll a number of Native voters whose qualifications were held to be doubtful. Clause 17 of the new Bill declared that "no person shall be entitled to be registered as a voter by reason of his sharing in any communal or tribal occupation of lands or buildings." This meant that an African would have to own property to the value of £25 or more on individual freehold tenure before he could qualify to be registered.

The Bill was opposed by the Independents, Sauer, Rose-Innes, Merriman and their followers, but was supported by the Sprigg party and by the Afrikander Bond. "Mr. Hofmeyr was not the man," says his biographer, "to object to the presence of Native representatives in the House, he believed in the principle of their representation; but there was a great danger which arose from the fact that, as a result of the franchise provision, the natives who wielded this power were to a large extent still sunk in barbarism. . . . We find him aiming at an alteration in the franchise, not indeed in the direction of a colour test, but rather of a civilisation test, and it was largely due to his exertions that the voters' roll of the Cape Colony was not swamped by a mass of illiterate barbarians, whose sole qualification was that they possessed communal property to the value of £25, and thus the politics of the Colony were not either reduced to a struggle between black and white, or perhaps, worse still, placed at the mercy of unscrupulous agents outbidding one another for the votes of an ignorant electorate."[2]

In his speech to Parliament, Hofmeyr used an ingenious argument in favour of the Bill. The Natives, he said, were subjected to disabilities as an inferior and criminal class. As such they were not deserving of the rights accorded to the highest class of freemen. "If the Kafirs were equal to the whites, then they were entitled to vote, but then the class legislation directed against them must be swept away. If they were not equal to the whites, then they were not entitled to vote, then the class legislation must be retained, and the power must not be given them to sweep it away for themselves."[2]

It is clear that Hofmeyr, like Sauer, Rose-Innes and Merriman, and even Jabavu himself, explicitly or implicitly believed that any form of mass struggle for Native rights was undesirable, and that the Natives should be prepared to remain in a minority in the electorate, if not permanently, at least for a very long time to come. They were prepared to salve their liberal consciences by insisting there should be at least what would nowadays be called a token Native vote. That class legislation was in itself directed primarily to keeping the blacks as an "inferior and criminal class" did not seem to trouble them.

The Registration Bill was passed in May, 1887, the Independents being the only members to vote against it. It resulted in some 30,000 Africans being struck off the voters' roll.

To prove the consistency of his logic and perhaps also, as we shall see later, for another reason, Hofmeyr then moved: "That this House is of opinion that all aboriginal Natives, registered or qualified to be registered at Parliamentary elections, be exempt from all special laws and regulations in respect of natives." Among such special laws he referred to the Native Pass Law, the Native Location Act, the Native Liquor Clause, and a law which said that Natives who desired to bequeath property might do so only under Native tribal law and not under European law.

These proposals of Hofmeyr were embodied in a Bill and eventually passed into law as the Native Disabilities Removal Act. It was regarded by Hofmeyr's critics as a measure serving the interests of the Cape wine and brandy farmers. The clause abolishing prohibition had been sandwiched in among a number of other provisions of a purely liberal character. This criticism is described by Hofmeyr's biographer as "unworthy." Whatever Hofmeyr's motives may have been, the Act was a boon to Native voters. It has been described as the Magna Carta of Natives in the Cape, and it is only in our own day that these rights have been placed in jeopardy. It is an interesting fact that Hofmeyr's descendant and biographer himself voted for the Native Laws Amendment Act of 1937, which placed the Natives of the Cape under the same class legislation as those of the three northern provinces.

Rose-Innes was among the nigrophilists who supported Hofmeyr's Native Disabilities Removal Bill on general grounds. But he sought, at first unsuccessfully, to secure an amendment in favour of the retention of prohibition for Natives. In this he had the unqualified support of Jabavu, himself a devout Wesleyan and a "temperance man." Again and again, Rose-Innes returned to the attack until he succeeded in getting legislation passed. In the meantime, some cynical statements were made on public platforms and in the Press on the question of alcohol and the Natives. Referring to a speech made by Hofmeyr at Kimberley in 1891, *Imvo* reported that the speaker had "hinted at the wisdom of a policy of doing away with the natives of this country by means of the deleterious drink popularly known as Cape smoke."* In fairness it must be stated that these were not Hofmeyr's own words, but only the interpretation that Jabavu placed on them.

At about the same time, the Johannesburg *Star* published a leading article advocating the extermination of the black population by means of alcohol. "In alcohol is to be found the only influence which may be trusted to sap the fund of seemingly infinite vitality [of the black man] which will overcome civilisation if civilisation does not overcome it."

The passing of the Native Disabilities Removal Act did not deter successive governments at the Cape from attempting further class legislation. In May, 1889, the Sprigg Government proposed "an effective pass law" which was to apply to registered voters as well as to the rank and file. The pass was to be shown on demand to any J.P., police officer, veldcornet, constable or (white) owner or occupier of land, on pain of

* Cheap brandy.

20*s.* fine, with the alternative of a month's imprisonment with or without spare diet and hard labour. "So nearly," wrote Jabavu, "has it become a crime for a Native to exist in the land which was once his own."

The agitation against the Bill was effective. A petition was drawn up and a deputation of Africans, headed by Jabavu waited upon the Government. The Bill was withdrawn.

O those sweet, far-off liberal days! It seemed that democratic government in the Cape was going to broaden down from precedent to precedent. At least so some believed. A writer in the *Cape Mercury* was full of hope for the future: "Men who claim to be in possession of the average share of common sense will not fail to catch the significance of this petitioning among Natives. It shows that the old days of lawlessness are being relegated to the limbo of forgotten things, and that a better era of loyalty to existing law, or fair and straightforward agitation against an obnoxious law, has begun. The final appeal of the future is not likely to be to the assegai and the rifle, but to the ballot box. A race that sets such store by litigation and oratory as the Kafir, is easily governed by even so complicated a code of laws as ours, provided that their feelings are not wantonly outraged and that they are treated with at least elementary justice."

Jabavu was now the acknowledged leader of Native opinion and *Imvo* a dominant factor in elections in the Eastern Province. But there were not wanting cynics who considered Jabavu a mere puppet dancing to the tune of the Europeans who subsidised his paper and dictated his policy. Thus, when the Bloemfontein *Friend* praised Jabavu's speeches and writings, the Port Elizabeth *Telegraph* replied with the following: "We neither doubt for one moment either Tengo's ability or his blackness; but the *Friend's* contributor may learn if he doesn't know that his 'ability as an editor' is due to the number of white 'coaches' who look after Jabavu. We pity the credulity of any reader who believes that the articles in the Kafir paper have not been submitted to 'Umlungu'* scrutiny. Not an article appears that does not contain sesquipedalian words that no Kafir this side of the Tropic of Capricorn could understand or would use—except on an Amateur Christy platform."

Imvo's only comment was: "This no doubt would be an

* White man.

61

additional feather in the cap of our Editor, if he troubled about such decorations." There was no attempt to deny the impeachment. It might have been urged that the long words in the leading articles were evidence that Jabavu did indeed write them himself. A European writing for Africans would certainly have tried to use simpler language.

Jabavu's claim that he would stand by principles and not by personalities was subjected to increasingly severe tests after July, 1890. In that month the Sprigg Ministry fell and Rhodes became Premier.

Rhodes had been sent to Parliament by the diggers on the diamond fields. He was determined to put through his programme of Imperialist expansion to the north. He had no natural sympathy for Africans and dealt ruthlessly with Native tribes who stood in his path. At the same time he was prepared to mouth liberal sentiments if it was a question of getting votes in the Cape. He is credited with coining the phrase: "Equal rights for all civilised men south of the Zambezi." According to William Plomer, the actual words used by Rhodes were: " 'Equal rights for every white man south of the Zambesi,' and thus he was correctly reported in the *Eastern Province Herald*. A copy of the newspaper was at once sent to him by an association of the Coloured voters at the Cape, and he was asked whether he had in fact spoken the words as printed. This was on the eve of a general election and Rhodes was bound to consider the importance of the Coloured vote. He therefore sent back the newspaper, on the margin of which he had written: 'My Motto is—Equal Rights for every civilised man south of the Zambezi. What is a civilised man? A man, whether black or white, who has sufficient education to write his name, has some property, or works. In fact, is not a loafer.' This is a peculiar and characteristically narrow definition of a civilised man, and it is sad to discover that Rhodes was capable of juggling with so important a statement simply in order to catch votes."[3]

The Sprigg Government was thrown out by a combination between Rhodes and other Independents on the one hand and the Bond on the other. It was rumoured that Rhodes had obtained the support of the Bond by promising to carry on their Native policy and raise the qualifications for voters. "The great question of the future," observed Hofmeyr, speaking to his white followers at Paarl, "is the electoral privilege of the franchise—whether we shall in future be governed by the blacks or by ourselves. The latter is what Mr. Rhodes is striving for, and he deserves the fullest co-operation of the Afrikanders. His heart is with us."

Jabavu's special friends and patrons, Rose-Innes, Sauer and Merriman, were now hand in glove with Rhodes and the Afrikander Bond in a combination which had come into power on the understanding that it was to make the future safe for white South Africa. *Imvo* began a campaign of special pleading which it kept up for years, trying to show that its three heroes were still the best friends the Native people had. Its task was rendered doubly difficult by some of the public utterances of these nigrophilists. For instance, Merriman, speaking to an audience of white farmers at the Port Elizabeth agricultural dinner in April, 1891, was reported as follows: "The question before the country was whether it was going to be a black man's country or a white man's country. (*Cheers.*) When he saw the farmers becoming disheartened and hiring their land out to Kafirs, the Colony becoming blacker, Natal a large native location helped along by coolies, and Cape Town becoming browner and browner every day, then he felt misgivings in his mind as to the future." Jabavu did not reply to this demagogic tirade by denouncing the opportunism of Merriman. Instead, he said that the future for the black man was not as rosy as Merriman had painted it.

When the new composite Government came into being, fears were expressed in Native quarters as to what would happen next. Jabavu tried to calm these fears. "With gentlemen such as Messrs. Sauer, Innes and Sivewright, whose principles are opposed to anything savouring of injustice to the natives, in the Cabinet, we have, we think, no reason to be apprehensive."

Indeed at first it seemed that the nigrophilists were not going to support the new Government in further anti-Native legislation. A certain P. J. du Toit, an extremist member of the Bond, moved an amendment to the Master and Servants Law, granting the power to farmers to thrash their Native servants. The Bill, which became known as the "Strop Bill," was defeated by thirty-five votes to twenty-three, Innes and Sauer and most of the former Independents voting against it. Hofmeyr and his Bond and Rhodes (to the pained indignation of Olive Schreiner) voted for it, as also did Sivewright, one of those "gentlemen . . . whose principles," Jabavu had written just two weeks before, "were opposed to anything savouring of injustice to Natives." Hofmeyr, according to his biographer, gave the Bill his "qualified" support.

But of this pact between nigrophilism and imperialism worse was to come. Hofmeyr stumped the country to get support for a new measure to limit the qualification of African voters. He wanted to give a second vote to all, black and white, who had passed the matriculation examination, and further additional votes to members of the learned professions. "Then the country would be saved from the threatened danger."

The idea of a higher educational qualification did not meet with much support. Among his own followers were some, like a certain van der Walt, who declared that "an educational test would only incite the Natives to learn, and then the work of purging the list would have to begin again." Certain Englishmen were equally suspicious: "Mr. Douglas said that the educational vote proposed by Mr. Hofmeyr was only a blind and the real object was to deprive the English mechanics of the franchise. Hofmeyr's whole move was intended to elevate the Afrikander Bond so that it could still further dictate to the English people of the Colony."

The proposed plural voting was therefore dropped and the Native Franchise Act of 1892 provided (1) that voters already on the roll should remain there, (2) that in future the property qualification should be raised from £25 to £75, while the salary qualification was retained at £50 per annum, and (3) that every applicant for registration should sign his name in the presence of the registering official.

The immediate effect of the measure (which was passed by forty-five votes to twenty) was shown at the registration of 1893 in a decrease of 3,348 in the number of non-European voters as against an increase of 4,506 in the number of Europeans. One rather interesting result of the signature qualification was the formation in certain districts of large evening classes, where Coloured and Native adults laboriously acquired the ability to write their own names.

The Act was another blow at the democratic rights of Africans in the Cape. And yet it had had the support of Hofmeyr and of those "old Cape liberals," Rose-Innes, Sauer and Merriman. Such was the effect of the unholy alliance between Rhodes, the Afrikander Bond and the Independents. Of the so-called nigrophilists who voted for the measure, Innes seems to have been the only one who had any scruples about the matter. "The franchise question very nearly produced a split in the Cabinet, Innes being pledged to oppose any restriction of the existing Native vote. It was only under persistent pressure from both Merriman and Sauer that in the end he was induced to acquiesce in the very moderate changes which, after much discussion, were accepted by the Bond."[4] "Sir James Rose-Innes supported this; he said, *inter alia*, 'The Bill contained no mention of colour, but they who supported the Bill trusted that it would neutralise the Native votes."[5]

Jabavu, thus faced with a situation in which his own favourite friends of the Natives supported a Bill which had the manifest objective of reducing the number of Native voters, failed miserably to put up any kind of fight against the passage of the Bill. The Port Elizabeth *Telegraph* was once more able to claim that *Imvo* had become "a mere Ministerial organ instead of a reflex of Native opinion." To the charge that he had weakly acquiesced in this reactionary measure, the harassed Jabavu could reply only: "If there had been a party sufficiently courageous to table a motion that no change at all should be made, that party would claim our support. Failing this, we had no option but to fall back upon the compromise which, maintaining the *status quo*, proceeds to legislate for posterity of which we know nothing and care less." The kindest comment on these unhappy words would seem to be that they were ill-considered. But as the expression of the standpoint of one who claimed to be a champion of Native rights, could there ever be a more damning statement? Because the Bill proposed to leave existing Native voters on the roll, Jabavu was prepared to accept it. Even the *Cape Times* professed itself shocked: "After this confession of indifference to the permanent effect of the coming legislation, the Government should abandon the saving clause in favour of those on the register and apply the purge boldly, unreservedly and at once. We shall see then how the *Imvo* folk like being treated as they are willing that their sons should be treated."

There seems little doubt that the Bill would have been defeated if the Independents had voted against it. But this would have meant voting with the Sprigg party against Rhodes and the Bond, and this the friends of the Natives were not prepared to do. There were things that meant more to them than friendship for Africans. As for Jabavu, it was clear that he was once more supporting individuals and not principles.

Jabavu adopted a similar churlish attitude towards a group of Coloured people who attempted to continue the struggle against the new law after it was passed, by means of an appeal to the Imperial Government in London to veto the measure as an infringement of the Constitution of 1853. Jabavu appears in this connection in a most unsavoury light, his racial bias against the Coloured people combining with his opportunistic attachment to his white political supervisors, who had seen fit to vote for the reactionary measure. The new move came from a Coloured group in Kimberley. They had sent emissaries to the Eastern Province to try to secure Native support for the petition. Jabavu advised the Africans to have nothing to do with it. "It is well known Natives trusted Messrs. Innes, Sauer and Merriman to do the best they can in a difficult situation to safeguard their interests. . . . To join in a movement by extreme men for an appeal would be treachery towards friends who have long stood by us. Natives cannot afford to deal with their friends in Parliament in that way; and they have wisely decided not to identify themselves with the doings of a small party of irreconcilables. We have no doubt their action . . . will commend itself to colonists generally, not excepting those of the Afrikander school."

The possibility of a united front between various sections of the non-Europeans has always been a major issue in the struggle for freedom of the black man in South Africa. The idea did not appeal to Jabavu. Whenever the Coloured people are mentioned in *Imvo* there are either references to bastardy, disparaging remarks, often only too well-founded, on the political ineptitude of the Coloured voters, or haughty advice tendered by one whose tremendous political experience and lofty principles were above reproach.

Actually the relations between the Coloured voters and the Bond were on a par with those that existed between the Native voters and the Independents. Hofmeyr cultivated the Coloured vote just as assiduously as Innes, Sauer and Merriman did the Native. And both Hofmeyr and Merriman were prepared to let their non-European supporters down when it would have been inconvenient to uphold their views.

In the General Election of 1893 an attempt was made for the first time to put up non-European candidates. In Paarl it was declared that a movement was on foot to unite everyone, "Moslems, Indians, Cape Men, Natives, Creoles and Coolies," in support of James Curry, the Coloured candidate. In Cape Town the Malays prepared to nominate Attoan Mah Effendi, a man of Turkish extraction. At that time there existed in the Cape a form of proportional representation known as the cumulative vote. Certain large constituencies returned more than one candidate and every voter was allowed to cast as many votes as there were candidates. Voters, if they so desired, might give all their votes to the same candidate. The Malays in Cape Town were threatening to use this device to secure the return of Effendi; and so Orpen's Constitutional Amendment Bill was hastily rushed through Parliament, abolishing the cumulative vote. Jabavu taunted the Malays for being so naïve as to let the cat out of the bag before election day. *Imvo* did not approve of Coloured candidates. They would take away votes from the white Independents whom Jabavu was pledged to support.

Hofmeyr was the only member of the House who spoke against Orpen's Bill. "His objection to colour was not so strong that he would object to see a well-educated man like the Effendi sitting in that House. If the Effendi was elected by the Malay community and he [Mr. Hofmeyr] had the good fortune to be re-elected . . . of which he was not quite certain . . . the Effendi was quite welcome to a seat by his side. That was a feeling which did not seem to actuate many other members of the House."[2] No doubt this daring statement on the part of Hofmeyr stood him in good stead with his Coloured constituents in the election a few weeks later.

To illustrate the other side of Hofmeyr's attitude to colour, the following anecdote is recounted by his biographer: "A deputation of his Coloured electors waited on him to ask whether they might become members of the Bond. . . . Mr. Hofmeyr made no reply; instead, he invited the deputation to dine at his house. The men saw the point; they felt that it was impossible for them to accept such an invitation, neither therefore could they expect to be treated in every way as the white man's equal."[2]

Behind the "Native question," as always, were the twin problems of land and labour. It was now more than a generation since the main boundaries of the Native reserves in the Eastern Cape had been established and the Native possession of these areas had become an accepted thing. But there was one region where Native occupation was more recent and less secure, and upon this territory the white farmers cast envious eyes. The fruitful region of Glen Grey had been settled by a section of the Tembu tribe at the close of the war of 1877. The system of land tenure had never been settled and Xhosas and Fingos had crowded in from all sides. It was this region which the Bond considered should be handed over to the white colonists. They put a motion to that effect in Parliament in 1889. This was unsuccessful and further attempts were made from time to time.

At the same time the labour problem was becoming more serious. The mines on the Rand and at Kimberley were crying out for cheap labour. Merriman, the liberal, was in favour of importing cheap white labour. In a debate in Parliament on State-aided immigration, he declared that "Kafirs were simply lazy, turbulent brutes who could not be managed. They got drunk and fought and turned a place into hell upon earth. Neither were Hottentots the sort of men they wanted, as they were unintelligent. . . . He suggested to the Government that a small shipment of Continental peasants (Italians preferably) should be immigrated as a trial. The country wanted cheap labour."

But Rhodes was a realist. He and the Bond set about solving the labour problem in earnest. The Glen Grey Act of 1894 has been described as the highest product of the co-operation of the two men, Rhodes and Hofmeyr. "The whole territory was to be split up into locations, and each location was to be subdivided into lots, indivisible and inalienable without the consent of the Governor. The ownership of a lot was not of itself to confer the franchise. Village councils and a district council were to be instituted . . . and a labour tax of 10s. was to be imposed on all Natives who did not go out as labourers for three months out of the twelve. By this provision and even more by the fact that the institution of fixed tenure would very soon produce a landless class, it was anticipated that the needs of the labour market would be met."[2]

Some four years later Hofmeyr, who by this time had quarrelled with Rhodes, said in a public speech that "he had never tried to deprive a Coloured man of his educational privileges; he had never joined in the insensate cry of 'equal rights for all white men south of the Zambezi.' . . . It was an open secret that if Mr. Rhodes could have had his way no black man would have had a vote. . . . He [Hofmeyr] never supported any measure to encourage forced black labour."[2] Apparently no one in the audience had the courage to remind him of the Glen Grey Act.

In 1895 came the Jameson Raid. The Independents, led by Sauer and Schreiner, now broke with Rhodes and united with Hofmeyr in a middle policy which approved of neither Rhodes nor Kruger and sought to secure the union of South Africa by peaceful means. The attitude of *Imvo* during the Anglo-Boer War, though it was apparently dictated by its political backers, was not in itself discreditable.

In their efforts to reconcile Boer and Briton, the Independents often resorted to the argument that it was bad policy for the white races to quarrel in face of their common enmity to the blacks. It was difficult for Jabavu to continue urging Native voters to give support to persons who used arguments of this nature. For instance, when Schreiner, in a speech on volunteering in September, 1899, said "he would be glad to see volunteers more efficient and perhaps at less expense, in order to be able to defend the country against what one might call the natural enemies of the country, the Native population," Jabavu had to argue through a whole column of *Imvo* in his efforts to explain away what he described as this "unguarded slip of the tongue."

Jabavu was more successful in putting forward a consistent policy in regard to the war. He found very useful ammunition to hand in statements made by the Campbell-Bannerman Liberals in England, who were strongly critical of the military attack on the Boer republics, the executions of "rebels" and the concentration camps. *Imvo* was full of quotations from the *Manchester Guardian* and other Liberal papers. Various sermons by pacifist parsons both in England and in South Africa were also quoted at length. *Imvo* was closed down by the military authorities in August, 1901, and did not resume publication until October, 1902, when the war had ended.

Jabavu continued in his political attachment to the Bond.

The Innes-Sauer-Merriman combination had broken up in 1898. Sauer was now a leading Bondsman and Innes was a Progressive. Both the Bond and the Progressive Party were interested in the Native vote. Jabavu supported the Bond candidates and attacked the Progressives. A leader-writer in the *Cape Argus* suggested that Jabavu was trying to hold the balance of power. "He began to fear that if the Progressives got too large a majority he would be rather left out in the cold, so he has been working hard to level up." Some years later the *Argus* again referred to "the strange combination . . . between the Bond and the Natives who follow the lead of Mr. Tengo Jabavu. These things are always curiously, we might say adroitly managed. The Bond officially has nothing to do with *Imvo* and Mr. Jabavu does not become a Bondsman; but there is some useful gentleman such as Mr. Sauer, who acts as a least common denominator, and the sum works out all right. . . . Bond views on Native policy are not such as could possibly commend themselves to the judgment of the Native elector if he were in a position to exercise his choice intelligently."

The granting of responsible government to the Transvaal and Orange Free State led to the union of the four provinces in 1910. The preliminary negotiations and drafting of the new Constitution resulted in furious arguments as to the future of the Cape Native and Coloured vote.

A National Convention met in 1908 to draft the new Constitution. The Cape representatives were expected to insist on the maintenance of the Cape vote. *Imvo* was optimistic as to the result. "That the existing rights and privileges of the Natives of Cape Colony will be safeguarded we have no doubt. We are equally persuaded that something, even though not on a par with what our Cape people possess, will be done for our Native friends in the other Colonies in the direction of securing for them some form of representation in the Union." In spite of the assurances given by the Cape representatives, many Natives remained nervous, and at public meetings continued to urge the Convention not to let them down. Jabavu deprecated such agitation while the Convention was sitting: "There would be reason for it when the proposals of the Convention are found seriously and unjustly to threaten the rights of any section of the people; but we fail to find any ground for Natives crying before they are hurt."

But Jabavu was proved wrong. In February, 1909, the

Convention produced the first draft of the new Constitution. Though the existing franchise in the Cape was retained, the non-Europeans lost their right to sit in Parliament. *Imvo* declared: "The Natives of the Cape have never returned men of their colour to Parliament, although they knew that they could do so, and that knowledge was of the essence of their peace, happiness and contentment under their Government; but the draft Constitution deprives them of these and stereotypes vicious, flagitious and immoral colour distinctions among the King's subjects, which spell the abandonment of the Cape's liberal Native policy. This should be strenuously resisted. It is a bad policy, too, to ignore the existence of the numerous Native people in the neighbouring colonies in the matter of representation."

There were very few of the white nigrophilists who continued to fight against the proposed colour bar in the new Constitution. The Cape Town branch of the Afrikander Bond passed a resolution, proposed by Hofmeyr, objecting to certain items, including the introduction of colour limitations concerning membership of Parliament in the Cape. This point of view was rejected by the Bond as a whole. The traditional Cape liberals, Sauer, Merriman, Innes, J. C. Molteno and others, having put up some sort of fight for the Cape franchise in the National Convention, now considered that they had done their duty and were prepared to accept the new constitution.

One suspects in the case of many of the Cape liberals that their nigrophilism was only skin deep. They expressed publicly their interest in maintaining the Cape Native vote. This vote had provided them with safe seats in Parliament. But in the last analysis they were prepared to sacrifice the principles of democracy which knew no colour bar for what they conceived to be more important things, among these the achievement of a "united" South Africa.

Of all the prominent political "friends of the Natives" only W. P. Schreiner fought the colour bar to the bitter end. And he was not an "old Cape liberal," but an ex-nigrophobe. Full tribute has been paid to him in a biography by Professor Walker. "In his younger days he had held such unsympathetic views on the Native question that he had shocked the liberals of the old Cape House; but from 1899 onwards, when he was forty-two years of age, he had begun to swing round, and long before the time of Union, had become a convinced supporter of the claims of civilised non-Europeans to full citizenship in a civilised state. He now fought the draft South Africa Act to the very gates of Westminster because he believed on general grounds that a close federation of small states was the best guarantee of liberty, and that . . . it was the only form of closer union that could save the Cape's liberal policy from being swamped by the illiberal policy of the other three provinces. . . . As for the comfortable doctrine that the Cape franchise was so firmly entrenched that it could not be harmed, he condemned the two-thirds majority clause as a trap. Northern opinion being what it was, if only a few Cape members betrayed their trust, Native and Coloured parliamentary rights would vanish."[6] And they did betray their trust—once more—in 1936.

When the draft Constitution was sent back for amendment to the Cape Parliament, Schreiner forced a division on the question of the proposed colour bar. His motion was defeated, only twenty voting for it and seventy-seven against. Among those who voted with the majority were the old-time liberals, F. S. Malan, J. X. Merriman, J. C. Molteno and J. W. Sauer. Finally, when the draft South Africa Act was submitted for ratification by the Cape Parliament it was supported by ninety-six votes to two. The diehards were W. P. Schreiner and J. Gordon Sprigg.

Schreiner went to England to try to induce Westminster to insist on modifications in the Constitution. The Africans also sent representatives to London, among them Tengo Jabavu and Walter Rubusana. They failed, as seemed inevitable. On August 31, 1909, *Imvo* declared: "The blow has fallen, and the British Government and House of Commons have passed the Union Constitution Act without the amendments we had hoped for."

Jabavu remained for a time in London and gave some lectures. Speaking at the New Reform Club, he "advocated that under the Union there should be manhood and womanhood suffrage in the case of the whites, and the Cape franchise throughout the Union in the case of the Natives, and said that under such a system Native predominance would be prevented" (*Imvo*, November 20, 1909). Jabavu's line, like that of the Cape liberals in general, was again clearly expressed: the Natives did not want predominance, they did not claim majority rights, but only such privileges as would not conflict with the maintenance of European rule.

Thus the African electors of the Cape lost the right to send men of their own race to Parliament, a right which they had never exercised. But non-Europeans might still be elected to the Provincial Council in the Cape Province. In the provincial elections in 1910 an African candidate was put forward for a Cape constituency. This was the Rev. Walter Rubusana, who stood for the predominantly Native constituency of Tembuland.

Like Jabavu, Rubusana had served his political apprenticeship as an agent of white politicians. Whereas Jabavu had worked for the Independents and then for the Bond, Rubusana had been employed by the Progressives. Born in 1858, at Mnandi in the Ciskei, he had been educated at Lovedale. He was ordained as a minister of the London Missionary Society in 1884. He went to the United States and was awarded the honorary degree of Doctor of Philosophy by the McKinley University, a Negro college, for a *History of South Africa from the Native Standpoint*. On his return to South Africa he continued to work in the Church and was one of those responsible for the revised version of the Xhosa Bible.

Jabavu was by no means enamoured of Rubusana's candidature for Tembuland. Rubusana had been a supporter of the Progressives and Jabavu considered him to be in the enemy's camp. At the same time, for *Imvo* to oppose the first African candidate who had gone to the poll would have been outrageous. He therefore took the line that the electors should consider Rubusana not as a black man, but on his merits. He considered that Rubusana was not wise in standing. "It would have been [better] for the Native candidate to feel that he was buttressed by a strong call from the electors—elements which seem to us to be lamentably wanting in the reverend gentleman's campaign."

In spite of this resentful attitude on the part of *Imvo*, Rubusana was elected. This was a great victory for the Native voters of the Cape. *Imvo* was forced to make some show of welcoming the result. "Congratulations to Rev. Walter Rubusana on his return for Tembuland . . . he has scraped his way in by a majority of twenty-five. A crusted old Progressive, he has to thank the South African Party for withdrawing their candidate when asked to do by his Progressive friends when they found themselves in a tight corner. . . . Whether he and his Progressive friends will continue to lick the boot that has thus kicked them remains to be seen." Thus the disgruntled Jabavu.

But *Imvo*, whether Jabavu liked it or not, was forced to give increasing public support to Rubusana, who had become an accepted champion of Native rights. *Imvo* published a lengthy and laudatory biography of the first black provincial councillor.

Nor were some of the old Cape liberals any more pleased than Jabavu to see the principle to which they had so long paid lip service thus put into practice. R. W. Rose-Innes wrote to the *East London Dispatch* deploring the election of a black man to the Provincial Council. He was appalled at the idea of a black man being allowed a salary, a free railway ticket with use of a first-class compartment and a lavatory and bedding such as European passengers used. Such things, he declared, would damage the Native cause and put the clock back.

It was the old story of liberalism in South Africa. The Natives must not put forward extreme demands: this would simply play into the hands of the reactionaries. But the reactionaries for their part had no scruple on this score: their demands were invariably extreme. So-called compromises, which have been made from time to time, have always resulted in a certain proportion of the demands of the reactionaries being conceded. Thus the history of South Africa ever since 1910 has been a continual process of whittling down of Native rights. That it would be possible by militant organisation and leadership under the banner of extreme demands to put a stop to this process or even to reverse it is an idea which has seldom attracted the support of South African liberals.

One of the results of Union was the birth of a movement to unite all politically-minded Africans in a single national organisation. But Jabavu would not support the new movement. Instead, he attempted to build up an organisation of his own, which he called the South African Races Congress. *Imvo* gave no publicity to the first meeting of the South African Native National Congress which met at Bloemfontein in January, 1912. The Congress had soon to face another drastic piece of anti-Native legislation in the Native Land

Bill of 1913, which proposed not only to stop "mixed farm-ing" (the share-crop system whereby Natives had the use of a portion of a white man's land, paying rent in the form of a proportion of the crop), but also to limit drastically the right of Africans to own land.

The new Bill immediately aroused a storm of protest from all genuine friends of the Natives. But Jabavu was tied to Sauer's chariot wheel and Sauer, as the new Minister of Native Affairs, sponsored the Bill. In the face of general Native indignation, Jabavu professed his approval of the principles embodied in the Bill. *Imvo* started once more on a campaign of special pleading. The measure was going to give the Natives land; not take it away; Mr. Sauer would not let the Natives down; and so forth.

Jabavu summoned a meeting of his South African Races Congress and got them to pass a resolution in favour of the Land Bill. But he could not carry the Native masses with him, even in the Eastern Province. A meeting of the Queens-town Vigilance Association expressed "alarm at the change in the Native policy of the country as outlined in the Native Lands Bill . . . and expressed itself as quite out of sympathy with the views of Mr. Jabavu." Jabavu replied that he had asked Native audiences whether they objected to the present Native reserves being confirmed, whether they were against more land being found for landless squatters and whether they objected to separate areas being set aside for black and white. In all cases they had answered, "No." He had not asked them whether they were in favour of Native land being permanently limited to a mere fraction of the area of the country.

The Land Bill was passed by a large majority. In the course of the debate Sauer was able to quote Jabavu as favouring the measure.

As had been foreseen, the illegalisation of share farming had immediate and drastic consequences for the Bantu, especially in the Free State. Thousands of African families were driven off the white farms. For months they wandered, homeless and starving, until they were eventually absorbed as labour tenants (semi-serfs) on the farms or as labourers in the urban localities. The land promised for evicted squatters was never provided.

His support of the Land Act brought about Jabavu's

political downfall. For thirty years he had been the acknowledged leader of African voters in the Cape. The avowed champion of Native interests, he had allowed himself to become ever more plainly the tool of a group of white politicians. He had dodged this way and that wherever Sauer led him. He had used his facile pen to gloss over and explain away this or that hostile statement or reactionary act on the part of his white cronies. He had defended or belittled the importance of the various pieces of anti-Native legislation for which his friends were responsible. He had poured scorn on other African politicians who were in the tow of rival white parties. He had opposed any form of unity between the Coloured and the Africans and he had sabotaged unity among the Africans themselves. He had travelled far from the brave beginning of *Imvo* when he had promised always to consider "measures more important than the individuals who propose or support them." All this he had got away with. But he could not get away with his support of the Land Act. Rebellion flared up among his own followers in the Eastern Cape. His policy was publicly repudiated by the majority of politically-minded Africans.

In 1914 Jabavu committed his crowning folly. In the provincial elections in 1914 he stood against Rubusana in Tembuland and let the white candidate in. He said that he had been requested by Tembuland voters to stand. But it was clear that he was splitting the Native vote. He declared that he would secure votes from whites as well as blacks. But the result was a foregone conclusion. Payn, the white candidate, received 1,004 votes, practically all white votes "with a sprinkling of blacks." The bulk of the black vote was shared between the African candidates. Rubusana got 852 and Jabavu 294. Thus the first, and only, African provincial councillor lost his seat.

Pathetically Jabavu protested in *Imvo* that it was "idle to make a scapegoat of a candidate who never thought of contesting the seat, but who, invited by a section of his countrymen, would not disappoint them," and so on. His protests did not avail. Nemesis had come upon him. The old man, broken in health, his influence lost, virtually retired from politics. He died in 1921, leaving his sons to carry on *Imvo* and the traditional policy of attachment to the white politicians, politely termed "intelligent statesmanship." His son, Professor Jabavu, has defended Tengo Jabavu's integrity in an interesting biography. He was undoubtedly a man of talent and the most outstanding figure in a generation of black South Africans. He could hit hard and, when not constrained by his political affiliations, did much to expose the injustices which Natives suffered. One of his most noteworthy achievements was his share in setting up the South African Native College at Fort Hare. For years *Imvo* carried on propaganda and Jabavu himself stumped the country to raise money for this scheme, which came to fruition in 1916.

CHAPTER VIII

THE ETHIOPIAN MOVEMENT

IT IS AN INTERESTING fact that the first Bantu mass movement on truly national lines was a religious one. What came to be called Ethiopianism was an attempt on the part of Christian Africans to set up their own churches independent of the white ones. Though some of these churches were purely tribalistic affairs or confined to particular areas, others made a nation-wide appeal to all black Christians and tried to unite people of all tribes and nations. Though outwardly religious, they were also to a large extent political in their appeal. They began as a revolt of the black members within the missionary churches. Bantu Christians almost always found that there were colour bars in the white churches; even some of the most enthusiastic missionaries insisted upon treating all members of their Native flocks as children, refusing to ordain black men as priests or, if they did so ordain them, always putting them in positions where they had to take orders from white superiors.

It was about eighty years ago, in the early 'eighties, that the black church movement began, in the eastern Cape, that part of Africa where the Bantu had been longest in contact with Western civilisation and where there was the largest number of Bantu Christians. By this time many Bantu had become thoroughly acquainted with the Bible and with theological dogmas and creeds. They had not failed to notice that the white missionaries were divided into many different sects and that these sects differed one from another on what were supposed to be important points of doctrine. Many Africans felt that they were just as capable of having their own views on these matters as the Europeans. No doubt they were. They felt too that a Bantu church would provide a field where they could develop their own ideas and express their own personalities without having to suffer the constant interference of white missionaries who claimed superior knowledge and understanding. At the back of it all, moreover, was the growing feeling of national consciousness and revolt against the whites, not only in religious matters, but in everything. The industrialisation of South Africa was beginning: Africans of many different tribes were meeting one another as labourers on the railways or in the mines at Kimberley and on the Witwatersrand. It was not strange that some of them began to think of national unity. The conception of a common church from which the whites would be excluded had a wide appeal.

When new ideas are in the air who can say who really discovers them first? Perhaps Nehemiah Tile was the pioneer. Born in Tembuland and baptised by the Wesleyans, he became a Methodist preacher. After a course in theology at Healdtown* he was sent back to Tembuland to work there for the Wesleyans. But he proved to have ideas of his own on religion and politics and in 1884 he was in trouble with his European supervisors. He was accused by the Rev. Chubbs of "taking part in political matters, stirring up a feeling of hostility against magistrates in Tembuland, addressing a public meeting on a Sunday, refusing to inform him [Rev. Chubbs] of his activities, and donating an ox at the circumcision of Dinyebo, heir to the paramount chief of the Tembus."[1] He was tried by a group of Wesleyan ministers. After a heated argument, he resigned from the Wesleyan Church and set up his own church, the Tembu National Church. He had the

* Healdtown, Wesleyan Native Mission School in the Ciskei.

support of the Tembu chief and of the tribe as a whole, and the first church building was erected at the royal kraal.

This Tembu dispute had ended in a mere tribal church but it initiated a movement with more far-reaching results. There were a number of breakaways from the white missions in different parts of the country. In one of these a young white missionary, Winter, played the chief part. He came to one of the Berlin mission stations in Sekukuniland, Transvaal, in 1889. "He was a typical example of the rash, over-sympathetic, over-zealous, headstrong equalitarian who easily does so much mischief."[2] In other words he appears to have been a genuine believer in the doctrines of Christianity. "Immediately upon his arrival, before he had gained knowledge of his work, or experience of the Natives, he jumped to the conclusion that the whites in general, and his own colleagues in the mission in particular, were too standoffish with the blacks. 'We ought to treat our flock not as inferiors but as equals,' he declared, 'at any rate those Natives who are Christians and have certificates of schooling.' Whether out of irresponsibility, or from the desire to make a bid for cheap popularity with the Natives, Winter proclaimed his views openly among them. They met of course with enthusiastic approval, and on the eager proposal of one of the Native ministers who had pushed himself into the van of the movement, Winter set up an independent Native Church. The first decision of the vestry on taking office was to dismiss Winter as an interloper, which may have opened his eyes to the folly of his action, but by then the mischief was done and the fatal precedent created."[2]*

In that same year in Pretoria a Native minister, Kenyane, broke away from the Anglican Church to organise an independent black religious community, taking with him his entire congregation.

The next outstanding name in the history of the Ethiopian movement is that of Mangena Mokone. He was born in the Transvaal in 1851. In 1870 he went to Natal and worked there for 10s. a month on the sugar plantations, "in order to buy a rifle."[1] After some months he went to Durban, where he worked as a domestic servant and attended night school. In 1874 he was baptised by the Wesleyans and took up preaching.

* On the subsequent history of Winter and his Sekukuni Church, I have not been able to get any further information.

According to reports, "he was specially endowed with spiritual power in preaching. On one occasion during the night service he had his congregation on their knees all in tears, until the neighbouring Europeans were drawn to the scene and one shouted, '*Vuka*, boy! *Vuka*, boy!'* and remarked to the others, 'The poor niggers are lying on their bellies.' The Rev. Rowe, the European missionary superintendent, was sent for and requested to replace the 'boy' Mokone by a better person who would not frighten the poor creatures with hell fire."[1]

Mokone afterwards went to Pretoria, and it was here that he began to resent the interference of his white supervisors. He saw that though in theory all were brothers in Christ in practice it was not so. The African missionary was not allowed the privileges of his white colleagues, and if he differed from them on any matter he was obliged to submit to their ruling.

It was at the end of 1892 that the great breakaway occurred. The occasion was a Wesleyan missionary congress held in Pretoria. The Native ministers found that they were excluded from the board of the congress, also that black and white meetings were to be held separately, whites having the right to attend the black meetings if they so desired, while blacks were to be excluded from the white meetings. Mokone and his indignant fellow African ministers withdrew from the congress to hold their own protest meeting outside. How could they preach the gospel of the brotherhood of all men when their own colleagues refused to practise it?

Mokone resigned from the Wesleyan Church and on the following Sunday, in November, 1892, he and twenty others founded the Ethiopian Church. "They called themselves Ethiopians because they interpreted the prophecy, that Ethiopia shall soon stretch out her hands unto God, to refer to the African races."[3]

The movement soon spread beyond Pretoria. A number of other Bantu parsons broke away from the Wesleyans and joined Mokone, among them J. Tantsi of Johannesburg. Mokone was advised to get into touch with the Tembu Church in the Queenstown district of the Cape. He went to Tembuland and met the Rev. Goduka, who was now the leader of the Church founded by Nehemiah Tile. On his return to Johannesburg he met people who were in touch with the African Methodist Episcopal Church of America. A young

* Get up, boy!

African woman, Charlotte Manye, afterwards Mrs. Maxeke, had gone to study at the Negro university at Wilberforce, U.S.A. Mokone heard of her through her relations in Johannesburg and through her he began a correspondence with the American A.M.E. It was soon proposed to unite the two Churches and this was decided upon at the 1896 Conference of the Ethiopian Church.

At this conference a new leader became prominent in the person of James Mata Dwane. He too was an ex-member of the Wesleyan Church. According to the official history of the Anglican Church in South Africa, "in 1894 Mr. J. M. Dwane, a Wesleyan minister, joined them [the Ethiopians]. 'Undoubtedly a prophet and a man of great gifts,' he had made the tremendous journey to England to collect money for a native undenominational college, a scheme of his own. When he returned the Wesleyan authorities put all the money he had collected into the common fund, and Dwane, disappointed, left them to become the leader of the Ethiopians."[3]

Dwane appears to have been a man of outstanding ability and energy. But he had in him an opportunistic streak. He and Makone struggled for leadership. The 1896 Conference decided to send three delegates to America, "to consolidate the union of the Ethiopian Church and the A.M.E. Church."[1] The three chosen were Mokone, Dwane and John G. Xaba. Each delegate was supposed to raise the money for his own passage to America and back, a not very democratic arrangement. Dwane was the only one who went.

He was welcomed with enthusiasm by Negroes in the United States. Addressing a vast audience, Dwane assured them "that the Africans would never allow the white man to ride roughshod over their country. Africans were rapidly imbibing civilised habits and would soon be able to run great civilised governments. Then they would say to the European nations, 'Hands off!' "[4]

When Dwane returned it was as General Superintendent for South Africa. This was resented by some of the Ethiopians, "who contended that he was sent to America on an important mission and not to receive office without sanction of his brother ministers." Moreover, "as the Rev. M. M. Mokone was the founder and supervisor of the Ethiopian Church, many expected that if any offices were to be created Rev. Mokone should be the first to be considered."[1]

Now the A.M.E. did not seem big enough to contain both Dwane and Mokone, but it was not till 1899 that the split came. In the meantime the work went on and progress was made under the supervision of Bishop Turner, a Negro who had been sent out from America. The new movement had not only aroused the hostility of the various white governments, who naturally feared the political consequences of any large-scale movement making for unity of the Bantu—though President Kruger is reported to have said, "Let the Kafirs preach to the Kafirs; why interfere with them?"[1]—but had also excited the envy of rival white missionary groups, who were annoyed when the Ethiopians took their African converts from them. The Anglicans decided to adopt new tactics to deal with the Ethiopians. In 1899 the Church Missionary Society in London declared: "It is our desire that when Native Christians in any country are sufficiently numerous and matured . . . the Church should become either independent or an autonomous branch of the English Church, in either case in communion with other Anglican Churches."[3]

This policy was soon put into effect in South Africa. Dwane came under the influence of Julius Gordon, Rector of Queenstown, who realising the tremendous possibilities of the Ethiopian movement, sought to draw it back within the fold of the Church. He explained to Dwane the doctrine of the apostolic succession; he maintained that the A.M.E. could not hand on episcopal orders—that is, make bishops—because they had never in the first place received them. He urged Dwane to seek admission for himself and his followers to the only catholic and apostolic church, the Church of England. Accordingly Dwane, much intrigued by the thought of episcopal gaiters, summoned a special conference of the Ethiopians at Queenstown, in October, 1899. Here he proposed that they should secede from the American A.M.E. and join the Anglicans as a semi-independent body, the Order of Ethiopia. There was opposition, but only from a minority. Apparently the ground had been well prepared. About thirty of the ministers present decided to follow Dwane. Mokone was in the minority of eleven who decided to carry on with the A.M.E.

The A.M.E. remains to this day a purely non-European Church organisation, largely dominated by American Negro influence. Its bishops are appointed from America. It has become moderately respectable and is tolerated by the authorities, though among its parsons are to be found a number such as Rev. J. Tantsi who have continued to play a prominent part in various political movements for national freedom.

The subsequent history of the Anglican Order of Ethiopia is not without interest. Dwane never became a bishop. The Anglicans deny that they ever promised to make him one. It seems clear that no specific promise was ever given by anybody entitled to speak with the authority of the Church as a whole. Dwane himself maintained that it was implicit in the agreement between himself and the priests who had urged him to break with the A.M.E., and he continued for years to campaign for the right of the Order of Ethiopia to manage its own affairs and to have its own bishop. In the meantime he and his followers found themselves once more working under white supervision. The trouble flared up in 1904. Dwane's supervisor, Mr. West, made a public complaint in April of that year against Rev. Dwane's "method of keeping accounts." The dispute continued and Dwane prevailed upon a conference of African ministers to pass a vote of no confidence in the supervising chaplains. When in 1905 the Bishop of Grahamstown sent two priests (Revs. Grant and Thompson) to administer Easter Communion to the Ethiopians, "Rev. Dwane would not supply Mr. Grant with an interpreter."[1] Dwane's next move was a circular urging the Ethiopians to refuse to take Communion unless it was administered to them by a priest of their own colour. The result of this was that Dwane lost his deacon's licence and was degraded to the rank of an ordinary parish priest at Zoloze. This seems to have been Dwane's final attempt to assert his control over the affairs of the order. Thereafter he remained a humble follower and died in 1915. The Order of Ethiopia continued to exist, but hardly to flourish. It is said that "the Ethiopians now have two weak points, they do not convert the heathen and they are exclusively Xhosa."[3] It is plain, moreover, that this branch of the Ethiopian movement has lost that one freedom which was the occasion of the origin of the movement— namely, freedom from white supervision in religious matters.

In justice to the Anglicans, it should be said that they, more than any other body of white churchmen in South Africa, have continued to take a public stand against the prevailing race prejudice and slave-driver psychology of the white rulers. As in all white churches, and as with the

Socialists and Communists, as we shall see later, the enthusiastic nigrophiles within their ranks have had to drag along with them an unwilling mass of white followers who, though they may not openly oppose work among the Bantu, are yet sufficiently South Africanised to regard such work as the specialty of certain people and not as the main task confronting the church as a whole. Those Ethiopians who joined them were not so much men of character like Mokone as self-interested place-seekers and climbers, concerned more with position, power and money than with the principles of Christianity. At the same time it would have been wise for the Anglicans to have given Dwane his bishopric. Africans have always been able to say, "You see, the white Christians never treat us as if we were really their equals." As lately as 1914 some Anglicans were still arguing the necessity of appointing Native bishops "to stem the tide of Ethiopianism." "Those most interested in Native work were in favour of this scheme—the creation of a missionary diocese in the Northern Transvaal, similar to those already existing in Kaffraria, Zululand and Basutoland—seeing in the eventual appointment of Native assistant bishops and archdeacons the only antidote to Ethiopianism."[3]

Apart from the Ethiopians, numerous other independent African churches sprang up in the 1890's. A religious movement, the African Christian Union, was founded in Natal by a Scottish missionary, Joseph Booth, who came there in 1890. Supported by various churches in turn, he came to Africa intending to establish "industrial missions." He converted a number of Zulus to his point of view and they issued a manifesto in September 1896, which Jabavu's newspaper, *Imvo*, reprinted. It began with a passage from Isaiah:

> *"Cry aloud, spare not . . .*
> *Warn my people of their transgressions. . . .*
> *A little one shall become a thousand*
> *And a small one a strong nation.*
> *I the Lord will hasten it."*

This was followed by a list of officers, some with addresses in America, others in Natal, including Dr. J. M. Nembula (treasurer) and Solomon Kumalo (district agent).

The aims of the organisation were stated in twenty-one points, among which were the following:

To unite together Christians of the African race and of various denominations in the name of Jesus Christ to solemnly work towards and pray for the day when the African people shall become an African Christian nation.

To provide capital to equip industrial mission stations.

To demand ... by Christian and lawful methods the equal recognition of the African and allied peoples to the rights and privileges accorded to Europeans.

To solicit funds [from Europeans] to restore Africans [in America] to their fatherland.

To place on record ... the great wrongs inflicted upon the African by the people of Europe and America and to urge upon Christians, who wish to be clear of African blood in the day of God's Judgment, to make restitution. ...

To develop the culture of tea, coffee, cotton, cocoa, sugar, etc., and to establish profitable mining or other industries or manufactures.

To establish transport agencies. ...

To engage European skilled labourers as servants to train and teach African learners any department of commercial, engineering, nautical, medical or professional knowledge, if found necessary.

To mould and guide the labour of Africa's millions into channels that shall develop the vast God-given wealth of Africa for the uplifting and commonwealth of the people, rather than for the aggrandisement of a few already rich Europeans.

Finally, to pursue steadily and unswervingly the policy AFRICA FOR THE AFRICAN, and look for and hasten by prayer and united effort the forming of the AFRICAN CHRISTIAN NATION by God's power and in his own time and way.

The manifesto ended by offering shares in the organisation at £1 each!

Naturally enough, the new movement met with violent opposition from the European Press, and Jabavu's *Imvo* was not backward in joining in the chorus of denunciation. "A union in which the religious sentiment is pressed into service to cover the most hare-brained business and political schemes. ... We should be guilty of a flagrant dereliction of duty did we not express the horror of our people of a movement on such dangerous lines, unfurling on behalf of an ignorant people at this time of day the motto of 'Africa for the Africans.'" The Ethiopian movement was described as "Mania Number Two," "Mania Number One" being the cattle-killing led by Nongqause forty years earlier. Jabavu poured scorn on this new manifestation of race exclusiveness. "The welfare of the land depends upon the enlistment of the best men . . . of whatever nationality . . . for its advancement," and so forth.

At the same time *Imvo* advised the Tembu Church to join up with one of the established, i.e. white-controlled organisations. "We have told the tribe before that so long as it stands there not attached to any one of the already existing religious denominations, so long will they labour under suspicion of propagating a political movement under the guise of religion, and so long will they be watched" [by the whites].

But as to the African Christian Union, which Jabavu castigated and stigmatised as mania, and as to their naïve manifesto, one may observe that if they were mad, yet there was method in their madness. To ask funds of Europeans in South Africa for the purpose of bringing back those Africans who were living in America may have been fantastic, but there is much in the manifesto that is essential to any sound African emancipatory movement, and who is to say that African Christians should not unite against the wrongs they suffer? Unfortunately it would seem that uniting is not easy for the Bantu. To-day, apart from the A.M.E., there are hundreds of purely Bantu churches. The same inherent splitting tendency which is the bane of Bantu political organisations has brought into being almost as many independent Bantu churches as there are Bantu parsons. In 1933 there were 272 independent Native churches on the Government register and probably many more unregistered. Thus it is that the Ethiopian movement and the rest count for very little in the situation to-day. But were all these little churches united in a single body, no government could afford to ignore them.

CHAPTER IX

POLL TAX REBELLION

THE BAMBATA REBELLION in Natal in 1906 may very well be taken as the turning point between two periods in the history of the black man in South Africa: the early period of tribal wars and fights against the white invaders, which ended in the loss of the country and the reduction of the Bantu to the status of an internal proletariat; and the second period, one of struggle for national liberation and democratic rights within the framework of present-day South Africa, where black and white intermingle in complex economic and political relationships. During the first period the Bantu fought as isolated tribes and on military lines. Though they did not meet the whites on equal terms, but opposed shield and assegai to the rifle and machine gun, at least they met them as members of independent tribes or nations having their own territory and military organisation. Some of the Bantu groups, notably the Zulus, Basuto and Bapedi, were powerful nations and compelled respect. During the second period the Bantu became helots on white-owned farms, vagrants, pass-bearers, people without rights in their own country. They were not allowed to carry arms, except as police "boys" in the service of the white man, and even then they must not use the gun, but only the assegai. Their big chiefs were reduced to mere salaried puppets, acting as tax-collectors and continuing in office only so long as they duly carried out the policy and orders of the white Government.

After the Boer War the chief problem that confronted the English financiers who had by this time established their political control over the whole country was the development of the gold mines. This raised inevitably the question of labour supply. Though the Natives had been robbed of their land by both Boer and Briton, they possessed still a certain amount of territory in the form of Native reserves. Also the squatting system was in operation—that is, white farmers permitted Natives to live upon their farms and pay rent by giving up a portion of their crops. The technique of labour indenture and forced labour had not been perfected. Consequently, the mine-owners were unable to obtain an adequate supply of cheap labour. It was decided to import labourers from China and by 1906 there were over 50,000 Chinese workers on the Rand. They came on three-year contracts and when not at work were shut up in compounds. Many of them escaped from the compounds and became robbers. An agitation arose for their repatriation and they were finally sent back to China.

The question of labour supply for the mines became now even more acute and various new measures were adopted by the authorities to oblige Africans to leave their homes and go to work for white employers. Poll and hut taxes were introduced in the different provinces. Failure to pay the tax was a criminal offence and every African had to carry his poll tax receipt with him wherever he went. In the Transvaal the tax was £2 per year per head, amounting in many cases to considerably more than a month's wages.

At the end of 1905 the Government of Natal decided on a tax of £1 per head on every male, irrespective of colour, over the age of eighteen years. The tax had the dual purpose of raising revenue and of forcing Natives into employment. Natal, like the other provinces, was suffering from the post-war depression, but in spite of this farmers complained bitterly of the acute shortage of labour.

The tax became payable for the first time on the first of January, 1906. Early in that month there were rumours of Native unrest and discontent with the new taxation. The Natal newspapers of the time make interesting reading. There were reports that the Natives were paying up well and that rumours of unrest among them might be discounted. Then, on January 20, came the news that Harry Smith, a white farmer, had been murdered near Camperdown. It appeared that Smith had decided to go to Maritzburg to pay his tax and had called his Native labourers together and taken them with him to pay their tax at the same time. A day or two later Smith answered a knock at his door. A Native wished to see him. When he opened the door he was stabbed with an assegai. He died of the wound and his assailant managed to get away. A rumour spread that this would be the signal for a general uprising of the Natives. A few days later large numbers of white farmers from the Camperdown district trekked into Maritzburg for safety. The authorities persuaded them that it had been a false rumour and they returned to their farms.

The newspapers again reported that the Natives were "paying up well." The Secretary for Native Affairs, touring Zululand, reported, "Everything appears most satisfactory in my opinion. The good results are in a measure due to the example set by Dinizulu," the paramount chief of the Zulus, who had paid his tax. On February 7 the *Natal Witness* still maintained that there was "no Native unrest" and that the stories of disaffection were all "lying rumours."

But three days later the same newspaper was compelled to admit that there had been a serious affray at Byrnetown near Richmond. It had been reported to the authorities that a number of the tribesmen of Chief Mveli had refused to pay their taxes. Police were sent to deal with this insubordination. They were attacked and two were killed. From different parts of the country came reports of refusals to pay. The leaders of the rebels in Mveli's country were two commoners, Majongwe and Makanda. They and a number of others escaped into the forests and troops were sent to hunt them down. Mveli himself was called upon by the military authorities to assist in tracking down his rebellious tribesmen. On February 15 the *Natal Mercury* in a leading article stated that "The fellow tribesmen of the fugitive participators in the Byrnetown tragedy are joining with the authorities in the efforts to effect their capture, the example being given by the Chief Mveli, to whom all credit appears to be due for the correct part he has played throughout the proceedings."

The two ringleaders in this affair were prominent members of a local group of Ethiopians. This particular sect, calling themselves the African Congregational Church, had come into conflict with Chief Mveli's father as far back as 1895. They had claimed that they were independent of the chief's authority because they were Christians, and this contention had been upheld by the Supreme Court. The Government had acted on instructions "received from the Queen that religion was to be fostered to the utmost among the Natives."[1] The result was the exact opposite of what had been expected by the authorities in England. The Ethiopians, because they had their own African church, were not under the control of the white missionaries. Nor did they come indirectly under Government control through their chief. "Is it surprising then," says Stuart, "that a group of barbarians with the merest veneer of Christianity, cut off from all effective controlling influences, should in course of time have developed rebellious tendencies?"[1]

David Makanda was a teacher of religion who had been turned out of the tribe by the chief on account of his intransigence. He had returned to the district about 1900 and had linked up with Majongwe, also called Mjongo, who was a well-known sawyer or wood-cutter. Together they had carried on an extensive practice in politics, religion and business. It was said that Majongwe had trained many hundreds of his fellow Africans as wood-cutters. The growth of the wattle industry in Natal had provided opportunities for this work.

The troops, following Majongwe's tracks, burned down huts as they pursued him and his followers into the bush. In the mountains they caught two of his people and, after a brief court martial, condemned them to death. Mveli and his men, helping in the pursuit, were forced to witness an execution which took place on the mountains in the early morning mist. As the shots rang out, says the reporter, "tears rolled down the black cheeks of Mveli the chief, as he raised his assegai in salute of the vindicated law."

But in the House of Commons in London, "Mr. Harold Cox asked Mr. Winston Churchill why two Natives had been shot in Natal after being tried by court martial instead of being tried before the civil tribunal. Mr. Churchill said that he had no information with regard to the alleged shooting."[2]

The Natal papers reported that a "sweeping movement" had been begun by the troops in different parts of the country, that the authorities were dealing with "sullen chiefs," who were being made to pay the tax as an example to their followers, that things were "settling down everywhere" and that there was "reassuring news all round." On February 21 the capture of Majongwe was reported.

In the meantime authority employed a heavy hand in dealing with Native unrest in the towns. On February 13 three Africans arrested in Durban were charged with "incitement to sedition." One of them, Uhlobezenke, was sentenced to six months' hard labour and fifteen lashes. "As accused left the dock he failed to salute the Magistrate, and when he was forced to do so by the interpreter did so very sulkily.

He was made to repeat the salute."[2] N. Zondi, charged with a similar offence, was given twenty lashes. At Maritzburg an African named Muzi was sentenced to twelve months' imprisonment and twenty lashes for "making assegais and uttering seditious language." In Newcastle a Native was "overheard by a white lady" discussing the rebellion with a fellow African. He was in typical African style carrying on a conversation with a friend the other side of the street and apparently failed to realise that passing Europeans might be listening. His sentence was six months' imprisonment and fifteen lashes.

In Durban an African was sentenced for making assegais. A riksha-puller was charged with "insulting the troops." A young Native was charged with "spreading false reports calculated to cause unnecessary alarm." He had written in Zulu to an acquaintance, saying, "I want you to tell me about the poll tax. . . . I want to go to the Zulu king because I am a soldier. . . . At Richmond the Europeans and Bantu have fought. . . . Nine Bantu have died. . . . I shall leave Durban and go to Zululand." The magistrate said that "young fellows like the accused were the cause of a lot of unrest, and he would have to be punished for it. He sentenced accused to six months' hard labour and fifteen lashes."[2]

While the police and magistrates were thus occupied in the towns, the troops were busy dealing with more trouble at Mapumulo, north of Durban, and at Ixopo in southern Natal. At Ixopo a number of Africans were brought before the court martial and tried for sedition. Two chiefs, Mskofeli and Mamba, were the most prominent of the accused. A newspaper correspondent declared that the evidence given in the trial showed that "one raw Native has been prepared to dip his assegai in European flesh, and his excuse has been what he calls excessive taxes." Mskofeli was fined 100 head of cattle for not bringing prisoners. Mamba was found not guilty.

Disaffection and resistance to the new tax continued. On March 9 it was reported that the Dumisa Natives, near Umzinto, were showing fight and that the young men of the tribe had disregarded the authority of the chief, who had ordered them to pay their taxes. The chief was then ordered to call an *indaba* (tribal gathering) and the officer in command of the troops addressed an audience from which the young men were however conspicuously absent. Officials sat by with basins and receipt books to receive the taxes. After the speech came the demand for payment. The audience sat in sullen silence. Some muttered, "We have no money to pay." Finally a young man, shamefacedly, came up with his £1. He was followed after a time by four others. That was all. The treasury was richer by £5. The audience was told to disperse, but to see that they paid up within a week.

At Mapumulo the Chief Gobizembe was in trouble because his tribesmen had "insulted the magistrate." "Gobizembe made no effort to deliver up the offenders. The twenty men he produced were taken haphazard, and two of them produced documents to show that they were in Johannesburg at the time when the Magistrate was insulted."[2] The artillery opened fire on Gobizembe's kraal at a range of 2,500 yards, and destroyed it. The chief was captured and forty *indunas* (headmen) surrendered. Gobizembe was fined 1,200 head of cattle and 3,500 sheep and goats. His tribe was dispossessed of two-thirds of his lands, which were shared between two new chiefs "hereafter to be nominated."

By the middle of March the trouble appeared to be over—except for a small affair at Umtwalumi, where the Natives had become "defiant." The troops began to return and were welcomed at Maritzburg and Durban by leading politicians.

The courts martial continued their work. Seven Africans at Ixopo were sentenced to death for sedition, but the sentences were commuted by the Government to long terms of imprisonment. This leniency created considerable dissatisfaction among the white colonists. The next to be put on trial were twelve of Majongwe's followers, who were held to be responsible for the deaths of the two white soldiers killed near Richmond at the beginning of the rebellion. On March 28 it was reported that they had been found guilty and sentenced to death. The next day there was a ministerial crisis in Natal. "The Government has resigned office in consequence of the Secretary of State [in London] having instructed the Governor to suspend the carrying out of the sentences of death passed by court martial on the twelve Natives" concerned in the deaths of the two white soldiers.

A tremendous uproar now broke out, not only in Natal, but among whites throughout South Africa. Protest meetings were held and resolutions passed. Briton and Boer made common cause against the Government in England. Christian clergymen joined in the protests. The Rev. J. G. Aldridge of Durban, in a Press interview, spoke of "this unwholesome humanitarian sentiment . . . this ignorance of the facts of our life." The *Cape Argus*, the *Cape Times*, the Johannesburg *Star* all joined the indignant chorus. Only the Bloemfontein *Friend*** struck a discordant note. "We can quite understand the present indignation, as the loyal little people have been accustomed to shoot Boers after a khaki trial, but to-day are not even allowed to shoot Kafirs until the Liberal Government is assured that the forms of law have been duly observed. The whole affair reads like a rehearsal of the judicial murders of which Scheepers, Baxter, Bester and scores of others were made the victims during the [recent Anglo-Boer] war. The summons to the Natives to witness the killing of their friends is a nasty replica of the procedure adopted in the military butcheries. The Natalians may rave as they like, but in no quarter, except of course the rebel Rand, will it get much sympathy."

But the opposition from London was short-lived. On March 31 came the announcement: "The Imperial Government leaves Natal freedom of action regarding the Native executions." The Natal Government returned to office and the executions were carried out. The twelve "were shot at Richmond in the presence of a large number of Natives, including chiefs, at midday on April 2, the firing party consisting of the comrades of the deceased. They met their death with fortitude." Majongwe himself, not having sufficiently recovered from his wounds, was unable to attend the trial. He was, however, subsequently tried by the Supreme Court, convicted and sentenced to death by hanging; the sentence was carried out in September.

The lull of the storm during March was only the prelude to the second and more important part of the rebellion. Though many of the chiefs had been "sullen" and some had gone in for deliberate sabotage, none had so far been prepared to place himself openly at the head of the rebellion. Stuart says: "As a section of the Native public appeared desirous of a change in the way they were being governed, it devolved of course on someone to take the lead. Who should this be? A Chief? Of course, for in a matter such as this it would be altogether foreign to Native sentiment for a mere commoner to do so. Look how Makanda and Mjongo had failed."[1]

* *The Friend* was founded in 1850.

The leader who now emerged was the chief of a comparatively small tribe which had its territory just north of Greytown on the borders of Zululand. This was Bambata, after whom the rebellion finally came to be named. In April, 1904, Bambata, on coming with his people to Greytown to pay the hut and dog taxes, had protested to the magistrate against furnishing information in connection with the census, and had declared, "If there is anything behind all this we shall be angry." J. W. Cross, the magistrate, had replied: "You may as well expect the sun to fall from the heavens as imagine that harm will come to you."

In August, 1905, Bambata was arrested following a faction fight in his ward. He was convicted and sentenced to pay a fine of £20, with the alternative of three months' imprisonment. About this time he visited his lawyer in Pietermaritzburg, from whom, it seems, he learned that his deposition from the chieftainship was contemplated.

When in September, 1905, the poll tax was proclaimed in the Umvoti (Greytown) division Bambata took the opportunity of reminding the magistrate of the statement that gentleman had made when the census was taken, asking him to reconcile the assurance then given with the demand for the poll tax that was now being made. The magistrate was unable to do this to Bambata's satisfaction.

The Greytown correspondent of the *Natal Mercury* reported on February 20, 1906: "Some surprise is created here at the Government not acting more promptly in the removal of Chief Bambata, whose repulsive presence and control near Greytown is not inviting to the local European population."

Bambata was officially deposed on February 23 and his relation Magwababa was appointed acting chief in his stead. On March 8 the *Mercury* reported that Bambata had been "cheeky," had refused to obey the Government's command and was courting trouble. "Recently he was ordered to report himself to the Secretary for Native Affairs at Maritzburg but he has not heeded the command." His followers had informed the court messenger that "they were sleeping on their assegais and that they would not be easily taken." On March 9 newspaper headlines announced: "Trouble at Greytown. . . . Bambata's Contumacy. . . . Small Column moving Out. . . . An Insolent Chief." Three days later the white public was informed that Bambata had just been missed by the troops and had taken to the bush. After that no more was heard of Bambata for some time.

Unknown to the authorities, he made his way, accompanied by his family, to the kraal of Dinizulu at Usutu and there had several interviews with the Paramount Chief, "being treated by Dinizulu in a markedly hospitable manner."[1] It was said that Dinizulu gave him instructions to go back to Natal, commit an act of rebellion and then flee to Nkandla forests, where Dinizulu's men would join him. Two young men were sent back with Bambata to Natal, one being Cakijana, who soon began to play an important part. Bambata's wife and child remained at Dinizulu's kraal.

Bambata arrived in the Greytown district on March 31. He raised an impi and captured the acting chief Magwababa and kept him prisoner. This was the signal for the rebellion to flare up again. Large numbers of European troops, also African soldiers recruited from the so-called "loyal tribes," were called up by the authorities. The Native police, or Nonqai, also played an important part in the fighting. There were a number of armed clashes.

On April 3 the troops were ambushed at Mpanza and some of them killed. Bambata then crossed the Tugela River to the Nkandla forests. Here Sigananda, an old man of ninety-six, was the local chief. His people were iron-workers and assegai-makers and had in the preceding January "expostulated with the magistrate in a violent and disrespectful manner because required to pay poll tax." Difficulty had been experienced in obtaining labourers from his tribe for the Public Works Department.

Sigananda was called upon by the Government to arrest Bambata and hand him over to the authorities. The old chief and his tribe replied to this by throwing in their lot with the rebels.

On April 18 Dinizulu sent a letter to the Government protesting his loyalty and saying that he was prepared to assist in suppressing Bambata. "Little did anyone suppose at this time," says Stuart, "that this communication, to all appearance brimming over with the deepest loyalty and affection, had issued from one who was actually committing high treason at the moment he sent it." Bambata and his fellow rebels declared that Dinizulu was with them, and many flocked to his standard on that account. Others, hearing of Dinizulu's public declaration, did not know where they stood. There can be no doubt that if Dinizulu had come out openly on the side of Bambata many thousands more would have joined in the rebellion. As it was there were signs of unrest in many parts of Zululand and Natal. On May 2, H. M. Stainbank, magistrate at Mahlabatini in Zululand, was killed while on his rounds collecting taxes.

Now the Government forces were closing in on Bambata's stronghold in the Nkandla forests. The most important and decisive battle of the war took place in Mome gorge. In a thickly-wooded mountain valley the followers of Bambata and Sigananda tried to defend themselves. One section of the Government forces drove the rebels up the valley, while another section cut off their retreat and mowed them down unmercifully with machine guns. About 500 Africans were killed in the fight, among them Bambata himself.

The whites claimed that they were civilised fighters and that the Bantu were barbarians. Particularly, they pointed to the fact that on some occasions the Natives had mutilated the dead. This did not prevent the representatives of civilisation from cutting off the head of Bambata and displaying it to convince the "superstitious Natives" that the leader of the rebellion was in fact dead and not invulnerable as he had claimed to be.

In spite of this, it was said that the Bantu still believed that Bambata lived. In June there was another serious rising, this time in Mapumulu, led by the chiefs Meseni and Ndlovu. It was not till the end of July that the Government finally suppressed the rebellion.

In all nearly 4,000 Africans lost their lives in the Poll Tax Rebellion. Of the Government forces only twenty-five Europeans and six Africans were killed in the fighting. The whole business cost the Government nearly a million pounds, a sum far in excess of the amount raised in poll tax.

Dinizulu was placed on trial in 1908. He was charged with high treason, public violence, sedition and rebellion, and with being responsible for the death of certain persons killed during the rebellion. The trial lasted many months, the Hon. W. P. Schreiner, ex-Prime Minister of the Cape Colony, being his defending counsel. Among those who interested themselves in his defence were the daughters of Bishop Colenso. "Owing to Dinizulu's enormous influence in Natal and Zululand, witnesses could be got to give evidence against him only with the greatest difficulty."[1] He was found guilty of high treason (a) by harbouring and concealing Bambata's wife and children for over fifteen months; (b) by harbouring and concealing the ringleaders Bambata and Mangati during the actual progress of the rebellion; and (c) by harbouring and concealing 125 named and other rebels at various times." He was sentenced to four years' imprisonment and a fine of £100 or a further twelve months' imprisonment. In 1911 he was exiled to the Transvaal, where he was given a farm on which to live. At the same time his salary of £500 a year was restored to him.

It is difficult to assess the role played by the Ethiopian movement in the Bambata rebellion. In the opinion of many of the more ignorant of the European colonists, the whole thing was engineered by sedition-mongers from America. Such an interpretation is of course fantastic, though those who advanced it claimed to have particular knowledge of what they called the "Native mind." They would never admit that it was the essential injustice of the poll tax which was in the first place responsible. During the course of the rebellion the Natal newspapers made many references to the Ethiopian movement. Under the heading, "Worse than Exeter Hall," the *Natal Witness* of February 15, 1906, referred to a leading article in the London Liberal daily, the *Tribune*. This article gave a history of the Ethiopian movement and "appears to sympathise with it."

Two days later the *Natal Mercury* published a cartoon in which Natalia, a sort of cousin of Britannia, points to a huge toadstool labelled "Ethiopianism," and says to the gallant Natal carbineer who stands ready with drawn sword, "We must get rid of that poisonous weed." In a letter headed "The Ethiopian Movement—the Cause of the Trouble," a correspondent wrote: "An evil star rose in the American firmament and sent its satellites to preach sedition in Natal." The writer went on to say that not all *amakolwa** were bad, but only those who followed the Ethiopians and other similar Churches. He declared that one such sect, the African Congregational Church, had treated "their old pastor, the Rev. S. Pixley, of Inanda, most shamefully," and they were now independent of European control. The country, he added,

* Native converts to Christianity.

97

was rotten with sedition. This statement was indignantly denied a few days later by James Dexter Taylor, the Secretary of the American Zulu Mission, who maintained that the African Congregational Church was not Ethiopian and that its members were on the best of terms with the Rev. Pixley and himself.

Another writer attacked the Church of the Province of South Africa, saying that the encouragement the Ethiopians had received from that body was sufficient to establish them in the country. "It only shows how the Church can, with the best of intentions, do an immense amount of mischief when acting on their own responsibility in connection with matters that are not exclusively confined to Church affairs. The South African governments were somewhat lax in neglecting to look into this inroad of the Ethiopian sect in the first instance, instead of being led into indifference by the simplicity of the churchmen." To these remarks the Bishop of Natal took exception. He replied with a long letter in which he gave an outline of the history of the Ethiopian movement. He pointed out that it was necessary to distinguish between the Order of Ethiopia, attached to the Church of the Province, and other groups of Ethiopians. "Rather it may be maintained that the Church of the Province, in guiding a large number of Natives into the paths of loyalty, has saved them from associating themselves with the dangerous political propaganda, the fatal results of which we have recently witnessed in Natal."

Another parson, James Scott, informed a public meeting "that Natal Natives were being sent to colleges in America. Over 150 young Natives were recently sent from South Africa, including twenty from Natal. This was one of the greatest dangers to the standing of the white men in South Africa. He would be loath to hinder any man getting education, but the fact to which he had drawn attention was a great danger to their future."[3]

In spite of all these efforts to blame Ethiopianism for the rebellion, the facts show that the struggle was in the main led by African tribalists and was the direct result of the imposition of the poll tax. It has been pointed out that an Ethiopian sect did play some part in the affair at Byrnetown, but that the rebellion did not seriously threaten the Government until the chiefs Bambata and Sigananda placed themselves at its head and the powerful Dinizulu gave it his support.

At the same time there was a section of the African community which was neither tribalist nor Ethiopian and which supported the rebellion, though perhaps not actively. We have seen how contact with European rule had produced in the Cape Province a new class of Westernised Africans who began to develop political forms of expression. At a somewhat later date a similar development took place in Natal. Some Europeans in Natal were not unaware that this new group was becoming more numerous and that its members might take the lead in fostering Bantu nationalism. Following the example set by colonial administrators in other parts of the world, they were prepared to give members of this class certain privileges which would mark them off from their unsophisticated compatriots and thus secure their "loyalty" and co-operation. The exponents of this form of *divide et impera* were the more intelligent and far-seeing colonists, usually educated men from England. The average white colonist did not see the necessity for a policy of differentiation. For him all Natives should be "kept in their place" and the educated black man was a monstrosity who should not be tolerated.

Even before the granting of responsible government in 1893, representatives of the colonists in the legislature sought to do away with the privileges enjoyed by those few Africans who were exempted from the operation of Native law. Accordingly, in May, 1890, a measure on these lines was introduced by the Secretary for Native Affairs. It was effectively opposed by Sir John Robinson and H. Escombe, who persuaded the Government to continue the established policy. In the same year the Government inaugurated a system of night schools for adult Africans, a progressive measure which has not been imitated by any of the other provinces to this day.*

Nevertheless, there were some educated Africans who refused to be placated by being allowed special privileges. One of the most distinguished of these, John Navuma Nembula, the first South African Native to qualify (overseas) as a medical doctor, joined the Ethiopian movement in Natal in 1896.

The first Bantu newspaper to be founded in Natal appears to have been the *Inkanyiso* (*The Enlightener*). It was apparently

* In view of very recent events, this statement needs qualification. See Chapter XXVII.

started in 1893, but the author has been able to obtain no further information about this paper.*

A Bantu newspaper called *Ilanga lase Natal* (*The Sun of Natal*) was started at Ohlange, near Durban, by John Dube in 1906. Dube, a parson in the Methodist Church[?], came to play an important part in the Native political movement. In the 1930's he was considered a "moderate man" and was one of the few African leaders, apart of course from chiefs, to be accorded the official support of the Government. In his youth he appears to have been rather more of a radical. He got into trouble with the authorities on account of certain articles which appeared in *Ilanga lase Natal* in connection with the Bambata rebellion. Commenting on the first battle between Bambata's impi and the Government forces, when four white soldiers were killed, *Ilanga* published the following: "A remarkable thing . . . is that the four troopers who were killed were all in the firing party at the execution of the twelve men at Richmond. What does this mean? Call it a remarkable coincidence if you please, but we regard it as having a very deep meaning, whether we are superstitious or not."

For this or for some other outspoken statement he was arrested. But he was released without being brought to trial. It is said that a member of the influential Shepstone family intervened with the Government and secured his release. This appears to be the only occasion on which he fell foul of the authorities.

Thus the Bambata Rebellion was crushed and the poll tax law remained in the statute book. But it was many years before it could be strictly enforced in Natal. It was not indeed until 1925, when the Union Government imposed a uniform poll tax on all the Natives in the Union, that the poll tax became really effective in Natal. And even then the Zulus did not accept it without renewed resistance, as will be seen in a later chapter.

* This is but one of the many Bantu newspapers of which the South African libraries have failed to preserve copies.

CHAPTER X

GANDHI AND PASSIVE RESISTANCE

THE FIRST INDIANS CAME to Natal in 1860 to work as indentured labourers on the sugar plantations. In the years that followed many more came out in the same way. "Although the Native races outnumbered the whites by ten to one, in the opinion of the planters efficient labour for the plantations was not obtained from that source."[1] So the white colonists welcomed the Indians. On the conclusion of their term of indenture many of the "coolies" remained in the country as hawkers, market-gardeners, domestic servants, etc. Numbers of them and their descendants subsequently got work on the railways and in the coal mines. In the sub-tropical coastal belt, an Indian peasantry, working small plots of land, soon became an important element in the population. Indian merchants and traders followed from India, trading at first among the Indian labourers, but afterwards carrying on business among the Zulus and Europeans as well. Many of these traders did well; some became very rich indeed. This was a development the colonists of 1860 had not bargained for. An anti-Indian movement developed among the whites.

In 1893, when the white settlers were granted responsible government, the first thing they did with their newly-won power was to limit the rights of the Indians. A tax of £3 a year was imposed on every Indian worker who had completed his term of indenture. A similar tax of £3 was placed on every Indian woman and on every child over sixteen years old. The object of this taxation was to force Indians to return to India on the completion of their contracts on the sugar estates. £3 was equal to about six months' wages of the average sugar worker.

In 1896 the Indians in Natal were excluded from the franchise. In 1895 the population of Natal was roughly estimated at 400,000 Africans, 80,000 Indians, and 40,000 whites. The franchise was not explicitly on a racial basis, but in practice only the white males had the vote. Africans, by passing certain "civilisation tests," could become voters, but not more than two or three ever qualified, and for the last decade or more there has been only one African voter.

While they were able thus to establish themselves in Natal, the Indians had little success in the Transvaal. A law of 1885 excluded Indians from citizen rights in the Transvaal Republic and forbade them to own land. In the eyes of Paul Kruger, it was their destiny to be slaves for ever. Here is a version of what happened when some of them came to lay their grievances before him. "One evening . . . four years after his triumph at Majuba . . . Paul Kruger laid aside his Bible and went to listen to the Indians who were waiting to speak to him in the courtyard of his official residence. They had dared to expect that he would receive them within the residence itself. . .˙ [The Indians] made speeches and talked of the rights of citizenship, which seemed to Paul Kruger to be decidedly beside the point. Soon his patience gave way. 'You are,' he shouted, 'the descendants of Ishmael, and therefore from your very birth you are bound to slavery. As you are the descendants of Esau and Ishmael, we cannot admit you to rights placing you on an equality with ourselves. You must remain content with the rights we grant you.' Having exhausted his references to the Scriptures few of his audience had read, the President of the Transvaal dismissed the 'coolie' merchants and tradesmen without further ceremony. Paul Kruger returned to his Bible."[2] The Indians, one supposes, returned to their homes, discouraged and bewildered. Plainly they had little to hope for while Kruger remained the President of the Transvaal.

But when the soldiers marched into the Transvaal and hoisted the Union Jack over Oom Paul's house in Pretoria the Indians may have hoped for something better. If so, their hopes were short-lived. In 1906 the Transvaal was granted responsible government and laws were passed immediately to restrict the entry of Indians into that province. A most humiliating pass law was introduced and other measures to prevent Indians coming. To such ends did it seem good to the whites of the Transvaal to employ the new measure of freedom granted to them by the Liberal Campbell-Bannerman government of Britain. It was against these Transvaal restrictions as well as against the Indian poll tax in Natal that the famous passive resistance movement, led by Gandhi, was directed.

About Mohandas Karamchand Gandhi a literature is growing up which may presently rival in quantity the literature about Napoleon. The Mahatma was born in 1869, the son of the temporary Prime Minister of a small native state of Southern India. His family managed to send him to London in 1887, and there he took a degree in law. Returning to India, he found his family out of favour and himself dependent on the living he could make as a lawyer. When he first came to Natal, in 1893, it was, as he thought, on a temporary visit to conduct a lawsuit on behalf of an Indian client. It chanced that his business took him to Pretoria. On his way there from Durban he had his first taste of the indignities to which Indians, whether labourers or lawyers, are subjected by the civilised whites of South Africa. Among other incidents it is recorded that he was pushed into the gutter by a policeman when he dared to walk on the footpath past the house of President Kruger. On his return to Durban, he found the Indian community there much alarmed over the new Indian Disfranchisement Bill. The Natal Indians were looking for a leader. Gandhi was inevitably chosen. He postponed his return to India and helped to found the Natal Indian Congress.

South Africa offered to the young Indian a natural field for his talents. By this time he had already begun to develop the ideas which were afterwards embodied in the programme of *satyagraha*, or soul-force, a doctrine which derived in part from Tolstoi and Ruskin and which might be called largely Christian, though the activities of the white "Christians" of Durban who were busily making things hot for Gandhi and his friends opposed a striking contrast to the dignified behaviour of the *satyagrahis*.

In 1896 Gandhi returned to India to collect his wife and family. While in India he published various newspaper articles describing conditions as he had observed them in Natal, and these were given considerable publicity in both England and South Africa. On his second arrival in Durban he was set upon by the mob and nearly lynched. He was saved from this fate by the action of a policeman and an Englishwoman, who protected him with her umbrella from the hail of stones and other missiles. The authorities took no steps to prosecute his assailants until they received a telegram from the British Colonial Secretary, Joseph Chamberlain, instructing them to do so. But Gandhi said: "It was natural for them to be excited and to do something wrong." He refused to support the prosecution and it was dropped.

The Anglo-Boer War which broke out soon after this provided an interesting revelation of how Gandhi's philosophy worked out in practice. "It must be largely conceded," he said, "that justice is on the side of the Boers, . . . but so long as the subjects owe allegiance to a State, it is their clear duty generally to accommodate themselves, and to accord their support to acts of the State. . . . Our rulers profess to safeguard our rights because we are British subjects, and what little rights we still retain, we retain because we are British subjects."

Thus the Indians were persuaded by Gandhi to support the war. An Indian Ambulance Corps was formed. The Indian stretcher-bearers proved invaluable to the British; they were mentioned in dispatches and awarded medals.

Gandhi took a similar line during the Bambata rebellion in 1906. This was essentially a revolt against the poll tax on the part of Africans and as such it was quite comparable to the struggle of the Indians against a similar discriminatory law. But Gandhi remained loyal to the British Empire. He again offered to the Government his service and those of the Indian community. Once more an Indian Ambulance Corps was formed. On this occasion Gandhi's action did help individual Africans, though politically the Africans had to thank him for leaving them in the lurch, for there were practically no European wounded. The war against Bambata was a slaughter carried out with machine guns against spears and shields. The whites had no desire to minister to wounded Zulus; without the Indian stretcher-bearers, these would possibly have been left to die. There were also hundreds of Africans who had been sentenced to flogging. The Indians ministered to their festering sores.

But in spite of the loyalty of the Indians, the colonists continued to regard them as pariahs and to legislate against them. Gandhi soon found himself involved in a more serious clash with the authorities.

The first great Indian passive resistance campaign in South Africa began in 1906, when the Transvaal Government passed a law making the carrying of a pass compulsory for Indians in that province. The law applied to every Indian, male and female, over eight years old. The pass-bearers had to supply their thumb-prints. Application had to be made immediately for certificates of registration. Every Indian was required to carry the pass on his person and to exhibit it when called upon by a policeman in any public place. In effect, the Indian was by the new law reduced to the status of the pass-bearing African.

The immediate response of the Johannesburg Indians was a mass meeting in the Empire Theatre, where Gandhi took the chair. At this meeting the famous Satyagraha Oath was taken, those present vowing that they would not apply for registration certificates and that they would passively resist all attempts of the authorities to enforce the "Black Act." The Johannesburg Chinese joined in the movement, since they too, as Asiatics, came within the scope of the new law.

Gandhi repaired to London to try to persuade the British Government to veto the measure. He interviewed Lord Elgin, the Colonial Secretary, who promised to withdraw the Act. But in January, 1907, the new Transvaal Constitution came into operation and the first Transvaal Parliament immediately re-imposed the law. The British Government now refused to intervene, Lord Elgin affirming that a self-governing state had "the right to go to the devil in its own way."

Thus the "Black Act" became law for the second time in July, 1907. The permit offices were picketed by the Satyagrahis. There were practically no registrations. The authorities alleged that there was intimidation, and moral intimidation there may have been, though no violence was offered by the pickets. To circumvent the pickets, Indians were permitted to register in their own homes. In spite of this, only 500 out of 13,000 Transvaal Indians registered. Thereupon Gandhi and Leung Quin, the Chinese leader, were brought to court and ordered, since they had not registered, to leave the country. They refused to go. The Government then adopted more drastic measures. Gandhi and other Satyagrahis were arrested and sentenced to imprisonment with hard labour. The gaols were soon full of them. The captive Gandhi was marched through the street, handcuffed and in prison clothes.

The Indians were feeling the full rigour of the law. Yet it was not they but the authorities who began to waver. Smuts, then Colonial Secretary of the Transvaal, proposed that the Indians should register voluntarily. If the majority agreed to do so, he would repeal the Act. But the Indians outside the gaol refused to act unless Gandhi was released. Gandhi was taken from gaol to Smuts' office. Smuts was polite, even pleasant. He told Gandhi that he would repeal the Act as soon as the majority had registered—at least that was Gandhi's version of that interview. Gandhi walked out of the office a free man and this was followed by the release of the other Satyagrahis.

Gandhi, now believing that he had a promise from Smuts, decided to accept "voluntary registration." But he found it difficult to convince his followers, for the Act had not been withdrawn and those who had taken the Satyagraha Oath had vowed not to register under any circumstances. Gandhi decided that he would be the first to register. But on his way to the office he was attacked by a group of Pathans, led by Mir Alam, who shouted that Gandhi had betrayed them. He was severely injured by the sticks of the Pathans, but he called the registration officer to his bedside and there gave his thumb-prints.

What happened now—or, rather, what failed to happen— confirmed the doubts of those of Gandhi's followers who had been difficult to convince. Smuts did not keep his promise. The "Black Act" was not repealed. Instead, it was stated that those who had registered would be exempted, but the others would be subject to the law, including all Indians who should come to the Transvaal in future. Gandhi and his followers thereupon took up the struggle once more. The Government was called upon to repeal the law, failing which the Indians would publicly burn their passes.

In August, 1908, the passes were dramatically burnt at a huge meeting in Johannesburg. In the midst of the smoke Mir Alam stood on the platform and expressed his contrition for his assault on Gandhi.

The Government's reply to the revival of passive resistance was the Transvaal Immigrants' Restriction Bill, which aimed at making it impossible for Indians, with very rare exceptions, to enter that province. This measure also the Satyagrahis determined to oppose. Indians individually and in groups began to enter the Transvaal openly in defiance of the new law. It was not only poor Indians or Indian intellectuals who took part in this movement. A group of Indian businessmen, headed by Parsi Rustomji, were arrested at Volksrust and ordered to leave the Transvaal within a week. Instead, they proceeded to Pretoria, where they were arrested again. Deported to Natal, they immediately crossed the border again and were then sentenced to three months' hard labour.

Deportation to Natal was useless against this new form of resistance, for as soon as the Indians were released in Natal they came back again. The Government then started deporting Satyagrahis to India, including some, even, who had been born in South Africa. This raised a furore in India, and the Government there passed a law prohibiting further migrations of indentured labourers to Natal, a measure which the Natal whites, for all their hostility to the Indians did not relish.

Passive resistance continued for years. Gandhi and the other Satyagrahis spent much of their time in gaol. In the meantime the Union of South Africa came into being and Smuts became its first Minister of Justice. Matters came to a head in 1913 when the Supreme Court decided that only Christian marriages were legal, thus reducing Indian women to the legal status of concubines. This brought the Indian women into the fight. At the same time the Indian labourers in Natal began to take strike action against the £3 poll tax. This purely proletarian side of the movement was perhaps less spectacular than Gandhi's imprisonments and fastings, but it was just as effective in bringing the authorities to order. It was led in the main by a Christian Indian, A. Christopher.

The first big strike occurred among Indian workers on the Newcastle coal mines. These were incensed at the treatment accorded to a group of women resisters who had marched to the Transvaal, where they were arrested and then imprisoned with hard labour. The Newcastle strikers formed the nucleus of a band, 2,000 in number, who, led by Gandhi, began a march to Volksrust. There were women among them. Two had babies and the babies died on the march, one from drowning and the other from exposure.

All the marchers, including Gandhi, were arrested when they crossed into the Transvaal. Numerous white sympathisers also found themselves in prison, including Henry Polak and the architect H. Kallenbach, two of Gandhi's friends in Johannesburg. Indian strikes broke out throughout Natal. The miners were sent back to the mines as prisoners, and put to work under the direction of the white workers and foremen, who were armed for the purpose. The mines were surrounded with barbed wire.

But the Government had shot its bolt and a world-wide storm of indignation now forced it to retreat. The Viceroy of India made a public speech attacking the South African Government. Smuts agreed to the appointment of a special commission, which recommended the abolition of the £3 poll tax and the restoration of the legal status of Indian married women. The Government acted on these recommendations and the Transvaal Indian pass law was also repealed.

That was not the end of the persecution of Indians in South Africa. Discrimination against Indians in the Transvaal continues to this day. In Natal their right to acquire land is limited to certain coastal districts. From the Orange Free State they are completely excluded. In the Cape they share the political rights and disabilities of the Coloured people. The events of 1913 have shown, however, the tremendous possibilities of the passive resistance weapon in the hands of those who are prepared to use it courageously, consistently, and with supreme patience.

CHAPTER XI

DOWN WITH THE PASSES !

IT HAS ALREADY BEEN noted how, in the years immediately following the Act of Union, a South African Native National Congress came into being and how this organisation conducted a campaign against the Native Land Act which was passed in 1913.

The forerunner of the National Congress was an ephemeral body, the Native Convention, which met for the first time in Bloemfontein in 1909 to discuss the impending union of the four provinces. This was the first occasion on which politically-minded Africans came together from all corners of South Africa to discuss common problems. To this meeting came Walter Rubusana from the Cape, John Dube from Natal, M. Masisi and J. Makgothi from the Orange Free State. In addition, were delegates from the Transvaal and from Bechuanaland. The convention submitted a number of mildly-worded requests to the Government.

Much of the Native organisation at this time seems to have been sponsored by white liberals and especially by those English who were opposed to the increasing control the Afrikaners were obtaining in South African affairs. Resolutions passed by Native organisations were invariably garnished with professions of loyalty to the British Crown. When Edward VII died, memorial services were held in the English churches. But Natives who attempted to enter a church at Bloemfontein for the purpose of taking part in the ceremony were turned away. A similar incident occurred at Cofimvaba in the Transkei, where Natives were refused admittance by the churchwarden when they tried to enter the English church. In reply to subsequent protests from Native Christians, the local pastor said that while in general it was not desirable that Natives should attend the same service as Europeans, an exception might have been made on this occasion. He therefore refused to endorse the action of the churchwarden.[1] In spite of incidents such as these, the majority of African leaders continued pathetically to believe that the English would protect them against the Dutch. A deputation of Transvaal Bantu waited on Lord Gladstone, the Governor-General, to express sympathy on the death of Edward VII. Under the new Constitution, four members of the Senate were to be nominated by the Government on account of their special knowledge of the Coloured (i.e. non-European) races. The deputation submitted a list of persons who would, they thought, be suitable. These included W. Hosken, who was a leading member of the Chamber of Mines, Vere Stent, former Editor of the Johannesburg *Star*, J. S. Marwick, a Natal Unionist, and W. P. Schreiner. But the South African Party Government, ignoring the suggestion, failed to appoint these Unionists to the Senate. Instead, it chose four S.A.P. men who as senators displayed so little interest in the non-Europeans that most people, even members of the House, were unaware of the nature of their appointment.

At the end of 1911 the movement which aimed at giving South African Native public opinion some more permanent form of expression began to gain ground. The leading exponent of the new propaganda was P. Ka I. Seme, a young African lawyer from Natal, who had returned to South Africa in 1910 after graduating as B.A. at Columbia University, U.S.A., and studying law in London. Writing to *Imvo* on October 24, 1911, on the subject of "Native Union," he declared: "The demon of racialism, the aberrations of the Xhosa-Fingo feud, the animosity that exists between the Zulus and the Tongas, between the Basuto and every other Native must be buried and forgotten. . . . We are one people. These divisions, these jealousies, are the cause of all our woes and of all our backwardness and ignorance to-day." He advocated the formation of a South African Native Congress and proposed an agenda for an inaugural meeting.

The South African Native National Congress at its first meeting declared that it was in favour of uniting all "Smaller bodies" in "this greater political and national body." Its aims were to unite all the different tribes in South Africa, to demand on behalf of black South Africans equal rights and justice and to put forward the political demands of the people on all occasions. Seme became Treasurer and Dube was elected President. The Secretary was Solomon T. Plaatje, a Tswana and a man of considerable literary ability.*

The Congress attempted to fight the Land Act by sending a deputation to England, though it ought to have been clear by this time that there was nothing to be hoped for from the British Parliament. For this purpose a hastily summoned meeting was convened at Kimberley. A second petition was drawn up also for presentation to the Prime Minister of South Africa. Dube, Rubusana, Msane, Mapikela and Plaatje were sent to London. They received no satisfaction and in the midst of their endeavours the First Great War broke out. Whatever slight interest they might have aroused in South African affairs rapidly evaporated. They returned, having accomplished nothing but one more demonstration of the futility of such attempts.

Nevertheless, at the close of the war, in 1919, another deputation was sent. Of those who had gone the first time in

* Among his works are *Mhudi*, a historical novel in English, and a translation of Shakespeare's plays into Tswana.

1914, only one, Plaatje, went again in 1919. The others were J. T. Gumede, L. T. Mvabaza, R. V. Selope Thema and the Rev. H. R. Ngcayiya. They succeeded in gaining an interview with Lloyd George and they made their way to Versailles, one of dozens of deputations from all over the world, among them a deputation of South African Dutch-Afrikaner nationalists, led by General Hertzog, whose business was to plead for a republic. The reply the Bantu representatives brought back from the British Colonial Office was "that the British Government could not interfere in the internal affairs of the Union of South Africa. They were advised to return to Africa and humbly submit the grievances of the black men to the Union Government."

Of the achievements of the Congress one of the most outstanding was the establishment of a national newspaper. The *Abantu-Batho* was actually founded by Seme with a capital of £3,000 subscribed largely by his patron, Queen Regent Natotsibeni of Swaziland. It was, of course, not the first Bantu political newspaper published in South Africa. Leaving earlier missionary journals out of account, that distinction is held by Jabavu's *Imvo*. But whereas *Imvo* was written in English and Xhosa only, *Abanto-Batho* contained articles in English and in the leading Bantu languages, Xhosa, Zulu, Suto, and Tswana. Its name too was a happy bilingualism—*abantu* meaning "people" in Zulu and Xhosa, while *batho* means the same in Suto and Tswana. A number of other Bantu newspapers were amalgamated with the *Abantu-Batho* from time to time. Thus D. S. Letanka's *Motsoaelle* (The Friend) was incorporated in 1912, and Saul Msane's *Umlomo wa Bantu* (Mouthpiece of the People) in 1913.

This unification of Bantu newspapers was highly desirable. Numerous small, inadequately financed papers had sprung up in different parts of the country. Many were ill-managed and few endured. It was better to have one good national paper than many local poor ones. *Abantu-Batho* attracted to itself many outstanding African journalists. Among those who were editors of the paper or regular contributors to its columns were Mweli Skota,* Saul Msane, Robert Grendon, R. V. Selope Thema and D. S. Letanka. Of these Letanka had the longest period of service on the paper, being Editor or Assistant Editor from 1912 to 1931.

* Editor of *The Black Folk's Who's Who*, published in 1932.

The growing literacy and political consciousness of black Africa was reflected in the wide popularity of *Abantu-Batho* in its early years. It did more perhaps than any other organ to break down tribal barriers. It popularised various national slogans at different periods: "*Vuk' Afrika!*" ("Wake up, Africa!") and later, "*Mayibuy' i Afrika!*" ("Let Africa come back!"). The latter slogan has been criticised as implying a return to the "good old days" of tribalism, to conquest by assegai, to backwardness and superstition. But few users of the slogan really mean it in that sense. What they aim at is the return of Africa to the Africans in the literal sense that they want their country back, or at least they demand that they, as the overwhelming majority, shall have the right to say how they shall be governed. "Africa for the Africans" did not become popular until it was taken up by the Pan-African Congress in 1959–60, though certain political groups, particularly those influenced by American movements, such as the Garvey movement,* have used it. "*Mayibuye*" has a peculiarly South African connotation.

The organisation of the S.A.N.C. (later called the African National Congress) was for many years loose and ill-defined. The congresses, held almost every year at Bloemfontein, usually were prepared to accept anyone as a delegate, provided he was non-European and had some sort of organisation behind him. At quite an early stage local and provincial branches of the Congress were formed. These recruited individual members in the manner of other political organisations. There has been little central control and the provincial bodies have been virtually independent, in fact if not in theory. As will be seen later, certain provincial sections of the Congress have been very active, while others were moribund; some have adopted militant lines of action, others followed a moderate policy. It has depended on local conditions and local leadership. The Congress has at different stages in its history been superseded by other organisations which claimed to speak in the name of the Bantu as a whole. But it has never been

* Marcus Garvey, Jamaican Negro leader who founded a movement in the United States which gained a considerable following in the 1920's. One point of its programme was the repatriation of the American Negroes to Africa. For this purpose, an old ship was acquired, which was to be the first ship of the Black Star Line. Garvey was later expelled from the States and returned to Jamaica. His most vociferous followers in South Africa were Professor James Thaele, a Suto, and McKinley, an American Negro, both living in Cape Town.

completely eclipsed. It still survives and can claim a longer record of continuous activity than that of any other national organisation of the South African Bantu.

The War of 1914–18 brought about big changes in the outlook of the black man in South Africa. The country was not the scene of much fighting. The Union forces attacked the German colony in South-West Africa and conquered it after a short campaign. There was a Boer rebellion which affected only a few districts in the Transvaal and Orange Free State and this was soon suppressed by the Government. All the fighting was over by July, 1915. The old policy of not allowing black men to bear arms was maintained, but thousands were persuaded to join the Native Labour Corps. These were sent overseas to dig trenches and do other jobs behind the front. About 700 of them never saw Africa again: they were drowned at sea when the troopship *Mendi* struck a mine and sank on February 21, 1917.

The Rev. Ray E. Phillips found the following in the war song of a Bantu tribe of the northern Transvaal:

> *"I went to France in the great war of the whites.*
> *Do you hear the thundering of the big guns?*
> *It is like the thundering of Heaven."**

Those who returned from Europe came back with new ideas. They had been in places where colour bars were unknown. Their eyes were opened. They did not at all relish returning to the old life of colour bar and pass law, of liquor law, urban areas law and poll tax. Nor did they fail to remember the promises of the recruiters who had induced them to join up for service overseas. They had been told that they would not have to pay poll tax any more, that they would be given grants of land and exemption from the pass laws. Naturally these promises were never kept. They had been made not by the Government, but by enterprising recruiters who had no authority to make such promises. It is even said that those who thus went with the Labour Corps were forced on their return to pay poll tax, not only for the current year, but also for the years of their absence from South Africa. After

* Quoted by Charlotte Leubuscher in *Der Sudafrikanische Eingeborene als Industriearbeiter und als Stadtbewohner.* Jena, 1931.

1918 there were thousands of black men in the country who were not willing any longer to endure the anti-Native laws, men who were prepared to stir up their fellow Africans to revolt against the system.

Apart from sporadic strikes by industrial workers, who felt acutely the burden of the rising cost of living, the chief expression of unrest during the hectic war and post-war years was the struggle against the pass laws. It will be remembered that passport laws for Hottentots were introduced by the British in the Cape in 1809 and that these laws were abolished by Ordinance 50 in 1828. Passes for the Bantu were first introduced in the Cape in 1817. These, however, were more of the nature of international passports in that they were made available to Africans living on the other side of the frontier who wished to seek work within the colony. These pass regulations tended to lapse, however, as the various Native territories, such as the Transkei, were conquered and absorbed. On the other hand, in the Boer republics of the Transvaal and Orange Free State pass and vagrancy laws obtained, comparable in their severity to the old pre-1828 regulations affecting Hottentots in the Cape.

Pass laws were often numerous and complicated. They were aimed at directing and controlling migrant Native labourers in the interests of European employers. They were considered a necessary accompaniment of the poll tax and reserve systems. A black man who was not working for a European was deemed a vagrant. By means of the pass system, he could be tracked down, punished and returned to his employer when necessary. In addition to passes showing where and by whom the bearer was employed, there were travelling passes, passes allowing the bearer to look for work, also special night passes allowing Africans to be out after the curfew hour at night.

These pass laws varied from province to province and even from town to town. The Cape Province had no general pass law for Africans residing within its borders, though some of the towns introduced pass regulations. In the Transvaal Republic Natives were forbidden to walk on the side-walks, though they were permitted to cross a side-walk to enter a building. Restrictive regulations of this sort are sometimes attributed solely to the Boers, but the extremely English Cape provincial town of East London had a municipal regulation forbidding the use of the sidewalk by non-Europeans, a law which was still being enforced as recently as 1920.*

The side-walk law has apparently lapsed in the Transvaal, though it was still in operation in 1905; for in that year the Native United Political Association of the Transvaal in a petition to the King complained that Natives were prohibited from walking on the footpaths of any street, "except in the case of respectable and well-conducted Coloured persons, not being aboriginal Natives."†

The petition availed nothing. In fact, the annexation of the Transvaal by Great Britain had no effect whatever on the status of the blacks. The Transvaal Native poll tax ordinance of 1905 imposed a tax of £2 per year on every African male, whether working for a European employer or not. Polygamous Natives had to pay an extra £2 annually for every additional wife. Every African male was obliged to carry his poll tax receipt with him wherever he went. Failure to produce it on demand rendered him liable to imprisonment.

The manner of the administration of the pass laws added to the feeling of resentment with which they were regarded by Africans. The rank and file of the police consisted in the main of young Afrikaners‡ recruited from the country districts. Often poorly educated and uncouth, they experienced, no doubt, feelings of inferiority in the more urban

* "An elderly Coloured man, who was charged with being on the sidewalk in Oxford Street, stated he was afraid to walk in the road on account of the motor cars, as he was old and lame. The court advised him in that case to keep clear of the principal streets. A fine of 5s. was imposed, the alternative being seven days' hard labour." *East London Dispatch*, January, 1920.

† The petition also states that lashes were inflicted in all cases of assault by Natives on whites, but not vice versa. The death penalty was inflicted in all cases of outrage or attempted outrage on white women, whereas comparatively brief terms of imprisonment were provided for similar offences by white men on Native women. Respectable Natives were excluded from first- and second-class compartments on the Central South African Railways. Natives were prohibited from purchasing landed property. Natives were not allowed to hold public meetings.

As a result of this petition and other agitation by and on behalf of Natives, a motion was passed in the British Parliament in March, 1906, instructing the Government to safeguard the interests of voteless Natives in colonies possessing responsible government. This resolution was more honoured in the breach than the observance. Anti-Native legislation was not repealed and the British Government did not interfere when further inroads were made on Native rights and privileges.

‡ It may be necessary to remind the reader that Afrikaner refers to the Afrikaans-speaking white man (Boer or Dutchman) not to the Native African.

environment, for which they obtained psychological compensation by lording it over the blacks. An African travelling about the country or out in the streets after nine in the evening was sure sooner or later to encounter a policeman and to be ordered in no very courteous language to show his pass. Even those few Africans, clergymen and the like, who were exempted from the pass laws, were liable to be accosted in this way. The exemption certificate was in point of fact only another sort of pass to be shown and did not exempt its bearer from the rough demand of the police. In the pass offices, which African workers must visit every month to renew their monthly employment passes, they are often dragooned, shouted at, sworn at and unpleasantly treated. Long queues of Africans are often to be seen at these pass offices. The Natives wait patiently sometimes for hours before they receive attention. Any African who attends accompanied by his white employer, however, goes straight to the head of the queue and is dealt with immediately. The writer has seen an African who dared to wear his hat in the pass office have it roughly knocked off by an official, who ordered him back to the end of the queue. E. H. Brookes writes: "Any form of pass system is likely to be felt as a genuine grievance—not only by educated Native leaders but by the illiterate masses; and it is because of the bad administration of the law. The manners of the police towards Natives require but little comment. Nothing could be more offensive than the way in which a Native, walking out on a Sunday afternoon with his friends, is suddenly and peremptorily held up to produce his pass. This production is quite uncalled for and unnecessary: it serves no purpose but the temporary magnifying of the policeman's self-importance. But the manner in which the document is called for instils into the mind, even of the apathetic 'kitchen boy,' a burning hatred of the pass and everything connected with it."[2] For the Bantu are a naturally courteous people.*

Thus it is not surprising that the pass law figured prominently in the list of Native grievances and that the African National Congress should make the abolition of passes one of the first points in its programme of demands.

The beginning of 1919 marked a high point in the Native

---

* In the Bantu speech there is no equivalent of the English "Thank you!" This is because thanks must be more elaborate and subtle: one word would be discourteous.

struggle against the pass system. The trouble had begun as far back as 1913, when the Free State Provincial Council empowered municipalities in that province to apply a pass law to Bantu women. Hitherto only the men had had to carry passes. This was a new move and it met with immediate opposition. The women followed a policy of passive resistance. They refused to carry passes. Hundreds were sent to prison, particularly in the towns of Bloemfontein and Winburg. At the latter place the prison became so full that the authorities were powerless to deal with the resisters. The struggle went on for many years. In 1920, the Congress newspaper, *Abantu-Batho*, reported that the women of the Free State were "again fighting the battle of freedom. In the district of Senekal at the Court of Marquard sixty-two women were sentenced to pay a fine of £2 each or go to gaol with hard labour for one month because they refused to take out residential passes and pay 6d. a month for them. The women refused to pay the fines and preferred to go to gaol, so they had to march twenty-four miles to Senekal, where there is a prison. Another group of 100 women will be charged with the same offence at the next session of the court."

This passive resistance on the part of the women was successful: the authorities were forced to withdraw the pass law for women. Prominent in this movement against the pass law was a young Bantu lawyer, Richard Msimang. He had taken his law degree in England and had returned to South Africa in 1912. Of the women who took part in it, no prominent names stand out. Bantu women on more than one occasion in the history of South Africa have shown remarkable courage and determination and they have been associated with many movements of a militant character. Their resentment against what they considered to be injustice has been bitter and persistent. Agitators have often taunted Bantu men with the fact that while they have continued to carry passes their women have got rid of passes.

In 1919 Native men in the Transvaal made the first serious attempt to fight the pass law by means of passive resistance. The movement, which was under the leadership of the African National Congress, assumed large proportions on the Rand and in Pretoria. Some interesting details of the campaign were given by a reporter in the *Star* of March 31, 1919: "Shortly after eight o'clock [in the morning] several thousand

Natives marched to the Pass Office and requested Mr. Laurence, for whom the boys have a great regard, to interview a deputation. Mr. Laurence agreed, and the ringleaders of the movement, ten in number, entered the Government official's office. They submitted their case, which did not appear to be a strong one. Their main grievance was the matter of passes. They contended that by having to carry a pass the Native was jeopardised in any effort he made to ameliorate his position. 'That,' said Mr. Laurence, 'was the sum and substance of their argument. I was sympathetic and listened to them patiently. I advised them that if they broke the law they would suffer in the long run, and that if they continued their movement of relieving boys of their passes I should have to step in as an official. The deputation then departed.'

"The crowd then proceeded to the big open space behind the Pass Office [Von Brandis Square] and held a mass meeting. A number of speeches were delivered, the general purport of which was that the Natives domiciled in town and along the Reef were not being fairly treated. 'Our voice,' said one speaker, 'is not heard and will never be heard so long as the present conditions exist. We count for nothing in Parliament, although we are the majority of the population of the country. We are increasing every day, and we have a right to be heard, and we will be heard.' The speaker and others went on to explain the tactics which it was decided to pursue: strike and decline to carry passes. The statement met with vociferous applause, and hundreds of boys* handed in their passes to the organisers.

"It must also be mentioned that the leaders emphasised that no violence must be contemplated. Boys then went round the crowd and collected a tremendous store of sticks and *sjamboks*. . . . The speeches over, 'Rule, Britannia' was sung, and then 'The King.' Cheers were enthusiastically given for the King, the Governor-General and President Wilson. Over the latter the Natives were clamorous in their cheering. The business of collecting passes was then continued, and pickets went up and down demanding the pass of every boy they met. Many Natives, though unwilling to 'part,' did so, deeming discretion the better part of valour. . . .

"During the forenoon the Native pickets proceeded to the suburban districts and 'collected' passes as they went along. They entered shops and demanded the passes of the Native

* "Boy"—South African term for adult male African.

employees. How many passes in all have been collected at the moment it is difficult to say, but certain it is that the number must run into a couple of thousand at the lowest estimate. The pickets are meeting with but little opposition; so it may be inferred that the majority of the Natives are in sympathy with the movement.

"Subsequently the police interfered, with the result that ten Natives have been arrested and are at the moment in custody at Marshall Square. It is understood the police are taking stringent action, and are determined to give short shrift to those boys who are interfering with their compatriots. Later, C.I.D. men arrested eleven Natives this afternoon in connection with the Native strike. The boys who were apprehended took up a defiant attitude, and declined to go to Marshall Square, but agreed to go to the Pass Office. The detectives and the procession started towards town. At Eloff Street the detectives changed their tone and challenged the recalcitrants to resist going to Marshall Square. The Natives at once gave in and went to the police station. There they were lined up and addressed by Major Cooke, who told them they had gone against the laws of the country and against the King, that they would be handed over to the police and punished for their traitorous actions."

Many more Natives were arrested, including numbers of women. Some were charged with "disturbing the public peace," others with inciting workers to leave their employment. Apparently a general strike was contemplated. Crowds swarmed outside the magistrates' courts where the trials were taking place, singing "*Nkosi Sikelela*,"* and demanding the release of the prisoners. On April 3 the South African Mounted Police charged the crowds and many, including women, were injured.

Rioting took place throughout the town, groups of whites

* "*Nkosi Sikelela*," the song popularised by the A.N.C., is now widely known among Africans and is referred to as the Bantu National anthem.
The Xhosa version is given below with a translation:

Nkosi sikelel' i Afrika,	*God bless Africa,*
Maluphakanyisw' uphondo lwayo.	*Lift up our descendants.*
Yiva nemithandazo yayo	*Hear our prayers*
Uyi sikelele.	*And bless them.*
Yiza Moya, yiza Moya	*Forward, Spirit, forward, Spirit*
Oyingcwele.	*Which art holy.*
Nkosi sikelela	*God bless*
Thina lusapho lwakho.	*Us thy children.*

and blacks coming into conflict. S. P. Bunting, solicitor and well-known Socialist, was mobbed by a crowd of whites as he was returning from the courts where he had been defending some of the prisoners. In the evening, at about five o'clock, "Natives in Vrededorp turned out and intercepted white men at the Fordsburg subway. They asked the first man they met, was he an Englishman? and meeting with a reply in the affirmative, that man being an ex-Army officer, they escorted him through the subway with raised sticks and cheers for the King. They refused to allow him to go to the assistance of another white man who had been knocked down and at whom Native women from the parapet were throwing bricks and stones. The Englishman, as soon as he got clear from the Natives, gave the alarm, and the police from the Fordsburg station ran to the subway, while a squadron of the S.A.M.R. was summoned from the town. . . . The police soon mastered the situation."[3]

Later "a nasty collision took place between Europeans and Natives at Vrededorp. It appears that fifty sanitary boys were returning from work when Europeans, according to present information, interfered with them. The boys were joined by other Natives and there was a fracas, as a result of which several Natives were shot and had to be taken to hospital, while several Europeans were injured and are also in hospital. No one was killed."[3]

It was reported that the position on the mines was normal, the Congress having failed to secure strike action there. The Chamber of Mines, with the concurrence of the Native Affairs Department and Government officials in the various territories, had invited "a number of responsible Native chiefs, who have gone into the question at present agitating the Native minds, and they condemn the movement to resist the pass laws. It is mainly due to the influence of the Native chiefs that the Natives on the mines have kept aloof from the present trouble."[3]

In a leading article, the Johannesburg *Star* pointed to the anomaly that Natives who struck work or incited others to strike were being imprisoned, whereas whites on strike at the same time were not being charged.

In all some 700 arrests were made. On April 25, Natives attacked, unsuccessfully, a police escort taking prisoners from the court-house to the gaol.

There was considerable ill-treatment of Natives by the police both in the streets and in the cells at Marshall Square. White civilians also took a hand in the pogrom, attacking and beating Natives in different parts of the town. Many meetings of the Congress were broken up by whites who used firearms. George J. Boyes was appointed by the Government in May to investigate the allegations of police ill-treatment of Natives. He exonerated the police "in view of the difficult circumstances," but said that the Government should take steps to modify the pass laws, as it appeared to him that the Natives were determined to resist.

In the inquiry Richard Msimang appeared for the Natives. Boyes congratulated the Natives on their selection of a representative. "At this inquiry he has throughout the proceedings shown great courage and ability both in leading the Native evidence and in cross-examining the police witnesses. He has been most courteous and polite to myself, as Commissioner, and the police authorities." Unfortunately, the 465 pages of evidence taken during the inquiry were never printed.

This movement against the passes, courageous as it was, did not bring about any change in the system. It did not spread to the mine Natives nor to centres outside the Rand and Pretoria.

There is a kind of naïve heroism in the spectacle of these thousands of black men assembled on Von Brandis Square, crying "Down with the passes!" but then, "No violence!" surrendering their sticks, setting about their defiance of injustice with songs of Britannia, with cheers for England's King and for President Wilson, only to have their meeting roughly dispersed by the police. There was no meanness in them, but a dignity which might well have made their conquerors ashamed. South Africa may be notorious for the ill-use and waste of her natural assets, but here is the most tragic instance. Of such material as the men of the Von Brandis Square meeting what magnificent citizens might not have been made if justice and magnanimity had been accorded them in place of the prevailing race hatred and intolerance.

CHAPTER XII

SOCIALISM FOR BLACKS

Apart from the passes, there were other and more fundamental causes of Native discontent in South Africa during the concluding years of the First World War. The cost of living rose rapidly. Prices went up while employers strove to keep wages at the old level. A commission appointed in 1919 to inquire into the cost of living stated that "the Natives are now realising that the purchasing power of a sovereign only equals that of 10s. as before the war, and on some articles even less than 10s." Black workers as well as white began to come out on strike. The white strikes were usually official, competently organised by trade unions with experienced leaders. The Africans had no trade unions to speak of. Their strikes were spontaneous affairs, with no trade union or organised backing. Usually they were completely illegal and the strikers were liable to imprisonment under the Masters' and Servants' Act.

Conditions in these years were favourable for the spread of socialistic doctrines among the Bantu.

Socialism, like Christianity, was a European importation into South Africa. Both the trade union and political wings of the South African Labour movement were established by immigrants, and they were organised in the same way as were similar bodies and movements in Britain. Some of the first craft unions in this country were branches of parent organisations overseas, and some of them, such as the Amalgamated Engineering Union, still are so.

White artisans from Europe were quick to adapt themselves to regarding their unions as organisations for maintaining the scarcity of their particular kind of skilled labour. Hence they were not slow to accept a colour bar which prevented non-Europeans from competing with them. They accepted also and without question the fact that all unskilled labour was performed by Africans or other Coloured persons at wage rates far below their own. From the 1880's onwards it was considered right and natural that the white artisan or overseer was entitled to 20s. a day or more for his work, while an African labourer was lucky if he earned as many pence. There must have been a general feeling, understood, if not explicitly, that the very high wages of the white worker were made possible only by the very low wages of the African worker. White trade unionists, therefore, coming on the scene had little difficulty in adopting the prevailing colour-bar mentality of the ruling race, and they cheerfully jettisoned the internationalist and equalitarian ideas of the British labour movement along with other trade union principles which had seemed well enough in England but which in South Africa seemed Utopian. When the South African trade unionists found it necessary to extend their activities into the political field (by the formation of local trades and labour councils and, later, of a Labour Party) there was no fundamental change in their attitude. The South African Labour Party, founded on a national scale in 1909, was nominally socialist and became affiliated to the Labour and Socialist International, but its socialism was, naturally, in conformity with labels on station benches, "for Europeans only."

The South African Labour Party was born of the political turmoil of the decade following the Anglo-Boer War. This was a period of political differentiation. The war had brought about a new economic and political situation in the territory of the old republics. The Chamber of Mines was now the dominating force. The mine-owners were seeking a solution of their labour problem. The future relations of white and black labour, of skilled and unskilled workers, were still in the melting pot. At the same time there was a serious shortage of Native labour for unskilled work. The modern system of Native labour recruitment, with its ugly background of land laws, poll-tax and pass system, had not yet been perfected.

The South African mine-owners proposed to solve their labour problem by importing Chinese labourers. This roused a storm of opposition and was countered by the suggestion that the mines should employ whites as well as blacks for unskilled work. F. H. P. Creswell took the lead in a movement in favour of such a policy. The authorities however, ignored the storm, went ahead and imported the Chinese. This led to further agitation in both Britain and South Africa. It is interesting to note that, while the British Liberals raised the cry of "Down with Chinese slavery!" most of the South African agitators, not at all concerned for the Chinese, cried vociferously, "We are ruined by Chinese cheap labour! To hell with the heathen Chinese!"

A hypothetical future Chinese question in South Africa was happily avoided by a Liberal parliamentary victory in Britain and by the granting of responsible government to the Transvaal in 1906. The Chinese were all repatriated. But the "white labour policy" remained, and as its exponent, Creswell entered the newly-formed Labour Party and became its parliamentary leader. Prior to this, Creswell had been neither a socialist nor a Labour leader; and he did not subsequently become a socialist. The fact that he was able at one stride to secure the leadership over the heads of old trade-union leaders was not without significance. It is the measure of the extent to which the Labour Party had already become even less "working class" than those who laid its foundations had intended.

The trade union stalwarts, however, were at one with the rest of the Labour Party in emphasising the menace of coloured labour. There were some, nevertheless, who exhibited traces of a socialist conscience, an unwillingness to identify themselves completely with the prevailing colour prejudice. Among these was W. H. Andrews, who spoke at Johannesburg, in 1911, at a meeting held "to protest against the encroachment of coloured labour in the skilled trades of South Africa." Andrews was reported as saying that "they were not there to ruin any industries, not to keep any section of the community down. They were there to say that a man who did certain work should be paid for the value of the work done, and not according to his colour or nationality. . . . The Government was guilty of a crime not only against the white people, but against the 'nigger' himself in forcing him to go to the mines and work for the benefit of the capitalist class. . . . He condemned the whole system of indentured labour."[1]

"Equal pay for equal work" and "the abolition of the indentured labour system" thus became the twin slogans of the white labour movement. Though some of the trade unions, notably the Typographical Union, at least in its Cape Town and Durban branches, did admit non-Europeans to membership, "equal pay for equal work" meant in practice the exclusion of the non-Europeans from the craft unions. Nor was any attempt made by the so-called "industrial unions,"

124

such as those in the engineering and building trades, to organise or admit to membership the unskilled Africans who worked side by side with their skilled white members.

"Abolition of the indentured labour system" was taken to mean, not that Native labour should be free (the Labour Party has never fought for the abolition of the pass laws, the master and servant laws or other feudal restrictions on the liberties of the African worker*), but that "the Coloured people and Natives should be kept in their own territories," to quote a phrase employed by Andrews at a lecture delivered in April, 1911.

There were still remnants of this policy even in the programme of the Left socialists who broke away from the Labour Party in 1915. There has always been in the ranks of the Left an unwillingness to face up to the fundamental labour problem of working-class unity, and a strong tendency to push the black worker out of sight and out of mind into some remote Arcadian Native territory, where presumably he would be able to live happily ever after "developing freely along his own lines," so long as these lines did not bring him back into the picture as the competitor of the white worker. The implications of such a policy were never taken seriously and what it amounted to in practice was that the African worker was either regarded as an enemy or simply ignored. As for the "abolition of indentured labour," the Labour Party, when, after the 1924 elections, it shared power with the Nationalists, did nothing to implement this programme so long and so loudly proclaimed.

Socialists and Labour men in Britain have at all times found difficulty in grasping the attitude of South African Labour on the colour question, and when prominent Labour leaders from overseas visited South Africa there were many awkward moments. Both Keir Hardie, who was on the Rand in 1907, and Tom Mann, who came out in 1910 and again in 1914, were shocked by the prevailing racial attitudes of white workers. Keir Hardie was greeted with rotten eggs because he was said to have advocated equality between whites and Indians. He was afterwards allowed to speak, however, when the workers found that he believed in "equal pay for equal work, regardless of colour or creed."[2]

* This statement is no longer true in view of recent developments in the South African Labour Party. See Chapter XXVIII.

Tom Mann fared better, for he had been invited to South Africa by the South African Labour Party itself. When Tom was advised to go carefully on the Native question because if he spoke too freely it might "spoil his tour," he replied by threatening to take the next ship home. The organisers of the tour capitulated and no attempt was made to censor his speeches.[3]

But if the rights of some millions of black workers could thus fortunately be expressed in a formula and forgotten, the claims of the Coloured workers, so much less numerous, so much more disconcerting, had always to be taken into account. The Coloured could not conveniently be consigned to some corner, there to develop along their own lines. Their presence was and has remained an embarrassment in South African politics, a thorn in the flesh of the white trade union leaders. Before the First World War the majority of skilled workers in the Cape were Coloured. Their votes had to be canvassed. So it has happened that both the Labour Party and the Nationalists when in opposition have been at much pains to present themselves as the supporters of the interests of the Coloured workers, only when in power finally to alienate Coloured sympathies by sponsoring, supporting, or at the least failing to oppose, anti-Coloured legislation. Both parties approached the problem of the Coloured by seeking to draw two dividing lines, one between Coloured and white, the other between Coloured and black. Both ended by drawing one line, thick and strong, between Europeans and all non-Europeans.

In the period 1913-14 the S.A.L.P. was growing in all the urban centres, including Cape Town. The Party in the Cape, following the tradition founded by the local Social Democratic Federation, not only sought the Coloured vote, but actually went so far as to admit Coloured persons as members. With the approach of the elections, due in 1915, a definite attempt was made to win the Coloured vote in the Cape, and this coincided with the "equal pay for equal work" campaign in the Transvaal.

In September, 1913, the South African Industrial Federation, representing the organised workers in the Transvaal, sent Harry Haynes and George Mason to investigate the labour position in the Cape Province. Mason on his return reported that the Coloured men in the Cape were "willing to stand up and organise and demand civilised white standards of wages."

He advocated that the skilled Coloured workers should be organised in the same unions as the whites, though he realised that Coloured workers, except for the most highly skilled, would tend, if rates of pay were equal, to be sacked before whites in times of depression. The remedy for this lay, he declared, in the organisation of the semi-skilled and unskilled, and he had advised the Coloured workers accordingly. "The low-paid Coloured unskilled man is a danger to the Coloured skilled man and the white workers too."

Developments in the Cape soon had repercussions in the north, and Labour Party speakers there were compelled to defend the new line before critical and sometimes hostile audiences. Andrews, always a model of logic and lucidity, explained the Party's policy at Germiston in December, 1913. He began by saying that the white race was morally responsible for the Coloured man (a fact of which many Europeans were uneasily aware), that many trade unions already admitted Coloured workers and that the S.A.L.P. in the Cape had had Coloured members for some years. He "took care to remind the audience that racial antipathies were not to be flouted, no social commingling was intended, but rather a logical step in the pursuit of the white ideal by a precaution which prevented the Coloured worker from being exploited by the capitalist to his own evil and to the detriment of the white worker as well. The racial instincts could have their full sway socially, while at the same time they extended to the Coloured man full economic and political equality." Thus a good time could be had by all concerned.

The Labour Party was careful to make it abundantly clear that this new approach to the Coloured worker did not imply that its attitude to the African and the Indian had changed in any way. The Indians must be got rid of, if possible, and the Africans must just go away into the country and develop quietly by themselves. The official report on policy, published in the *Worker* in January, 1914, declared that only those Coloureds would be admitted who had given "practical guarantees that they agree to the Party's policy of upholding and advancing white standards. . . . Nothing should be done to attract Coloured people to the Party at the expense of the white ideals. We cannot shirk the responsibility which circumstances place on the white race in this country. The white population must at present, and for a long time to come, bear the responsibility of guiding the destinies of the country, and this responsibility will not be lessened by the indiscriminate admission of large numbers of Coloured people in all stages of civilisation into our political institutions."

The Natives, on the other hand, were to be segregated; there was to be no extension of the Native vote; legislation of the "most stringent character" was advocated, "prescribing heavy penalties, without distinction of sex, for cohabitation of whites with Kafirs"; squatting and "Kafir farming" were to be abolished and Natives prevented from owning land in areas occupied by whites. The Labour Party envisaged a rapid growth of the white population, the eventual elimination of the Coloured as a significant economic class, and the seclusion of the Natives in their own reserves, where they would be given educational facilities and training in agriculture.

This utopian programme was on all fours with the segregation programme subsequently formulated by Hertzog and idealised by Professor Edgar Brookes.* Neither the Labour Party nor the Nationalists, be it noted, ever made any attempt to carry out those idealistic portions of the scheme which promised the black man adequate land and the opportunity to develop along his own lines. Nor was it to be expected that they would. But they did support and force through Parliament various pieces of discriminatory legislation embodied in the programme. In practice, therefore, their programme became purely reactionary and the ideals were conveniently thrown overboard.

But though the majority of South African Labour men and socialists might observe no incongruity between promise and performance, between principle and the prevailing anti-colour prejudice in which they participated, it was inevitable that here and there was to be found one who took his socialist principles so seriously as to be driven to protest. And here it is possible to draw a very close parallel between the Christian and socialist movements in South Africa. There have always been, there are to-day, hundreds of thousands of professing Christians in this country, white people who attend church and are members of the various organised religious bodies.

* In his early days Brookes supported Hertzog's segregation policy, but afterwards recanted. It is said that he lost his professorship at Pretoria University College as a result. In 1937 he was elected to the Senate by the Native electors of Natal.

But to the overwhelming majority of these it never seems to occur that there is anything incongruous between church membership on one hand and race prejudice and support of the colour bar on the other. But it is plain that the fundamentals of Christian teaching are irrevocably incompatible with colour bar practice, and so there have always been some thoughtful Christians who are prepared to champion the cause of the blacks. Significantly enough, a high proportion of them were born overseas.

Prior to 1915 there had been occasional speeches on street corners* and isolated articles in the Labour Press from time to time, advocating a more strictly "working class" attitude towards the blacks, but as far as the records show no serious or sustained attempt on the part of white socialists to convert the African workers to socialism or to organise them in trade unions. But, during the First World War, a new and more realistic type of socialist activity developed. In 1915 a group of Left socialists broke away from the South African Labour Party and founded the International Socialist League and its newspaper, the *International*. The occasion of the split was the war issue. The League was anti-war. But there were other causes of difference. The new organisation soon developed a keen interest in the African workers, or at least this was the case with some of its more radical members. Two of these in particular became extremely active in carrying the socialist message to the Africans. They were David Ivon Jones and Sidney Percival Bunting.

These two men of outstanding personality have left their mark on the South African Labour movement. Jones had previously been Secretary of the Labour Party. He had come to South Africa from Wales some years earlier on account of his health. He learned to speak Zulu and soon became intensely interested in the African people. He believed that the black workers of South Africa were soon to take their place among "the iron battalions of the proletariat" in a world-wide struggle against capitalism.

Bunting came of a Nonconformist family who had taken an active part in the Liberal movement in Britain in the

* "Jock" Campbell, a socialist from the Clydeside, is said to have preached unity between black and white workers. He flourished in Johannesburg between 1905 and 1915. His meetings, however, were attended by white workers and not by Africans.

nineteenth century. Jabez Bunting, his great-grandfather, had been a leader of the Wesleyans. His father, Sir Percy Bunting, founded and edited the *Contemporary Review*. His mother, Mary Hyett Lidgett, came also of Methodist stock. Both father and mother led lives of unceasing devotion to unpopular causes and it was in such an atmosphere of strenuous activity in the service of others that Sidney Bunting had grown up. He first came to South Africa on military service in 1900. After the War he remained, took a law degree and practised in Johannesburg.

Jones and Bunting, with the help of the International Socialist League, started in Johannesburg an organisation known as the Industrial Workers of Africa. Its slogan was *"Sifuna zonke!"*—We want all! It was their hope that this would soon grow into a large trade union of unskilled workers on the lines of the America I.W.W.* Their hopes were not fulfilled. The Government sent spies into the organisation. One of these became Secretary and another, Luke Messina, subsequently gave perjured evidence against Bunting and others when they were arrested in connection with the famous "bucket strike."

The bucket strike was a stoppage of work by the Johannesburg "night-soil boys," as they were called. These were the days before water-borne sewage became general in the Golden City. African sanitary workers, feeling the pinch of the rising cost of living and inspired no doubt by a successful strike of the white municipal workers, downed buckets and demanded 6*d.* (or according to other reports, 1*s.*) a day more. The authorities drafted in Native police as scabs. But there were not enough of these to do more than attend to schools, hospitals and the like: private residences had to be neglected. The growing stench in the city assailed the noses of all citizens. The strikers, numbering 152, were arrested and sentenced to two months' imprisonment under the Masters' and Servants' Act. The chief magistrate, MacFie, addressing the bucket-carriers after sentence had been passed, said: "While in gaol they would have to do the same work as they had been doing, and would carry out that employment with an armed escort, including a guard of Zulus armed with assegais and white men with

* The Industrial Workers of the World organised seamen, lumbermen and other casual or migratory workers. It flourished in North America during the 1900's, but ceased to be an important organisation after the First World War.

guns. If they attempted to escape and if it were necessary they would be shot down. If they refused to obey orders they would receive lashes as often as might be necessary to make them understand they had to do what they were told."[4]

The authorities then took action against those whom they considered to be the instigators of the strike. Five Africans (leaders of the African National Congress) and three Europeans (members of the I.S.L.) were arrested and charged with incitement to violence. Their names were N. D. Ngojo, A. Cetyiwe, H. Kraai, D. S. Letanka, L. T. Mvabaza, S. P. Bunting, H. C. Hanscombe and T. P. Tinker. The preliminary examination in the magistrate's court on a charge of incitement to violence attracted great attention and the occasion was made use of by the socialists to put over to the general public as much propaganda as possible. Bunting's legal knowledge stood the accused in good stead. The Crown tried to show not only that the socialists, working through the Industrial Workers of Africa, were the chief cause of the bucket strike and a strike of Native miners which followed it, but that they were responsible for a dozen other happenings all over the Witwatersrand, where Africans had gone on strike or rioted in protest against passes and other wrongs. The accused had no difficulty in showing that they had played no direct role in any of the strikes or riots; in fact, their first knowledge of the bucket strike had been a report which appeared in the Press. They were concerned to propagate the doctrines of socialism and industrial unionism. They believed in strike action, but only when it was prepared by adequate trade union organisation. They had considered that the Natives were not well enough organised for strike action and had advised accordingly. As the case proceeded the Public Prosecutor looked more and more foolish, and though the accused were committed for trial, the Attorney-General refused to prosecute and the charges were withdrawn. Incidentally, the charges had been based largely on the evidence of the African detective, Luke Messina, who broke down and confessed that he had made a false affidavit against Bunting at the instance of the authorities.

Bunting and Jones continued to have difficulties, not only with the police, but also with their fellow members of the International Socialist League, many of whom doubted the wisdom of this direct approach to the black worker. But the two intransigents were not discouraged. They persevered with their self-appointed task, trying to educate the white workers in general and their fellow socialists in particular on the importance of what they called the black proletariat. Jones started night classes for Africans, teaching them to read and write. He got them to write on their slates: "Workers of the world, unite! You have nothing to lose but your chains and a world to win." But few Natives actually joined the League. They felt uncomfortable and shy at white meetings. The Industrial Workers of Africa did not long survive the bucket strike, though in 1919 their Cape Town branch was still able to help in organising a strike of Cape Town dock workers.* It is certain that the constant police attention which the organisation enjoyed was effective in scaring Africans away.

In February, 1920, there was a big strike of African miners. Over 40,000 came out. The strike was broken by a simple device. A police cordon was drawn round every compound. Each group of Africans thus isolated was told that all the rest had gone back to work. In the absence of an African miners' union or central strike committee, this method eventually succeeded, though not without bloodshed. European civilians also joined in the fray, attacking "with revolvers and other weapons" a meeting in support of the strikers which had been called by the African National Congress at Vrededorp, Johannesburg.

There was the usual scabbing by white workers on black strikers and, as Bunting said, "no single clear call from any trade union leader." "The demands of the Natives are vague," he wrote. "The strike is undoubtedly an instinctive mass revolt against their whole status and pig level of existence. The Native Congress has had very little to do with the movement other than to hold a watching brief. The strike is in no man's control. Organisation within the compounds there is, of course, but of necessity there can be very little definite organisation between mines owing to the *cordon sanitaire* of police ringed round each compound."

The strike was peaceful at first, but "violence is provoked at last." The police trying to force an entrance into the compound at the Village Deep Mine were met by the

* See Chapter XV.

132

resistance of the Bantu miners. Eight Africans were reported killed. Rumours were "insistent" that the strikers on several mines had been driven down below at the point of the bayonet.

The I.S.L. issued a magnificent *Don't Scab* leaflet, largely the work of Bunting, which appealed to the white miners to refrain from breaking the Native strike. The leaflet said: "White workers! Do you hear the new army of labour coming? The Native workers are beginning to wake up. They are finding out that they are slaves to the big capitalists. Food and clothing are costing more, but their wages remain the same, away down at the pig level of existence.

"But they want to rise. Why not? They want better housing and better clothes, better education and a higher standard of life.

"They have seen the white workers getting more and more wages to meet the rising cost of living. They have noted that our power is due to organisation and they are following suit. They are uniting in a new Army of Labour.

"White workers! Do not repel them! The Native workers cannot rise without raising the whole standard of existence for all.

"They are putting aside their tribal differences and customs; they are entering the world-wide army of labour. They are putting aside sticks and assegais and are learning how to withhold their labour unitedly with folded arms. They are learning how to win the respect of white people by peaceful picketing and organisation. They are falling into line with the trade union movement of the whole world. It is an insult to the trade union movement to bring in troops when any workers go on strike, as if they were unreasoning savages. The fact that they can combine proves they are nothing of the kind.

"When white workers go on strike they enrol Special Constables. Do not allow yourselves to be enrolled as Special Constables against Native strikers. It is an insult to your own Labour movement.

"White workers! On which side are you? When the Native workers are on strike we are all thrown idle. Thus they prove that all sections of Labour are interdependent; white and black solidarity will win!

"White miners! Don't you feel humbled when you cannot

go below because your hammer boys won't go down? Learn the lesson! Your interests and theirs are the same as against the boss.

"Back them up! The Chamber of Mines will be asking you to take up the rifle to dragoon the Native strikers. Don't do it! That would wreck the Labour movement in this country.

"Be on the side of labour, even Native labour, against our common capitalist masters. The Natives have shown that they can stop the mines as well as you can. Get them on your side.

"Beware! The Chamber of Mines may use the crisis to break the white unions. They may march the Natives back to the kraals under armed guard and starve them into submission on the road. Meanwhile, the white workers will be starved into accepting the masters' own terms.

"Therefore, DON'T SCAB! DON'T SHOOT! Don't take a rifle against your own hammer boys, and see that if the Natives are sent back to their kraals they go by train, where they may be under public inspection all the time."

But the tragedy was that this moving appeal fell upon deaf ears. The sorry scabbing continued. The belief, implicit in all Marxist propaganda, that fundamentally the interests of all workers are one, was never questioned by Bunting and the few who worked with him then. But the white workers believed that they had nothing in common with the blacks. A realist, one not obsessed with Marxist doctrine, might have pointed out that the white miners earned ten times as much as the blacks, that many of them employed black servants in their homes, that a victory of the black miners would have increased the desire of the mine-owners to reduce the status of the white miners, since any increase in black wages would have to be met either by a reduction in white wages or by a reduction in profits. Such was the reality of the situation which the white workers, consciously or not, understood very well.

In 1920 Ivon Jones left for Russia and later died there of consumption. For some years Bunting remained the only prominent leader of the International Socialist League who was genuinely interested in work among the Africans. At a later date, however, the struggle for the inclusion of the black worker within the ranks of the socialist movement was revived. This came about some time after the I.S.L. became the Communist Party of South Africa.

CHAPTER XIII

BULHOEK AND BONDELSWARTS

A CONSIDERABLE FERMENT OF ideas and notions, political and otherwise, was stirring among the Bantu in the decade following upon the end of the First World War. All sorts of political movements arose, some of only local and temporary significance, others more enduring. Finally, one big movement spreading over the Union swallowed them all up. This was the I.C.U., which is described later. Some of these local and ephemeral organisations, however, were extremely interesting and of significance for the historian. Of these the Israelite and Wellington movements deserve our attention.

It has been observed that the struggle for racial freedom in South Africa has often taken a religious form. An instance of this the Ethiopian movement, has been noted. The shooting at Bulhoek occurred in May, 1921. In the events leading up to this bloody massacre the elements of land hunger, Ethiopianism, and primitive tribal ideas about salvation by supernatural forces were inextricably combined. To say merely that a religious sect known as the Israelites came into conflict with the white authorities is an over-simplification of what was in fact extremely complex. For the origin of the Bulhoek shooting we must go back to 1909, when a dismissed African Methodist preacher, John Msikinya, visited America and returned to South Africa as "Bishop" of an American Negro sect, "The Church of God and Saints of Christ."[1] He was joined by Enoch Mgijima, who lived in Bulhoek location, near Queenstown. Halley's comet appeared in the sky at about this time and Mgijima preached "that Jehova was angry, and that unless men turned to their ancient religion there would be disaster. The New Testament was a fiction of the white man's and they must worship on the model of the Israelite patriarchs who in their day had been liberated by Jehovah from the yoke of oppressive rulers."[1]

With the death of Msikinya, in 1918, the organisation split and Mgijima was expelled from the American parent Church. He thereupon founded his own sect, known as the Israelites, and soon gained a large following in the eastern Province of the Cape and also in the Transvaal. The group met every year on the Bulhoek commonage, near Queenstown in the Ciskei, to celebrate the passover. In 1920 they assembled as usual, celebrated the passover and then built huts and settled down to live upon the commonage. The authorities tried to move them, but they steadfastly refused to go, saying that they had gathered at Ntabelanga (Bulhoek) at Jehovah's orders, there to await the end of the world for which they were preparing for it was near.

Commenting on the coming clash, the *International* of December 17, 1920, says: "Preparations are being made by capitalism to commence a wholesale bloody slaughter. . . . The Native is inarticulate, and, like ourselves in our corresponding period of culture, his aspirations to progress are manifested in a religious form. . . . Yahweh could always beat the enemies of the original Israelites provided no 'chariots of iron' were used against him. They were the ancient tanks, and if against such crude implements of warfare Jehovah was quite powerless, how does He stand against machine guns and bombing planes? The Native Israelite rebels will be rudely taught that 'no saviour from on high can help them,'* and in time will learn that their only strength lies . . . in economic organisation."

The Government, through the Native Affairs Department, offered free railway passes to the Israelites if they would return to their homes. Leaders of various African organisations, including the African National Congress, fearing trouble, urged them to leave. But the fanatic Israelites would not listen to advice, even from Africans. They would not move from the common.

To them in May, 1921, came a large force of police supported by Defence Force units. They were once more ordered to go. The Israelites replied: "Jehovah tells us that we are not to allow you to burn our huts, or drive away our

* Quotation from "The International," the Communist song.

people from Ntabelanga, or allow you to arrest the men you wish to arrest." Armed with such swords and spears as they had been able to make for themselves out of old cart wheels and the like, they charged at the police and soldiers. The soldiers waited until they were a few yards away and then opened fire on them with rifles and a machine gun. One hundred and sixty-three Israelites were killed and 129 were wounded. A cinema film was taken of the proceedings, but was not subsequently shown in public. Meanwhile, the women and children were at prayer in the temple. Those who had not been killed were arrested and tried. Mgijima and two other leaders were sentenced to six years' imprisonment and 100 others received various shorter sentences.

Though most of white South Africa seemed prepared to accept the shooting as a matter of course, as one more episode in the struggle to keep the Native in his place, there were strong protests from a number of quarters. Arthur Barlow, Labour M.P. for Bloemfontein, asked in Parliament for an inquiry into the shooting. This was refused by General Smuts, then Prime Minister and Minister for Native Affairs. The Johannesburg *Star* printed a leading article which became famous. Four socialists were arrested at Cape Town for issuing a leaflet headed "Murder, murder, murder! . . . The Bulhoek Massacre. . . . Christians slaughter their Christian brethren."

The *Star*, a paper controlled by the gold-mining interests, is capable at times of quite a high degree of liberalism on matters that do not immediately affect mining shares. Its Editor attacked General Smuts in strong terms. "The full and gruesome details of the bloody affair at Bulhoek have created a painful impression. . . . We are not dealing with the phrase-maker and visionary, but with the practical man of affairs who, as head of the Government, assumes full responsibility for the acts of its servants, Colonel Truter and General van Deventer [in charge of the police and soldiers]. . . . When General Smuts rebukes Mr. Barlow, and accuses him—than which no more serious accusation could be made by one white man against another—of 'fomenting ill feeling between the races,' he is sheltering himself behind a mischievous fallacy. Racial ill-feeling will never be fomented by the knowledge on the part of the Natives that there are Europeans who are honestly anxious to see that they are justly and fairly dealt with. On the other hand, we can conceive of nothing more calculated to do permanent harm than any impression that the Prime Minister—who is also directly responsible for looking after the interests of the Natives—regards such grievous loss of life as occurred at Bulhoek with much less concern than if Europeans had been involved, or is determined to shield subordinates who may be proved to have been guilty of a gross error of judgment."

The writer of the article further expresses the opinion that the authorities should have taken a firmer line at the beginning by "stopping any illegal squatting when Natives first began to drift into Bulhoek" and says that the "real question is the handling of the operations when they actually started. . . . We cannot understand the statement that 'so many thousands' of natives tried to overwhelm 'so many hundreds of police.' It has been understood that the total number of males, including boys and elderly men, at Bulhoek was under 500; and the police, we know, numbered 800, with artillery and machine guns. Then with regard to the Prime Minister's statement that 'The police held their fire to the last,' surely it would have been wiser, and certainly more humane, to fire earlier. A preliminary volley might have checked these foolish people at comparatively small loss of life. Colonel Truter must have known this. By waiting until the mob were only a few yards away, and then directing rifle and machine gun fire on to them, it meant that most of these natives would either be killed or badly wounded, and this is what happened. Over two-thirds of them were mown down—the more fortunate ones killed outright, the others horribly mutilated with abdominal wounds and shattered limbs. If the object of those controlling the operations had been to destroy or mutilate as many of the Israelites as could be disposed of in the shortest possible time, they could scarcely have acted otherwise. . . . These miserable, deluded people defied the Government and invited death. They were a crazy little band of religious fanatics and passive resisters, such as will arise at times in all countries and among all peoples; and their own people condemned them and demanded that firm action should be taken against them. There was the less reason therefore 'to make an example,' if this was the motive of the police authorities, and to enforce such ghastly punishment. The Prime Minister somewhat unctuously concluded his statement with the following observation: 'I hope that however regrettable the incident may be, it will be brought home to every part of the population of South Africa that the law of the land will be carried out in the last resort as fearlessly against black as against white,' to which the House, with equal unction, uttered a pious, 'Hear, hear.' . . . If it were conceivable that several hundreds of Europeans had been killed and wounded in a collision with the police there would be no question about an inquiry; and it would be most unfortunate if the Government conveyed the impression that they hold native life so much more cheaply than that of the rest of the community."

The Editor of the *Star* was not prosecuted. For one thing, the article had been carefully phrased, and for another the *Star* was the leading unofficial organ of the Government. But the Cape Town socialists, who had said very much the same sort of thing in less guarded words, were prosecuted. At their trial the Judge remarked: "If the *Star* is the product of an educated and the leaflet of an uneducated man, then I must say it is the strongest argument for education in this country that I have come across." The jury found two of the socialists guilty: Harrison, who had a number of previous convictions, was sentenced to a fine of £75 or six months' imprisonment, and Driburgh to £10 or fourteen days. But the sentences were suspended pending a decision of the Court of Appeal as to whether the Placaat, a relic of Roman-Dutch law introduced in 1754, under which they had been convicted, was still in force in South Africa. The Appellate Division found that the Placaat was not in force and the two were acquitted.

As to the Israelites, they were not all exterminated. Some survived and the sect still has a following to-day in certain districts. In the Native districts of Johannesburg the Israelites may frequently be seen on Sundays, walking vigorously in procession, bearing crosses of wood bound with strips of blue and white cloth. The votaries are themselves clad in long, white, flowing robes, with sashes of blue. They are a reserved and secretive sect who resent any interest shown in their doings, so that little is known of them or their beliefs to-day.

In the same year that Enoch Mgijima and his followers opposed their home-made spears to the machine guns at Bulhoek, another organisation offering salvation to the black man was founded, this time in the Transkei. But while Mgijima had relied entirely on supernatural forces, such as Jehovah, and supramundane powers, such as comets, Wellington Butelezi taught that American Negroes were coming to save Africa and that they would arrive in aeroplanes.

Of Butelezi it was said that at school in Natal he had been nicknamed "Bootlaces" and had been the object of his comrades' mockery. Of his earlier political history prior to 1921 nothing is known, but in that year he appeared in the eastern Transkei, earning his living as an *inyanga*, or Native doctor. The *inyangas* were of two kinds: some were herbalists and worked cures by drugs that they concocted for themselves; others treated their patients by spells and incantations.* According to Monica Hunter,[1] Butelezi said that he was from America, that his name was Wellington, and that he had been educated at the University of Oxford and Cambridge. He professed ignorance of the South African Native languages and when addressing his meetings was obliged to make use of an interpreter. However, occasionally forgetting himself, he would break into floods of fluent Xhosa. He told his followers that all Americans were Negroes and that they would be coming soon to set their brother Africans free from the rule of the white man. They would arrive in aeroplanes. When they came "the Europeans would be driven into the sea" and the Bantu would not have to pay poll tax any more. Looking into a crystal, he professed to see the planes on their way. But his hearers could not see them yet as they were still too high up. They must be patient. Presently, to the great joy of the people, the promised aeroplanes did in fact appear and flew fairly low over the country. They had been sent by the South African Government, who wished to overawe the Natives. But to Wellington's credulous hearers they seemed confirmation of his words, and served greatly to increase his prestige.

He taught also, following in a small way the footsteps of Nongqause, that all white fowls and pigs must be slaughtered. This the people hastened to do. There was a glut of pig fat. All who joined him received membership badges on payment of the membership fee of 2s. 6d. He prophesied that "fire would come down from heaven and burn up all pigs that had not been killed, the owners of them, and those without membership badges. Members' names were written in a large

* See *Black Hamlet*, by Wulf Sachs.

book which was to be sent to Pretoria to the Governor-General, and thence to America."[1] The movement was religious. Wellington conducted the services and combined prophecy with collecting the half-crowns. His agents went throughout the Transkei, urging people to stop paying the poll tax and to refuse to send their cattle to be dipped,* advice which in both cases had a strong appeal for the Bantu, most of whom did not understand the reasons for the cattle dipping and regarded it as one more unjust imposition of the white man's rule.

As time passed and the expected Americans failed to arrive the movement gradually died away. The most interesting thing it attempted was the setting up of schools, called American schools. Run and controlled by Africans, these schools were a new thing in the Transkei, where all schools had hitherto been run by missionaries. The schools perished through lack of funds and, probably also, lack of teachers. Elsewhere in South Africa there are some schools conducted by African Churches, notably those of the A.M.E.

The Wellington movement was short-lived. Its collapse was hastened by the expulsion of Wellington himself from the Transkei. To-day it is only a memory, though it is said that in certain districts it is still rare to see a white fowl or pig.

No prophet or priest was concerned in the revolt of the Bondelswart tribe in 1922. The Bondelswarts were a Hottentot tribe of South-West Africa. The German colonists were able to subdue them only after a long period of "bitter and insistent fighting,"[2] in which the Bondelswarts gave a good account of themselves. Even after they had been conquered the tribe continued sullenly resentful, while under German rule they were repressed, exploited and conscripted for labour in the usual way until 1919, when the Union Government took over the German colony of South-West Africa under a League of Nations mandate. If the tribe had hoped anything from this change of masters, they were speedily disillusioned, for the policy of the Union Government proved every whit as oppressive as that of the Germans had been.

An imposition that was especially resented by the Bondelswarts was the dog tax, which exacted £1 per annum for one dog owned and payment at a higher rate for more than

---

* To kill ticks, the bearers of East Coast fever and other diseases. A Government regulation.

one, up to £10 for five dogs owned. Since the Bondelswarts were people who lived in the traditional Hottentot way by herding cattle and by hunting, this heavy dog tax thus struck most shrewdly at their means of gaining a livelihood and accordingly excited furious resentment, which culminated in 1922 in a general refusal to pay the tax.

The subduing of the dog tax revolt offers a glaring example of betrayal of the principle of trusteeship on the part of a mandatory Power. In May, 1922, General Jan Christiaan Smuts, "Father of the Mandate system," sent a force of nearly 400 men, armed with four machine guns and accompanied by two bombing planes. To the mechanised slaughter that then took place even the determined Bondelswarts could offer no manner of resistance. Over 100 men, women and children were killed outright and many more mutilated or seriously injured. No white man died.

But the rattle of the machine-gun fire and the sound of the bomb explosions travelled round the world and four months later the incident had a sequel at the League of Nations Assembly when a Negro of Haiti, a Monsieur Bellegarde, rose to tell the story of the Bondelswarts and "made a courageous and impassioned appeal that even now stands as one of the models of eloquence in the Assemblies of the League."[2]

As a result of this appeal, the League of Nations Assembly adopted, on September 30, a resolution calling for an inquiry and ordering South Africa, as the mandatory power concerned "to do everything possible to relieve the suffering of the victims."[2] Some sort of inquiry was duly made and reports submitted, one in English and one in Afrikaans. At its next session, however, it developed that the Mandates Commission was not at all satisfied with these reports, which revealed certain inconsistencies—inconsistencies of which the Union Government must have been aware. The only way to get at the truth of the matter appeared to be to summon some survivors of the Bondelswarts to appear before the Commission and relate their version of what had occurred, since they could not submit a written report. Against this project, however, the long distances and the time that must elapse before such a plan could be carried out were urged, and, more cogently, the argument that thus to listen to the Bondelswarts themselves *"would undermine the prestige of the mandatory Power concerned."*[2] Nothing further was done.

But the father of the Mandate System did not emerge well from the incident. And the poet Roy Campbell, when Smuts published his philosophy of Holism, found the apt comment:

> "*The love of nature burning in his heart,*
> *Our new Saint Francis offers us his book.*
> *The saint who fed the birds at Bondelswart*
> *And fattened up the vultures at Bulhoek.*"

CHAPTER XIV

RAND REVOLT AND "WHITE SOUTH AFRICA"

BETWEEN 1907 AND 1922 a series of clashes took place between the white gold-miners of the Witwatersrand and the mine-owners, which equalled in bitterness anything in industrial warfare to be found elsewhere in the world. The background of this industrial struggle, which finally found a political solution in 1924, was something more than the mere hostility between Capital and Labour. It was the traditional class struggle intensified and distorted by the peculiar racial and social conditions of South Africa.

The colour bar, as a social system, was not introduced into South Africa by the Welsh, Cornish and Australian miners and artisans of the Witwatersrand, who fought the mine-owners between 1907 and 1914. The colour bar had its genesis in the old system of Coloured slavery in the Cape. It was perpetuated and intensified and given religious sanction by the land and labour policy of the trekking Boers, who opened up the hinterland in the nineteenth century.

The situation in which the white worker found himself after the political complexion of South Africa had been finally settled by the war of 1899—1901 and the granting of responsible government to the ex-republics in 1906 has been succinctly described by a British Labour peer and Fabian socialist.* "The imported European mine worker," he says, "found himself in a community whose traditional first principle was and is that the white man is an aristocrat, admitting the black to no equality in Church or State, and doing no manual labour; that the black is an inferior species of animal and must be kept so. He taught the black to stope, to work machine drills and sharpen tools, and all the jobs of the mine, and took contracts for work which the black man did under his direction—at Kafir wages. . . . The mine manager, however, does not see white men and black men, he sees only grades of labour —and it is the technique of his training, from which he could not depart, to try to reduce his labour costs by the most economical blending of dear grades and cheap. He had the impiety to attempt to take the Kafir out of his traditional South African place and to use him to blackleg the white man. Why not? He is not a sociologist or a politician, he is a capitalist organiser of industry. South African racial tradition and trade union principle, therefore, invariably coalesce in demanding that the Kafir shall not be given such opportunity to improve his status. A conventional colour bar is established by collective bargaining in the mines, and it is demanded that it shall be made stable by the sanction of the law."[1]

The mine-owners did not see "white and black men"; they saw only "grades of labour." Moreover they had behind them from 1907 to 1924 governments which on the whole were sympathetic to their interests. It was not possible or expedient for them to sack all the white miners . . . they needed the higher grades of labour, the skilled engineer and so on; but they sought to whittle away bit by bit the privileges of the rank and file of the white miners. There were a number of ways of doing this, and they were all attempted, one at a time or simultaneously. They could try to put Africans on to doing more skilled types of work (drill-sharpening was a case in point, and there were many bitter fights over this); they could attempt to dilute white labour by increasing the ratio of black to white workers (this was the main grievance in 1922); and, failing both of these, they could try to reduce the wages of the white workers.

The struggles of the white workers on the Witwatersrand reached peak points in the great strikes of 1907, 1913, 1914 and 1922. The general miners' strike of 1907 was a response to

* Lord Oliver, in *The Anatomy of African Misery*, 1927.

a new regulation that one miner should supervise three drilling machines. At the same time reduced contract rates were proposed. These proposals involved at the same time dilution of white labour, an extension of the field of skilled work for Africans, and a reduction in white wages. The strike was lost.

The July strike of 1913 began on a single mine, the New Kleinfontein, where the question of Saturday afternoon work was the grievance, but it soon spread to all the mines, and ended in a general strike of white labour on the Witwatersrand. Imperial troops were used in an attempt to suppress the strike and considerable bloodshed followed. The Government, however, caught unprepared and with inadequate military forces at its disposal, was forced to conclude a truce which left the industrial situation practically unaltered, with "no victimisation" for the strikers and Government compensation for the scabs.

The uneasy truce was ended in January, 1914, when Smuts and Botha forced a "show down," nipped an incipient general strike in the bud, imprisoned large numbers of the workers' leaders and kidnapped and deported to Europe nine prominent trade unionists.

The industrial struggles on the Rand in 1911-14 form a fascinating chapter in the history of South African labour. The temptation is strong to digress from the main theme, to tell the story of how Mary Fitzgerald led the "Pickhandle Brigade," to recall the martyrdom of Labuschagne, the battle of the Rand Club, the siege of the Trades Hall and other spectacular happenings* of those turbulent times, but the record of such events will help us little in our study of relations between black and white workers. For the Africans were but spectators whose fate was being decided, incidentally, by the battles they witnessed, though indeed it is doubtful whether many of them realised this. In general, the black workers suffered neither personal abuse nor injury. They were not summoned by either side to bear part in the fray. In a Wild West film our attention is on the gun-play, on the heroes and villains, not on the cattle, which to be sure are stolen and recovered at intervals as the drama proceeds, but which nevertheless are merely incidental background from the point of view of the film story.

* You may read of them in *Comrade Bill*, by R. K. Cope, pp. 133-42, and in *Grey Steel*, by H. C. Armstrong, pp. 159-66.

In the July strike of 1913 there were, however, two incidents in which Africans figured. That strike had started at the Kleinfontein Mine, where George Mason had succeeded in persuading the black miners to strike with the whites. In a lecture given nearly three years later, Mason "recalled that shortly prior to the July, 1913, strike the Federation of Trades had initiated an agitation, at his own instigation, against Native and Coloured artisans in Johannesburg and had succeeded in ousting many from the trades here. That was his outlook on the Native question then. In the July strike, however, they had discovered that the interests of the white workers were bound up with those of the Native. They found that they could not stop Kleinfontein Mine without Native co-operation. He therefore appealed to them, and they responded almost to a man, and the mine was stopped."[2] (The lesson was not lost upon George Mason, who, it will be remembered, was one of the two men sent down to the Cape by the Federation in September, 1913, and who returned to advocate the organisation of the Coloured workers there.) But history has no record of a similar co-operation on other mines when the strike became general, nor is there any mention of the Native miners in the terms of settlement. The Kleinfontein incident, while it may have been the first occasion on which African workers had agreed to refrain from scabbing or to come out in sympathy when Europeans were on strike, was certainly not the last instance of such co-operation on the part of the black workers—co-operation which while it was of vital importance to the effectiveness of the white strike action, yet remained unacknowledged by any demand of the white strikers on behalf of the black workers. This fact can occasion little surprise to any who are familiar with the prevailing white South African indifference to the condition of black South Africans. In almost all cases of this sort the Europeans have similarly ignored the Africans in the final settlement, have not inquired what demands the Africans had to make on the employers, have failed to support them in subsequent strikes which the black workers fought on their own behalf, and have even, and that not infrequently, scabbed against them.

The other significant incident in the July strike occurred when Park Station was burned down by the strikers, "in order," it was said, "to prevent the trains running." When he saw the white mob approaching, an African railway attendant took fright, fled into the building, was trapped by the flames and burnt to death. Evidently he was not called upon to "join the strikers."

The high-handed methods of Smuts and Botha were successful in crushing the strike when it was continued in January, 1914, but at the cost of their popularity with the electorate. Early in 1914 the Labour Party secured a majority in the Transvaal Provincial Council and the swing to the Left continued until August of that year. It is, moreover, extremely likely that the Botha Government would have suffered defeat in the General Election of 1915 if the war with Germany had not broken out. As it was, Smuts and Botha were able to stage a "khaki election" and the Labour Party was hopelessly defeated.

After the war the struggle between the Chamber of Mines and the white workers broke out with renewed fury and culminated in the Great Strike and Red Revolt of 1922.* This powerful strike lasted longer, was if anything more bitterly fought, and raised more clearly the fundamental issues at stake than any of the previous struggles. It ended, as had happened in January, 1914, in an abortive general strike, associated on this occasion with an armed revolt which was suppressed by the Government only after considerable loss of life on both sides. Once more it was followed by the inevitable swing-over to political action on the part of the white workers and their middle-class and agrarian supporters of the programme of a "White South Africa." This time no world war intervened and there could be no lucky khaki election to save Smuts and the mine-owners from the Nemesis of defeat at the polls.

The strike was precipitated by an announcement from the Chamber of Mines that they intended to repudiate the *status quo* agreement, which defined the ratio of white to black labour, and to retrench 2,000 white miners.

In the ranks of the white workers in this 1922 strike there were three main schools of thought. First, there was the orthodox trade union leadership, headed by the S.A. Industrial Federation and the Joint Strike Committee. Its methods were essentially reformist. Secondly, there was the

* For accounts of the Rand Strike of 1922, see in addition to sources already quoted, *The Story of a Crime*, published by the Transvaal Legal Defence Committee, 1924, and *Red Revolt*, by S. P. Bunting, 1922.

"Council of Action," a group of intransigents who had been expelled from the Mine Workers' Union for conducting "illegal strikes" prior to January, 1922. This was a small but active group, led by Spendiff, Fisher, Shaw and Wordingham. During the strike it was joined by the communist leader, Andrews, and during the final stages of the strike its headquarters were the offices of the Communist Party. It believed that the strike could not be won unless it developed into a general strike (of the white workers). It was not directly hostile to the Natives; and its leaders, on more than one occasion, tried to stop the spasmodic attacks on Natives which characterised the penultimate stages of the struggle.

The third group consisted of the "commandos," which were bodies of strikers organised, as far as industrial conditions would permit, on the lines of the traditional military organisation of the Voortrekkers. Since 1914 there had been a rapid increase in the numbers of Afrikaners employed on the mines and by this time they formed the majority of the white workers. They had close links with the countryside and their relatives on the farms gave gifts of food to assist the strikers. The commando members were Afrikaner nationalists to a man. Their leaders were openly nigrophobe and it was largely due to them that the main slogan of the strike became "For a White South Africa."

The "reformist" leadership of the Federation was swept aside at an early stage by the militant Council of Action and the commandos, who tended to coalesce both organisationally and ideologically as the strike proceeded. The Afrikaner strikers sang the "Red Flag" in English to the tune of the old republican "Volkslied," and the "Marxist socialists," not to be outdone, refurbished an old May Day banner so that its slogan read, ironically enough, "Workers of the World *fight and* unite *for a White South Africa!*" At the same time some of the Parliamentary Labourites, who had largely been eclipsed as representatives of the workers by the new militant leadership emerging from below, now sought to come back into the limelight with a political slogan. Bob Waterson's famous "Republican Resolution," carried amidst scenes of tremendous enthusiasm at a meeting in the Johannesburg Town Hall in the fifth week of the strike, proved a fiasco. It called upon the Nationalist and Labour Members of Parliament to proclaim a republic and form a provisional government.

148

The proposal was rejected by the canny parliamentarians, but it served to indicate the lengths to which this fusion of ideologies had gone among the workers.

The strike proper lasted for eight weeks and was followed by a fortnight of armed revolt. At quite an early stage of the strike it was clear that nigrophobia was running high. The writer of this book marched in the "Citizens' Commando" and remembers vividly how the Native onlookers scattered as the commando came down the street.

When the strike broke out few Africans can have realised that a battle was being fought over them and their future. It must have seemed to them that the white men were fighting among themselves as they had done during the Anglo-Boer War, though this time, strangely enough, they saw English-men and Dutchmen fighting on both sides. Africans were prepared to look on and enjoy the fun when the strikers marched past with banners or when pickets raided workshops to pull out scabs. When the strikers turned on them in anger they must have been as disconcerted as spectators at a boxing match would be if one of the boxers broke loose and attacked the audience.

As for the African mine-workers, many of them found themselves unemployed as a result of the strike. The Chamber of Mines repatriated thousands to their homes in the territories, partly to be sure to save the cost of feeding them and partly to get them out of the way while the strike was on, a demonstration of the power of organised action which might inspire them to similar resistance at some future date. Among those who remained in the compounds rumours began to spread, echoes of the attacks by strikers on Africans which became increasingly frequent as the strike continued and the commandos got into their stride. Sometimes all the residents of a compound would turn out in alarm to repel a threatened attack by a strikers' commando. Often it happened that the commando was merely marching past the compound intent on other business. But the mere sight of Africans proved sometimes sufficient to rouse the strikers' ire, and so interracial clashes, useless and meaningless, took place, as one might say, by accident. However some of the attacks upon Africans were made deliberately by certain groups of strikers. African workers going about their ordinary business found themselves set upon, assaulted and sometimes fired at. Many demanded their passes from their employers and said that they wished to go home. Among these were the sanitary workers in the municipal compound at Vrededorp, who said that they had been threatened "when they went out with the night-soil plant." As a result, parts of Johannesburg went without sanitary services for a time.

The first serious clash between white and black occurred on February 12 at Apex on the East Rand, and there was another large-scale fight at Fordsburg on the next day. On March 7 there were serious fights at Brixton and the strikers, armed with rifles, attacked the compound at the New Primrose Mine. In the clashes on March 7, three Europeans, seven Natives and one Indian were reported killed and thirty-six Natives and six Europeans wounded.

Both the Government and the strike executive published warnings against attacks on Natives; and the members of the Council of Action risked their popularity with the strikers by intervening in many a fracas which threatened to develop into a serious clash. A statement was issued by the official strike committee, Augmented Executive, stating that reports had reached them from many parts of the Witwatersrand to the effect that bodies of strikers were attacking Natives wantonly and without any reason or cause. These acts had, without doubt, caused considerable feeling among Natives, particularly in the Fordsburg and Vrededorp areas of Johannesburg, and the position in the various compounds nearby was viewed with the utmost concern. The Executive therefore instructed all strikers that such conduct must cease forthwith and any striker observing anyone of his party attacking Natives must see that the offender was handed over to the authorities without delay. It could not be too strongly urged, the statement said, that the provoking of Natives to disorder would have far-reaching consequences in so far as the whole community was concerned and would provoke ill-feeling on the part of the general public to the industrial cause.

S. P. Bunting, almost alone among communists, sought to counteract the growing anti-black feeling with his articles in the *International*, the communist newspaper.

In Cape Town white trade unionists called big meetings and collected funds in aid of the strikers. The Coloured and Native organisations called rival meetings to protest against the idea of a "white South Africa" and the pogrom which they believed was taking place on the Rand. The I.C.U. (the new non-European trade union) held a mass meeting on the Cape Town parade, where a resolution was passed condemning "the murderous onslaught on defenceless, peaceful non-Europeans" and urging the Government to protect their lives. It declared that the colour bar was responsible for the trouble on the Rand and should be abolished, and ended by calling on every Native and Coloured man to assist the authorities while giving unswerving loyalty to Government, King and country. A resolution moved by communists in the crowd, urging support of the strike "because defeat would mean defeat for all classes, both black and white" was rejected.[3]

It has been maintained by some critics on the Left* that the anti-black pogrom was deliberately stimulated by the authorities, who used *agents provocateurs* for this purpose in an attempt to draw a red herring across the trail. There may have been some truth in this, notwithstanding the Government statements at the time, but it is highly probable that clashes between black and white would have developed in any case, with or without C.I.D. assistance.

Those who believed that the strike was or should have been a purely working-class affair of strikers *versus* the Chamber of Mines were little more than a voice crying in the wilderness. They were simply swamped in the rising tide of anti-Native feeling. To have advocated the unity of the workers, black and white, against the bosses would have sounded fantastic to all parties concerned, and so the "visionaries" contented themselves with saying: "Leave the Natives alone; the mine-owners and the Government are the enemy." Perhaps there was a grim logic in the attitude of the average white striker who felt that he was fighting to maintain the *status quo* of the aristocracy of white workers against the overwhelming numbers of the blacks, as well as in the attitude of the African National Congress, the A.P.O., the I.C.U. and other organisations of the non-Europeans who called meetings to protest against the White South Africa campaign and the "anti-black pogrom on the Witwatersrand."

Nearly a generation has gone by since the Rand Revolt, and those who saw in it a movement harmful to the future of the black worker can point to the sequel for confirmation of

* E.g. R. K. Cope, in *Comrade Bill*. Cape Town, 1943.

their views. In 1924 the Smuts Government was defeated at the polls by an electoral "Pact" between the Labour and Nationalist parties. At once a so-called "civilised (i.e. white) labour policy" was introduced and Africans in Government employ were dismissed by the thousand. In 1925 came the Mines and Works (Colour Bar) Act which finally established in the law of the land the principle that the right of a man to do skilled work depends on the colour of his skin.

The British Labour peer quoted above summarised the position in 1927 as follows: "The high white wages, it is uncompromisingly recognised and stated, can only be paid on condition of Natives alone being employed for all unskilled and semi-skilled labour, and being paid at a sweated wage. The mining industry sets the standard of wages for all white South African skilled labour, and a ratio between white and black wages of from over ten to one down to six to one runs through the whole structure of industry. (The ratio of the wage of skilled and unskilled labour in Britain averages fifteen to eleven.) This direct dependence of the white worker's very high wages (the highest in the world) upon the very low wages of the Native labourer is the secret of the philosophy of the industrial colour bar, extensively applied previously in practice, and recently embodied in legislation at the demand of the white South African Labour Party. That party is now firmly established as a section of the European aristocracy of South Africa —combined with the mine-owner and the farmer in exploiting the native African on the basis of an industrial economy and a theory of social relations derived direct from slavery. The Labour Party may not, perhaps, desire to exploit the Native, but it is doing so, through the operation of the conditions thus begotten. Not unnaturally, it prefers doing so to having its own wages reduced, which, in the evolved conditions under which alone the mining industry can be fully maintained, is practically the only alternative."[1]

CHAPTER XV

"I SEE YOU, WHITE MAN!"

FOLLOWING UPON THE UNSUCCESSFUL pass resistance movement on the Reef in 1919 came other less notable disturbances here and there about the country. The cost of living had risen beyond all bounds. There had been no comparable increase in wages, particularly in the wages of the Africans. If the white workers suffered hardship during this period of inflation, the black workers lived in misery. Discontent was general. In such favourable circumstances, the I.C.U. movement came into existence. Founded at Cape Town, in 1919, as a trade union of dock workers, it soon developed into a general all-in union for non-European workers, under the title, "Industrial and Commercial Workers Union of Africa." In the end it came to lose its strictly industrial character and become a political mass party of national emancipation. In fact for a number of years it replaced the African National Congress as the chief political party of the Bantu people.

With the name of the I.C.U. is inseparably associated that of Clements Kadalie. A Native of Nyasaland, he was among the founders of the movement. Full of restless energy, a born orator, a capable organiser, he was able to overcome the disadvantage of being unable to speak the South African Bantu languages.

Kadalie himself has given* an account of the founding of the I.C.U. "I was walking down Hanover Street, Cape Town, with two friends. . . . We met a police constable who had something to say to my friends. I interfered and the constable pushed me off the pavement. We decided to report the constable, but while we were discussing the matter a European passing by asked who was assaulted. We told him. . . . He said that such behaviour on the part of the police was the reason why there was no friendship between black and white in this country. He handed me his card and we took the number of the policeman and reported him to his sergeant. That was the

* In a speech at the Seventh Congress of the I.C.U., reported in the *Workers' Herald*, May 17, 1927.

beginning of the I.C.U. The European gentleman was none other than Mr. A. F. Batty. After talking things over with Mr. Batty, we decided to start a non-European trade union, and the first meeting was held on January 7, 1919, with Mr. Batty in the chair. . . . Mr. Batty made it plain that he wished this to be a purely non-European trade union, and he would only identify himself with it in as far as he could give advice. That night twenty-four members joined and we collected £1 4s., which was next day deposited in the Standard Bank. The second meeting was held on January 25 and I was then appointed first Secretary of the I.C.U. Mr. J. Paulsen, who was foreman at the Union Castle Docks, was appointed Chairman. From that time Mr. Batty never interfered with the internal affairs of the I.C.U."

In December of that year, 1919, some 400 dock workers went on strike at Cape Town. At that time the majority of dock workers at this port were Natives. They began to organise themselves about the middle of 1919. Two organisations were in the field—the Industrial and Commercial Union and the Industrial Workers of Africa. The latter, which was only a branch of a Johannesburg organisation,* was less strong than the new locally founded I.C.U., by which it was presently absorbed. The strike, which had the support of the Cape Federation of Trades, was partly a demand for increased wages and partly a protest against the export of foodstuffs at a time when prices in South Africa were rising rapidly. It would thus be not inapt to describe it as an attempt to kill two birds with one stone: to raise wages so that the workers could afford to pay the higher prices for food, and to stop prices going higher by keeping food in the country. The white trade unions had been discussing the need for combating the rising cost of living, but it was the Natives who took action first, as it was also they who felt the pinch more acutely.

On December 4 the Federation of Trades had adopted a resolution calling upon trade unionists to refuse to handle foodstuffs for export. The immediate occasion of the strike was the order to load a large quantity of jams, fruits and other foods to be shipped to England on the *Norman*. The Federation held a council meeting and the men concerned, employed by the stevedoring companies and the Union Castle Company, struck work. The crane-drivers ceased work

* See Chapter XII.

in sympathy and those members of the unions who were at work on loading the *Armadale Castle* left the ship. Work all over the docks was at a standstill. The Port Superintendent offered an increase of wages to 6s. per day. This was refused. The strikers held a meeting and passed a resolution demanding 8s. 6d. a day for Native and Coloured employees and 12s. 6d. for foremen.

But on January 9, 1920, the *International** had to report: "The strike has been a failure, the cause of which is the treachery of the white workers." The Cape Federation of Trades had made a mistake in not assuring sufficient support on the part of the white unions before "asking such self-sacrifice from the Native fellow workers." This failure of the National Union of Railway and Harbour Servants, a white union, to rally the active support of the dockers is described as disappointing. The paper adds that "Brother Stuart, the Secretary of the Cape Federation, has played the game as far as he could." The Socialists, at their annual conference, held in Johannesburg, passed a resolution "calling upon the various federations and the N.U.R.A.H.S. to deal with the shameful scabbing on Native and Coloured strikers by white workers." The Secretary of the Railwaymen, however, replied, that "The strike of the Native workers at Cape Town docks was not organised by this Union nor by the Federation of Trades here. . . . The resolution [passed by the Federation] which we promised to assist, called upon all workers not to handle food-stuffs for export . . . there was no intention of calling a strike . . . the workers should have stood by when such traffic was offered." But no explanation was offered as to how the workers could have "stood by" without going on strike.

Another instance of scabbing by white workers on black strikers which took place at about the same time and to which the Socialist resolution also referred, was at Kimberley, where Native and Coloured drivers working for the municipality and the railway cartage contractor struck for a minimum wage of £2 per week, an increase of 25 per cent. on what they were then earning. White railwaymen "were found to drive the wagons with perishables, although adequately warned that they were scabbing, and so far N.U.R.A.H.S. have done nothing in the matter officially."

* Socialist organ.

Though almost all the strikes reported ended in failure there was not any abatement of the strike fever, which was indeed the product of conditions of distressful urgency.

In February, 1920, Native students at a missionary institution at Kilnerton, near Pretoria, went on a hunger strike "for more food." A few months later there were riots at Lovedale, where the theological students set fire to the buildings as a protest against bad bread. In the Cape Province Natives were reported to be organising everywhere. At East London the Bantu trade union was said to be 2,000 strong, and local white socialists were invited by the Native leader, Dr. Rubusana, to address a meeting at which some thousands of Natives were present.

In this atmosphere of dissatisfaction the newly formed I.C.U. spread from Cape Town like a veld fire over the Union of South Africa, first to the seaport towns of Port Elizabeth and East London, then to the country districts of the Central and Eastern Cape Province, then to the Orange Free State, then to Johannesburg and the Transvaal. In the words of a writer in the London *Times*: "The genuine grievances of the South African Natives provided the hotbed in which the I.C.U. flourished. Rack-rented Natives in the urban locations, underpaid Natives in Government employ, badly treated Natives on European farms, flocked to join the movement." One section of the workers, the miners, the I.C.U. hardly touched, and in this important respect it fell short of what the African National Congress was able to achieve at Village Deep in 1920.

The I.C.U. was still in its infancy when it had to mourn its first African martyrs, killed in the shooting at Port Elizabeth in October, 1920. Their leader at Port Elizabeth was Masabalala, a well-educated African in the employ of Lennons,* where he was liked and respected. He was a good speaker and popular at meetings. Addressing an open-air meeting of the I.C.U. held at Korsten, just outside the city, "he stressed the necessity of agitating, educating and organising the Bantu and other non-European sections of the community if any redress of their grievances was to be obtained. He passionately urged them to link up with the Amalgamated Industrial and Commercial Union, which had come into being

* Wholesale chemists.

three months previously, and to demand a living wage. At the close of the meeting, at which there were present a few plain-clothes constables... a resolution demanding a minimum wage of 10s. per day for all adult non-European workers was . . . adopted. It was announced . . . that there would be another mass meeting at the same place on the following Sunday, when Masabalala and possibly Clements Kadalie would address them."[1] But this meeting never took place. On the following Saturday morning Masabalala was arrested by the police, on instructions from Pretoria. No reason was given for the arrest, nor was any charge made. Bail was refused. Black and white workers were alike indignant. Crowds gathered in front of the City Hall. In the afternoon the crowd, some of whom were armed with knobkerries and sticks, moved towards the police station where Masabalala was held. What happened next is not known precisely. Someone, it is alleged, fired a revolver. This the police took as the signal to fire. The shots killed twenty-one persons and injured many more. The injured were left to lie until their friends took them to hospital.

It was in 1923 that the rapid growth of the I.C.U. began, when the organisation began to advance into the country districts and into the northern provinces.

The advance of the I.C.U. into the Free State was the occasion of another of those periodic massacres of Natives by which civilised white South Africa asserts its right to rule over the inferior races. The trouble in Bloemfontein in April, 1925, began with a beer raid in which the police clashed with a group of Natives, and one of the latter was shot dead. The Natives responded by rioting and demolishing the location police station. For a time the location was held by the inhabitants, black men and women who armed themselves with sticks and stones and prepared to repel an attack by the white citizens of the town. The police and armed civilians advanced on the location. Five Natives were killed and twenty-four were wounded. The usual judicial inquiry followed. A large number of witnesses were examined and the following statement was made:

"There is no doubt at all that the firing was begun by the irresponsible armed civilians who were present. Some of the police, hearing the firing, were under the impression that the order had been given, and also began firing. As soon as the firing broke out the police officers immediately did everything they could to stop it, and after two or three minutes all firing had ceased. Captain Seabrook had found it impossible with the limited number of men at his disposal to keep the civilians in check, and many of them had broken through at various points and seized the opportunity afforded by the advance to fire at the Natives. Others on a *kopje* in the rear of the forces also took part in the firing, and so did two armed mounted men in the direction of Monument Hill. In our opinion this firing by civilians was the gravest and most deplorable feature in the whole of this unfortunate happening. The police and special constables were quite capable of handling the situation, and the intervention of armed civilians was not only unnecessary, but entirely wrong. It gravely hampered the police in carrying out their duties and we are afraid it has left a legacy of bitterness behind upon the Native mind which it will take a long time to efface. It may be suggested that these civilians considered the town was in danger from the Natives and that they were assisting the police to repel that danger, but if they did think so, it was their duty to place themselves under the orders and control of the police officers, as so many of the respectable citizens of Bloemfontein actually did. We are afraid that the conclusion is justified by the evidence that their object was rather to 'get at' the Native and punish him than to protect the town, and in any case their action is to be condemned in the strongest possible terms."

At East London and at Bloemfontein the I.C.U. put forward demands for a minimum wage. Negotiations with municipal councils and chambers of commerce yielded no fruit, but the actions were not without political consequence, for at its conference at Johannesburg, at Easter, 1925, the South African Trades Union Congress passed a resolution supporting the Bloemfontein demand. This was the first public recognition of the existence of the I.C.U. by a white workers' organisation.

The I.C.U. headquarters was now transferred to Johannesburg and in 1925 its annual conference was held there. By this time the organisation had become so popular that numbers of leaders of other organisations, many of them previously hostile, came flocking in. Among these were A. M. Jabavu, son of Tengo Jabavu and now Editor of *Imvo*, and A. W. G. Champion, who had previously been Secretary to the Native

Mine Clerks' Association.* Champion was later to play a significant role in the affairs of the I.C.U.

In July, 1926, Tielman Roos, Minister of Justice in the Nationalist Government, threatened to bring in a "sedition Bill" to stop the agitation which was gaining ground among Natives. "The education of the Native does more harm than good," said Mr. Roos. "The worst enemies of the Natives are the white nigrophilists, who are numerous in certain Churches. The Sedition Bill would, in the case of the white men, apply only to very extreme instances such as the few hundred Bolsheviks who are inciting the Natives. . . ."[2]

The Press reported a meeting held by Thomas Mbeki of the I.C.U. at Middelburg, Transvaal. Mbeki's speech was given great prominence and was said to have "aroused considerable indignation among a section of the white population. Unless the leaders of this organisation adopt a milder tone it is feared that there will be trouble."[2] Mbeki was reported to have declared that "their object was to organise the Natives industrially, since the I.C.U. was founded solely and principally on industrial lines. They were endeavouring to better their conditions of living and obtain a higher rate of wages." Referring to the meat and mealie meal porridge that Natives lived on, he exclaimed, " 'O God, what is the matter with you black people?' To obtain better conditions, it was useless to act individually. . . . He advised his hearers to send a deputation to meet the Town Council and place before that body the question of higher wages."[2]

It was against such agitation that the proposed legislation was directed. Tielman Roos' Sedition Bill eventually took the form of a special section of the new Native Administration Act.

In August the Government declared that Kadalie himself must be subject to the pass laws. He was told that he would have to get permission from the Native Affairs Department if he wished to move about the country. He applied for a permit to enter Natal. This was refused. Kadalie decided to defy the Government. He went to Durban, where he was received with tremendous enthusiasm by some 8,000 supporters of the I.C.U. After addressing a number of meetings, he returned to Johannesburg in triumph, the authorities having failed to arrest him in Natal. A large meeting in the I.C.U. hall in Johannesburg celebrated this victory. Among the speakers

* An organisation fostered by the Chamber of Mines.

who congratulated him was S. P. Bunting of the Communist Party. In the course of a lengthy speech, Kadalie declared that the best way to deal with the pass laws was simply to defy them. He denounced the Pact Government, which was pursuing a reactionary policy towards the Native workers and that in spite of the presence of three Labour members* in the Cabinet. "No government in the world is sympathetic to the workers except the Government of Russia," he declared.

But a few days later Kadalie was arrested, taken back to Durban and there charged before the local magistrate. He was found guilty of entering Natal without a permit and fined £3, with the alternative of a month's imprisonment. Against this finding Kadalie appealed and was successful in getting the magistrate's decision set aside. The grounds of appeal were that he had been in Natal less than seven days and that he had gone there for a "business purpose."[3]

During 1926 the I.C.U. had to deal with its first large-scale internal crisis. The question of policy came to the fore. The movement had reached the stage where something had to be done to satisfy the rank and file. The Africans had welcomed this hope of deliverance from their misery. Thousands had joined the movement: they had paid large sums in subscriptions. Money was being spent like water. But no positive gains had been achieved for the masses. Since the early dock strikes at Cape Town and Port Elizabeth there had been no strikes at all. No attempt had been made to take direct action on a mass scale against the pass law or against any other of the slave laws.

Two schools of thought emerged: the left wing believed in direct action, strikes, the burning of passes, refusal to pay taxes, etc.; the right wing was all for a policy of *hamba kahle* (go carefully). In practice, the believers in *hamba kahle* were not able or willing to produce any concrete plans. Nothing was done. Disillusion spread among the rank and file. But as people grew disillusioned in one district, as their enthusiasm waned and they ceased to pay their subscriptions, the I.C.U. moved on to new, untouched districts. So that it happened that by the time that the I.C.U. was flourishing in the Transvaal it was already losing members in the Cape, except in Cape Town itself, where membership increased in 1924.

* W. Madeley, F. H. P. Creswell, T. Boydell.

A writer in the *Workers' Herald*, the I.C.U. organ, complains: "When one knows the fact that the I.C.U. was first established at Cape Town in 1919, and that up to 1925 the Cape Province was the backbone of this national industrial organisation, one desires to know what has gone wrong with the Cape. In all the big towns of this province the I.C.U. had a large membership and the enthusiasm for the cause was predominant everywhere. Cape Town, Port Elizabeth and East London, and even small branches such as Adelaide, were the leading branches of the organisation in every respect. But of a sudden the Cape has made a halt; I was almost tempted to say it is dead. Who is responsible for this? Is it the rank and file or the officials?" The real reason should have been obvious: members were tired of paying subscriptions and getting nothing for their money.

The left wing began to demand a change of policy. It wanted action, something to revive the dying enthusiasm of the rank and file, to justify the existence of the I.C.U. and its leaders. The left wing was led by communists, members of the workers' revolutionary party. By 1926 four of these were on the National Executive Committee of the I.C.U. The communists demanded not only a militant policy of struggle and no more *hamba kahle*, but also a change in the internal organisation of the I.C.U. They wanted to curb the power of the leaders, of Kadalie and some provincial secretaries, who, they declared, were acting as dictators. And, most important, they wanted the control of finance to be put on a sound basis, for it had become an open secret that scores of minor leaders in all parts of the country were helping themselves liberally to the funds of the organisation.

At the same time other influences from outside were at work upon the I.C.U. The Government had grown alarmed at the rapid growth of the movement. Members of the C.I.D. were appointed to watch the I.C.U. There is no doubt that many African police spies came into the ranks and even became leaders, occupying responsible positions and sharing in the intimate councils of the movement. In addition to this Government-inspired spying, there was the interference, more or less well-intentioned, which came from large numbers of private individuals who witnessed with increasing nervousness this manifestation of the growing will to unity among the Bantu. It was amazing to see how, almost overnight, so many Europeans, hitherto seemingly indifferent to the plight of the Africans, now emerged as philanthropists, became "interested in the poor Natives" and wished to "do something to help them." Joint councils were organised, welfare clubs* sprang up, missionaries and parsons came out openly with appeals for a Christian attitude towards the blacks, and certain "good people" who had never before displayed any interest in African trade unionism now became interested in the internal affairs of the I.C.U. and much concerned for its welfare, which concern they expressed by attempts to influence the policy of Kadalie and other leaders. Among these were religious people, college professors, humanitarians and the like. They saw in the I.C.U. a powerful influence for good, if only those extremists and communists who were leading the organisation astray could be eliminated.

Kadalie, who had become by 1926 a power in the land so that newspapers accorded him as much publicity as they gave to any Cabinet Minister, was not unwilling to be influenced by their suggestions. He was not immune to the subtle flattery of being spoken to courteously almost as if he were the equal of these humanitarian representatives of the ruling race. He was persuaded, some say against his better judgment, to listen to these people. They told him that Government hostility could be attributed only to the presence of certain communists and agitators among the leaders of the I.C.U. They told him that if only he would get rid of these "reds" all would be well with the I.C.U. The Government would tolerate—nay, even recognise—the organisation. The I.C.U., thus freed of its red incubus, could affiliate to the International Federation of Trade Unions, with its headquarters in Europe, and this improved status would lead ultimately to recognition from the white trade union movement in South Africa. All this and more also was urged upon Kadalie. But what perhaps influenced him and the other *hamba kahle* leaders more than any of these persuasive arguments was the communists' vociferous criticism of the I.C.U.'s financial system. The radicals ceased not, in and out of season, to demand popular control of the union's funds and stricter supervision of the finances. Kadalie decided that the communists must go or cease to be communists. By various manœuvres, he set about achieving this end.

* The Bantu Men's Social Centre, Johannesburg, for instance.

On December 16, 1926, a meeting of the National Council of the I.C.U. was held at Port Elizabeth. A detailed account of that meeting is given in the Communist Party paper, the *South African Worker*, for December 24, 1926:

"A long agenda . . . had been prepared for discussion, but barely a third . . . was touched upon during the meeting. Practically the whole of the council business centred round two particular items—namely, the policy of the I.C.U. in relation to the Communist Party, and the invitation from the League against Colonial Oppression for delegates to be sent to the forthcoming Brussels conference.

"Indications soon made it clear that these two items were going to show a cleavage of opinion, and later events fully bore this out. In a gathering of thirteen delegates (the total council is composed of nineteen), Kadalie, National Secretary, opened the discussion on the above-mentioned points by remarking that he had come down from headquarters determined to see a definite policy laid down with regard to relations between the I.C.U. and the Communist Party. He maintained that communist members interfered with internal I.C.U. affairs, and said he believed that the Brussels conference was a Bolshevik affair financed by Moscow.

"The General Secretary, J. LaGuma, pointed out that such was not the case, that the conveners of the Brussels conference were of all shades of opinion, and that the South African Trades Union Congress and the African National Congress had accepted the invitation. To turn down the matter in this fashion was simply tantamount to forcibly preventing the non-European masses of South Africa from making common cause with their oppressed fellows elsewhere. In any case, their delegates would not be bound by opinions expressed or decisions arrived at unless they so desired, whilst they would undoubtedly greatly benefit from the knowledge and experience gained.

"At this stage Kadalie jumped up in a furious rage and proceeded to attack certain of the delegates present. He then left the room and the meeting broke up in disorder. When things calmed down somewhat, it was decided to adjourn for half an hour and to instruct the General Secretary to communicate with Kadalie, calling upon him to be present and to apologise for his behaviour. Upon resumption, the requested apology was tendered after some delay.

"Soon, however, it became apparent that the interval had been utilised by certain delegates for framing direct attacks on the communists present. A little later confirmation of this arrived in the form of a resolution, moved by A. P. Maduna, Provincial Secretary for the O.F.S., and seconded by Champion, to the effect 'That no member of the I.C.U. shall be a member of the Communist Party.' An amendment was thereupon moved by T. Mbeki that 'no official be expelled by reason of his being a communist.' On a vote being taken, Maduna's motion was declared carried by six votes to five."

The Communist Party members, being now required to resign from either the I.C.U. or the Party, refused to do either. On being told that they were therefore expelled, they retired in good order, singing "The Red Flag." After the departure of the communists, the National Council meeting broke up in confusion, abandoning all idea of further sessions. Of avowed communists on the National Council there were five. In addition to LaGuma, were E. J. Khaile as Financial Secretary, Thomas Mbeki as Transvaal Provincial Secretary, John Gomas as Cape Provincial Secretary and R. de Norman, an Indian member of the Cape Town Committee. Of these Mbeki and de Norman soon revoked their decision against resigning from the Communist Party and thus retained their jobs in the I.C.U.

The extent of communist influence in the I.C.U. was revealed by the attitude adopted to the expulsions by the local branches of the I.C.U. In a number of urban centres where the communists were well-known, meetings of I.C.U. members protested against the expulsions. There was an immediate sequel at Port Elizabeth, when, on the following Sunday, the I.C.U. held an open-air meeting at Korsten location. The expelled members asked permission to state their case, alleging that the rank and file were being kept in ignorance of what had transpired. The request was refused and they thereupon proceeded to hold a meeting of their own alongside, to which hundreds of Native workers flocked, listening attentively to what they had to say. At the conclusion of this meeting the following resolution was passed unanimously: "This mass meeting of members of the I.C.U. held on Korsten *kopjes* hereby calls upon the National Council of the I.C.U. to reinstate unconditionally the communists expelled from the organisation. . . . It further wholeheartedly endorses the following demands as enunciated at this meeting: (*a*) no interference with officials' political views, (*b*) no exercise of autocracy by officials towards branch executives and members, (*c*) I.C.U. to be represented at the Brussels conference, (*d*) passive resistance to be organised in conjunction with other bodies of African people against pass laws and other oppressive legislation."

The Communist Party then issued a manifesto "to the Native workers and oppressed peoples of Africa—to the members of the Industrial and Commercial Workers Union of Africa." The manifesto declared that the officials had been expelled "for no other reason than because they were active members of the Communist Party. . . . Every member of the I.C.U., including Kadalie, Champion and others, knows full well that these comrades have given their whole life and energy to the building of the I.C.U." There followed an exposition of the Communist Party's policy and programme. "The Communist Party is not in opposition to the I.C.U. It appeals to all Native workers to join up and help to build a still stronger I.C.U. The C.P. is a political party, whereas the I.C.U. is a trade union. Nearly every member of the C.P. is a trade unionist and some hold office in the trade union movement. No other trade union has ever suggested that they should be expelled. You are told you cannot serve two masters. Your expelled officials have never served two masters, but only one—the downtrodden workers of Africa."

In a leading article, the *S. A. Worker* declared that "so widespread indeed has been the indignation aroused among the rank and file that it has only been with considerable difficulty that the Communist Party has persuaded active fighters in the I.C.U. ranks not to leave the union. . . . The whole of the I.C.U. machinery has now been flung into a state of chaos, and this at the very time when the Government is training its heavy artillery for an opening cannonade against all non-European workers." The last sentence refers to the projected Native Administration Bill.

Back in Johannesburg, Kadalie faced the rank and file at a crowded meeting in the I.C.U. hall. Mbeki was in the chair. Uproar prevailed almost from the start. It proved too much for Mbeki to handle, and he vacated the chair in favour of Kadalie, who became virtually the sole speaker. He refused a hearing to the expelled officials and requested

Bunting and other white communists to leave the hall because they were whites. They refused to do so.

Writing in the *S. A. Worker*, Bunting gives an account of Kadalie's speech: "The racial cue was followed throughout, for it can always be counted on to arouse some support. The *white* communists were attacked, no doubt in the hope of dividing the black ones from them. 'We will beat the *white* workers at their own game,' said the speaker, and '*white* men call me a "good boy" '—as if *black* men did not!

"And again: 'What do *you Natives* want with communism? You want more wages, better conditions, repeal of pass laws, etc., not communism, the meaning of which 65 per cent. of you do not know' (and he was careful not to tell them)—as if communism were not just *the only way to get these things*, and as if it were a white man's affair instead of being equally or more in this country a black man's—he did not tell them that."

And of course there was no mention of the group of whites, members of the Joint Council* and others, including (as Kadalie years afterwards confessed on a public platform at a time when he was once more seeking communist help) the well-known novelist, Mrs. Ethelreda Lewis, who had persuaded him to expel the "reds."

Twice at this stormy meeting, when the opposition grew too vociferous, a band, evidently held in readiness for the emergency, played loudly to drown the speakers. Another of Kadalie's manœuvres, however, proved his undoing. "This branch meeting," he argued, "has no say in the acts of the National Council; only a conference can review them." To his chagrin he was taken at his word, and a motion was proposed referring the matter of the expulsions to the forthcoming I.C.U. conference for review. This was ruled out of order. A member, who diverted the angry audience to smiles by opening his speech with the words "Jesus said . . ." moved

* Joint Councils, i.e. formed of Europeans and Africans. These were started by a group of Christian liberals in Johannesburg, among whom were Howard Pim and J. D. Rheinallt Jones. The aim was to bring together Africans and Europeans to discuss their mutual problems. In practice, the Europeans always predominated on these bodies. Their work of promoting good relations between the races was carried out in general by diplomatic means, by approaches to this or that local body or to the Government in connection with particular grievances of Africans. After the formation, in 1928, of the Race Relations Institute, with its headquarters in Johannesburg, the Joint Councils worked under the ægis of that body, of which Professor Alfred Hoernle was Chairman.

that the National Council's decision be accepted as final. Kadalie put this to the vote, but obtained little support. Uproar ensued, in which the cry for "Reference to conference" could be heard. In the end Kadalie was obliged to put both motions and reference to the conference was carried.

Bunting concluded his article with what has proved a prophetic utterance: "What is happening in the I.C.U. is not a mere flash in the pan peculiar to local circumstances, but is on all fours with the similar fate in most other countries of unions whose bureaucratic leaders have made themselves snug, gone yellow and led them through the wide gate and along the broad path that brings them to—what may appear to be superficial prosperity, but really means, as fighting organs against capitalism, their absolute destruction."

Nevertheless, the expulsion of the Communists did not appear to do any immediate harm. The I.C.U. fire continued to spread to the farthest corners of South Africa, and even through the Rhodesias to Nyasaland where an African who distributed the I.C.U. paper, *The Workers' Herald,* was sentenced to three years' imprisonment for doing so. At the time of the expulsions the I.C.U. had perhaps fifty thousand members. In 1927 the numbers were doubled; in 1928 they were doubled again. Almost a quarter of a million strong, the I.C.U. reached its zenith and then the crash came.

But in the early months of 1927 the restless Kadalie was still busy consolidating his position against the communists and preparing for still greater triumphs of membership and finance. He failed to see what was coming.

The Seventh Annual Congress of the I.C.U. was held in Durban in April, 1927. This congress may be considered to mark the peak point in the career of the I.C.U. About 200 delegates from all parts of the country attended and the Congress lasted five days. Champion, in welcoming the delegates on behalf of the Durban Branch, claimed that the branch had a membership of 26,000 and was so strong that the I.C.U. need have no fear of financial difficulties.

Kadalie had made strenuous efforts to get a prominent European to open the Congress. He had written to the Mayor of Durban inviting him to do so, with every protestation of loyalty. "Our people, the Natives of South Africa and in particular members of the I.C.U., place our loyalty to the King and British love of freedom and justice first and above all and all the time. . . . We are entirely opposed to revolutionary methods—in fact, we dismissed a few members who showed revolutionary tendencies, and so on the agenda of the conference in Durban we have a motion making it impossible for the members of the I.C.U. to be in any way connected with the Communist Party." The Mayor hedged: he would be away from Durban on the opening day. Very well then, would he send his deputy? The badgered Mayor came out openly with his objection: he did not approve of their preamble—that famous preamble based on de Leon's "Preamble of the Industrial Workers of the World" and adapted for the I.C.U. by Cape Town Communists many years earlier. Other attempts to get a white man of satisfactory eminence failed and the Congress was opened by an African.

One incident of the Congress, though not of major importance, will serve to reveal the racial attitude of many I.C.U. members at this time. It has been seen how Kadalie was able to achieve the expulsion of the "reds" by playing on the theme of racial hostility. At this Congress a white labour leader, a Norwegian, S. M. Pettersen, a business man and small shipowner, bore credentials from the S.A. Trades Union Congress as their fraternal delegate. His record was good. He had organised a seamen's union, largely of non-Europeans, of which he was Secretary. From the floor of congress a Free State delegate, Keable Mote, rose to challenge Pettersen's right to be present. In extenuation it must be remembered that at all public meetings of Africans the members of the I.C.U. were accustomed to hearing the entire white race denounced in no measured terms, even by the *hamba kahle* leaders, whose platform utterances to Native audiences abounded in demagogy and radical phrases of the most belligerent character. It must also be borne in mind that the I.C.U. members had no training on the relations that should exist between their own trade union movement and the white trade unions. At this stage it was the fact that most members were still so politically inexperienced as hardly to be able to distinguish friend from foe among the white men. Certainly the subtler degrees of radicalism escaped them. The difference between out-and-out radicals, such as the communists, and mildly liberal sympathisers, such as the members of the Joint Councils, were not within their comprehension. Nevertheless, some of the delegates at the

168

Congress realised that there seemed to be a flaw in the logic somewhere. "Delegates should be careful what they say," urged J. Mzazi of East London in supporting Kadalie's contention that Pettersen should be welcomed in their midst. "Here we have passed a resolution in favour of the 'Hands off China' movement, and Comrade Kadalie has been elected to go and place our case before the white workers of Europe. Yesterday this very Congress dispatched fraternal messages to the white workers in conference at Cape Town, and to-day you attempt to shut out Comrade Pettersen. What kind of topsy-turvy methods are these advanced by Comrade Mote now?"

Mote, however, continued to object to the presence of the white man and it was clear that he had the support of the majority of the delegates present. Kadalie, coming to the rescue, "trounced Mote in such a manner that he looked like a naughty boy." He regretted the illness that had unfortunately prevented the attendance of Comrade Champion, who would certainly have told the Congress of the valuable help which Pettersen had given him with I.C.U. work. But the congress decided by thirty-six votes to thirty-five against Kadalie's motion and Pettersen was compelled to withdraw. An incident trivial in itself, but of importance as revealing the political *naïveté* of even politically-minded Africans at this time.

The question of the expulsion of the communists was dealt with at Congress in a debate on a recommendation from the National Council "that ordinary members of the I.C.U. be not allowed to identify themselves in any way with the Communist Party." Being interpreted, the recommendation meant that Congress was asked to endorse the action of the National Council in expelling the communists in the previous December. The only voice raised against this resolution was that of de Norman, the Indian delegate from Cape Town. He had been among those expelled, but had subsequently renounced membership of the C.P. in order to return to the I.C.U. His chief argument now was that Kadalie had himself been responsible for bringing the communists in. He contended also that Congress had no right to interfere with the political opinions of members. Only five delegates voted against the recommendation of the national executive.

When Congress did at last get down to the main business

169

of discussing plans and policy, the matter of action to be taken in opposition to the Government's new Segregation Bills was discussed. The so-called "ginger group," led by the former communist, Thomas Mbeki, and A. Maduna, urged strong action. "People are tired of these bad laws," said Mbeki. "They cannot endure this injustice any longer. The failure of the African National Congress was due to too much prayer and no direct action. For God's sake, don't turn chameleon! Are you going back to the masses and ask them to pray, or will you tell them to depend on their numerical powers?" He was certain that the masses would not accept (Kadalie's remedy) a day of prayer! He quoted the example of India, where the people had gone in for passive resistance. The idea of a general strike might make certain of the delegates tremble in fear, but there was no alternative if they wanted their freedom.

Maduna, supporting Mbeki, said that appeals to the Union and Imperial Governments had been tried before by other organisations and had proved useless. Deputations to Europe had been sent at the expense of the poorest people in the country, only to achieve nothing. All such endeavours and diplomatic "paraphernalia" had proved futile. Drastic action was needed.

Kadalie took the platform and with his facile eloquence made much use of demagogy and radical phrases to prevent the meeting from following the radicals. He was in favour of observing a day of prayer as protest "against this inhuman and undemocratic action of a civilised country." "No, no, no. That is too mild, Chief," shouted several delegates. "All right," replied Kadalie; "if you want to lead a bloody revolution, I am going to follow you, but mark you, if I do follow you I am going the whole hog. I am not a religious fanatic, as I ceased to pray in 1910, and I will not pray again until we are a free people by fair means or foul."

A number of delegates, specially those from the Free State, supported Mbeki. They thought the rank and file were well prepared for strike action. On the word from the leaders they would be ready. Others were more cautious. One said he suspected the words of the "ginger group" "because he had heard the names of Lenin and Trotsky being used." He feared the members might be imbued with the communistic spirit.

There was, however, fairly general opposition to the

day of prayer, so that Kadalie was obliged to delete the reference to praying and propose a day of formal protest. This was carried, against Mbeki's motion, by a fairly large majority. Kadalie's influence was still at its height.

On the perennial question of the pass laws Left and Right were once more aligned in opposite camps. Kadalie, introducing the subject, said that after all this talk about revolutions he held that if there was a grievance that warranted a revolution it was the pass laws. "After this Congress we must kick up the dust about these abominable laws." He suggested that a strong deputation should be sent to the Government to inform them that they would no longer tolerate the unjust laws. But he could tell his hearers beforehand what the Government's reply would be. The next thing would be to test the matter in the law courts. "Let us show the civilised world that we are prepared to take this matter even to the House of Lords. If we fail to draw sympathy and redress from all these channels, then, and then only, should other means be resorted to." But his hearers were weary of petitioning and disillusioned as to their chances in law courts. All Kadalie's noisy bluster had failed to conceal the essential barrenness of his proposals. He had to consent to withdraw his motion and to see it replaced by a somewhat more radical one proposed by the Indian, de Norman. This condemned "*in toto* the Native pass laws . . . as being unjust, iniquitous, brutal and a disgrace to any civilised country," instructing the National Council "to appoint a deputation to interview the Government" and, failing satisfaction, "to organise a passive resistance movement throughout the Union."

The presence of a minor Native chief, Diniso Nkosi, of a section of the Swazi tribe in the Barberton district occasioned a number of speeches. Mbeki said that this chief was a most loyal member of the I.C.U. and that all his people had joined also, in spite of warnings from the Native Commissioner, who had threatened to eject them from their land if they did so.

One of the most important results of the Congress and one that was to have far-reaching results for the I.C.U., results that certainly were not foreseen at the time by Kadalie or any of the other leaders, was the decision to send Kadalie to Europe. At this time the white trade unionists of the country were represented by two main bodies, the Trades

Union Congress with its headquarters in Johannesburg, and the Cape Federation of Labour at Cape Town. When nominating a representative of South African Labour to attend the annual International Labour Conferences held in Geneva, it was the practice of the Government to allow these bodies to send a representative alternately. The idea of allowing a black worker to go had never been mooted. The Congress now registered a protest against this partial attitude on the part of the Government which thus ignored the "real workers" of the country and resolved to instruct its National Secretary, Mr. Clements Kadalie, "to proceed to Geneva to submit the claims of the non-European workers who are the victims of merciless exploitation of both capitalism and the white labour policy of the Pact Government." Kadalie was also instructed to carry on an intensive propaganda tour throughout Europe and even to the United States.

Two months later, in June, 1927, Kadalie left for what became a triumphal tour. His journey is said to have cost hundreds of pounds. He visited England, Paris and Geneva. In England he was welcomed by the leading trade unionists, who were impressed by the membership roll of the I.C.U. He was fêted and made much of by certain labour sympathisers, of whom more will be heard later. Flushed with success and the pleasure of being listened to with respect as speaking for more than 100,000 black workers, Kadalie was inspired to ask the British trade unionists to send back with him one of their number, an eminent leader, who would make a platform tour of South Africa accompanied by Kadalie. This was a plan which would have considerably enhanced the prestige of the I.C.U. and also of Kadalie. But the coal-miners were on strike in England and prominent trade unionists were all too busy to spare time for touring South Africa. No suitable man could be found. However, Kadalie, before he left England, extracted a promise from the trade union executives that they would send him a man. It was not until the end of 1928 that this promise was fulfilled and then the British trade unionist, when he did arrive, was not the kind of man Kadalie had asked and expected.

During Kadalie's absence, spontaneous strikes, not led by the I.C.U., broke out here and there among Native workers in the Transvaal and Natal. It was only to be expected that the masses would take action at last. The flame of revolt had been fanned by the I.C.U. All over the country meetings had been held proclaiming the coming of the new age of unity when Africans would rally and throw off the burden of oppression. The new doctrine of constitutional methods did not chime in with the angry mood of the workers nor with the tone of speeches at purely Native meetings. On June 16, 1927, there was a one-hour strike by 1,500 African workers in Durban Docks, in protest against the arrest of twenty of their number for failure to pay the poll tax. In northern Natal a large number of coal-miners went on strike, but the strike was disowned by I.C.U. headquarters at Durban. There was a further strike in July at the Johannesburg railway goods yards, the strikers demanding more pay and better food. The "complaints and Research" Secretary of the I.C.U., H. D. Tyamzashe, was soon on the scene, not to encourage the strikers, but to persuade them back to work, with the promise that their grievances would be discussed in a few days' time. The strikers indignantly rejected this advice. Nevertheless, the strike was broken by blackleg labour within the space of twenty-four hours.

A week later the I.C.U. organ, the *Workers' Herald*, pointed out in a leading article that "the reasonable attitude of the I.C.U. officials at the recent Kazerne strike should prove to the Government that they were not dealing with a lot of hotheads, but that they are dealing with men who are anxious to assist both employer and employed."

In spite, however, of such attempts on the part of the I.C.U. leadership, which, carrying on the *hamba kahle* tradition, endeavoured always to give that organisation the outward appearance of an innocuous body interested only in co-operation with the Government and opposed to all forms of extremism, it was inevitable that the spread of the movement should be viewed with apprehension by farmers, missionaries and others. Farmers' organisations, particularly in Natal and the Orange Free State, threatened drastic action against any of their labourers who joined the I.C.U. The Johannesburg *Star* was prepared to adopt a more tolerant attitude, especially as the I.C.U. had little or no influence among the Natives in the gold mines. In a leading article, in September, 1927, reference is made to a speech by a well-known Roman Catholic missionary. "Everywhere," said Father Huss, "the Native is no longer seeking knowledge, but only revenge against the Europeans. Where at one time I would have been heard with respect, I am faced with bitter antagonism and bombarded with questions, and this is symptomatic of the new attitude of thousands of Natives, through the growth of this deadly threat to the peace of the country, the I.C.U." The *Star* "considers that this generalisation is exaggerated," for did not Father Huss himself admit that the Transkei is so far "free from the I.C.U. menace." The article concludes: "We imagine that there has been a good deal of quiet, intensive propaganda work by certain Europeans among certain Natives, but the vast majority of the Natives are not responsive to the doctrines and ideas of communistic socialism as proclaimed from Moscow. It is also worth remembering that all avowed communists were expelled from official positions in the I.C.U., whereas an avowed communist* holds the chief executive appointment in the European Trades Union Congress. The work being done by Joint Councils of Europeans and Natives provides a useful corrective to the tendencies deplored by Father Huss. The extension of that work and the carrying out of some of the recommendations put forward will do more to remedy the excesses of the I.C.U. than anything else."

June, 1927, was marked by the holding of the first non-European conference at Kimberley. It was called by Dr. A. Abdurahman, the well-known leader of the Cape Coloured people, and D. D. T. Jabavu, Professor at Fort Hare Native College, and was an attempt to bring together representatives of all the non-European organisations in South Africa. The chief organisations which sent delegates were the African People's Organisation (Coloured, led by Abdurahman), the Cape Native Voters' Association (Jabavu), the African National Congress, the South African Indian Congress and the I.C.U. The I.C.U. attended "with reservations." There was considerable rivalry between the I.C.U. and the A.N.C. and they did not take kindly to the idea of co-operating with that body. Champion made the big speech for the I.C.U. He declared himself to be an extremist, and at one stage he questioned the right of certain Europeans to sit on the platform. Apart from elaborate oratory, the conference produced very little. It did not achieve any real co-operation

* W. H. Andrews. The S.A. Trades Union Congress was subsequently renamed the S.A. Trades and Labour Council.

among Africans, Coloureds and Indians. But it did suggest the possibility of a non-European united front being achieved at some future date in South Africa.

CHAPTER XVI

DECLINE OF THE I.C.U.

THOSE DISINTEGRATING FORCES which had been at work within the I.C.U. for some time were beginning to appear on the surface at the time of Kadalie's return from Europe in November, 1927. Certain local leaders had taken advantage of his absence to entrench themselves in various ways. In Natal, and especially in Durban, where the Africans had always seemed more politically conscious than their fellows on the Rand, the branch had continued to grow, but in the Transvaal and the Orange Free State the decline was obvious. The Government too was tightening up the various anti-Native laws. The new Native Administration Act, with its "hostility clause" aimed ostensibly at agitators who sought to create feelings of hostility between black and white, was gazetted within a few days of Kadalie's landing in Cape Town. A few weeks previously Solomon ka Dinizulu, the paramount chief of the Zulus, obviously acting on Government instructions, had officially warned his tribesmen against joining the I.C.U. In March, 1928, it was announced by Kadalie that the I.C.U. would now be reorganised on proper trade union lines. This held out the prospect that the organisation would in future take up in detail the grievances of special categories of workers. It was a progressive move and long overdue. It was doubtless intended by Kadalie to counteract the feelings of disillusion which had followed upon the disowning of so many spontaneous strikes by the I.C.U. leaders. The decision, however, was never carried out.

For a time, interest was centred on a renewed attempt to secure affiliation of the I.C.U. to the South African Trades Union Congress. In the negotiations Kadalie played his hand badly. The Native workers had good friends in the T.U.C., who, though in a minority, were prepared to do what they could to influence that body in favour of the African workers. The I.C.U. applied for affiliation on the basis of 100,000 members. As the T.U.C. had a total membership of less than 30,000, it was clear that if affiliation were to be granted on this basis, the I.C.U. would completely dominate the white unions. Clearly the Natives had a moral right to a majority in a body claiming to represent the workers of South Africa. Equally clearly, this was not the way to set about the business. It was obviously necessary first to insert the thin end of the wedge. Kadalie was advised to apply for affiliation on the basis of a few thousand members. In any case, it was pointed out, the I.C.U. had not, in fact, 100,000 members in good financial standing. But Kadalie insisted on his point of view.

The T.U.C. appointed a sub-committee to prepare a memorandum on the subject. This was presented to the conference in April and endorsed. It rejected the I.C.U. application for affiliation, but declared in favour of joint meetings from time to time between the two bodies to discuss matters of mutual interest.

In the meantime, the I.C.U. held its Eighth Annual Congress at Bloemfontein in April, 1928. It was not a harmonious gathering, even less so than the congress of 1927. The effects of increasing disintegration were becoming apparent. Much time was spent on squabbles over delegates from what were alleged to be "dud" branches. Kadalie encountered strong opposition when he moved "that this Congress of the I.C.U. sends fraternal greetings to the S.A. Trades Union Congress now in session in Johannesburg and pledges itself to work for the unification of all trade unions, irrespective of colour or nationality, into one trade union congress of all workers." He declared that the I.C.U. would knock at the door of the S.A.T.U.C. until the door was opened to them.

While Kadalie had been absent in Europe, his rival, Champion had still further entrenched himself in the organisation. Kadalie, who had exercised a dominating influence in the affairs of the union, now found Champion a difficult customer to handle. Hitherto there had been only one bull in the kraal, now there were two.

A Native of southern Natal, urbane, slow-moving, slightly obese, an indifferent speaker but a competent organiser, Champion, as has been noted, had not entered the I.C.U. until its success had seemed assured. He was by nature cautious, evasive, concerned with power, no natural revolutionary. He owned a little property. Throughout his career, he never voluntarily adopted a revolutionary role, though it happened more than once that such a role was thrust upon him. Essentially Kadalie's inferior in intellect and courage, he would in normal circumstances have been no match for Kadalie. But at this time the scales were weighted in his favour and he was not slow to avail himself of the opportunity. By the end of 1927 it had become sufficiently obvious that Champion was now Kadalie's rival for the leadership. It was equally obvious that the growth of the I.C.U. in Natal provided a steadily increasing source of revenue and that Champion's services were exceedingly valuable. To get rid of Champion without losing Natal was the problem. Early in 1928, Kadalie took the bull by the horns, but the bull proved too strong for him. Himself a Native of Nyasaland and unable to speak the South African Bantu languages, Kadalie found his facility as an orator in English of little avail against Champion's appeals to the Zulus in their native tongue.

Champion was summoned before a disciplinary tribunal appointed by the Executive to carry out a wholesale "cleansing" of the I.C.U. The tribunal removed him from his post as Secretary for Natal pending the next annual conference of the whole organisation. But Champion had no intention of waiting for the conference. He persuaded the majority of the Natal branches to rally to his support. At first, there was some talk of retaining nominal affiliation to the head office, while securing "financial autonomy" for Natal. But this idea was abandoned and so the I.C.U. *yase* Natal came into existence, a completely independent organisation with Champion in control.

The secession of Natal, the largest and the only flourishing branch of the I.C.U., was a blow to Kadalie. It was soon followed, moreover, by an epidemic of splits and breakaways throughout the country. Everywhere local leaders declared their independence. Apart from the loss of Natal, the most serious damage was the secession of a group of branches in the northern Orange Free State under the leadership of Keable Mote, the "Lion" of the O.F.S. The I.C.U. was soon in a hopeless state of collapse and confusion. Secretaries were bolting with cash, the union's furniture was being sold to pay lawyers' fees. The loss of Natal had meant the loss of the bulk of the paying members.

The events that led up the the final debacle were full of drama and tragedy. Anarchy prevailed. Individual leaders competed for power. They fought to obtain control of the I.C.U. And as they fought, the I.C.U. vanished before their eyes until there was nothing to fight over.

In the midst of the pandemonium, in July, 1928, the long-awaited British trade unionist arrived. Kadalie's hopes rose as he went to meet the man who might restore his prestige and help him once more to bring the I.C.U. together under his sway. The newcomer was a Scotsman, W. G. Ballinger, of the Motherwell Trades and Labour Council. He had been sent out by a group of British trade unionists and labour sympathisers, including Winifred Holtby, author of *Mandoa! Mandoa!* His mission was to act as "adviser" to the I.C.U. Temperamentally cautious and orderly, a careful and slow speaker, but no orator, having no previous experience or direct knowledge of South African conditions, he was literally appalled by what he found. His was a difficult task and one from which a skilled diplomat might well have begged to be excused. Ballinger was no diplomat. Having sized up the situation, he applied himself with dogged conscientiousness to the Augean stables. The deeper he penetrated into the inextricable muddle of faulty accounts and missing records, the more depressed he became. But he had no idea of giving up the task. The I.C.U. had already gone far on the road to the "absolute destruction" foretold by S. P. Bunting on the occaison of the expulsion of the communists who had wished to set the finances on a satisfactory basis. To save the I.C.U., the Natal secessionaries must be brought back. Mote and others had to be pacified. Most urgently, the finances had to be put in order. In addition, there were all manner of tactical problems to be faced. Ballinger found himself attacked from the right and from the left. The left wing did not scruple to accuse him of being an agent of the reformists;

they knew he had the support of the people who, in 1926, had advised Kadalie to expel the communists. The Government, the farmers, the capitalists, the police—in short, the white population in general—regarded him as a dangerous agitator who had come from his own country to stir up trouble with the Natives in theirs. The I.C.U. officials regarded him with deep suspicion, firstly as a white man and secondly as one who found too many faults in the internal organisation of their union.

There was some agitation in Parliament for Ballinger's expulsion from the country. He had been admitted on a temporary passport which had to be renewed at intervals. After a time, however, the authorities came to hold the opinion that Ballinger was not so dangerous an agitator as they had at first suspected. At the Orange Free State Nationalist Party Congress, speaking to a motion to banish Native agitators, the Prime Minister, General Hertzog, stated: "Far from there being any reason for expelling Mr. Ballinger, he is, perhaps, to be welcomed."

It was soon clear that relations between Ballinger and Kadalie were not going to be happy. The chief point stressed by Ballinger in his cautious public speeches was that the I.C.U. was now being reorganised on new and saner lines and that it was making an effort to live down its bad past. Such statements were not flattering to the Native leaders who had built up the I.C.U.

When he made attempts to make contact with employers' organisations and public bodies, in order to present the grievances and desires of the Native workers, Ballinger was always having flung in his face the remarks made by I.C.U. leaders at Native meetings. Such unhelpful remarks were often reported at length in the newspapers, which could scarcely fail to relish the confusion in the I.C.U. On October 22, the *Star* reported that the Volksrust District Farmers' Union had refused to give Ballinger a hearing after he had been invited by the executive of that body to address their annual meeting. Ballinger gave a Press interview in which he said: "Certain members of the executive explained that the reason I was not allowed to speak was that a number of the members had produced newspaper cuttings of speeches made by the I.C.U. speakers, and it was argued on those speeches that it was no use attempting to negotiate with people who talked so wildly. It was my intention to make a reasoned appeal to the farmers, pointing out that the Native was an important factor in the economic development of South Africa. . . . The union's refusal to hear me after I had been invited to speak to them, and had travelled to Volksrust at considerable personal inconvenience and expense, was discourteous to say the least of it. After all, the I.C.U. to-day is a different organisation from that of six months ago. It is making a real effort to become a trade union, a definite negotiating body, and the Volksrust farmers made a big mistake in refusing to hear me."

The same idea was expressed in a speech made at a conference of superintendents of Native locations, held at Bloemfontein on November 14, 1928. "Mr. Ballinger, adviser to the I.C.U., said he was glad to address people who were in close contact with the Natives. . . . The I.C.U. of to-day he urged, should be allowed to develop on trade union lines. If this were done, they would have an incentive to take their proper place in the civilisation which the Europeans had brought here. If this was not done, the Native would be driven into violent organisation. For him, communism had no danger. The I.C.U. was formed as a mass organisation in 1919—all body with very little head or feet. It developed and became truculent. Natives were told that they would get farms if they joined the movement, which had no real leadership. It had at one time an income of £15,000, a sum which many trade unions would be glad to have. The legal fraternity had battened on the movement. In Natal, one legal firm had in four months collected £3,334 11s. in fees from the I.C.U. . . . To-day . . . the tactics of the movement had been changed. . . . 'Give the I.C.U. a chance to prove itself in the new form with its new methods,' said Mr. Ballinger. Delegates should not judge the movement by some of its old leaders, who went about the country breathing fire and murder."[1]

Kadalie, who cannot have relished hearing his leadership described as "very little head" any more than he liked to hear his organisation belittled and condemned, had to bear all this. Much as he disliked and resented criticism and advice, he realised that in Ballinger lay his only chance of ever regaining the I.C.U. The effect of Ballinger's moderation was to make Kadalie break out into violent leftism in his public speeches. This was his way of kicking against the pricks of white tutelage

and control which he resented. When he had lorded it over the
I.C.U., undisputed and popular leader of hundreds of
thousands of Africans, he had seen the necessity for tactical
reasons of abandoning the path of extremism, strike action and
the like, and, pursuing a policy of conciliation, had advocated
petitions and days of prayer. Now that his authority was
undermined within the organisation, and when he needed
above all things to reassert his influence over the rank and file,
he naturally returned to his earlier and more congenial role
of platform thunderer. An instance of this is furnished by the
Onderstepoort strike, which broke out in the first week in
October, by which time Ballinger had been three months in
the country.

Onderstepoort was a Government veterinary laboratory and
farm near Pretoria. It employed a number of Natives as
unskilled or semi-skilled workers. The bulk of these workers
had joined the I.C.U. branch in Pretoria. It was decided to
approach the management for a rise in wages and a deputation
was appointed, consisting of five workers, who were to be
accompanied by Moroe, Secretary of the Pretoria Branch, and
Phoofolo, Transvaal Provincial Secretary. The management
refused to hear the deputation and dismissed the five workers
concerned. As a result of the dismissals, which were a clear
case of victimisation, the other Native employees gave notice
to cease work—in other words, they went on strike in sympathy
with the men discharged. Kadalie hastened to Pretoria from
Johannesburg. He was met at Onderstepoort by a body of
police armed with clubs and revolvers. "I asked if I might
address the men," Kadalie told a newspaper reporter, "and
I was told that if I was going to urge them to go back to work,
I might do so. I said that I was not going to do that and that
the I.C.U. would protect the men. My words seemed to
cause a commotion. The police looked threatening and I was
told to clear out. I went away with my friends and the police
followed us." Two days later, it was announced that the
Government had taken drastic steps at Pretoria, that the
Native strikers had been put in prison and that Kadalie might
possibly be arrested. The next day, seventy-one of the seventy-
five who went on strike were fined 10s. each, with the alternative of seven days' imprisonment. They were defended by
George Findlay. All those who were convicted were dismissed
from employment. There was some talk of appealing to the

Supreme Court, but it was finally decided not to do so. "We realised," said Ballinger, "that there was little hope of a favourable decision in the matter." .

The Government decision not to negotiate with the I.C.U. during the Onderstepoort affair was taken by General Kemp, Minister of Agriculture. The question whether other Government departments would "recognise" the I.C.U., in the sense of being willing to hear I.C.U. representations on behalf of Native civil servants, became during the next two months a major political issue. The I.C.U. had approached Walter Madeley, the Labour Party Minister of Posts and Telegraphs in the Pact Government, in connection with the conditions of Native employees in his department. Now, it happened that at this time an internal crisis was developing in the ranks of the Nationalist-Labour Pact. It will be remembered that a coalition had been established between the Nationalist and Labour Parties in 1924. The Labour Party had three of its members in the Cabinet. During 1928 a quarrel arose within the Labour Party itself between the National Council of the Party and the majority of the Labour Members of Parliament, led by Creswell. The latter maintained that the Labour Parliamentary caucus had the right to decide questions of policy. The Council opposed to this the assertion that the Labour members of Parliament should take orders from the National Council of the Party—that is, that they should be responsible to the Party as a whole. Madeley was the only Labour Cabinet Minister who supported the claim of the National Council. The quarrel between the Creswellites and the Councilites split the Labour Party throughout the country. As a new general election was approaching, it became necessary for the Government party, the Nationalists, to try to heal the split, or, if this proved impossible, to decide which of the Labour factions they were going to support. It was the Madeley episode that finally decided the matter.

Madeley must have realised that he would annoy his Cabinet colleagues if he received the I.C.U. deputation. Hertzog, the Prime Minister, declared afterwards that he had spoken to Mr. Madeley about the I.C.U. "The I.C.U., to my mind, was not a trade union. It was really a political organisation with members recruited from every walk of life. The question here was whether we were prepared as a Government to allow a Native body like that to come and represent to us

what wages should be paid to our employees in the service."
He had advised Mr. Madeley accordingly.[2]

Nevertheless, Madeley decided to go ahead. He would not deal with the I.C.U. direct, but through the South African Trades Union Congress. Accordingly, a telegram to that effect was sent to the I.C.U. "Steps were at once taken by the I.C.U. to satisfy the stipulation and . . . when Mr. W. G. Ballinger (adviser), Mr. Clements Kadalie (Secretary) and other officials of the I.C.U. appeared at the General Post Office to see the Minister, they were accompanied by Mr. W. H. Andrews, Secretary of the Trades Union Congress. Mr. Madeley again made it clear that he was not dealing with the I.C.U. direct . . . it was agreed that Mr. Andrews should act as intermediary for the I.C.U. in the subsequent discussions."[3]

The subtle distinction between meeting Kadalie alone and meeting him in the company of Andrews was apparently too fine to appeal to Hertzog. In a furious rage, he demanded Madeley's resignation. Madeley refused to go. The whole Cabinet was therefore forced to resign and was reconstituted without Madeley. General Hertzog was out of office for three hours.

At this point in our history, it is interesting to recall, by way of contrast with this unsympathetic attitude towards the I.C.U. displayed by Hertzog when Prime Minister in 1928, the utterly dissimilar attitude of Hertzog, as leader of the Opposition, at a time when the Nationalists were looking for support and felt that every vote was needed in order to defeat Smuts. In July, 1921, Hertzog wrote to Kadalie, enclosing a donation to the I.C.U. funds, with the words: "My only regret is that I could not contribute more liberally. The feelings expressed by you on behalf of your union I much appreciate in connection with my endeavours in Parliament; and I sincerely hope that these may contribute to a proper and true realisation of the intimate connection in which those stand who are represented by your union and myself in relation to the common good of South Africa. It is for us by our common endeavours to make this country, that we both love so much, great and good. In order to do that, we must not only ourselves be good and great, but we must also see that there is established between the white and black Afrikander that faith in and sympathy with one another which is so essential for the prosperity of a nation. It is my sincere desire that that faith and sympathy shall exist and to that end I hope to exert all my influence. With best wishes, Yours faithfully, J. H. M. Hertzog." This letter was reproduced in facsimile in the *Star* of February 7, 1929.

Similarly, in 1921, Dr. D. F. Malan, leader of the Nationalists in the Cape Province, sent the following telegram to an assembly of Natives at Queenstown: "No race has shown greater love for South Africa than the Natives. Therein he, the Native, assuredly is a pattern of true patriotism and is entitled to take his place side by side with the Nationalists in the common political arena."

This higher patriotism, transcending the bounds of race and colour was naturally and conveniently forgotten when Hertzog and Malan came into power, with the help of the I.C.U., in 1924. Thereafter they proceeded to legislate against their fellow black Afrikaners in a series of reactionary laws hitherto unparalleled in South Africa. However, the mere fact that Hertzog and Malan, responsible Afrikaner Nationalists, were capable, even with motives of self-interest, of expressing such sentiments towards the African I.C.U. is an instance not merely of the opportunism of politicians which indeed needed no fresh demonstration but of the more hopeful fact that racialism, in spite of all that has been said to the contrary, is only skin deep.

But, to return to the unhappy situation of the I.C.U. in the last months of 1928, it must now be recorded that Ballinger's presence did not put a stop to the series of secessions. In October of that year, the Cape Town, Bellville (Cape) and Lydenburg (Transvaal) branches broke away from the I.C.U. In November, a "unity conference" among Ballinger, Kadalie and Champion was held in Durban. According to reports, the talks were cordial. But it is not surprising that unity was not . achieved.

For a period, Kadalie and Ballinger worked in uneasy partnership. "So far as he can, he [Kadalie] restrains his fiery tongue. When recently, he broke out and attacked General Hertzog fiercely, he was advised by his European friends to apologise, and he did."[4]

But soon the irritated Kadalie quarrelled openly and violently with Ballinger. Kadalie thereupon left the I.C.U. taking with him the bulk of the remaining membership. He left

Ballinger in control of the I.C.U. organisation (such as it was), the organ (the *Workers' Herald*) and the debts!

On February 13, 1929, the I.C.U. published a statement headed: "The true facts concerning the resignation of Mr. Kadalie from the General Secretaryship of the Industrial and Commercial Workers' Union of Africa." The statement bore the signatures of Bennet Gwabini, Joe Kokozela and Geddes Tholutshungu, Administrative Secretary, Organising Secretary and Financial Secretary respectively. The domestic quarrels which led to Kadalie's resignation are described in some detail. There had been innumerable disputes about money and the administration of the finances of the organisation. On January 5, Kadalie had asked for a year's leave of absence. He "stated that he anticipated trouble and legal proceedings against him by his wife; and it was his desire that when such matters came up before the public eye, he should not be officially connected with the organisation. He made a long confession, in the midst of which he broke down in a gush of tears." He was granted the twelve months' leave on half-pay, and it was agreed that he should as far as possible continue to assist in propaganda work during his holiday.

But on January 25, the members of the National Council of the I.C.U. were surprised to see an article in the Johannesburg *Star* headed: "Clements Kadalie resigns Secretaryship of the I.C.U. Objects to Policy of Servitude." In a letter to the National Council, Kadalie stated: "After mature consideration, I find I can no longer remain the General Secretary of the I.C.U., since I cannot subscribe to its present policy of servitude, as conducted by those now at the head of affairs." Interviewed by reporters, he said: "I founded the I.C.U., built it up, and have no regret in handing it over to those who are now pursuing a policy which is diametrically opposed to that which was adopted and reaffirmed consistently year after year by the annual congress of the organisation. . . . We have always wanted, and now more than ever, a fighting policy. The present policy is in conflict with that adopted by Congress. . . . Many measures decided upon have not even been attempted. We were, for example, to approach the Government asking for the suspension of the pass law for six months, and if that were not conceded we were to have had protest demonstrations throughout the country, the members to burn their passes in public." He declared that as a loyal member of the I.C.U., he took serious objection to certain business of that organisation being relegated to a coterie of Europeans and Natives who assembled in the Bantu Men's Social Centre.* "The I.C.U.," he emphasised, "has no right whatever to delegate its functions to the Bantu Men's Social Centre in the matter of the pass law agitation. . . . A militant policy within the law is what the I.C.U. wants."

In replying to Kadalie's charges, the Ballinger section began by attacking him on personal grounds. The document makes a number of statements about disputes between the General Secretary and the Committee. These bear the stamp of office quarrels, such as whether motor-car petrol had been used on errands connected with the I.C.U., and so forth. It then goes on to deal, not very convincingly, with some of the political issues confronting the I.C.U. It refers to "a conference, consisting of representatives of the Joint Council of Natives and Europeans, of the African National Congress, of the South African Trades Union Congress, which had met the I.C.U. and passed certain resolutions, praying, for one thing, the Prime Minister and Minister of Native Affairs to receive a deputation of the Conference on the suggested abolition of passes. Mr. Kadalie knows that the Conference (and particularly Professor Brookes and Mr. Ray Phillips, both of them Joint Council members) took the most active part in moving all the Government machinery to effect an early reception of the Conference deputation. But Mr. Kadalie omits to tell that nothing and nobody has so unstintingly contributed obstacles to the effective working of the Conference as himself. It was his stupid speech at Lichtenburg, when he so impertinently vilified the Prime Minister, which almost broke up the deputation. As a matter of fact, the situation was saved only by his offering to be omitted from the personnel of the deputation." The document is significantly silent on the subject of pass-burning.

The season of alarms and excursions connected with the resignation of Kadalie culminated in a dramatic finale. At a large open-air meeting on Sunday, February 10, 1929, Kadalie promised the audience that on Wednesday, the 13th, he would resume the General Secretaryship of the Union, sweep out the good boys who had installed themselves in the office, and bring

* Bantu men's club in Johannesburg, the meeting-place of the Johannesburg Joint Council.

in his own staff. The new officials were announced as follows: Assistant General Secretary, T. B. Lujiza; Financial Secretary, J. A. LaGuma; Organising Secretary, A. P. Maduna; Assistant Organising Secretaries, Keable Mote and Thomas Mbeki; Complaints and Research secretaries, Doyle Modiakhotla and H. D. Tyamzashe. On Wednesday morning, nothing happened at the I.C.U. office. On Thursday morning, the *Rand Daily Mail* appeared with the headlines: "Clements Kadalie's Hectic Day. Resumes Secretaryship of I.C.U. in Morning. Arrested Later. Spends some Time in Cells on Drunkenness Charge."

Kadalie's difficulties were now legion. But he had still many loyal followers. Few, if any, of the popular leaders remained with Ballinger. The men of action, the organisers, men of Kadalie's own restless ilk, demagogues and firebrands that they were, went with Kadalie, or launched out on their own up and down the country with small one-man-show versions of the I.C.U.

At Easter in 1929, Kadalie gathered his followers together at Bloemfontein, where the Independent I.C.U. was then formed. In his efforts to obtain financial support from white sources, he once more took up a left line in public. Having broken with that section of white nigrophilists whose advice had led to his expulsion of the communists in 1926, he now returned to his earlier policy of co-operation with the "reds". But he found that now the communists were much less willing to help him.

In May, 1929, the Independent I.C.U. applied for affiliation to the League Against Imperialism, which had its headquarters in Paris. In his letter, Kadalie gave a new version of the split in the I.C.U. 'During my visit to Europe in 1927, it was thought necessary that a European adviser should be brought out to this country to assist us to put the administrative machinery on sound lines. Mr. W. G. Ballinger, of Motherwell, Scotland, was appointed to that position. Instead of being a valuable asset to the movement, Ballinger has disintegrated the whole movement, which is now split in two divisions.* The trouble arose in that Ballinger fraternised with the boss class, who all along before the advent of Ballinger fought for the union's destruction. Instead of encouraging us to pursue our militant policy as hitherto, he desired us to worship

* Three, with Champion's I.C.U. *yase* Natal.

at the shrine of capitalism. A break was inevitable. The militants formed themselves into the Independent I.C.U., of which body I was elected General Secretary. . . . At our Bloemfontein Congress it was decided that we affiliate with the League Against Imperialism. . . . Above all, it should be borne in mind that the desire of all African workers is to link themselves up with revolutionary international labour. We fully realise that we are an integral part of the proletariat, so we pledge ourselves to do all in our power to build a huge militant trade union in Africa—an organisation that must have as its object to fight capitalism to the bitter end."

Kadalie displayed equal facility in attacking the communists and in talking their language; he did both alternately as suited his book. The letter quoted above was followed a week later by another in which Ballinger is described as a "capitalist dictator." "The Chamber of Mines," wrote Kadalie, "got hold of him. All African workers are rallying to the good old cause of revolutionary trade unionism. Ballinger has succeeded in getting a few men, but all the leaders of the I.C.U. are with me and we are now conducting vigorous propaganda work. . . . What about cabling us £200 on receipt of this letter to enable us to carry on the good work we began ten and a half years ago?" Kadalie did not get his affiliation to the League Against Imperialism, nor, what was of more moment to him, the £200 he had asked for so ingenuously. The South African communists wrote at the same time to the L.A.I. advising against giving financial support to Kadalie. They regarded him as a spent force and had, moreover, good reason to doubt his sincerity in his new role as revolutionary.

Kadalie, after some adventures at Pretoria, where he was charged with "creating feelings of hostility" between the races, retired to East London, where he still had many loyal supporters. With him went his old lieutenants, Tyamzashe and Maduna.

Ballinger, left with the remnants of the old I.C.U., continued for a while to sort records, to deal with debts. But the veld fire had burnt itself out. It was useless to blow upon the ashes. Ballinger turned his attention to journalism, to research into Native economic conditions and other matters. With Howard Pim and other Joint Council leaders, he played some part in setting up a Bantu co-operative society on the Witwatersrand.

Though the I.C.U. had ceased to be a national organisation, some of the sections into which it had split still possessed a certain remnant of vitality, notably the I.C.U. *yase* Natal, led by Champion in Durban, and the Independent I.C.U. under Kadalie in East London. The scene now shifts to Natal, where the Bantu were fighting the beer laws.

In Natal, as elsewhere in South Africa, there were then, as there are now, special laws concerning the making and drinking of beer by black people—that is to say, laws which did not apply to other sections of the community. The possession of wine or spirits by an African was a criminal offence. A limited amount of beer-brewing for private use only was permitted, but the sale of such home-brew was forbidden. It is obvious that no law and no police force, however powerful, can ever prevent the manufacture of beer. The ingredients, yeast and grain, are common foodstuffs. Beer-brewing has always gone on. In the towns, many Bantu women make a good living by brewing and selling beer to Bantu workers. Their occupation is, of course, illegal. In spite of every device of concealment, the beer being hidden under floors, under beds, in privies, they are continually being arrested, fined and imprisoned. In 1930, the number of Africans sentenced for being in possession of liquor was 35,777. By 1935, this number had greatly increased. In spite of this persecution, beer-brewing remains a lucrative profession and one of the few industries which is predominantly in Native hands.

In 1928, a number of municipalities in Natal, taking advantage of a new provincial law, decided to engage in the municipal brewing of *utshwala* (Native beer). Beer canteens were opened in Durban, Pietermaritzburg, Greytown and other centres. At the same time, all home brewing was made illegal. This at once roused the ire of the women in the towns. They banded together, called for a boycott of the canteens, pulled their men into the fight. The I.C.U. *yase* Natal was forced to take up the struggle. It was a national struggle in a very definite sense. The canteens, which had their origin in the desire to control beer-drinking and to prevent orgies of drinking, were understood as an attack upon the economic basis of the developing urban Africans. The income from the sale of beer would now go to the municipalities. That these latter promised to use the money for the development of various amenities for Africans did not impress the indignant beer-queens, who saw their income thus stolen from them. What now happened was that all the resentment of the masses against the whole burden of slave laws and colour discrimination was focused on one particular point. The beer laws, the police who administered the beer laws, the Government of white supremacy which lay behind it all—these were the enemy to be attacked. There was a general stirring of the Natives in southern Natal. The I.C.U. there grew more popular every day.

The first round in the fight was provoked by an incident that seemed quite irrelevant. At Greytown, in March, 1928, some bewildered and resentful Africans entered the European cemetery one night and smashed a number of tombstones. It was admitted by the police in the subsequent inquiry, and the point was emphasised by the Johannesburg *Star*, that the I.C.U. was in no way responsible for this destruction of the tombstones, the only connection being that one of the men responsible had at one time been an organiser of the I.C.U., from which organisation he had been expelled some time before the tombstone affair.

This desecration of graves roused considerable hostile feeling among Europeans, and the white ruling interests who had witnessed the growth of the Native union with uneasy resentment now made the incident a pretext for a general attack upon the I.C.U. Public meetings of white citizens were held in Greytown and other Natal towns. Violent speeches were made. I.C.U. offices were raided and I.C.U. members beaten and ill-used by the white mob. Furniture and other property of the union was carried into the streets and there burned. At Weenen six whites were arrested in connection with an attack on the local I.C.U. office. Each was sentenced to five days' imprisonment or a fine of £1. A collection was made by the whites outside the court-house and the fines were paid.

Meanwhile, the boycott of the hated municipal canteens went ahead. Native women picketed the canteens and refused to let men enter. The canteens sold practically no beer at all. The police interfered and fights developed between them and the women, the latter using sticks and stones with good effect.

Matters came to a head at Durban in June, 1929, when a white mob attempted to storm the I.C.U. hall and offices in

Prince Edward Street. They met with strong resistance from the Africans and in the fighting two of them were killed. News of the attack spread rapidly through the city and large bodies of blacks and whites joined in the fight. A number of I.C.U. members were besieged in the union's hall. Fearing that those inside would be taken and butchered by the whites, the Natives of the Point Dock area organised a black relief column which tried to force its way into the hall. The police opened fire with revolvers upon the advancing relief column and they were forced back, leaving a number of dead and wounded lying in the street. In all, six Africans and two Europeans lost their lives. The besieged occupants of the I.C.U. hall eventually surrendered to the police.

The judge who conducted the commission of inquiry blamed the white mob for what had occurred. "It must be apparent . . . that had the irresponsible whites not beleaguered the I.C.U. hall, thereby virtually imprisoning a large number of blacks, and had they not attacked the hall by throwing bottles at them through the windows, there would have been no armed sortie by the blacks from the hall. McCabe and Summins would not have been killed and others injured. There would not have been a reinvestment of the hall by the whites, no relief column of blacks would have rushed to the scene from the Point and no conflict would have taken place between the police and the mob on the one hand and the relieving column of blacks on the other. I do not overlook the fact that when a sortie was made from the hall, McCabe was cruelly butchered to death and Jamieson terribly ill-treated and tortured, but the white mob was likewise guilty of gross excesses. The Native who was with the relieving column and who was seen to carry and use a firearm (I assume he did, although the evidence is not conclusive on the point) was subsequently overtaken and done to death in an inhuman manner, and, after the relieving column was in full flight, it was pursued and attacked by the white mob, many of them in motor cars."

In spite of these bloody affrays, the canteen boycott went on for many months. In September, 1929, African women of Weenen attacked the municipal beer hall there. They were arrested and fined £5 each, a sentence which furnishes an instructive contrast with the fine of £1 imposed by the same court earlier in the year on the six whites who had shared in the attack on the I.C.U. office and the beating of the members.

Disturbances continued. It was said that the Africans in Durban were refusing to pay their poll tax. Though it was now November, many had not paid their tax for the current year, 1929. From the Government point of view, the situation was unsatisfactory. The new Minister of Justice, Oswald Pirow, decided to quell the unruly Natives of Durban by a display of force and by an experimental taste of the tear gas that was the latest addition to the Government's armoury. Accordingly, on November 14, 1929, Pirow, employing the latest technique in travel no less than in handling Africans, made his famous journey by aeroplane from Pretoria to Durban. At Durban, he took charge of an armed police battalion which paraded the streets and conducted a house-to-house search for tax-defaulters. No resistance was offered, but thousands of curious black folk lined the streets to see the procession go by. Suddenly, with no warning, the police flung a couple of tear-gas bombs into the midst of the crowd. The tear gas was effective. The crowd ran. Hundreds came the next day to pay their taxes. Pirow's police had proved the usefulness of the new weapon.

Incidentally, it is said that one group of police entered the I.C.U. office and roughly demanded to see Champion's poll tax receipt. He produced the receipt and offered cups of tea, which were refused.

It was at the end of 1929 that the Government introduced a new parliamentary measure which was intended to help the authorities in suppressing the Bantu liberation movement. This took the form of an amendment to the old Riotous Assemblies Act, and gave the Minister of Justice the power to order any individual, white or black, to leave any particular part of the country if he, the Minister, considered that his continued presence there might lead to the creation of "feelings of hostility" between the European and non-European sections of the community.

The new law came into force in May, 1930, and was used against Champion, who was ordered to leave the Province of Natal. He went to Cape Town and afterwards to Johannesburg. The ban remained in force for three years, after which Champion returned to Durban and resumed the leadership of the I.C.U.

This deportation of Champion, like so many of the other deportations ordered by Pirow during his term of office as

Minister of Justice, revealed on the part of the authorities a complete lack of understanding of the real situation. The beer riots, for which a certain amount of responsibility might possibly have been attached to the I.C.U- (though they were so clearly the product of strong indignation on the part of the African women that it is certain they would have occurred whether Champion had been there or not), took place in June, 1929. It was not until September, 1930, that the deportation order was issued. But early in 1930, if not indeed before this date, Champion had already renounced any sort of revolutionary role. In May of 1930, the Government had warned the I.C.U. *yase* Natal in regard to the tone of speeches at meetings. The I.C.U. replied regretting "misunderstandings" between Natives and the Government. These misunderstandings would disappear, they said, if the Government would send officers personally to interview the I.C.U. The trouble had all been caused by the English officials of the Native Affairs Department in Natal, from whom the Government had evidently received incorrect reports. The letter concluded by stating that "the Native leaders of the I.C.U. have perfect confidence in the Nationalist Government." This referred to that same Government that had come with tear gas and bayonets to collect taxes in Durban only six months earlier! Champion held aloof from the anti-pass campaign which developed in Durban under communist leadership during 1930.* His organisation took no part officially in the pass-burning in December of that year. Champion was, in fact, playing Kadalie's policy of *hamba kahle* and using his power to hold back the Africans from action, at the time when it seemed good to Pirow to deport him.

In evidence of the truth of this statement, it must be noted that the deportation of Champion was opposed by the Mayor of Durban, the Rev. A. Lamont, who interceded with the Minister of Justice on his behalf. J. S. Marwick, M.P., and the Natal *Mercury* both vigorously opposed Lamont's action, which was in any case useless. Pirow refused to alter his decision.

Champion himself, thus cut off from his I.C.U. *yase* Natal, moped like some poor exile of Erin sighing for his lost country. But about his attitude there was nothing heroic. He refrained from taking any part in political activities and was careful not to offend the Government. He did, however, go so far as

* See Chapter XX.

to contribute a serial article to the African Nation Congress organ, *Abantu-Batho*. The article, entitled "The Story of My Exile," was full of nostalgia and self-pity. It began with a quotation: "Greater love hath no man than that he should lay down his life [his liberty] for his friends." The article recorded that he had been given fourteen days' grace to leave Natal. He applied for permission to re-enter Natal to put his affairs in order and to see his family at Inanda. This was granted and he was allowed to visit his home between December 18 and 31, 1930, on condition that he "have no communication with and take no part whatever in the affairs of the association known as the Industrial and Commercial Workers Union *yase* Natal, or with any similar association . . . and attend no public meeting and take no part whatever in politics . . . and daily at five o'clock in the evening report himself personally to the officer for the time being in charge of the police station at Inanda." Champion accepted these humiliating conditions and spent a few days in Natal. His deportation order was renewed for another year in September, 1931, and again renewed in September, 1932. In all, he was an exile for three years. The ban would probably have been maintained indefinitely had not Smuts succeeded Pirow as Minister of Justice after the gold-standard crisis early in 1933, when Champion was allowed to return on the understanding that he should "behave himself." In the interval the agitation against the beer halls had subsided. These are now patronised by the majority of Africans in Durban, though illicit beer-brewing continues.

Meanwhile, at East London, Kadalie's dying candle gave one last revolutionary flicker in a general strike of railway and harbour workers early in 1930, an account of which is given by Monica Hunter.[5]

The workers, who were demanding an increase of their daily wage from 3*s.* to 6*s.* 6*d.*, were called out on January 16 by Kadalie's Independent I.C.U. Kadalie cabled for funds to the International Transport Federation and to the League Against Imperialism and also appealed to the Trades Union Congress, Johannesburg, asking them to prevent European scabbing. It was claimed that 1,500 workers were out. Blackleg labour, consisting of sixty Zulus from Durban, various European and Bantu casual labourers, and sixty European schoolboys who had the time of their lives acting as stevedores, was employed. I.I.C.U. agents at Port Elizabeth and in the Transkei urged the Africans to abstain from scab labour. The strike spread to employees in all types of work. Meetings were held twice daily: "in the morning a religious service, in the afternoon a political meeting."[5] These meetings were attended by thousands of persons and were reported by the police and in the Press. Kadalie urged the strikers to avoid drink and not to use their sticks.

Many of the strikers were monthly employees and were thus liable to imprisonment under the Masters' and Servants' Act, but, except in isolated cases, they do not appear to have been prosecuted.

At the end of a week, the strike committee was able to claim that 96 per cent. of the workers were out, though later the employers said that the figure was only 86. Some food was distributed, but it was plain that the Bantu were feeling the pinch. On the 24th, some began to return to work. The committee decided to employ pickets. But on the 26th, Kadalie and eight other leaders were secretly arrested and charged with incitement to public violence, or, alternatively, with promoting hostility between Natives and Europeans. Bail was refused. From prison, Kadalie ordered the strikers to return to work.

In the trial which followed, all the accused were acquitted on the latter charge, it being argued that the word " 'bloody' applied as an adjective to Europeans was not inciting because Bantu 'become used to it in their work, a white employer often using it to urge his labourers to get a move on' and that the struggle was an economic, not a racial, one."[5] Kadalie, however, was found guilty of incitement to public violence and sentenced to a fine of £25, or three months' imprisonment with hard labour. The other leaders were acquitted. Kadalie had throughout the strike tried to restrain the strikers from any act of violence, and in fact no such acts had been committed. It was only at the last, when announcing the committee's decision to commence picketing, that Kadalie had, warning the strikers that the police would shoot, urged defiance of authority. It was on this speech that the conviction was secured.

The net result of the strike was that one firm raised the minimum wage paid to African unskilled labour from 3s. to 3s. 6d. per day, and that those railway employees who had not gone out on strike received extra pay for the strike period.

Some strikers lost their jobs. The whole affair was damaging to the prestige of the I.I.C.U. Though this was not apparent when Kadalie, returning to East London in May after his trial at Grahamstown, was welcomed by a mass meeting 4,000 strong. White employers distrusted this enthusiasm for Kadalie and urged the Government to deport him under the provisions of the Riotous Assemblies Act. No action was taken and it was rumoured that Kadalie had come to an understanding with the authorities. The part he played in helping to break the back of the Communist Party's pass-burning campaign at Bloemfontein at the end of the year is related in a later chapter.*

Thus, its leaders overawed, its ranks split into numerous sections, its membership practically gone, the I.C.U. faded out from the revolutionary movement in South Africa. While it lasted it had, more than any other movement of the Natives, raised the prestige of the African and put fear into the heart of the authorities. For a time, it had even seemed that it was going to change the whole face of South African political and industrial relations. Persecution helped to kill it; but the forces of internal disruption were a more fundamental cause of its collapse. It illustrated, as all other mass movements of the African have illustrated, the tremendous disparity between the urgent desire for change on the part of the downtrodden blacks and the inadequacy of their political leadership.

As all other mass movements have illustrated, though none more grievously, the spectacular career of Kadalie with its meteoric ascent to a position of power as the trusted leader of nearly a quarter of a million Africans, though it may be the most extreme example, is not untypical of the career of many African leaders who have risen only to prove more apt at promise than performance. Kadalie had great talents. Intelligent, versatile, passionate, he possessed those qualities of personality which drew others to him and made him a natural leader of his fellows. Yet his rapid rise to power must be ascribed not only to his natural gifts of charm and persuasive oratory, or to these combined with his personal ambition, but to the whole situation in which the Bantu people found themselves at this time. Their great need then, as it remains their great need to-day, was for leadership. At the time when Kadalie came to them, this need was fresh and strong, un-

* Chapter XX.

196

impaired by the disillusions and betrayals which have since been their lot. For a brief period, Kadalie was able to satisfy this need. His fiery tongue roused a wave of enthusiasm in those who had been hopeless. On the crest of this wave, secure and confident, admired by Africans, respected and flattered by Europeans, rode Kadalie, drunk with the heady wine of success. But he was, for a complex of causes in which the main ingredient must have been a desire, conscious or unconscious, to arrest that moment of time, to remain for ever borne forward on the acclamations of the multitude, unwilling to carry out the mass resistance he had promised. To resist now was to risk all. Later! Later the time would come. He failed to understand that the time had already come when he must act or lose all. The mounting wave crashed, but not against the barriers that held the Bantu in misery. It fell amidst the rocks and pools of intrigue, incompetence, mismanagement and dishonesty. Kadalie, failing to take the current when it served, had lost the venture. The masses sank back into sullen suspicion. But of this tragic tale of Kadalie, the most tragic feature is that the opportunity he thus squandered was unique in the history of the black man's struggle for freedom in this country. Black leaders are needed. Who can doubt that they will arise? But it may be that never more will it fall to the lot of any leader to enjoy a trust so absolute as was given to Kadalie. Remembering the I.C.U., the Africans are wary. No single mass movement of the black workers in South Africa has ever even remotely approached the power that was in the I.C.U.

CHAPTER XVII

HAMMER AND SICKLE

THE INTERNATIONAL SOCIALIST LEAGUE, which has hitherto figured in these pages as a small group of Europeans who were more or less anxious to spread the Marxist gospel among the Bantu workers, became merged into the new Communist Party of South Africa in 1921.

The nigrophilist group in the party was pushed very much into the background by the 1922 strike and the exciting events which followed it. There had never been a black party membership. Bunting was playing almost a lone hand, and even he had been partly persuaded that the white Labour movement was really swinging left. There was a campaign for the release of the strike prisoners, of whom there were some hundreds still in gaol, many of them threatened with the death sentence. Tom Mann, the veteran socialist leader, came out from England to help in the struggle. Huge meetings were held in the Johannesburg City Hall and elsewhere—meetings in which not a single black worker could participate. Three of the strikers, Lewis, Hull and Long, died on the scaffold singing "The Red Flag." Feeling against the Smuts Government ran high. When the Nationalist-Labour election pact was formed, the Communist Party did not hesitate to support it.

The communists were agreed that the immediate objective must be the defeat of the Smuts Government; nothing else was so urgent. Both the Labour Party and the Nationalists were known to be anti-Native in outlook. But for the moment even they seemed to be learning the lessons of solidarity, at least in the Cape, where large numbers of Natives and Coloured people had the vote. Even before the strike, in October, 1921, Cape Town Labour Party district committee had invited the representatives of all labour unions (black workers) to meet them in the Trades Hall. Judging by the attendance, the suggestion was made at the most opportune time. The gathering was presided over by Mr. Thomas Boydell, M.P. Supporting him were Mr. Charles Pearce, M.P., Dr. Robert Forsyth, M.P., and Mr. John Lomax, M.P.C. Representatives of non-European labour unions included Clements Kadalie and a number of other prominent Native and Coloured leaders, as well as "Bennet Ncwana, Editor of *The Black Man*, a Native paper published in Cape Town."

It is not clear from the report what exactly resulted from this conference, or what the Labour leaders offered. Ncwana says: "Relations between the South African Labour Party and Native workers were plainly outlined by Mr. Boydell and other members of the party. The representatives of Native unions spoke very strongly against the attitude of the Labourites in the north. Another matter of importance was the consideration of sending delegates to the forthcoming conference of the party to be held in Johannesburg." Actually a Coloured delegate, but no Native, did attend the conference as representative of one of the Cape branches, but his presence at the Johannesburg meeting did not bring about any noticeable change in the north.

The Nationalists too were prepared to drop their nigrophobia for the time being for the sake of getting Native votes in the Cape. They became uncommonly friendly. The letter written by General Hertzog to Kadalie sending a donation and good wishes to the young I.C.U. and asking for co-operation for the "common good of South Africa, . . . this country, that we both love so much," has already been mentioned, as has Dr. Malan's telegram of greetings to an assembly of Natives at Queenstown* These were but two outstanding incidents in the general campaign of friendliness which was carried on by the Nationalists at that time.

So, while maintaining their criticism, the communists did what they could to help the Nationalists into power, an act which most of them lived to regret. In their election manifesto, they said they were out "to bury Cæsar [i.e. Smuts] not to praise the Pact." They pointed out that the Smuts Government "has frankly governed the South African people, White, Indian, Coloured and Native, with the sword. Its career of bloody repression of the workers is without parallel in any other part of the British Empire with the exception of India. . . . In a country so politically backward as South Africa from the working-class point of view (though advanced from the

* These two messages were effectively quoted by Colonel Deneys Reitz eight years later at a time when the Nationalists were openly stimulating anti-Native feeling in a bitterly-fought election campaign.

capitalist point of view), the defeat of the South African Party Government will in itself mean an appreciable step forward in the march towards complete emancipation. . . ."

There is little mention of the Natives in this manifesto. Some members of the party fought strongly for the inclusion of definite demands for the Native workers. But the majority were in favour of toning these down as much as possible so as not to offend the susceptibilities of the white voters to whom the C.P. was appealing. Among the crimes of the Smuts Government are listed the massacres of the Natives at Bulhoek, Village Deep, Port Elizabeth, and the slaughter of the Bondelswarts. There is a list of "certain planks which, though figuring in Labour platforms in the past, now seem to be liable to be neglected in the scramble for place." Among these are two which applied to Natives—"abolition of pass and passport laws and mine-workers' records of service,"* and "extension of educational facilities to all sections of the population."

But the movement within the Communist Party in favour of coming out openly and unequivocally and on all occasions as the champion of Native rights continued to grow. Once the Pact had got into power, in June, 1924, this movement gained in strength. The Labour Party now had two seats in the Cabinet. Nevertheless, it soon became increasingly clear that the new régime was to be just as reactionary as the old one in its attitude to the Native people. At a national conference of the Communist Party, held in Johannesburg at the end of 1924, the nigrophiles were able to challenge the old leadership of the party.

At the three previous annual conferences, a resolution had been carried applying for affiliation to the South African Labour Party. This application had been three times rejected. The Communist Party of South Africa was now a section of the Communist International (Comintern), with headquarters at Moscow. The policies of all sections of the Comintern were supposed to be guided by decisions made by international conferences held in Moscow, or, when such conferences could not be held, by the Executive Committee of the Communist International, the E.C.C.I. The "line" in Britain was to seek affiliation to the British Labour Party,

* The latter a comparatively unimportant grievance of the white miners, put in here so that the white workers might not feel unduly offended at being asked to help in the struggle against the pass laws.

and, though conditions were obviously quite different in South Africa, where the Labour Party was hardly socialist in practice and made no claim to represent the millions of black workers, the same line was adopted here. This was the beginning of a period of tutelage for the South African communists. It was to lead in the future to important consequences for the C.P.S.A. As time passed, so the influence of Moscow grew. Theses and resolutions in great numbers were produced. Elaborate directives were issued for creating revolution in different countries. Members of the C.P. looked more and more to Moscow for a lead, and in the end many of them came to adopt an almost religious attitude to the pronouncements emanating from Moscow. That time, however, was not yet.

By 1924 the C.P.S.A. had not yet had time to mature in the new tradition. Moreover, the Comintern had not yet devoted any special attention to South Africa. The colonial theses and directives were still in the future. Discussions at the party conference were therefore untrammelled by any considerations of orthodoxy, except for a feeling on the part of some members that it would be a good thing to do in all things as the British C.P. was doing, and hence to continue to apply for affiliation to the Labour Party of South Africa.

To this there were three groups of opposition. Firstly, Bunting and his supporters. Secondly, delegates from the Young Communist League, the junior section of the party. Thirdly, the party delegates from Cape Town. The Y.C.L. had suffered from an internal conflict six months before the conference on the question of the Natives. Some of its members wanted to work among the Native youth and to bring the blacks into the organisation. Others said that the blacks should be organised in a separate body and the existing Y.C.L. kept for whites only. The dispute had been referred to Communist Youth headquarters in Moscow. The Young Communist International frowned on the idea of segregation within the youth movement in South Africa, and accordingly the young nigrophilists went ahead in their endeavours to "capture the Native youth," a task which in practice proved to be much more difficult than they had imagined. However, they had managed to convert two promising young Africans, Stanley Silwana and Thomas Mbeki, and these were present at the conference.

In Cape Town, communist interest in the Bantu had been increasing for some years. The I.C.U. was flourishing there. The white socialists had helped the I.C.U. to draw up a constitution on I.W.W. lines. Natives and Coloured had defended the communist platform against attacks by white hooligans. In the Cape there was a growing feeling that the non-Europeans were the "real proletariat and that any association with the Labour Party would be dangerous." From Cape Town to attend this conference came S. Buirski, a foreign-born member of great eloquence and persistence, who argued the case for a strong Native policy. Bunting found that he had valuable allies.

By a narrow majority the conference decided not to renew the application for affiliation to the S.A. Labour Party. In the minority were W. H. Andrews, C. F. Glass and a number of old white trade union stalwarts.

From this time the Communist Party lost white members rapidly. W. H. Andrews resigned the Secretaryship early in 1925, though he retained his membership of the party.

In 1924, the I.C.U. came to Johannesburg. The first Witwatersrand Branch was started by Silwana and Mbeki, assisted by the young white communists. Kadalie came north in 1925 and decided to make his headquarters in Johannesburg. For a time, he and the communists co-operated closely. The communists were, at this time, the only whites who were really interested in the I.C.U. and the leaders of that movement liked to have white men on their platform. Also the rank and file of their members liked to hear what the communists had to say. The I.C.U. was still fighting to establish itself. It had not yet decided to become respectable.

But the change came quickly. At the end of 1926, Kadalie decided to break with the communists and to expel the "reds" from the I.C.U.

Communist work within the I.C.U. had brought few converts to the party and after the break and the expulsions, the white revolutionaries were left fairly high and dry. Only one means of contact with the Natives was left to them, the C.P. night school. This had been started in 1925 in the Ferreirastown slum, in a Native Church building hired on week nights for the purpose. The building had no electric light. There enthusiastic white communists bent their energies to teaching by candle-light, semi-literate Africans to read involved passages in Bukharin's *ABC of Communism*. The organiser of this school and general factotum in Native work was T. W. Thibedi. He had been a member of the I.S.L. in the old days. For years he had been the only black man in the party. Now he proved himself a remarkably competent organiser. Gradually the Communist Party began to get an African following. Africans were to be seen wearing the five-pointed star with the hammer and sickle.

In 1927, the Nationalist-Labour Pact Government passed the so-called Hostility Law. Clause 29 of the new Native Administration Act stated: "Any person who utters any words or does any other act or thing whatever with intent to promote any feeling of hostility between Natives and Europeans, shall be guilty of an offence and liable on conviction to imprisonment not exceeding one year or to a fine of one hundred pounds or both." Presumably this gave the authorities the right also to seize and destroy newspapers and books circulating among Natives. There was no intention of using the law against whites who incited race hatred against blacks. Such incitement is an almost daily occurrence in South Africa, but in no instance has anyone been charged with such an offence. On the other hand, the law was used against persons who protested against the unfair treatment of blacks.

Tielman Roos, who as Minister of Justice had piloted this new law through Parliament, was known among whites as a sentimental and not unkindly politician with a reputation for liberalism and honesty. He had gone into opposition in 1914 because he disapproved of Smuts' pro-war policy. His liberal ideas did not, however, extend beyond the colour bar, as witness the following extract from a speech he made in Johannesburg in 1928: "There is a Native menace in South Africa, and the whites will be driven into a big united white party to create a bigger and more potent weapon to fight for what we believe in . . . we will rule the Natives. . . . Every white man in South Africa is an aristocrat and people who are rulers and governors cannot be proletarians." Referring to Kadalie's apology to General Hertzog for a militant speech made at Lichtenburg, Mr. Roos declared: "I would be insulted if a Native apologised to me."

Tielman Roos' new act was used for the first time in Cape Town against two Africans, Stanley Silwana and Bransby Ndobe, and a Coloured man, John Gomas. Gomas was one of the communists who were expelled from the I.C.U. in 1926. Silwana has been mentioned in connection with the Young Communist League and the founding of the Johannesburg branch of the I.C.U. These two were now playing a leading part in the affairs of the African National Congress in Cape Town. The Congress had been revived in the western Cape after the collapse of the I.C.U. and was now the chief mass organisation through which the communists were carrying on propaganda. Ndobe, a young Basuto, was organiser of the A.N.C. in the Western Province.

Trouble had developed at Paarl, early in 1928, as the result of a Native being shot dead by a white policeman. Police in the Cape had been armed with revolvers and instructed to "shoot when necessary." The policeman had accosted three Natives late at night and one of them had been shot. The *Worker* reports: "The constable was removed to a place of safety after the indignation of Coloured and Native residents of Paarl had risen to tremendous heights, but he was not placed in custody." Only after the African National Congress had held demonstrations of protest was he arrested and charged. Eventually he was acquitted by a white jury.* As a result of speeches made at the protest meetings, the African leaders mentioned were arrested and charged with "creating feelings of hostility." They were all sentenced to three months' imprisonment without the option of a fine.

In the meantime, the communists were making headway in Johannesburg. They began to reap the harvest of their three years of struggle to establish themselves as a predominantly African organisation.

Their newspaper, the *South African Worker* was revived on a new basis. It was now a Native paper. More than half the articles in it were printed in the Bantu languages: Xhosa, Zulu, and Suto. Gone were the white compositors. In their place appeared an old Native printer and his boy, who turned the handle of the old-fashioned printing machine in the Party office in Fox Street. It was not perhaps from a printer's point of view a very elegant paper, but it was the first real communist paper South Africa had seen. The paper was edited by Douglas Wolton.

The school too was moved to the party office and grew rapidly under the guidance of Charles Baker, a schoolmaster

* In South Africa all juries are white.

from England. He had lived in South Africa for many years and taught in Government schools up and down the country. A militant atheist, his chief business in life was to denounce religion as the "opium of the people." Now on the ground floor of a slum tenement he ran this night school for adult Africans. There were not enough desks to go round: the pupils sat on the floor. Blackboards there were none: the comrades blackened the walls. Lessons, given by inexperienced but enthusiastic teachers, were interrupted by intermittent incursions of the curious. Night passes were a nuisance. Every adult African, if he wished to avoid arrest after nine in the evening, must carry a special pass signed from day to day by his employer. Many employers would not sign passes for their workers to attend a communist school. The teachers had to make out passes for all pupils, a laborious business and time-wasting. Later special forms were printed to ease this difficulty.

In the country also the Communist Party was making progress. At Vereeniging communists were refused admission to the location by the superintendent. So they held a meeting outside the location which was attended by 2,000 location residents. Several hundred joined the party, including many women. At Potchefstroom, the location went over *en bloc* to the communists. Thibedi had gone there to hold a meeting and had addressed a gathering of more than 1,000 people. Interrupted by detectives and hauled off to the charge office in a motor car, he was followed by the entire audience. A mêlée ensued between the location superintendent and some women in the audience, which now became menacing. Truncheons were drawn and used. The crowd agreed to behave quietly if three of their number were allowed to accompany Thibedi to the charge office. Thibedi was charged with inciting hostility between the races. Bunting defended Thibedi at Potchefstroom and secured an acquittal. The magistrate, Mr. Boggs, took up a liberal attitude. He said there was perfect freedom in South Africa for all races to enjoy full rights of speech and assembly. If the Natives felt oppression by pass laws or any other Government acts, there was no law to prevent them organising for the repeal of such measures, provided they organised constitutionally. The Communist Party was a legal organisation in this country, and if the European or Native wished to join it, there was nothing to prevent their doing so.

Hundreds of Natives crowded the court and lined the streets outside the whole day long; and when the verdict was declared, there were scenes of tremendous enthusiasm. A meeting was held immediately on the market square and addressed by Wolton standing on a wagon on which a red flag was flying. A group of whites who had been present in court watched sullenly. Wolton's words roused their anger and they began to interrupt him. He addressed them as "fellow white workers," but this infuriated them and they thereupon attacked the wagon and assaulted Wolton. Both whites and blacks then scattered to obtain a supply of sticks from a nearby wagon. The fight became general and the police intervened. Finally, the communists led the crowd back to the location. As a result of this affair, practically every man and woman in Potchefstroom location joined the Communist Party. White leadership has often proved a hindrance to the communists, for Natives have learned to be suspicious of the white man, even if he claims to be their friend. They feel that, however friendly he may seem to be, he must have some sinister motive: at the best, he is probably trying to make money out of them. But here they had witnessed white communists being assaulted by the local whites, whom they knew for their oppressors. This had proved to them that the communists were genuinely their friends. Another factor which had greatly increased the Party's prestige among the Africans was Bunting's defence of Thibedi. A lawyer who could win a case and actually get a black man out of the hands of the police must indeed be a man of great power and influence.

Another incident which took place at Paardekop, a country location, illustrates the difficulties experienced by the police in coping with white agitators among the Natives. Thibedi and Baker went there to attend a public meeting of the local branch. Mounted police were present, but did not interfere until the meeting ended, when they informed Baker that he had infringed the Urban Areas Act, and that accordingly they would arrest Thibedi! To Baker's question as to why they did not arrest him, the reply was that Thibedi was a Native! After further argument, the police took both Baker and Thibedi in charge, together with seventeen other Natives, and marched them off to the superintendent's office. That gentleman was not to be found, having gone off to Standerton.

The police then marched their captives to the police station at Platrand, a distance of fifteen miles. Here the Natives were locked up without food or blankets, and next morning fined half a crown each by the police. Thibedi was released with the others and he and Baker were ordered to appear before the magistrate a week later. The charge, however, was withdrawn.

At the same time the Johannesburg communists were breaking new ground in the field of Bantu trade unionism. Hitherto Native unions, such as the Industrial Workers of Africa and the I.C.U., had been rather loosely organised political parties rather than trade unions in the strict sense of the word. They had taken in every black man who cared to join and they had made little or no effort to organise the workers in particular trades or industries. But now an attempt was made to organise proper trade unions. The prime mover in this new venture, apart from the invaluable Thibedi, who seemed to have a genius for getting people together, workers in a particular industry, women, location residents, or whatever were needed at the moment, was Bennie Weinbren, a white communist. He drove a laundry van and began his trade union career by organising his fellow white laundry workers and starting the Native Laundry Workers' Union. Other small unions were quickly added to the list during the early months of 1927— Native bakers, Native clothing workers, and Native mattress and furniture workers.

The headquarters of all these new unions was in the Communist Party offices at 41A Fox Street, Ferreirastown, which, with the night school, trade union meetings and other activities, became the rendezvous of hundreds of Johannesburg Natives. At first many of the new adherents were rather vague as to the nature of C.P. membership. Asked to prove that they were members of the party, they would produce a trade union card or night school pass. It was all very shocking to some of the Comintern purists, but as time went on things began to sort themselves out. The new unions were eventually organised in a Non-European Trade Union Federation, of which Weinbren was the Chairman and Thibedi the chief organiser. At the inaugural meeting, W. H. Andrews was in the chair.

It was found that the African workers in the so-called "secondary" industries were the easiest to organise. Though often classed as unskilled, they are really quite skilled and it is not easy to replace them at short notice. They are usually location residents and have their wives and children with them, though they may not have severed completely their ties with the countryside. They constitute the nearest approach to a true Bantu proletariat in South Africa. In contrast to the more shifting and semi-peasant miners, building labourers and railway construction workers, here to-day and gone to-morrow, always preoccupied with cows and land, these urban workers were comparatively quick to grasp the idea of trade union organisation.

The growth of Native unions at this time was helped by the new Wage Act. This was passed by the Nationalist-Labour Government in 1925 in order to raise the wages of white unskilled and semi-skilled workers and to force employers to give work to whites in preference to blacks.

The purpose of the Wage Act was, of course, to raise the standard of white labour, and it was always assumed that if employers had to pay more they would prefer white to black labour. It must be conceded, however, that the first Chairman of the Wage Board, F. A. W. Lucas, did not share this view. In practice, the operation of the Wage Act has benefited the blacks as well as the whites, for though the proportion of black workers in certain industries has been reduced, those who remained have obtained higher wages; while in other industries the blacks have held their own or even increased in numbers in spite of the higher wage standards. African workers have benefited from the fact that South Africa has enjoyed an uninterrupted wave of industrial expansion ever since the abandonment of the gold standard in 1933. Whites have tended to move into the more highly-paid or more pleasant occupations and Africans have stepped into their places. In industries such as laundering, where the work is considered hard, the European has not tended to replace the African, who thus enjoys the higher wages now made compulsory by law.*

Before deciding what minimum wages were to be fixed for different occupations, the Wage Board held meetings in the different industrial centres. Representatives of the employers and of the workers were asked to lay whatever information

* A careful study of the more recent activities of the Wage Board, how-ever, will probably reveal a tendency to fix wages on rather lower levels for grades of work now accepted as usually performed by Africans.

they wished before the Board. The new unions took advantage of this machinery, which gave Bantu workers for the first time the opportunity of bringing their grievances officially to the notice of the authorities. This too contributed to the rapid growth of the African unions, so that towards the end of 1928 the new Non-European Trade Union Federation was able to claim 10,000 members on the Rand.

In spite of certain improvements brought about by the action of the Wage Board, the workers found that in most cases strike action became necessary to remedy grievances. Sometimes the workers had to strike in attempts to force employers to pay the legal wage! Many of the smaller strikes were successful. Some of the larger ones were complete failures; though even the failures did not at first damp the enthusiasm of the new trade unionists. In May, 1928, Native workers in a number of Johannesburg clothing factories ceased work and demanded payment for Good Friday, when the factories had been closed. They were out for only half a day when the demand was granted. There was a "lightning strike" at a large laundry against working overtime without pay. One of the workers was dismissed and the police were called in. Threats of a further stoppage, however, secured the reinstatement of the worker.

In further strikes which occurred in the clothing factories the communists had opportunities of trying out their theories of the unity of labour irrespective of colour. The trouble began at Germiston, near Johannesburg, on May 18, when three white girl workers were dismissed by the management of the African Clothing Factory because of their organising activities on behalf of the Witwatersrand Tailors' Association. The W.T.A. was a purely white union, but its Secretary, E. S. Sachs, was a member of the Communist Party. The white workers, the majority of whom were women, ceased work and demanded that the three dismissed girls should be taken back. On the management's refusal to do this, the white workers of the three other clothing factories in Germiston came out in sympathy. On the third day of the strike, officials of the Native Clothing Workers' Union visited the African Clothing Company and held there a meeting of the Native workers, who agreed to come out in sympathy with the whites if the white union desired it. A deputation then visited the white strikers to get their opinion. They agreed unanimously, amid cheers, to call on the Native workers to strike. The result was a complete stoppage of work. In all 400 white workers and 120 black workers were involved. The management was forced to capitulate. The three dismissed workers were reinstated and it was agreed that there would be no victimisation of the strikers, whether black or white.

This victory was hailed by the communist paper as an example of the solidarity of labour. It must be noted that the Natives struck to help the whites and not for any demands of their own. A week or two later the white clothing workers in Johannesburg had an opportunity of showing whether they were similarly prepared to strike to assist their fellow black workers. This strike also began as the result of the dismissal of a worker, but this time a black worker. Some 250 Native workers stopped work. The police on this occasion came quickly to the help of the employers. The Chairman and Secretary of the Native Clothing Workers' Union, Gana Makabeni and Thibedi, and four others were arrested and charged under the Riotous Assemblies Act. Seventy-five of the strikers were charged under the Masters' and Servants' law and sentenced in every case to ten days' imprisonment or a fine of £1. The white workers did not come out in sympathy and the strike was called off a week later.

In July, Weinbren brought about the amalgamation of the two unions of which he was chairman, the white and Native laundry unions. The two unions were to retain their separate identity within the new body, while being represented on a joint committee. It was hoped that this would prove a precedent which would soon be followed by other white and black unions. This hope was never realised and after a time the laundry union itself dissolved again into the original two unions.

Towards the end of 1928, J. A. LaGuma was brought up from the Cape to be secretary of the Non-European Trade Union Federation. This was resented by Thibedi, who had up to now acted as secretary of most of the unions and also as general manager of the Federation. The organisation began to experience some of those internal dissensions which had at one time, according to communist theory, been believed to be the monopoly of "reformist" bodies such as the I.C.U. In spite of these difficulties, the Federation continued to function, and further strikes, some of them successful, took place. On September 25, the African, Indian and Coloured workers at the Transvaal Mattress Company, which employed only non-European labour in its mattress section, struck successfully to enforce payment of wages as laid down by the Wage Board. In October, employees of another furniture factory secured payment for overtime by means of successful strike action.

On the political field, the communists were equally active. Two representatives of the non-Europeans had been sent to the conference of the League Against Imperialism in Brussels in 1927. The two chosen were J. A. LaGuma and J. T. Gumede. Gumede was President of the African National Congress. He had in the past figured as a Crown witness of the "good boy" type in a case in which Ivon Jones was before the court. In the eight years which had passed since this incident, he had apparently become better acquainted with the white radicals. After attending the Brussels conference, LaGuma and Gumede visited Soviet Russia. Gumede, taken on a tour of the Asiatic parts of Russia, saw there that non-Europeans, some of them as dark-skinned as he was himself, enjoyed the same political and social rights as Europeans. The lesson was not lost upon him. In February, 1928, he returned to South Africa a convinced and enthusiastic supporter of the communists. He held numerous meetings all over the country and did much to popularise the communist and the Soviet idea among members of the A.N.C. Within the Congress, however, he encountered the inevitable opposition. The more conservative members banded against him and worked for his removal from the presidentship. At the conference of the Congress, held in Bloemfontein at Easter 1928, the chiefs, in what was in effect the "upper house," discussed the growing influence of the communists and passed a motion disapproving of the growing "fraternisation" between the A.N.C. and the Communist Party, "European or non-European." The mover of the motion said: "The C.P. has brought Russia to the stage it is now. The Tsar was a great man in his country, of royal blood like us chiefs, and where is he now? Kadalie has driven the communists out of his ranks. If the A.N.C. continues to fraternise with them, we chiefs cannot continue to belong to it." Another chief was overheard saying: "It will be a sad day for me when I am ruled by the man who milks my cow or ploughs my fields." Thus the Bantu aristocracy. In reply,

President Gumede pointed out that recently the author of that very Native Administration Act just condemned by the chiefs had declared the communists to be the only opposition to his Native policy that he feared; and that Government, S.A. Party and Chamber of Mines Press alike hated the C.P. because it spoke not for royalty, but for the masses, for all workers white and black, for workers' unity, and against acts of oppression such as Bulhoek. After Gumede's speech the chiefs withdrew their motion, but they and other right-wingers continued to grumble about communist influence until the conference ended. An interesting side-light on this conference is provided by the incident of a letter from Kadalie proposing a meeting of the national councils of the I.C.U. and the A.N.C. The proposal was eventually accepted, though when Kadalie addressed the gathering as "Comrades" this provoked hearty laughter from the chiefs, the term suggesting that Kadalie himself was not altogether free from communist influence.

Early in 1928, the Communist Party got in touch with an organisation in Basutoland, the *Lekhotla la Bafo* or League of the Poor. In this British Crown colony or protectorate there were three political groups among the Natives: firstly, the chiefs, more or less conservative, concerned for their prestige and usually on the side of the British Government, on the good-will of which they were dependent for their positions and salaries; secondly, the Basutoland Progressive Association, representing the middle classes, small business men, teachers and officials—in fact, most of the educated Basuto; thirdly, the *Lekhotla la Bafo*, which claimed to speak on behalf of the masses of tribal peasants. The two most active individuals in the League of the Poor were brothers, Maphutseng Lefela and Josiel Lefela. As far as can be gathered from the records of the C.P., it was, almost inevitably, Thibedi who first established contact with the Basutoland organisation. The Lefela brothers were great writers and for a period of years they filled columns of the *S.A. Worker* with reports in Suto on events in the protectorate. *Lekhotla la Bafo* carried on its work under great difficulties, meeting with opposition not only from the British authorities and the chiefs, but also from the "progressives." The old-established Basutoland paper, the *Mochochonono* (Comet) refused to publish their reports, as also did the two Johannesburg Bantu papers, the *Workers' Herald*, organ of the

I.C.U., and the *Abantu-Batho,* organ of the A.N.C. It was the communist *S.A. Worker* which first gave them the much-needed publicity. In August, 1928, the League of the Poor held a conference at Mapoteng in Basutoland, at which Gumede was the chief speaker.

Meanwhile, the Pact Government continued to prosecute black and white radicals under the hostility clause of the Native Administration Act. But the law had not been adroitly worded and the police found it increasingly difficult to secure convictions. Malkinson, a white communist, had distributed copies of a pamphlet, *What is this Communist Party?* at the A.N.C. Congress at Bloemfontein. Malkinson was charged under the hostility clause. After a lengthy trial, he was found not guilty. Writing to the *S.A. Worker,* Malkinson reported: "A Native witness, Matebe, called by the Crown, was asked what his impressions of the pamphlet were and what it urged him to do, and whether the particular passages quoted excited his feelings. To all these questions Matebe, who had evidently read and understood the pamphlet well, gave answers that word for word turned out in my favour—that is, in the favour of the Communist Party; showing that the C.P. stands not for race, but for class; urging the Native workers to unite with the white workers in order to speak with one voice to the master class, whether white or black; that the pamphlet only described the conditions of the workers as they actually were and held no horrors for him, as he knew all these since he was a child, and he was brought up and lived under the conditions stated. . . . We called no witnesses; we asked no questions. The Crown case was as weak as it could possibly be under the circumstances."

Undiscouraged by the result of the Malkinson case, the authorities, this time in Cape Town, made another attempt to get a communist into gaol for "creating feelings of hostility" between the races. This time the accused, Brown, a Coloured man, was charged in connection with a speech he had made on Union Day, May 31, 1928. The Government had chosen this day, the eighteenth anniversary of the Act of Union, to celebrate the passing of the Flag Bill. For nearly a year, British and Dutch had been quarrelling over a flag. The Nationalist Minister of the Interior, Dr. Malan, had introduced a Bill to abolish the Union Jack as the official flag of the Union of South Africa and to substitute a new flag which would not embody the British emblem in its design. Violent opposition had developed among the English, particularly in Natal, and the Labour members of the Government, also English, had threatened to rebel. Finally, a compromise flag was designed to conciliate all parties. Van Riebeek's orange, white and blue flag was the basis of the design. In the centre a small Union Jack, together with small replicas of the Orange Free State and Transvaal republican flags, was inserted to represent the past. The hoisting of the new flag was celebrated throughout the country by demonstrations of unity and joy on the part of the South African Europeans. In Pretoria, the rival generals, Hertzog and Smuts, spoke from the same platform. The African National Congress and the Communist Party in Cape Town staged a rival demonstration at which the new flag was denounced as "a symbol of the unity of Boer and British imperialism." Earlier in the year, the Coloured people had rioted against the introduction of the first edition of the new flag, the one that omitted the Union Jack, and feeling still ran high. In his speech, Brown was alleged to have said: "To hell with General Hertzog! To hell with General Smuts! I wish they were both six feet under the ground." Brown was found guilty by the magistrate, but his verdict was reversed by the Supreme Court.

In the Transvaal, while the ranks of the Communist Party were swelled by hundreds of Native recruits, chiefly from the smaller semi-rural locations, few adherents were gained from among the Bantu intellectuals. For this there were several reasons. For one thing the intellectuals were more consciously nationalist than the rank and file. For the workers it was enough that they saw white communists facing the white hooligans and the law courts. They realised that the C.P. was something different from the ordinary white man's party. In any case, the party had by now become increasingly black in composition. Many of the country branches were organised by Native communists. Only occasionally a white communist would come to address a meeting. Nevertheless, the intellectuals maintained their theoretical objections to a party in which whites still obviously played a leading role. But there were more practical reasons. These African intellectuals in many cases regarded politics as a career, and it was clear to them that the C.P. did not offer the same opportunities of economic advancement as the Congress and the I.C.U. The communists were always short of money, but they did not go in for taking collections so frequently as did these other organisations, partly because they did not wish to appear in the eyes of the masses as a money-making concern. The financial scandal of the I.C.U., now in process of decay, was in the minds of everyone. The C.P. had no wish to be thought a second I.C.U. Going even to the other extreme, they failed to ask for money when they badly needed it and when the rank and file would gladly have given. Their few remaining white supporters had to dig more and more deeply into their pockets. When the Party had money, it spent it on propaganda, leaflets, newspapers, hire of halls, and was never in a position to offer big salaries to organisers, a condition which, while it had certain advantages in that it discouraged the entry of African opportunists, out to line their pockets rather than to serve the cause of their people, tended to make all black intellectuals fight shy of the movement. The most important cause, however, that operated in making the black intellectuals feel the wisdom of keeping their distance from the C.P. and all its doings was the unfailing regularity with which the communists were in trouble with the police, that same phenomenon which, operating in the contrary manner upon the black masses, tended to make these feel that the communists must be their friends. Africa has still to produce a large class of Bantu revolutionaries who, like the intelligentsia of Tsarist Russia, will be prepared to sacrifice their comfort, safety and freedom for the cause of Bantu emancipation.

In the ranks of the party the best Bantu communists were always those who had not been spoilt by serving an apprenticeship in the Congress or with the I.C.U. The best of all were rank and file Bantu members, often semi-literate, who received their education through the party and had never been in any other organisation. But of the intellectuals who came into the organisation in 1928 and who thereafter played an important part in its history were four who must be mentioned: Albert Nzula, Edwin Mofutsanyana, S. M. Kotu and John Marks. Nzula was an African of outstanding ability, though he had grave faults of character which were later to prove his undoing. A teacher at the A.M.E. Mission School at Wilberforce in the Transvaal, he attended a communist public meeting at Evaton in August, 1928. He was much impressed by the fact that Wolton had continued to address the meeting even when rain began to fall. Writing to the *S.A. Worker* a month later, he says: "After reading through *Communism and Christianism*,* I have come to the conclusion that every right-minded person ought to be a communist. I have hesitated all the time because communism has been misrepresented: I have been brought up on capitalistic literature, which is never satisfactory when it tries to explain working-class misery. I am convinced that no halfway measures will solve the problem. . . . I am prepared to do my little bit to enlighten my countrymen on this point." A competent exposition of his intellectual approach.

Kotu and Mofutsanyana were honorary officials of the C.P. in Potchefstroom. The location superintendent refused to allow them to sleep at their homes in the location because they were communists, and, as the law did not allow them to sleep in the town where they were employed, they had for a period to sleep out on the veld, until they finally obtained a ruling from the local magistrate. "that a member of the Communist Party as such should not be classified as an undesirable person." Mofutsanyana was to prove one of the most loyal and steadfast of communists; but he was slow, not gifted with eloquence, and lacking in drive. Kotu, of more mercurial temperament and a good platform man, did not last in the party so long as Mofutsanyana.

The only African woman who played any part in the communist movement at this time was also a Potchefstroom recruit, Josie Mpama. Her people were old residents in the location and the authorities found it difficult to deport her.

Of the numbers of African workers who came into the Party at about this time, three were to play important parts in the future of the movement. Gana Makabeni, Johannes Nkosi and Moses Kotane were workers who were attracted to the party through the trade unions, and they received most of their education, political and otherwise, at the party night school. Kotane, who was an avid reader and who never failed to turn up at the school with abstruse passages of political argument which he requested his teachers to elucidate for him, was later to become one of the party's theoreticians, proving himself capable of holding his own in arguments on doctrine with the best of the white intellectuals.

* A naïve and somewhat patronising book by Bishop Brown, who had been unfrocked by the Episcopal Church of the United States of America because he declared he could reconcile the teachings of Jesus of Nazareth, Charles Darwin and Karl Marx. This book did not, one would have thought, provide any very attractive introduction to prospective communists.

The Communist Party held its Seventh Annual Conference in Johannesburg in January, 1929. There were thirty delegates, twenty black and ten white, representing, according to a report of the credentials committee, nearly 3,000 members.

CHAPTER XVIII

BUNTING IN THE TRANSKEI

FOLLOWING THE CONFERENCE at the beginning of 1929, the Communist Party prepared for a new kind of election campaign. The term of office of the first Nationalist-Labour coalition was at an end and elections were fixed for the forthcoming June. The C.P., now predominantly Native in composition and mainly interested in Native affairs, turned its attention to the Cape. In that province alone did a certain number of non-Europeans enjoy the privilege of voting, though even there only whites were allowed to stand as candidates. It was decided to contest Cape Flats, a constituency near Cape Town and having a large Coloured and Native electorate, and Tembuland, the Transkeian constituency in which half the electors were Natives. Wolton was to fight Cape Flats and Bunting Tembuland.

The Tembuland campaign must be regarded as one of Bunting's outstanding achievements. It ended in his defeat, but a defeat which was in a sense a personal victory. The Communist Party had been until now a party of the large towns and of the smaller urban locations. In places like Potchefstroom, contact had been made with a number of Bantu farm labourers and labour tenants. But in no instance hitherto, with the exception of some visits to Basutoland's *Lekhotla la Bafo*, had the red flag been carried into the Native reserves. The Transkei is by far the most important of South Africa's Native territories. It has a population of over a million Bantu and only some 20,000 whites; it extends nearly 200 miles from east to west and over 100 from north to south. In the course of the campaign, which lasted for three months, Bunting sent frequent reports to Johannesburg, and these appeared in the *S.A. Worker*. He was accompanied by his wife and by Gana Makabeni, whose home was in the Transkei. Makabeni acted as Xhosa interpreter. They hired a motor van and Native driver in Durban and set out to lead a sort of "caravan life," as Bunting described it. They entered the Transkei on March 8, 1929.

"On entering these 'sacred territories,'" wrote Bunting, "the police began their attention at once, no doubt on advice from Durban or 'higher up.' Wherever we made a halt, they scrutinised our Native passes and our car licence, and at Umtata, the capital, they threatened us all with prosecution, and eventually arrested our driver for entering the Transkei without a permit, although he, like Comrade Gana, was born here. The case was timed to hamper our movements and is still pending. Eddie Litshaba is out on £10 bail, though the maximum fine is £1. Our slightest move is watched and reported by the police from place to place. Moreover, the chief magistrate informed us on our arrival that our campaign was discountenanced by the authorities, who would refuse us any facilities or any information beyond what we were legally entitled to. The chiefs have been told to take no part in the election campaign—and their salaries are at stake! Of course, we knew that before, but it is more unblushing than we expected. The European population generally, too, with one or two exceptions (not communists, but at least professing some sort of liberalism or labourism), are more vulgarly hostile than I for one quite realised they would be: they have not so far offered us violence, like the aristocrats of Potchefstroom, but have already repeatedly threatened to shoot us. The Christian parsons appear among the most reactionary of all. Generally the whites seem to consider themselves . . . to be 'the' people of the country. As for the Native people, whose own reserve we supposed this to be, our general impression so far is that they are more held down here than anywhere else in South Africa. By a long régime of 'segregation' and congestion, all the stuffing seems to have been knocked out of them—so at least the authorities probably flatter themselves: perhaps we should rather say it is bottled up, with a very heavy official hand on the cork.

"There is no branch of the Congress; the I.C.U. broke up some time ago (although some still say they 'vote for Kadalie'); and there is no other Native organisation except official bodies like advisory boards, and, especially the 'Transkeian General

Council' or *Bhunga*, a Native mock parliament controlled by white officials, which seems mainly concerned in praying the Government to make some petty reforms which the *Bhunga* has no power to make itself. . . .

"The Native voters consist mostly of lawyers' clerks, teachers, recruiting clerks, etc., and perhaps tend to consider themselves a superior caste, but we have already urged on them the duty of using their 'privilege' in trust for the whole of their people, and this we hope most of them will do, secretly, though openly they may have to kowtow to their bosses. As for the mass of the Natives, they are already ours wherever we establish contact.

"We held our first meeting on the 6th on the market square, Umtata, the two halls having been refused to us. Amid a running fire of white shopkeepers' jeers, etc. (although their customers are almost exclusively black), the big Native audience heard us gladly—never had they heard such a gospel, least of all from a white man. Our speeches became the talk of the whole district, and we propose, though everywhere the whites beseech us to depart from their coasts, to go from village to village delivering a like message. The police for their part will do their d——est to shut us up.

"More than ever we can see how completely these territories, with all their officials and paraphernalia, are to-day mere appurtenances of the Chamber of Mines. The people have just so little land per family, and are taxed just so much, that they can only subsist by sending their men to the mines. And the whites simply batten on the couple of pounds brought home by each mine-worker after his dreary contract has expired."

A few days after writing this, Bunting, Makabeni and Mrs. Bunting were arrested and charged under the hostility law for speeches made at a meeting, and, in the case of Mrs. Bunting, for distributing *Imperialism in South Africa* and the C.P. programme, and convicted by the chief magistrate, Welsh, and sentenced—Bunting to £50 or six months' hard labour, and the others to £30 or three months each. Fortunately, they were able to bail themselves out and go on with the campaign pending an appeal to the Supreme Court. In the course of the trial, a verbatim report of the meeting, taken down by a local newspaper correspondent, was handed in by the police, but the magistrate refused to allow it to be read in court because of the large Native audience present.

They visited the mission station at Buntingville* where the parson in charge was the second white man in the Transkei "to behave decently to us, even in giving us a small hall to hold a meeting in, the weather being dreadfully bad."

On to Queenstown, still pursued by the police. A couple of Bantu "police boys" had been told off to follow them about. Gana writes: "When we stop they watch us and see what kind of food we eat and how we go to bed. When we camp for the night, they have to do likewise. If we divide up our party, they do the same, one following Bunting, another following me. I went up and down the same street (in Queenstown) so that the people could see what I was doing, and the C.I.D. man kept following me without any shame until the shop boys laughed at him. He had no time for a meal and had to eat out of a paper bag."

After covering a wide area, they returned to Umtata, only to be arrested again for practically all the speeches they had made since the previous prosecution. Again they were convicted and allowed out on bail pending appeal. Fortunately, Bunting managed to get the appeals postponed until June 24, after the election. "But such tame speeches! I can't help wondering how many years of imprisonment Lord Olivier,† say, or even the Editor of the *Star* would be doing if he came here, or where else in the world a candidate is brought to court for every election speech."

The African voters made up half the electorate and there were a few Coloured voters as well. There were two other candidates, the official Government (S.A. Party) man, Payne, and an independent, Hemming. It seemed therefore that Bunting had a good chance of winning the seat, for it was clear from the start that he had the sympathy of the overwhelming majority of the Bantu inhabitants. But Bunting received only 289 votes, enough to save his deposit. On the face of it, it was not a victory, but it was a creditable performance if one considers the facts. All the forces at the disposal of the Government were used to discredit him. Officials openly entered the lists against him—a thing which would have provoked a crisis in South African politics if it had happened to, say, a Boer Nationalist candidate in an ordinary election campaign.

* Named after Jabez Bunting, Wesleyan divine, an ancestor of S. P. Bunting.

† Author of *The Anatomy of African Misery*.

Bunting was already in Umtata and the election campaign was in full swing when the chief magistrate said to the *Bhunga*: "People will come among you from all over the country, some even from overseas, and will try to tell you about new doctrines. . . . They do not care whether you are going through bloodshed and tears as long as they can get you to adopt their doctrine. . . . Your needs will become disturbed. . . . The Governor-General is in a position to deport a person who makes himself a nuisance. . . . I would like to remind you of the agitation which is going on round about us just now and ask you to use your best efforts to try and quell it."

Reporting the result of the election, the *S.A. Worker* said: "The shadowing everywhere by police, their interruption of the candidate's speeches (sometimes they actually addressed his meetings themselves) and their personal interference between him and the electors actually had the effect they must have contemplated—of frightening the Native voters and Native people in general from his meetings. Many even leading Natives visibly shunned our candidate owing to the tick-like presence of the C.I.D.; and not a few voters continued so scared that, wishing to vote for Bunting, they dared not go to the poll at all.

"Apart from that, the constant arrests and legal proceedings, taken altogether, lasted some five weeks—a big slice out of a campaign lasting little more than three months. Owing to the necessity of being constantly at or within call of the court at Umtata, Bunting had to rely on scratch meetings often at less than twenty-four hours' notice.

"Election leaflets given to voters were brazenly taken away from them by the detectives, who would also come up and listen to private conversations, and intimidate bewildered voters just before our candidate came up to them.

"When Bunting applied for inspection of the record of the preparatory examination which was still pending, he found that it was not at the magistrate's court at all, but at the office of the police, who had already typed on the front sheet, in anticipation of the court's decision, 'Committed for trial,' on a number of charges, two of which had not yet figured at all in the proceedings! It was a common thing to see a magistrate in the middle of a case go off to lunch in company with the prosecutor and police officers."

The Buntings and Makabeni won their appeal at the

Supreme Court, which held that there had been no intention on the part of the appellants to promote feelings of hostility, as they were merely preaching the doctrines of communism, which was a recognised political faith. As a result, some fourteen further charges made by the authorities at Umtata against the three communists were dropped.

Meanwhile, Wolton was campaigning on Cape Flats. On his way there he called at Durban, where he was immediately arrested, together with his interpreter, the District Secretary of the Natal I.C.U., Caleb Mtyali, on the usual charge of contravening the notorious Section 29 of the Native Administration Act. It was alleged that at a public meeting of the I.C.U. he had "advised Natives to follow the example of Russia, overthrow the Government and set up their own government, with black soldiers and policemen." The accused were committed for trial, but some months later the case was dismissed by the Attorney-General, who refused to prosecute.

While in Durban, Wolton helped to establish there a branch of the C.P. Of those who joined up, many were said to be members of the I.C.U. and thus now gave allegiance to both organisations.

In Cape Town, Wolton was confronted with an electorate absolutely different from Tembuland. Cape Flats was a sprawling, semi-urban constituency on the borders of Cape Town. It included the two Cape Town Native locations of Ndabeni and Langa, and there was also a considerable Coloured vote.

The communists concentrated their main efforts at Ndabeni, where the municipality had recently raised the rents, in order, so it was said, to persuade the inhabitants to remove to the new location at Langa. Wolton led a procession of some hundreds from Ndabeni to the Cape Town City Hall, to present a memorandum to the Mayor and Council. There was much enthusiasm at Ndabeni and communist hopes were high. Election day proved a great disappointment. As usual in South African elections, there was wholesale bribery of the electorate by the large political parties. Numbers of Wolton's most enthusiastic supporters went over to the enemy. On the morning of election day, the Treasurer of the Ndabeni Branch of the C.P., who had figured prominently on Wolton's platform a few days before, was seen piloting a car bearing the S.A.P.

colours, brazenly helping to collect voters for the other side. Wolton got only ninety-three votes and forfeited his deposit. He left for England shortly afterwards.

In the general election in which the Tembuland and Cape Flats campaigns had been mere side-shows, the Nationalists had produced as their trump card the so-called "Black Manifesto," a document which relied for its effect entirely on anti-Native feeling. In January, 1929, Smuts, the leader of the South African Party, then in opposition, had made a speech at Ermelo in which he had said: "The day will surely come when we shall not think of the south of the Limpopo only, but when the British states in Africa will all become members of a great African Dominion, stretching unbroken throughout Africa."

In reply to this outburst of Rhodesian principles, a manifesto was issued over the names of Hertzog, Roos and Malan. It stated that "the man who puts himself forward as the apostle of a black Kafir state—of which South Africa is to form so subordinate a constituent part that she will know her name no more—cannot possibly hold another doctrine than that of equal political rights for all Kafirs and white men everywhere on an equal footing. It must be clear to everyone that no leader of any party whatever that aims at such an object as has now been expressly and unequivocally announced by General Smuts can co-operate in an endeavour such as we are putting forth to make South Africa safe for the white man." There followed various figures showing the enormous black and insignificant white population of the British colonies in central Africa.

In spite of the record of Smuts in dealings with the Bantu, which no eloquence or special pleading could have made to seem even mildly liberal, it was in vain that the S.A.P. denied the impeachment. In South Africa whoever shouts anti-Native first and goes on shouting loudest always wins the support of the electors. Deneys Reitz, one of Smuts' chief supporters in Parliament, used all his eloquence to no effect. "They had the distorted spectacle of a Government going into the general election with a distorted version of a single speech as its sole political platform. With this cock-and-bull story, the Prime Minister was going to stump the country for the next six months telling the people that the South African Party were the apostles of Kafirdom. It seems to me to be the last desperate throw of the bankrupt gambler. . . . So far from wanting to swamp the white races, General Smuts' plea was for the white men in the southern continent to stand together for mutual protection." Reitz then quoted the letter sent by Hertzog to Kadalie in 1921 and the friendly telegram sent by Malan to a Native meeting. He did not, however, go so far as to remind anyone of the Bulhoek massacre or of the murder of the Bondelswarts!

Hertzog appealed to the electors to give him the two-thirds majority necessary to alter the Constitution of the Union of South Africa. He put forward four Bills which proposed (1) to abolish the Cape Native franchise, (2) to give the Natives of the whole Union certain limited representation through white senators, (3) to place the Coloured people on a separate voters' roll, and (4) to make certain changes in the Native Land Act of 1913.

The new Bills were supposed to embody the principle of segregation, and to "allow the Natives to develop along their own lines." The Smuts party, still hampered by that thorn in the side of the white politician in South Africa—the Coloured people—could not effectively reply to this. Though they were every bit as anti-black as their opponents when in the north, in the Cape they had still to rely on the Native and Coloured vote. The Nationalists were elected. They had been helped by the fact that white South Africa had had an unusual run of prosperity since 1924 as a result of the world boom in trade and the prosperity of the gold and diamond mines. The Labour Party ceased to be an important factor after the election. Its attitude on the colour issue had definitely cut it off from the support it might have got in the Cape. In the north, it could not hope to compete, though it tried hard, with the openly reactionary Afrikaner Nationalists.

As a result of the elections, the Nationalists came in with a complete majority over all other parties in the Lower House. But they did not get the two-thirds majority of both houses voting together which was necessary for putting the four Bills on the statute book.

Before this election the spate of anti-Native measures had to some extent been blocked by quarrels between the different groups in Parliament, but now there was nothing to stop a whole flood of reactionary legislation. The prospect looked unhealthy for the Native agitators.

At about this time, C. F. Andrews, the well-known leader of white liberal thought in India, paid an unexpected tribute to the South African communists. Addressing the Indian Trade Union Congress, he referred to his recent visits to South Africa and Europe and said that, except for his objections to "class war" and "open violence," he had "personally far more sympathy with the communists than with other labour parties in England and Europe. For while the right wing of the Labour Party constantly wavered with regard to the vital questions of 'imperialism' and 'racial superiority' and 'white labour,' the communists never wavered for a single moment with regard to these three essential matters. Already in South Africa I had found the same thing: the only Europeans in South Africa who really and honestly were against what is called the 'white labour policy' and were ready to admit Indians, Cape Coloured and Bantu on equal terms were the communists. Therefore my whole heart went with them in South Africa; and to-day it goes with them in Europe in their splendid struggle against these deep-rooted evils of race and colour prejudice and imperial domination."

Meanwhile, in Johannesburg the prosecutions of communists continued. Nzula had given up his post as headmaster of a Native school at Evaton and had come to Johannesburg, where he was helping Baker with the night school. In February he had delivered a lecture to the scholars on "Hertzog's Native Bills." On the evidence of the inevitable Native police spies, two of whom had joined the school, Nzula was charged and found guilty of "inciting to hostility" between the races. Baker appeared as witness for the defence. He contradicted the evidence of the two detectives who alleged that Nzula had used the words "hate the enemy" and "fight the white man." The trial was held two months after the lecture. One of the detective-spies admitted that he could not understand English very well and neither had made notes at the time. The defence maintained that Baker's evidence should be accepted by the court. The magistrate, however, preferred to believe the Crown witnesses. Nzula was sentenced to a month's imprisonment with hard labour, or a fine of £10. After the judgment, Baker wrote an article in the *S.A. Worker* headed "That Stinking Deal." He used very strong language. "Nzula was found guilty by Magistrate Backeberg (not Backveld!). . . . The magistrate, biased from the start by his class and hereditary prejudices.

refused to accept it [Baker's evidence], declaring in his ruling in the court—although he has discreetly left this out of the record—that 'Mr. Baker could not possibly have heard the lecture since he as chairman was occupied in keeping order.' Such a ruling, of course, is nothing more than an exhibition of magisterial imbecility, and as such it would never have done to let it appear before the judges on appeal. . . . Only an imbecile or an idiot would argue that in the absence of any evidence of disorder, and there was none, that the chairman could not follow the lecture—which he did and took notes as well." It is not surprising that Baker was charged with contempt of court. He was fined £10 by the Supreme Court, which he was allowed to pay in instalments.

The Communist Party by now numbered among its members many Africans whose political knowledge and understanding was small. It began to seem that the Party might be swamped by members who had little or no knowledge of Marxist principles and theory. The suggestion came from Moscow that the Party should remain a small and select body of trained revolutionaries working through a larger mass body. In this way, the communists would be enabled to preserve the purity of their doctrine while at the same time, through the larger organisation, giving a clear lead to the masses on all questions. It happened that this new suggestion from Moscow which was tantamount to an order came at a time when Bunting while in Tembuland had already tentatively founded an organisation called the League of Native Rights, a "designedly innocuous organisation," he called it, "with the preservation of the Native franchise and universal free education as the prime objectives," the Communist Party's interest in the scheme not being advertised but not necessarily concealed either. To the communists in Johannesburg the idea seemed good and they set about founding a new mass organisation to be called the League of African Rights. It was inaugurated by a public meeting in the Inchcape Hall, Johannesburg. The League called upon all to join who were interested in the struggle of black men for freedom in Africa. It drew up a "petition of rights" with demands for the abolition of the pass laws and land laws, extension of the vote and free education for the Bantu. On the lines of the Chartist movement in England, it proposed to get a million signatures to the petition and present it to Parliament. It took for its slogan "*Mayibuy' i Afrika*" (Let Africa return), and for its flag a black, red and green emblem. The song of "*Mayibuye*"* was sung to the tune of Clementine. It was immediately joined by J. T. Gumede, of the A.N.C., who was made President, and by Doyle Modiagotla, of the Ballinger I.C.U. who became Vice-Chairman. The Secretaryship was held by the communists Albert Nzula and Edward Roux. Charles Baker was Treasurer. The new organisation seemed well and truly launched according to Moscow specifications and the needs of the situation. The Communist Party, while duly represented in the leadership, was not conspicuous there.

But it seemed that this was not at all what Moscow had desired. The new L.A.R. was a success from the start. Political fever among Africans was still running high. The Natal beer riots in June had inflamed Bantu public opinion. The I.C.U. was breaking up, but there were thousands of Africans who were looking for just such an organsiation which would rally all the forces of the national movement. Thousands of petition forms were issued and signatures began to come in from all over the country. In the midst of it all a telegram from Moscow ordered the immediate dissolution of the League.

The communists were dumbfounded, for they had acted, as they thought, on instructions from Moscow. But like good Leninists they obeyed orders. Petition forms, as they came in, were dropped in the wastepaper basket. And the chance was lost.

In Government circles, there was growing dissatisfaction with the working of Clause 29. There must have been nearly 100 prosecutions under the Act. From all these only a handful of convictions had resulted, and most of these only because they had not been taken to appeal. In Bunting's final appeal the Supreme Court at Grahamstown had laid it down that in order to secure a conviction the Crown must show not merely that certain words uttered might have the effect of creating

---

* *Mayibuye!*
Tina Sizwe esi ntsundu
sikalel' i Afrika
eyahlutw' obawo betu
besese bu' mnyameni.

An approximate translation runs:
  Let it come back!
We the people who are brown bless Africa,
which was taken from our fathers when they were in
darkness.

Mayibuye, mayibuye,
mayibuy' i Afrika!
Makapele namapasi
Sitoli nkululeko.

Let it return, let it return,
let Africa return to us!
Down with passes.
We demand freedom.

hostility, or in fact had created such feelings, but, further, that it was the intention of the person charged to create such feelings of hostility between the races. Furthermore, if anyone spoke against the actions of the Government or against any particular white person, that did not constitute an infringement of the law, because that would bar all legitimate protests against grievances which might exist. Throughout the history of race relations in South Africa the judges of the Supreme Court, with very few exceptions, have shown themselves more liberal than either the Government or the local magistrates. In his numerous tussles with the law Bunting had, since 1915, been convicted a dozen times under one law or another. But of these convictions, no single one was upheld by the Supreme Court. Judges in South Africa, even when South African born, are usually men of experience and culture. They have been to universities overseas and have a wider outlook than the average South African magistrate, policeman or Member of Parliament.

The Government therefore decided on a new method of dealing with agitators. Tielman Roos, reactionary but sentimental Minister of Justice in the first Hertzog Government, had retired. His successor was a young and forceful man, a lawyer of some skill and possessed of a militarist turn of mind, Advocate Oswald Pirow. He it was who marched at the head of the Durban police on the occasion of the trial use of tear gas bombs. Pirow now gave notice of the introduction of a new law for dealing with recalcitrant communists and Native leaders. It took the form of an amendment to the Riotous Assemblies Act and gave the Minister of Justice power to order any individual to leave any magisterial district within seven days and for a period not exceeding one year, if, in the opinion of the Minister, his presence there might lead to the creation of "feelings of hostility between the European inhabitants of the Union on the one hand and the Coloured and Native inhabitants of the Union on the other hand." There was no limit to the number of magisterial districts from which an individual could be banned: it might be a whole province or even the whole Union. If at the end of a year the Minister desired to renew the ban for a further period, he could do so by issuing a fresh notice. The new law thus took the decision as to whether any person was creating feelings of hostility out of the hands of the Supreme Court and placed it in the hands of Pirow. It was an extension of the principle of "government by decree" and a step on the road to dictatorship in South Africa.

The proposed new legislation met with the united opposition of all the parties within the Bantu national movement. On the other hand, it had the support of the leader of the opposition in Parliament, General Smuts, who had already suggested in a public speech that the Native Administration Act should be "tightened up." In November, 1929, the African National Congress, the Communist Party and both the Kadalie and Ballinger sections of the I.C.U. made a united front against the Bill. On November 10 at the conclusion of a huge meeting in Johannesburg an effigy of Pirow, bearing the inscription "*Umbulali*" (tyrant) was burnt "to the accompaniment of voluminous shouts of derision." At this meeting both Ballinger and Kadalie spoke. The communist Kotu was in the chair and, acting as judge for the occasion, directed the burning of the guy. As the flames rose, Natives rushed forward to belabour the burning fragments. The affair nearly resulted in the deportation of Ballinger, whose presence in South Africa the authorities were just beginning to tolerate. He protested afterwards to the communists that the burning of the effigy had been sprung on him as a surprise, which was undoubtedly the case. This meeting was followed by others in Pretoria, Durban, Cape Town, Kroonstad and Johannesburg a week later, "just as successful but only more bitter as, following immediately after the police raids at Durban,* they must have been."

Commenting on the widespread agitation, the *S.A. Worker* said on November 30, 1929: "There can be no mistaking the feelings of the masses. They are quite alive to the issues involved. All the talk and propaganda carried on in the capitalist Press misrepresenting the communists will not confuse the minds of the masses of the African people. They realise that it is not 'Moscow gold' that is the cause of the trouble, but the RAND GOLD which demands cheap labour; that it is the pass laws, the taxation without representation, the low wages, the police bullying, colour bars, etc., that are at the back of the trouble; the complete landlessness and helotry of the Native population that are the potent factors in the present troubled state of the country; that it is Pirow and his clique, the

* See Chapter XVI, "Decline of the I.C.U."

disseminators of racialism, the apostles of 'white South Africa' and nigrophobia that are the agitators that ought to be deported."

Dingaan's Day had by this time become a recognised occasion for counter-demonstrations by Africans to the usual celebrations by the descendants of the Voortrekkers.* In this year there were Native meetings in many quarters on December 16. The Johannesburg demonstration exceeded all expectations. "A meeting commencing at 10 a.m. and continued until 4 p.m. preceded the procession. The enthusiasm was maintained throughout. Pirow came in for special attention from the speakers. His Riotous Assemblies Amendment Act Bill and Durban raids were denounced, as barbarous and only possible in a country whose basis was slave labour." Thus the report in the *S.A. Worker*.

In Cape Town the effigy burning at Johannesburg inspired the burning of straw figures of Smuts and Hertzog, which were duly committed to the flames at a monster meeting on the Grand Parade. Banners demanded "No taxation without representation" and "Down with Pirow's Bills!" The city authorities had refused a permit for the procession, but in spite of this over 1,000 marched with band and banners through the main streets—thus defying the authorities. "Ndobe, who led the procession, must be congratulated on a fine display of courage." There was only one European in the procession, though two or three had attended the meeting.

There were no clashes between white and black except at Potchefstroom, where the local white mob, which has already figured in this history, attacked the defenceless meeting with guns and revolvers. In his report of the affair, Edwin Mofutsanyana wrote: "We had heard rumours that a gang of white hooligans, organised by a certain prominent white citizen of Potchefstroom, would break up our meeting, but then similar rumours were heard in all centres. Early on Dingaan's Day morning, however, before the meeting started, there was present a large number of whites and we had a presentiment that trouble was ahead.

* These descendants, however, in 1938, proved no very dignified heirs of the Voortrekker tradition. The Voortrekkers often accepted help from Native chiefs like Moroka in the Free State, yet when the Centenary Voortrekker wagon reached Thaba. 'Nchu and Dr. Moroka, the grandson of that same chief who had assisted the Voortrekkers, offered the gift of an ox to their centenary feast, the gift was ungraciously refused.

"I got on the platform and before I got very far with my speech, the whites began shouting in Afrikaans 'You lie!' and 'Shut your mouth, Kafir!' I managed to go through my speech however. The next speaker was Marks.* He appealed to the police, who were present, to deal with the hooligans, but in vain. At about the same time a comrade touched my coat from behind and I looked back. A white man was just taking aim at me with a revolver. I jumped off the platform. The next thing I saw was Marks coming down from the platform head foremost. Several revolver shots rang out and I saw a man crawl on his knees, his leg completely broken by two shots. The Natives made a rush for the whites, who were now running away. The police now became quite active and tried to calm the people. After the affray, I discovered that six more people were injured beside the one shot in the leg. The latter, Hermanus Lethebe, died in hospital on December 22. The others were not so seriously wounded and are now recovering.

"There was great excitement after the meeting and things were assuming an ugly outlook when the magistrate arrived on the scene and spoke to the Native people and assured them they were going to receive justice. . . . Later a white man was arrested and charged with murder. He was Joseph Weeks, a brother of the location superintendent."

Six months later Joseph Weeks was tried for murder before a visiting judge and a white jury at Potchefstroom. The evidence showed that Weeks discharged the contents of his revolver at the Natives and was reloading when he was arrested. No evidence was given that any other person had fired the shots. In spite of this, the jury returned a verdict of "Not guilty." Similar verdicts are not uncommon in South Africa.

CHAPTER XIX

AGITATORS AT THE CAPE

EARLY IN 1930, the publishing office of the *S.A. Worker* was transferred to Cape Town. During 1929 the paper had been issued as a, rather irregular, monthly, but now an attempt was made to publish it weekly. The name was altered to

* J. B. Marks, an African.

Umsebenzi (Worker, in Xhosa). It was a very small paper, but it soon achieved a large circulation. The producers found a cheap means of illustration in hand-made lino-cuts. It was hand-set by local communists and printed by a Coloured "rat-shop" printer—that is one who employed Coloured labour and did not pay wages as laid down by the S.A. Typographical Union. The officials of this union made various efforts to prevent the communists from renewing their supplies of type, but always ways and means were found to secure necessary equipment, and the little paper struggled on, becoming the most widely read of Bantu papers.

The Africanisation process within the Communist Party continued apace. A sustained effort was made to translate the ideas of the social revolution into the Bantu idiom, to make the Party not only for the Africans but of the Africans. The slogan "*Mayibuye*" became the battle cry, supplemented by occasional reference to the "black republic" and to a "democratic Native republic, with equal rights for all races." The "*Mayibuye*" song was sung at meetings of Africans and Europeans. The paper began a lively campaign against the payment of poll tax and for the burning of passes on Dingaan's Day.

By this time the I.C.U. had become negligible, except in Natal, though even there it was steadily losing members to the Communist branch, and in East London, where Kadalie retained a following, though much depleted after the failure of the strike on January, 1930. In the Western Province of the Cape, the African National Congress was the popular organisa tion among Africans and also among certain sections of the Coloured people. Communist influence in the Cape A.N.C. was considerable. Elliot Tonjeni and Bransby Ndobe, the two young and militant leaders, co-operated closely with the C.P. *Umsebenzi* became to all intents and purposes the organ of the Congress. Wherever they went throughout the country districts of the western Cape, Congress agitators took with them copies of the communist paper and sold them at meetings. Local branch officials became agents for the sale of *Umsebenzi*. White employers and land-owners noticed their workers reading the little paper and soon showed their disapproval. They referred to it contemptuously as the "*Kafir koerantjie*."* The "*Mayibuye*" song too became popular among Coloured

* *Koerantjie*, diminutive of Afrikaans *koerant*—newspaper.

farm labourers and was translated into Afrikaans with adaptations.*

The Congress branches spread out from Cape Town along the Garden Route, the name given on railway guides to the route from Cape Town to Port Elizabeth, through Worcester, Knysna and Oudtshoorn. Along the Garden Route, though the mountains and forests are fair, the conditions of the Coloured farm labourers are otherwise. Badly paid and badly treated, Coloured and Native flocked to the Congress banner. Ndobe and Tonjeni would go to one centre, hold meetings, organise a branch, and collect enough money to take them on to the next town or village.

At Paarl, near Cape Town, was one of the older branches. Mention has been made of the agitation there at the beginning of 1928, when a Coloured man had been shot in the street by a white policeman. A similar event occurred there again in February, 1930. Police officers in Paarl were charged with cruelly beating non-European prisoners, men and women. They were tried before a judge and the usual white jury. In summing up, the judge indicated plainly that he thought four of the accused were guilty, but they were all acquitted by the jury and the judge was forced to discharge them.

Congress agitation, largely economic in its demands, for wages were pitifully low, spread to Worcester, Rawsonville, Barrydale and other centres. The daily newspapers reported that all records had been broken in the issue of licences for revolvers and guns to Europeans. Special telephone lines between Worcester and Cape Town were placed at the disposal of the police. An incident at Rawsonville had served as the signal for the rush to arms. There white farmers had broken up a Congress meeting with violence.

Beer became an important political issue, as it had in Natal the previous year; though in the Western Province the circumstances were a little different. In Natal the fight had

---

* *Ons bruin mense, seuns van slawe,*
Vra ons eie land terug,
Wat gesteel is van ons vaders
Toe hul in die donker sug.

Gee dit t' rug nou!
Gee dit t' rug nou!
Weg met al die slawerny/
Pirow kan ons nie ophou nie:
Afrika sal vryheid kry.

Which may be rendered:
We brown people, sons of slaves,
Demand our own land back,
Which was stolen from our fathers
While they were sunk in darkness.

Give it back now! Give it back now!
Away with all the slavery!
Pirow can not stop us:
Africa shall have freedom.

been for Native beer against municipal beer. Here it was Native beer *versus* the farmers' wine. The notorious "tot system" prevails on the Cape wine farms. Coloured labourers are forced to accept part of their wages in the form of a ration of wine. Temperance organisations in South Africa, waging war upon this practice, have long tried but with no success to get legislation passed to prohibit the tot system. The vested interests of the wine farmers are too strong for them, as they are also too strong for the opposition of a section of the Dutch Reformed Church. In the Western Province illicit Kafir beer drinking is not only against the law, but also against the interests of the wine farmers. It was therefore no coincidence that the wave of anti-black feeling and the large-scale issue of arms to civilians should be accompanied by beer raids on an intensive scale. It is also probable that the increased resistance which the police now encountered in the course of these raids was due to the increased political consciousness which the activities of the Congress agitators had aroused in the farm labourers.

The shooting which took place in Worcester on May 4, 1930, and which resulted in the deaths of five non-Europeans, was the subject of a magisterial inquiry, during which evidence was given not only by the police, but by Congress leaders. It is therefore possible to get a fairly clear idea of the sequence of events which led to the shooting. Tonjeni, giving evidence, said that armed white civilians had participated with the police in a beer raid on April 5. A black man had been killed. On Sunday, May 4, the news was spread that a Native had been seen at the Congress meeting carrying a rifle. This was enough to create a furore among the white population. Strangely enough, the man, by name Manzini, was subsequently shown to be an "ex-member" of the C.I.D. and no trace of the alleged rifle was ever found. A group of white police and detectives went to the meeting to arrest Manzini. After the arrest, two of the police remained with the meeting "to report the speeches." They were attacked by members of the crowd, who were incensed at this summary arrest of one of their number, who certainly had no rifle when he was taken and who, as the Congress members believed, was merely an ordinary unoffending member of the audience. The two policemen finally got away, as a result of the intervention of Plaatjes, Chairman of the Worcester Branch of the Congress.

The police then committed the inexcusable provocation of marching into the Native quarter with fixed bayonets. Of course they were attacked. They opened fire and five Natives were killed.

In his evidence, Captain Barter, the officer commanding the Worcester police said: "On May 2 Major Thomas arrived from Cape Town and we discussed the activities of Native agitators and the carrying out of liquor raids. As a result of a report on May 4 I mustered all available men, I instructed each man to load with five rounds of ammunition, and if it was necessary to fire, I would give one blast on my whistle and three blasts to cease fire. Each man was to take deliberate aim at a man attacking the police, to aim low and to fire to hit him." Asked why he thought it was necessary to march into the Native quarter again after the two policemen had got away safely, he said: "If they had not gone there people would have thought they were afraid."

Following the shooting, a hue and cry developed among the white citizens of Worcester. Armed civilians patrolled the streets. They assaulted a number of Native and Coloured people whom they encountered, but their main objective seems to have been to lay hands upon Ndobe and Tonjeni. One such civilian, who was wandering round with his rifle taking pot shots at Natives, was arrested by the police and fined 5s. by the local magistrate for being in possession of a rifle without a licence! He was complimented by the magistrate for his public spirit in coming to the help of the police. He said that he was trying to shoot Tonjeni. Humorists among the Natives said that he was fined because he missed!

Ndobe and Tonjeni now had some difficulty in escaping from Worcester. The armed whites placed a picket at the station and examined all departing Natives. The two leaders remained hidden in the non-European quarter. They managed by means of a Coloured woman to get a message through to the communists in Cape Town asking for a motor to fetch them on a certain evening. To disarm suspicion, the car must be driven by a European. The plan was successfully carried out and the two leaders got safely away. The *Cape Times* glibly concluded that the Congress was now dead in Worcester because people were no longer to be seen wearing the Congress badge. Naturally, the badge was not worn openly. To wear it at that time would have been to court death at the hands of the whites. But the people's continued loyalty to the Congress was shown by the fact that Ndobe and Tonjeni were thus able to lie hidden for four days while no one betrayed their hiding place. Another Congress member, Abel Simpi, wanted by the police for the part he had played in the fighting, escaped into the mountains. For ten weeks the police sought him diligently, but he fled from one hiding place to another and was not to be found. Coloured "trap boys" were sent to work for the various farmers, with the object of tracing him, but the farm labourers would not betray him. Finally, a small Coloured child, bribed by a packet of sweets, revealed his whereabouts.

As for the man with the rifle who was supposed to have started all the trouble, Manzini, the "ex-member" of the C.I.D., a small paragraph in the *Cape Times* on June 25 stated: "The Attorney-General has declined to prosecute in the case of Chief Manzini, who was charged with inciting to violence. Manzini was released from gaol this morning." But "if ever there was a case," commented *Umsebenzi*, "where on the face of things Government seemed guilty of a 'frame-up,' it is this."

Meanwhile, the Criminal Investigation Department had thought up another and more effective method of crushing the Congress. They found a useful agent in the person of "Professor" James Thaele, the President of the Western Cape Branch of the African National Congress. Thaele was a Basuto who had studied at Lincoln College in the United States, where he had gained the degrees of B.A. and B.Sc. Back in South Africa, he established a college in Cape Town with himself as the sole professor. The college had gone by now, but Professor Thaele remained. He was a facile person and for a time he flirted with the radicals. In July, 1929, he was in Johannesburg and there addressed the students of the communist night school. In view of his subsequent role as the great opponent of communism, it is interesting to report what he said on that occasion. "Professor Thaele congratulated them on belonging to the intelligentsia of the African race who understood the meaning of exploitation and could get down to work. His sympathies were entirely with the Communist Party. It was the party destined to bring forward in the near future a far-reaching change in social conditions. He did not believe in compromising on matters of principle and what he was saying there he had not hesitated to say publicly elsewhere. The people of Russia, who formerly groaned under Tsarist tyranny, now enjoyed freedom and they could appreciate the fact. Communism meant the emancipation of the struggling workers and the levelling up of the oppressed races. Because it stood for this levelling-up process, the Communist Party was hated by the capitalists. . . . They must read and, study the literature of the Communist Party " (*S.A. Worker*, June 31, 1929).

But the flowery speeches of 1929 did not in 1930 prevent Thaele from engaging in a campaign against the radicals in Cape Town. This campaign may have been in part merely an episode in Thaele's personal struggle for leadership of the A.N.C. Here the two young militants, Ndobe and Tonjeni, were threatening to eclipse the professor in the eyes of the majority of the members. There were constant allegations by the C.P. that this campaign was carried out in close co-operation with the C.I.D. and that Thaele frequently visited the C.I.D. office in Cape Town.

The African National Congress as a whole, as has been noted, was faced with the problem of communist penetration. Gumede, still the official President, found himself assailed on all sides. Matters came to a head at the annual national conference at Bloemfontein in April, 1930. The main question was whether or not Gumede was to be re-elected President of the A.N.C. The radicals who supported him included Nzula from the Transvaal, Gomas, Ndobe and Tonjeni from the Cape. Support came also from Champion, who, for reasons arising from the situation of the I.C.U. in Natal, was opposed to Seme, Gumede's principal rival for the office.

Gumede, to win support at Bloemfontein, might have compromised, but he did not. In his address to conference he advocated "defence of the Soviet," demonstration wherever possible, strikes, refusal to pay taxes, the burning of passes, and "struggle for a Black Republic." This caused consternation among those whom the communists dubbed the "good boys." The Rev. Mahabane, in the chair, seemed determined to allow the "reds" to speak as little as possible. The Bloemfontein *Volksblad* (Afrikaans Nationalist daily) reported: "The left wing is not being allowed to speak much, and their propositions are nipped in the bud by the Speaker." Even Ndobe and Tonjeni, who arrived direct from the battlefield of the

Western Cape, were unable to sway the conference. Ndobe, for forgetting himself and smoking in "parliament," was excluded from conference for a whole day and consequently lost his seat on the executive. When it came to the election of President, Mahabane himself decided who were entitled to vote. Seme was elected by thirty-nine votes against Gumede's fourteen.

Thaele himself did not go to Bloemfontein. When Ndobe and Tonjeni returned to the Cape, the fight began in real earnest. At first it seemed that the radicals might carry the day. A meeting of the Cape Town Branch, called to hear a report of conference from the delegates on their return from Bloemfontein, pledged their support to Gumede by over 200 votes to three. But Thaele was not to be beaten. A week later, he attempted unsuccessfully to get a resolution passed to debar communists from speaking on the Congress platform. The particular communists he had in mind were Brown, Gomas and Ngedlane (the last a resident of Ndabeni location), who had managed to retain membership of both C.P. and A.N.C. Thaele's strength was on the Parade where the Congress held daily meetings. Ndobe and Tonjeni, away on organising work in the country, could speak there only occasionally, whereas Thaele was always on the stump and had become well-known to the audiences. The burden of his refrain was that the communists were the agents of the "white man." Bitterly the communists resented this. Yet it was difficult to fight Thaele. They pointed to the parallel situation when communists had been expelled from the I.C.U. in 1926. "What argument did Kadalie use before the rank and file to justify his opposition to the 'Reds'? It was the same argument of the 'white man' which Professor Thaele is using to-day. . . . Kadalie played upon the natural feelings of the rank and file who suffer bitter oppression under the colour bar and the white dictatorship. Naturally the rank and file, not knowing anything of the C.P. and its policy, supported him. But while he was shouting anti-white to the Natives he was hobnobbing with the novelist Mrs. Ethelreda Lewis, with the Native Affairs Department, and with other representatives of white imperialism."

At the same time Ndobe and Tonjeni, though they defended their own militant line, were not prepared to declare themselves communists. They too felt the force of the "white man" argument—if not on themselves, then on the masses. Though they continued to accept help from the C.P., they were not prepared to defend the Party publicly except at meetings in the country, where Thaele was not known. In Cape Town, they generally kept silence on the subject of the communists or said merely "The Communist Party has never done any harm to the African." An understatement little calculated to prevail against Thaele's flowery eloquence.

Thus it came about that Thaele gradually gained the upper hand in Cape Town. There was an open break with the communists and rival meetings were held on the Parade. A communist meeting was attacked by Thaele's followers and their red flag was burnt. The communists retorted by a lino-cut cartoon in *Umsebenzi* showing Pirow as a policeman setting his dog, Thaele, on the Native workers and the Communist Party.

In the country Thaele had not so much influence with Congress members. But an incident at Worcester, on June 22, 1930, raised his prestige considerably. All Congress meetings in the country districts of the Western Province had by now been forbidden under the Riotous Assemblies Act. The Congress had its own property at Worcester and proposed to hold a private meeting there, for members only. Thaele was the chief speaker. "In spite of this, the *dorp* was full of police armed with tear gas bombs—they have been openly practising bomb-throwing during the last two weeks. Crowds of white farmers thronged the streets, hardly troubling to conceal their revolvers." Thus *Umsebenzi* of June 27.

Thaele had posted guards at the entrances to the Congress grounds, but some Europeans, headed by a newspaper reporter, pushed their way in. The police used this as an excuse to declare that the meeting had become public and was therefore illegal. They proceeded to arrest Thaele. The next day three more arrests were made. The four were charged with contravening the Riotous Assemblies Act. Interviewed after his arrest, Thaele told a newspaper man that the Congress guards had "let him down." Poor guards! For a black man to bar the way to a white man is dangerous enough at ordinary times in South Africa, and in Worcester at that time to do so would have been an act of notable heroism!

Thaele's temporary absence from Cape Town was welcomed by the communists, who profited by it to attempt to heal the breach in Congress ranks. *Umsebenzi* reports: "Since the Worcester arrests there has been a better spirit in the Cape A.N.C. . . . At a meeting on the Parade a Congress speaker, who only a week before was damning the communists for all he was worth, was urging support for the Communist Party because it was obviously the enemy of the Government and therefore the friend of non-Europeans."

But the Worcester prisoners, against whom the charge was subsequently withdrawn, were released on bail a month later. Thaele returned to Cape Town. Relations between C.P. and Congress grew rapidly worse. The "reds" within the organisation found it more and more difficult to remain there. In spite of his almost daily Parade harangues against white men in general and communists in particular, the Professor yet found time to appear on the municipal election platform in support of a European, a Mr. Bloomberg, and he had Bloomberg's election posters stuck up in the windows of the Congress Hall in Caledon Street. The left wing did not fail to point out the inconsistency, but a little thing like that did not seem to trouble Thaele at all.

With public meetings banned in the districts round Cape Town, Ndobe and Tonjeni moved further east. A branch of the Congress was established at Graaff-Reinet and interest was revived at Riversdale. Owing to the influx of large numbers of Coloured people who joined the A.N.C., *Umsebenzi* began to publish reports in Afrikaans. The farmers were becoming alarmed at the growing unity between Native and Coloured, and attempts were made to stir up ill-feeling between the two sections of non-Europeans. At Suurbrak two of the Congress leaders, Moses and Plaatjes, were set upon by a mob of thirty whites and 100 Coloured, presumably chiefly employees of the whites, and beaten up. In general, however, the non-European united front held firm.

Meanwhile, at Cape Town the struggle within Congress led to a complete rupture. In September, Thaele convened a special executive meeting in Cape Town to purge the Cape A.N.C. of all "bolshevistic elements." The bulk of the country branches were not represented. A Worcester delegate, P. Vumazonke, was present and voted against Thaele's motion. Ndobe and Tonjeni were as usual away organising in the country. According to a report given by Thaele to the *Cape Argus*, the following resolution was adopted at the close of a discussion which lasted several hours: "Having noticed the spread of bolshevistic tendencies among the non-Europeans in the Western Province, Congress is of the opinion that leaders and propagandists with communistic doctrines should not be allowed to address meetings organised by Congress. Further, that the sale of literature published by communists should be prohibited on premises owned by Congress, and that copies of this resolution be sent to all branches in the Western Province."

It was decided that B. R. Ndobe, formerly Provincial Secretary, should be suspended for a year, owing to his constant advocacy of the policy of the Communist Party, by the spreading of communist literature in spite of repeated warnings, and his action in applying for a passport to travel to Moscow without the knowledge of the officials and rank and file of the Congress; and that pending Ndobe's disavowal of bolshevistic tendencies, Elliot Tonjeni be appointed Provincial Secretary.

The oddest feature of this decision was that Ndobe and Tonjeni had been like twin brothers in their relations with the communists. Both had shown "bolshevistic tendencies," both had contributed articles to *Umsebenzi* and both pushed the sales of the paper in the country districts. Now Thaele attempted to divide them by deposing one from office and putting the other in his place. A clever move, but not all men are venal. On September 19, the two replied by the following letter, which appeared in *Umsebenzi*:

"DEAR COMRADE EDITOR,—We understand from a resolution which appeared in the *Cape Argus* of September 8 that while we were busy fighting the Pirow ban, Thaele was busy on the other hand assisting his bosses in their game of suppressing the voice of the toiling masses of this country.

"We wish to declare that the so-called 'executive meeting' which suspended Ndobe from office does not represent the African National Congress in the Western Province. Therefore its decisions are null and void. The attempt of Professor Thaele to betray the toiling masses of this country will be opposed and exposed before the African people. If we allow this to pass unchallenged it will mean that we too are wolves in sheep's clothing.

"A circular letter has been sent by Thaele to all branches

of the A.N.C. in the Western Province. In this letter nothing is said against the Pirow law or the prosecution of Comrade Tonjeni under the R.A.A. Nothing is said on behalf of the thousands of men and women who have been thrown into the army of the unemployed. Nothing is mentioned about demonstrations on Dingaan's Day. Nothing is suggested as to what steps should be taken against taxation without representation. The masses are not told how to struggle for a Black Republic.

"One of us [Tonjeni] has received a letter informing him that he has been appointed Provincial Secretary in the place of Ndobe. Tonjeni here states publicly that he will not be a party to this plot and refuses to accept such office. We are directing our forces against the Government of exploiters.

"Thaele has also called upon the branches not to read or buy *Umsebenzi*. We wish to declare that we stand solid behind our fighting newspaper. Long live *Umsebenzi*! Long may it expose the agents of the Government!

"BRANSBY R. NDOBE
(Provincial Secretary, A.N.C.).
"ELLIOT TONJENI
(Assistant Provincial Secretary)."

At the same time a group of nine leading Congress members in Cape Town sent a letter to the *Argus* repudiating the resolution expelling Ndobe.

Thaele's call for a boycott of *Umsebenzi* resulted in fierce battles in half a dozen villages in the Western Province. In certain centres where the radicals were in the majority on the local committee the paper continued to be sold. In others, Thaele's followers held the reins and the sale of the paper was officially prohibited, though in many of these individual stalwarts continued to sell the paper in spite of official sneers. *Umsebenzi* reported that some centres which took the paper one week, burnt it the next, and distributed it again the following week, according to whether the radicals or the good boys gained the upper hand. But the communists had the advantage in this fight, in that the A.N.C. had no paper of its own.*

Oswald Pirow, the Minister of Justice, was now making full use of the dictatorial powers granted him by the amended

---

* For the fate of *Abantu-Batho*, see Chapter XXVII.

Riotous Assemblies Act. At first he had confined himself to banning meetings, but finding that this had not the desired effect, he now began to prohibit particular Congress leaders from entering certain areas. In October, a notice was served on Ndobe and Tonjeni prohibiting them from entering the districts of Worcester, Robertson, Swellendam, Montagu and George for a period of six months. The Minister had managed to pick his deportees more astutely on this occasion. Steadily the orders of banishment were extended to cover almost all the Cape Province with the exception of towns like Cape Town and Port Elizabeth, where it was felt that Congress agitators could not do much harm. After the banning of the principal leaders, members in the different localities tried to carry on with the work of the Congress under increasing difficulties. A number of branch secretaries then received notices to leave their homes, among them Plaatjes, the Chairman at Worcester. Finally, the whole movement was beaten into sullen silence. Tonjeni had to go to live at Port Elizabeth and Ndobe was deported to Basutoland.

Ndobe and Tonjeni were eventually forced right out of the A.N.C. They found it impossible to break Theale's grip on the Cape Town branch. He had expelled or suspended all who would not agree to Ndobe's expulsion, protests from the country branches notwithstanding. On November 7, the left wing formed a new organisation, known as the Independent African National Congress (Cape), to which the most active country branches became affiliated.

At the end of November, there was a clash between white farmers and supporters of the I.A.N.C. at Oudtshoorn. Ndobe and Tonjeni were both present and they continued agitation in spite of numerous attacks upon their meetings by white civilians. The police then took action and banned them from the district.

CHAPTER XX

DEATH OF NKOSI

WHILE IN THE CAPE the communists fared thus, the party was trying to work up a nation-wide campaign for the burning of all passes on Dingaan's Day. This form of passive resistance had been tried before, by the African National

Congress in Johannesburg in 1919. It had resulted in the breaking up of the meeting by the police and the arrest of some 700 of the pass-burners. It was realised by some of the communists that pass-burning was a heroic measure, a dangerous weapon, a two-edged sword. It could prove effective only if carried out on a really big scale. If an individual destroyed his pass, he would be at once arrested and imprisoned. It would be a personal protest, a heroic gesture, but useless. Even if many individuals burned their passes their sacrifice would be in vain. The only hope of success lay in the burning of all passes at the same time. But the Party felt that its influence was now strong enough to make the venture worth while. "You cannot imprison millions," they said. In addition to considerable support in various small towns and in the country districts (though not in the reserves, where in any case the question of passes was not so important), they had strong branches in Johannesburg, Pretoria, Bloemfontein, and now in Durban. As early as July *Umsebenzi* was calling, "Prepare to burn passes on Dingaan's Day!" and as the weeks went by the slogan was regularly repeated.

In Bloemfontein the C.P. had been making headway ever since the Malkinson case in 1928. Malkinson himself had been an enthusiastic propagandist and he had converted a number of capable Africans, among them three leading members of the local Independent I.C.U. (Kadalie's I.C.U.), Ntela, Taabe and Mateta. As December 16 drew near, there appeared to be something in the nature of a communist landslide in Bloemfontein. Crowds attended the communist meetings and hundreds joined the Party. *Umsebenzi* made record sales. The authorities felt impelled to act. They began by trying to deport Ntela, whose home was in Basutoland. On November 17, he was told to pack up his possessions and prepare to leave the Union of South Africa, "to which country he must never return." When he asked on what authority he was being deported, he was told by the C.I.D. that instructions had been received from the Minister of the Interior. The detectives read to him extracts from the Native Urban Areas Act and the Riotous Assemblies Act. Malkinson, though not a lawyer, immediately took up the case. He was shown a warrant in which Ntela was charged with being a prohibited immigrant, under a clause of the Immigration Act of 1913, designed for Europeans, which stated that anyone who could not read and write might be declared a prohibited immigrant. Ntela was given a passage in English to read. He did so successfully. In the end he was discharged and allowed to remain in Bloemfontein. It seemed that the authorities in that city had yet to perfect their technique for dealing with Native agitators.

But a week later, Pirow came to the rescue of the local police. The Bloemfontein *Friend* reported: "Communism has gained a firm hold on hundreds of Natives in the Bloemfontein locations during the year, and there is every reason to believe that the movement is spreading, particularly among the younger Natives. Communist leaders in locations have spared neither time nor energy in propagating and cultivating their political creed among Natives, and, in addition to public meetings every week, they make house to house visits. Their intention, openly expressed, is to burn or otherwise destroy passes on Dingaan's Day. Yesterday the police served on two of the leaders notices under the Riotous Assemblies Act, which prohibit them from attending any public meeting in the district of Bloemfontein during November and December. The two leaders are Sam Malkinson (a European) and Isaiah Ntela (a Native)." But the campaign continued.

In Durban, too, that stronghold of Champion's I.C.U. *yase* Natal, the communists made converts. To that centre they had sent from Johannesburg, early in 1929, the young Johannes Nkosi, one of their few Zulu-speaking members. Born in Natal in 1905, Nkosi had been farm labourer and kitchen "boy." Quite early in life he had come to Johannesburg, where at the age of fourteen he had taken part in the Congress pass-strike. He joined the Communist Party in 1926 and attended the night school.

Nkosi's relations with Champion are interesting. In the early months of 1930, the I.C.U. *yase* Natal was still a big organisation in Durban and the newly formed C.P. branch a comparatively small affair. The great popular leader of the Durban Africans was already trying to play safe, though he seemed still to have some sort of sneaking regard for the radicals. To the big I.C.U. meetings, held on Sunday afternoons on Cartwright's Flats and attended by some thousands of Natives, Nkosi would come with his bundle of *Umsebenzi* and ask Champion's permission to sell them. Sometimes permission would be given, sometimes refused, according to whether Champion was at that particular moment in a rebellious mood or feeling the wisdom of placating the authorities. When refused permission to sell the paper, Nkosi would write a pathetic letter to the head office in Cape Town. He could not see why Champion was so timid. If only he were in Champion's place, he would tell them all to burn the passes! But Nkosi and Champion were of such different grain.

The Durban C.P. acquired a new hall in September and the crowd began to come to the communist meetings. In that same month Champion was deported. If the Minister of Justice had displayed any perspicacity, it would have been Nkosi whom he deported and Champion would have remained to keep the Durban Africans tame. But now Dingaan's Day drew near and Nkosi was in charge of the situation.

In preparation for the pass-burning, the C.P. called a "united front" conference in Johannesburg on October 26. It was held in the Inchcape Hall with Nzula in the chair. The *Cape Argus* reported that "delegates from all four provinces attended and resolutions were passed pledging all present to take part in an active war against the pass laws throughout the Union 'with the aim of smashing them for all time.' Supporters of the campaign said they were prepared if necessary to go to prison in defence of their principles. The conference decided on mass demonstrations on Dingaan's Day in the principal centres of the Union. The whole African population is to be asked to take part in a mass burning of passes and a general downing of tools on that day, particularly in mines, works and factories."

In addition to communist groups and trade unions, various branches and individual leaders of the Congress and I.C.U. joined in the campaign. Even the respectable *Imvo* was drawn into the fight. It advertised the conference and wished it success. In an editorial, it referred to the "repressive laws that the Government has seen fit to perpetuate in the teeth of the strongest opposition from those who have suffered under this yoke of bondage. . . . The damnable pinpricks and inconveniences suffered by all classes of Natives in their daily lives in the country of their birth are considered petty grievances by the so-called superior cultured race who delight in 'keeping the nigger unspoilt.' Why grumble when violent forms of protest have ultimately to be resorted to, and the aid of communists solicited? We do not love communists as such; but a white man would never hesitate to snatch a nigger's hand that saves him from drowning. Neither would a black man hesitate to call in a communist, or any other hated and despised person for that matter, who helps him to discard his yoke of bondage." A. M. Jabavu was becoming militant!

The Government now became uneasy, especially about the growth of communist influence in Bloemfontein and elsewhere in the Orange Free State. Dumah, a communist agitator, had been rousing the northern part of the O.F.S. Big meetings were held at Kroonstad and even Keable Mote (of chequered history*) was so much influenced by the popular movement that he had appeared on the Party platform and spoken in favour of a mass meeting on this particular "day of liberation." All seemed to be going well. But now the Government put a spoke in the communist wheel. Nothing had been heard of Kadalie for months. After the East London strike and Kadalie's return from prison, he had, except for a single fiery outburst at Pretoria in June, remained in obscurity with his Independent I.C.U. in East London. It was freely rumoured that the Government had threatened to deport him to his native Nyasaland if he gave any more trouble. Suddenly, however, like a bolt from the blue, he appeared in Bloemfontein. On December 7 he addressed a meeting of 600 Africans in Bloemfontein location. He warned his hearers against the communists and declared himself against the campaign for burning passes on Dingaan's Day. The Government, he said, would manage to find space in gaol for the law-breakers. He declared that the Natives could do nothing until they were properly organised. They must join the I.C.U. and have no more to do with the communists. He warned them against clashes with the Europeans.

The communists were furious. *Umsebenzi* broke out in denunciation of Kadalie's "dastardly behaviour." He was described as a "hireling, tool and 'good boy' of the white imperialists," and it was alleged that he had been sent to Bloemfontein by the Native Affairs Department. Kadalie's influence in the Free State capital was no longer what it had been, but still strong enough to cause a serious breach in the united front. The Bloemfontein masses did not flock to join the I.C.U., but neither did they rally to burn their passes on Dingaan's Day.

* Mote, the "Lion" of the Free State, broke away from Kadalie in 1928. See Chapter XVI.

The only centre which finally responded in a big way to the communist call for the burning of passes was Durban. A meeting was called on Cartwright's Flats. The meeting began at 11 a.m. and continued into the afternoon. It was enthusiastic, but quiet and orderly. Passes were handed in and collected in bags. The organisers prepared to form a procession and march through the town. At this moment a large force of the Durban Borough Police, both European and Native, which had been held in readiness, marched on to the Flats and attacked the meeting. Nkosi on the platform tried to control the crowd. The police were armed with pick handles and assegais and (at least some of the whites) with revolvers. Nkosi was shot and struck down while still on the platform appealing to the crowd not to offer violence. The Natives then resisted with sticks, stones and other missiles. In dispersing the huge gathering, the police killed or mortally wounded four men and seriously wounded twenty others. The names of the killed were Johannes Nkosi, Ben Pani, James Mhlongo and Joseph Sofili.

H. Krikst, who was present at the meeting, gives the following first-hand account of what happened there: "The meeting started at 11 a.m. very peacefully, and went on for a long time. Towards 4 p.m. the crowd was tremendous. As they were putting their passes into bags, the Native police charged, making towards the table on which the speakers were standing. I saw Nkosi struck down from the table. The police used knobkerries; while the crowd picked up stones. When the crowd was dispersed I saw them pack the wounded on a lorry. I followed in my car. There was a trail of blood dripping from the lorry. The lorry waited outside the police station for three-quarters of an hour or more. Then they were removed to the hospital. I wired to Bunting in Johannesburg. He replied, 'Save Nkosi at all costs. Spare no expense.' Nkosi died the following day. He had previously regained consciousness. He kept on saying, 'My head! My head!' "

The hospital doctor, who gave evidence at the subsequent inquest, was asked whether during his service in the Great War he had ever seen the dead more horribly mutilated. He stated that he had seen *some* worse cases. All of the deceased had been hacked all over the body with some stabbing instrument, the skulls of all were severely fractured, while none had less than seven serious wounds. The evidence of numerous witnesses went to show that the mutilations had been inflicted after the wounded men were removed from Cartwright's Flats. In the case of Nkosi, it was alleged that while still on the platform he was fired at by a police officer. He was removed from the scene of the fight apparently suffering from a single wound only, what seemed to be a bullet wound in the body. But when he died his skull was seriously fractured and his head and body were covered with deep gashes.

Though thousands saw Nkosi attacked, no one was ever charged for this evil deed. The Borough Police publicly denied that they had used revolvers. Some of the Natal boroughs still had their old municipal police. Unlike the Government police (South African Police), they were not supposed to carry firearms, and, even if they had, it was not surprising that they denied having done so on this occasion.

Not content with the bloody result of this unprovoked attack, the authorities followed up the killing by the arrest of thirty-two Africans who were present at the meeting, whom they charged with "incitement to violence." In the course of their trial some of the arrested men tried to make public the fact that fire-arms had been used. One pointed to a police officer present in the court and said: "That man pointed his revolver at Nkosi and fired at him." Though the usual newspaper reporters were present, no mention of this dramatic statement subsequently appeared in the daily Press in Durban or elsewhere. Twenty-six of the accused were found guilty. Four were sentenced to six months' hard labour without the option of a fine; and others received shorter sentences. A huge crowd of communist supporters attended the trial, and the police took advantage of the occasion to arrest some 130 of them, eighty-four of whom were charged under the pass law. By destroying their passes, they had marked themselves out for persecution.

With Nkosi dead and most of the local leaders arrested or deported, the branch at Durban seemed doomed. Headquarters at Johannesburg tried very hard to keep things going there. Gana Makabeni was sent to Durban, but in a few days he too was arrested and charged under Section 17 of the Urban Areas Act of 1923, which states that if in the opinion of the police any Native is "an idle, dissolute or disorderly person" he may be brought before the Native Commissioner, who may order his deportation to his country home, on pain of imprisonment if he should return to the district from which he has been deported within a period of two years. The operation of this section is entirely in the hands of the Native Affairs Department and the Native Commissioner may refuse to allow the Native concerned to be represented by a lawyer. The onus is upon the Native to rebut the allegation made by the police. If he fails to do so, it is assumed that the police evidence is true. Makabeni was deported to his home in the Transkei. A number of other leaders sent from Johannesburg were similarly deported. Finally, the C.P. was compelled to send a white member to Durban to keep together what was left of the local organisation.

This was no easy task. The landlord of the communist hall ordered his tenants to quit. The Party was left without local headquarters. Desperate attempts were made to go "underground." But the Durban Native communists did not care for secret meetings. They wanted to shout their defiance to the world. They wanted to show that they had burnt their passes, that they were not afraid of the police. Spies in their ranks, themselves immune from arrest, called public meetings to which the remaining communists came. The meetings were surrounded by the police, all participants marched off to the Native Affairs Department and then deported as "disorderly persons." It was only necessary for the police to state that they had been present at communist meetings for the Commissioner to agree to their deportation. Detective-Sergeant Arnold, known to the Zulus as *Tshaka*, directed the police activities. He had previously boasted that he had "squashed the I.C.U. menace." Now he was doing the same with the "communist danger." Letters sent from Johannesburg to Durban communists were opened, copies made and produced in the Native Commissioner's court as evidence that men were communists.

In spite of the terror, more passes were burnt. One communist returned from a tour of the neighbouring villages with a bag full of passes. Arrests were an almost daily occurrence in Durban. On February 20, *Umsebenzi* reported: "Fourteen arrested communists were marched through the streets under police escort. They sang '*Mayibuye*' and gave three cheers for the Communist Party. The 'good boy,' Rev. John Dube, watched them from his Chevrolet motor car, but they took no notice of him. Three more leaders, Philip Thompson, Mitchell Kubheka and Ruben Mlungisi, have been arrested."

On April 22, 1931, an official bulletin on the position in Natal was issued by the Department of Justice. It stated that "the communist movement was at its zenith in December with a membership of some thousands of Natives. The whole of the Kadalie faction had gone over in a body to the communists in November, and the I.C.U. *yase* Natal secretly joined up in hundreds, as did a large following of the African National Congress. The police action on December 16, coupled with the subsequent trial of thirty Natives for public violence, also the raid on the onlookers during the trial, had a moral effect on the general Native population, causing hundreds to break away from communism. Then on January 8, action was commenced against all communist leaders who addressed meetings, and most of the leaders were proceeded against and deported to their homes. This action shook the foundation of communism in Durban, the party being unable to procure leaders with any influence. The actual number of Natives attending communist meetings to-day has fallen to a handful. An attempt is being made by the party at their headquarters in Johannesburg to improve matters in Durban and to re-organise, but it is considered doubtful whether such efforts will meet with any success.

"The I.C.U. *yase* Natal has dwindled in numbers and influence until its strength to-day is described as of little consequence. Since the deportation of Champion, the leading officers and organisers have quarrelled frequently for supreme power, resulting in undercurrents being revealed to the masses which alienated the bulk of the I.C.U. following. The attendance at open-air meetings has fallen from approximately 2,000 to some 250, and most of the latter are not members. Practically no fees are being paid into the coffers of the organisation by members.

"The African National Congress to-day is considered to have little or no influence among Durban and coastal members, and all the originally appointed Natives in the organisation have resigned their offices. The Independent I.C.U.—Kadalie movement—does not now function on the coast of Natal. The police continue to keep an accurate check on all these movements, and developments are reported at once to headquarters.

"Incidentally, a movement which is not to be coupled with the activities of communist agitators, but which is doing considerable good among the Natives, is the old Natal Native

Congress. This organisation has a membership of some 200, who are led by the Rev. John Dube, and who are steady and most law-abiding."

The communists made further efforts to "go underground." There were still a few enthusiasts who had escaped the police net. Some half-dozen were got together into a "district committee." Among them was a young man called Radebe, who had been a most enthusiastic agitator since January and who seemed to bear a charmed life. He appeared to be a "house boy" and had addressed meetings in his white apron. Though he was very conspicuous, he was never arrested and the other communists began to suspect he was a spy and *provocateur*. Then their suspicions were set at rest. Radebe was arrested and deported to his home at Umkomaas on the South Coast. Some of his comrades saw him off at the station. A few days later he was back again, disguised, wearing dark glasses and without his white apron. Surely, the comrades thought, here was a true Lenin. He was invited to the next secret meeting of the underground district committee. He was not present at the meeting. When the committee ended their deliberations and came out to the street, there, waiting for them, were *Tshaka* and a group of Native detectives with hand-cuffs ready. All the Native members of the secret committee were thus delivered into the hands of the police. This was the end of Radebe's role as spy and *provocateur*. But he had done a lot of damage before the end came.

But it was becoming increasingly difficult for the police to make use of the Urban Areas Act for deporting communists. A deputation of white communists called on the chief Native Commissioner to protest against the deportation of Natives merely because they were communists. The deputation threatened to expose the high-handed methods of the police and appealed to "British fair play." The Chief Commissioner was not a bad sort. He promised to give instructions to his junior that in future evidence as to political sympathies would not be permitted when Natives were brought for deportation by the police. Every case would be "considered on its merits." In other words, the police would have to prove that the African concerned was in fact an "idle, dissolute or disorderly person" without reference to the Communist Party membership card found in his possession or to the fact that he had associated with communists or been seen at a communist meeting.

The District Committee followed this up by keeping a continual watch on the Native Commissioner's Court. There was always a danger of a communist being arrested and deported, without his comrades knowing anything about it. When an arrest occurred, a white communist would try to be present at the "trial" to give evidence as to the "good character" of the "accused." Such is the importance of white prestige in South Africa that even a white who is also a communist must be treated with respect in a "Native court." A number of *Tshaka's* projected deportations were thus defeated. Even some of the arrested members of the district committee were saved. Though pass-burning was still talked of in a general way, it was now agreed that Party functionaries —in fact, all known Party members—should comply as far as possible with the pass and poll tax regulations. For any member to burn his pass would be to invite imprisonment and deportation.

The district committee started an "illegal paper" in Durban, a duplicated sheet in Zulu, *Ndaba zamaKomanisi eTekwini* (Durban Communist News). Contact was maintained as far as possible with the deported members in the country districts. One of the leaders, James Mbete, had been deported to Pinetown, twenty miles to the north of Durban, and there a small but enthusiastic branch was organised. Contact was made also with some of the prisoners in gaol. Released men brought news from others still inside. A letter was even smuggled out and subsequently published in *Umsebenzi*.

Although open communist meetings had now become impossible there was always the I.C.U. The I.C.U. *yase* Natal had been allowed to continue its meetings. Though the authorities did not entirely approve of that organisation, they probably regarded it as a useful safety valve. All the fire had gone out of the I.C.U. speakers, but large crowds went to the meetings every Sunday, and there the communists were able to sell their newspaper and distribute their leaflets.

But the attempt to revive the C.P. in Durban was not a great success. The campaign had been too costly, the losses too crippling. Over 200 of the most active communists had been deported. Others who were in prison were deported immediately they were released. The movement had now to depend on the comparative immunity from deportation enjoyed by the two or three white communists. And before long Pirow was using his powers under the Riotous Assemblies Act to get rid of these also. Finally, even the whites had to "go underground."

Thus the pass-burning campaign ended in seeming failure. On the Rand a few hundred passes had been burnt, but heavy rain had prevented the anticipated large meetings. In Pretoria also little had been done. At Bloemfontein the intervention of Kadalie had effectively destroyed the movement. In the Cape Province the pass system was not in force, anyway. The net result of the campaign seemed to be the destruction of the Party's most militant branch, the death of a young leader, the imprisonment or deportation of many others: on the whole a setback to the Party. Liberal reformists among the Europeans, Native sympathisers of all kinds, also reformists among the Africans themselves were not slow to point the moral. They accused the Party of having led their Native members wantonly into trouble and suffering.

Were the Communist Party to blame for what had occurred? Could they have anticipated the brutal action of the police against Durban's passive resisters? Ought they to have realised as Dingaan's Day drew near, that they had not in fact the backing that was needed for such action? At the preparatory conference held in October over 600 delegates had displayed great confidence and enthusiasm. Bunting remarked then: "But what are 600 among these millions?" Would the millions follow their lead?

It is difficult to give a decided answer to these and similar questions. In a country where oppression of the Africans is so thoroughgoing and universal any message advocating resistance, any glimpse of hope, is eagerly welcomed by the masses. They flock to the banner. But this ready enthusiasm and acceptance of plans does not imply that depth of comprehension, that steadiness of devotion to the cause, which can alone provide a sure foundation for such mass resistance. The campaign was too rapid, its seeming success too facile. Paradoxical though this may seem, it gained adherents too easily. Its success was in the nature of a flash in the pan. Preparation should have been continued over a much longer period. The resistance should have been the fruit of a movement of long standing and not itself the occasion of the growth of the movement, as in many districts it was. That much may be conceded to the critics, those liberals who criticised yet themselves did nothing towards the abolishing of the pass laws. It is certain that the I.C.U. in the fullness of its power, with a quarter-million of adherents all over the country, could have carried out a nation-wide pass-burning and by passive resistance have abolished the system.

But as to the action itself, the question must be considered: what alternative offered? Either the pass laws must be endured or they must be resisted. The Party advocated passive resistance, the refusal to bear passes, willingness to endure imprisonment for the cause. It would seem that this is the way, the only way in which the pass law may be effectively fought. It is the way the women took, successfully.* It is the way of Gandhi and his *satyagrahis*. But such passive resistance requires a self-control and iron determination which must necessarily be the result of more than a few months' training. Against the provocation offered by the police on Cartwright's Flats the newly-won passive resisters were powerless. The technique of first attacking a peaceful meeting and then charging the participants with incitement to violence was calculated to succeed. No one could have foreseen that the police would actually bludgeon their victims to death.

CHAPTER XXI

MOSCOW SETS THE PACE

In the meantime, the Communist Party was facing an internal crisis. Between 1925 and 1930 it had seemed likely that Bunting's *tour de force* would lead to the establishment of an indigenous Communist Party predominantly African in membership and interests. Whites, of course, there were, but these had to a very large extent thrown in their lot with the non-Europeans—as far as the colour of their skins enabled them to do so. An African's comment on Bunting, "He has a white skin but a black heart," was typical of the way in which he and other white communists came to be regarded at this time. Whites still played a role in the Party out of proportion to their numbers, but their predominance in the leadership diminished as African leaders were recruited and trained.

* See Chapter XI.

These came from the ranks of the workers as well as from the black intelligentsia.

This very interesting and significant growth of an African revolutionary party was now paralysed by the active intervention of the Moscow Comintern. The socialists had affiliated to the Comintern in 1921, at the time when the Internationl Socialist League and a number of smaller Left bodies were merged in the Communist Party of South Africa, but for a number of years guidance from Moscow was only of the most general kind. In 1928, however, the South African communists were forced to adopt the slogan of a "Native Republic." This in itself would have done little if any harm to the Native side of the movement, though definitely closing the gates to the white workers, if it had not been accompanied by a violent campaign against an alleged "right danger." This unfortunate transfer to South Africa of an ultra-left policy which had its origin in Soviet politics but which had no justification in this country, resulted in Bunting's removal from the leadership of the Party in 1931 and to his expulsion nine months later.*

The new so-called "Bolshevik" leadership, Douglas and Molly Wolton and Lazar Bach, proceeded to purge the party of all "right-wing, social-democratic and vacillating elements"; it successfully smashed or antagonised the new African trade unions which had been built up by the communists on the Witwatersrand; it made any sort of co-operation between the party and other bodies, whether white or black, impossible; and it drove away almost all the Africans who had been attracted to the Party under Bunting's leadership. The night school dwindled.

Together with Bunting, a number of other leading white communists were expelled from the Communist Party. These included B. Weinbren, who with Thibedi had first organised the Non-European Trade Union Federation; S. Malkinson, the energetic leader at Bloemfontein; E. S. Sachs, Secretary of the militant Garment Workers' Union; and W. H. Andrews, who at this time was Secretary of the South African Trade Union Congress.

In spite of their depleted forces, the communists made strenuous efforts to carry out the tasks set them by the Comintern. They organised the unemployed in Johannesburg.

* See *S. P. Bunting, a Political Biography*, by Edward Roux.

Diamond, the popular leader of the white unemployed, was now in prison. In May, 1930, he had led a huge demonstration of white and black unemployed, the first of its kind in Johannesburg. Shouting the slogan, "We want bread!" and attempting to enter the Carlton Hotel and the Rand Club, the demonstrators clashed with the police. As a result of this affair, Diamond was sentenced to a year's imprisonment. Other white speakers were now put on this task of organising the unemployed, the most successful being Molly Wolton. Small and fiery, a brilliant platform speaker, she attracted large crowds, who delighted in the quick repartee with which she parried occasional heckling. Meetings were held outside the Labour Exchange. Similarly African speakers carried on propaganda outside the Pass Office. Demonstrations were planned, the idea being to bring black and white unemployed together and then to proceed to the various authorities (municipal and Government) to demand measures of relief. The demonstrations always began well, but it was noticed that the whites (mostly Afrikaners) were not keen on marching with the Natives. A procession consisting of approximately equal numbers of both races would start off, but by the time it reached its destination most of the whites had vanished and only a handful of white communists remained to give the demonstration its "united" character.

Nevertheless, a certain temporary co-operation was achieved between black and white workers. There was a successful attempt to collect food for the unemployed on Christmas Eve, 1932. Led by a white communist, between fifty and 100 persons, over a third of them were whites, marched through the streets followed by a wagon to carry any food which might be obtained. Various business houses, bakers, butchers, and grocers were visited and asked to give Christmas gifts to the workless. Quite a good load of food was obtained and this was afterwards shared out among those who had accompanied the wagon. When the march was ended some of the old Afrikaners insisted that the Natives should be given their proper share, "*want hulle het ook saamgekom.*"* The point was that there was no one else to lead the white unemployed and many of them were prepared to accept communist leadership even though this involved association with the Natives. How different was the position a few years later when fascist

* "For they also came with us."

257

agitators became active among the white unemployed, preached the usual racial hatred and sometimes succeeded even in driving the communist leaders away.

In May, 1932, Douglas Wolton went to prison, on a charge of criminal defamation. The charge was based on an article headed "Dingaan's Day Prisoner Brutally Beaten by Gaolers at Krantzkop" which had appeared in *Umsebenzi* in September, 1931. The article stated that "comrade Ntyakuya, one of the thirty-three prisoners arrested in connection with the Dingaan's Day activities in 1930, convicted and sentenced to five months' hard labour at Krantzkop Gaol, Natal, was one of the prisoners who was brutally maltreated whilst in gaol. Eyewitnesses state that some of the prisoners were lashed to blocks of wood and sjamboked until big holes were made in their flesh. Comrade Ntyakuya, at all times physically weak, was unable to stand this frightful torture and the continual beatings affected his heart, and he finally died in gaol without any medical attention before his sentence was completed. Due to the agitation of the prisoners and the serious threat of a strike in the gaol, following the death of this comrade, some improvements were made in the gaol conditions, but the comrade largely responsible for exposing these brutalities was given a further sentence of one month."

The witnesses for the Crown were the Resident Commissioner at Krantzkop and a number of prisoners and warders. Wolton relied on the evidence of some of the Dingaan's Day prisoners, in particular Cyrus Moroko and Emanuel Ntombela. The local district surgeon gave evidence that a Native died in gaol of bronchial pneumonia. Under cross-examination, Moroko contradicted himself and the court was not prepared to accept his statement that Ntyakuya had been thrashed or that he did not receive medical attention when ill. The evidence of Ntombela seemed more reliable, though it also failed to show that the dead man had been thrashed. He stated that he had known Ntyakuya in Durban when he was a member of the Communist Party. At the road camp Ntyakuya looked ill, but was forced to work. Once he was so exhausted that he sat down and could not go on working. He was sent back to Krantzkop. Previously he had complained frequently that he was ill, but had been ignored.

Referring to the general treatment of the prisoners at Krantzkop, Ntombela said: "Communists did not receive the same treatment as others. We who had taken part in the burning of passes were lined up by ourselves and when the food came we had to wait until all the other prisoners had received their rations. When we complained, the gaoler told us if we were not satisfied, to go to the Communist Party and get more. Every time we complained, this remark was repeated. We were then thrashed with sjamboks and sticks for no reason at all. Once the warders tied me to a tree with my toes just touching the ground and thrashed me with a stick until it broke." He mentioned further thrashings and being poked in the ribs with a stick. At the conclusion of his evidence, Ntombela removed his coat and shirt and showed a number of big scars on his back.

Wolton was found guilty by the magistrate and sentenced to four months' hard labour, three and a half months of which was without the option of a fine. The case was taken to appeal before Justices de Waal and de Wet in the Supreme Court in Pretoria. In the course of their judgment, in which they upheld the decision of the lower court, the judges referred to a cartoon which had appeared in the same issue of *Umsebenzi* as the article complained of. The cartoon showed a black man drawing a wagon in which sat a fat white man labelled "farmer." By the side walked a policeman with a long whip and in front walked a missionary with the reins in his hand. The judges considered that the cartoon was an incitement to race hostility. Under it was printed a quotation from a Nationalist orator: "I submit that the Native is happiest when he works for the white man."

During the latter half of 1932, the most exciting events took place in Germiston location. This location had previously escaped the attention of the communists because of all the Reef locations it was the most difficult of access, its superintendent rigorously insisting that no one not resident there should enter it without a permit. So far the communists had failed to make any contact there. In September, 1932, a vacancy occurred in the parliamentary constituency of Germiston. The Nationalist Government was in a bad way because of the gold-standard crisis. The Government was trying to keep on gold. The English pound had been devaluated and the South African pound, based on gold, was worth about £6 in London. This suited the South African Reserve Bank and certain sections of the South African capitalists.

But it did not suit the Chamber of Mines, who were still forced to pay wages and buy supplies in South Africa at the rates set by the undevaluated pound. The Smuts party, backed by the mine-owners and most of the political and financial forces in the country, was trying to force the Government off gold. The Germiston by-election therefore became a critical issue, for on its result might depend the whole future of the Government and the gold standard. A Nationalist had been returned for the seat at the previous election.

The Communist Party decided to contest the election with an African "demonstrative candidate." Africans, of course, had no vote in the Transvaal, nor were they allowed to stand for Parliament. But the communists maintained that the majority of the inhabitants of Germiston were Africans and if they had votes they would return a communist. Accordingly, John Marks was nominated as the communist candidate and the campaign went ahead. Meetings were held among both white and black workers. Voting forms were issued to the Natives in the locations. A public meeting for whites was held on the Germiston market square, but it was broken up with violence by the Nationalists. More successful were meetings at the railway workshops, where the audience consisted mainly of English-speaking artisans. The whites were urged to write "communist" across their ballot papers. Most of them replied that they preferred to vote S.A.P., because, though they did not think very highly of the Smuts party, they wanted to show their disapproval of the Government, which had been cutting the wages of the railway workers. But they were prepared to give the communists a hearing.

But the main idea was to get at the Natives in the location. Risking capture by the superintendent, communists entered the forbidden territory with leaflets calling meetings on vacant ground just outside the location. The local grievance which the communists exploited was the age-old lodger's tax, which at this time of unemployment was causing extreme annoyance to the location inhabitants. Under the Urban Areas Act municipalities are entitled to levy a tax on all persons, men and women over eighteen years of age, not being tenants or their wives, who reside in a municipal location. The tax at Germiston was half a crown per lodger per month. Tenants there built their own houses on plots in the location for which they paid a monthly ground rent to the municipality. If a tenant had a relative or friend staying with him, he would have to pay lodger's tax. The same applied to his own children when they were over eighteen years of age. At times of chronic unemployment, as in 1932, the people were unable to pay the tax. Many sons and daughters could remain at home only illegally. To discover the illegal "lodgers," the police made frequent raids on the location in the small hours of the morning. All who were liable to lodger's tax and had not paid it were convicted and imprisoned. When raids were feared, many, both men and women, left the location at night and slept out on the veld. Transvaal nights can be bitterly cold.

Here was a genuine grievance and the communists made the most of it. Huge crowds attended the meetings, which were held just outside the location. The location women had set up a special committee to fight the tax and with this committee the communists collaborated. A procession of women marched through Germiston and called upon the magistrate asking for the abolition of the tax. Meetings within the location were broken up by the police. The authorities tried also to stop the communist meetings. On Sunday, October 16, a large meeting was in progress when a number of police arrived on the scene. These included some plain-clothes detectives and two police officers in uniform, Captain Brown and Lieutenant Fourie. They couldn't order the meeting to disperse, as it was not being held inside the location. Nor, since the meeting was orderly, could they interfere on the grounds that there had been a breach of the peace. So they began themselves to interrupt the speakers. To be heckled by police officers in uniform was a new experience for the communists. But Molly Wolton was more than a match at repartee for any policeman. Soon she had the crowd laughing at the slower-witted police officers. Then an African policeman was put up to shout down the speaker with a rival speech telling the people to go "to watch the football match." But they preferred to stay and hear the talk about the lodger's tax. The police then demanded the pass of the African communist, Jeffery Movene, who was acting as chairman and interpreter. The communists, how-ever, knowing that Movene had no pass and not wishing to lose their interpreter, formed a cordon round the platform and tried to keep the police off. Molly Wolton continued to speak and the plain-clothes men, Europeans, pressing closely against the cordon shouted rhythmically "Shut up! Shut up!" A number of African detectives were also present and these, plainly acting under instructions from the white officers, now began to create disturbances here and there among the audience. The meeting became a rough-and-tumble. Finally Movene, Molly Wolton and Roux were arrested and taken to the location police station, where various charges were laid against them.

The prisoners were led off, still struggling, to the accompaniment of boos and jeers from the crowd, which followed. As the procession pased along a location street an African bystander laughed mockingly. He may have said something too. Two white policemen ran towards him. He ran a few yards to his hut, went in and closed the door. The police followed, opened the door and entered. People outside could see through the open door that the police were striking the man's face with their handcuffs. Then the door was closed. After a little while, the police came out alone.

The arrested communists were charged with "resisting arrest," with "inciting feelings of hostility between Natives and Europeans" and (in the case of Movene) under the Urban Areas Act and the Poll Tax regulations. The communists in turn proposed to lay charges against the police, of unlawfully shouting and breaking up a public meeting and with assault upon a number of women who had stood in cordon round the platform. The cases were referred to the Attorney-General, and he, wisely from the point of view of the authorities, allowed the whole matter to drop.

When nomination day came, it was found that there were four official candidates in the field. Besides the S.A.P. and Government candidates, there were a nominee of the Labour Party and an Independent. The communists made an attempt to nominate Marks, knowing full well that he would not be accepted, but in the hope of getting in some more propaganda. The task of proposing the Native candidate fell to the writer of this history, who was fortunate in getting away with only a few minor cuts and bruises at the hands of the Nationalist mob.

Election day was fixed for November 30. On November 5 the Minister of Justice took a hand in the election campaign on behalf of the Government candidate. He issued an order to five of the leading "reds" to leave the Witwatersrand for a period of one year from November 12. Those thus singled out were Issy Diamond, Douglas Wolton, F. W. Kalk, E. R. Roux and E. S. Sachs. The first four were Party members. Issy Diamond, a lively local barber, an excellent platform speaker and quick at repartee, had achieved much in his efforts to organise the unemployed. Wolton was the new Party leader, Kalk a secretary of a white trade union, Roux an agitator and the manager of *Umsebenzi*. The fifth, E. S. Sachs, was the Secretary of the Garment Workers' Union and had been expelled from the Party for "right deviations," in 1930, at the time of the expulsion of Bunting. All five were Europeans. Though Sachs was not technically a communist, it was really he, more than the communists, who was undermining the Government's chances in the Germiston election. The communist propaganda campaign would not affect the question of who would represent Germiston in Parliament. But a strike had broken out among the garment workers in Germiston. Sachs was the Secretary of their union. Most of the garment girls were Afrikaners, and they and their mothers, fathers and brothers had mostly voted Nationalist at previous elections. The police had used their usual brutality in trying to suppress the strike. On one occasion mounted police had been used and had actually ridden down a white girl striker. This had roused the ire of the white workers and made the Government very unpopular. So by including Sachs in the list of banned persons, Pirow was trying to kill two birds with one stone. He would stop the agitation in the location and he would get rid of the leader of the garment workers, who was helping to undermine the position of the Nationalist candidate. Of the four communists who were banned one, Wolton, was not at the time in Johannesburg at all and had consequently played no part in the election campaign.

The three "reds" actually left the Rand for a few days only (in the case of the writer not even that, for he remained in Johannesburg and played hide-and-seek with the police for a fortnight). An application was made to the Supreme Court to test the validity of the ban. The matter then became *sub judice* and the banned persons were able to return pending the decision of the courts. The Transvaal Division of the Supreme Court decided in favour of the Minister, but appeal to the Appellate Division, with the usual law's delays, prevented the order from being carried out for another ten months. By that time Smuts was Minister of Justice and he withdrew the ban imposed by Pirow.

The election proved an overwhelming victory for the South African Party. The Nationalists came second with the Labour Party candidate and the Independent nowhere. The communists stated that their candidate had received 3,000 votes in the location. This was only an estimate. In the general terror and commotion, it was not possible to collect all the voting papers.

The defeat at Germiston and the growing gold-standard crisis so undermined the position of the Government that it was forced, like the Labour Government in England in the previous year, to form a "national coalition." This led to the fusion of the two big parties, Nationalist and S.A.P. and a Cabinet in which Hertzog and Smuts shared the honours. The extreme or "purified" Nationalists eventually broke away under Dr. Malan and re-formed the old Nationalist Party.

Events continued at Germiston location. On November 13 a meeting of residents inside the location was broken up with violence by the police, and some 300 men, women and children were arrested. Most of them were subsequently released, but twenty-two were charged and some of them imprisoned for "public violence." For a few weeks the communists gave up trying to hold their Sunday meetings outside the location, but in January, 1933, they tried again. By now the authorities had thought up a new plan for stopping this propaganda. On January 18, half a dozen communists came from Johannesburg to hold a meeting. They took up their position outside the location and waited for a crowd to collect. People were slow to come, because it was not generally known that a meeting was to be held that day. Then about twenty African men arrived in a body. They were armed with sticks and were led by a man, nicknamed "Mac," who was recognised as the Native sergeant of police in the location, though on this occasion he was not wearing his uniform. The newcomers wasted no time in speech. They set about the little party with their sticks and finally drove them off. In the midst of the attack, a pair of white policemen arrived and stood looking on with approval. When asked to stop the assaults, they refused and added: "You people came here at your own risk." Black and blue, their soap boxes smashed, their banners torn, the communists managed at last to get away. The men with sticks were employees of the Germiston municipality. They had been ordered by the location superintendent to hold themselves ready that afternoon to attack the communists.

The next day a news item appeared in the *Rand Daily Mail*. It was reported that a group of African mine-workers, incensed at the communist visits to Germiston location, had attacked the communists and ordered them away from the location. The heading was "Communists not Wanted!"

To protest against the attack upon the communists and the increasing number of police raids for lodger permits, the location inhabitants called a meeting on Wednesday, January 25, inside the location. Without any warning, the meeting, a large one, was attacked by the police, led by the Superintendent himself flourishing a revolver. A section of the crowd did not run, but answered the police attack with sticks and stones. A number of shots were fired by the Superintendent, possibly by the police. Some eighteen Africans were wounded, five of them seriously. Among the latter was an old woman who was wounded in two places. Later she died of her wounds.

These efforts on the part of the authorities effectively crushed all open agitation against the lodger's tax for the time being. Turton, the Superintendent, was subsequently acquitted on a charge of culpable homicide, arising out of the death of the old Native woman. During the trial *Umsebenzi* reported, "There is a rumour in Germiston that the Native police sergeant, 'Mac,' who took a leading part in breaking up communist meetings some months ago, is now lying dangerously ill in hospital. It is alleged that he was assaulted by the location superintendent because his evidence at the trial was not to the liking of his *baas*. If he lives, perhaps Mac will not be such a good boy in future."

In the meantime, Wolton's principal lieutenant, Lazar Bach, had been sent down to Durban to direct communist activities in Natal. The movement there, what was left of it, was now entirely underground. For this work Bach was well-trained, for he had been an active underground worker in Lithuania, and the South African Communist Party regarded him as its leading expert on subterranean tactics. He sent long reports to the Central Committee about his activities. Some of the statements in the reports were afterwards criticised and declared to be false, but they were probably only the exaggerations of an enthusiastic revolutionary who was prone to see in every little incident evidence of the "ever deepening crisis and the upsurge of the toiling masses."*

The Government continued to tighten up the various laws and regulations by which it proposed to suppress agitation among Africans. At the beginning of 1932 the Natal Native Code was amended and a number of new features added. Alterations of the code apparently did not require an Act of Parliament but could simply be drafted and put into effect by the Native Affairs Department. Three of the new items which the communists considered were particularly directed against the revolutionary movement were described in *Umsebenzi* as follows: "The Governor-General (in practice, the Minister of Native Affairs) now has the right—(1) to suppress agitation against the Government by arresting any Native considered 'dangerous to the public peace,' and without trial imprisoning him for a period of three months, with the right to re-arrest him on a warrant on the same charge at the end of every three months' sentence—that is, to keep Native agitators (revolutionary fighters of the working class and peasantry) in gaol for an indefinite period; (2) to divide or subdivide any tribes or to create new ones (the old imperialist policy of 'pacifying' militant tribes, of granting certain privileges to some tribes in order to divert the growing national revolutionary movement and struggle for land which is developing in the reserves and rural areas into counter-revolutionary inter-tribal wars); (3) to prevent Natives from reading any literature which in the opinion of the 'Supreme Chief' (i.e. the Governor-General) may create agitation among them (aimed to ban the circulation of *Umsebenzi* and all revolutionary organs)."

The first of these regulations amounted to a suppression of the old privilege of *habeas corpus*, at least as far as Natives were concerned. It meant that a Native in Natal (and it seemed that the Natal Code could now apply equally well to the Transvaal and Orange Free State) could now be arrested and imprisoned without trial for as long as the authorities wished. Actually, this new provision of the Natal Native Code has never been put into practice. It remains in the Government's legal armoury for use should it ever be required.

---

* To quote *Umsebenzi*, which by this time consisted mainly of long political theses contributed by the Woltons or by Bach and had thus ceased to be a newspaper in the ordinary sense of the word.

With regard to the second point, it is undoubtedly true that there is still a considerable amount of intertribal fighting in certain parts of Natal. This is in part simply a carry-over from the early days before the white man came. But there is probably some truth in the communist contention that such intertribal warfare (like intercommunal hostility in India) is at least in part due to land hunger and Government interference with Native tribes and chiefs.

The third point, like the first, has never been tried out in practice by the Native Affairs Department. Though copies of *Umsebenzi* may have been quietly seized by the authorities from time to time, there has never been any public notice forbidding the circulation of communist papers in any Native reserve. In 1938, the police destroyed a quantity of literature published by the Watch Tower movement and intended for mine Natives on the Witwatersrand, but as this literature had been imported from abroad they were able to do so under the Customs regulations without reference to any law specially affecting Africans.

Towards the end of 1932, the Durban organisation of the Communist Party was able to establish contact with a number of Native reserves in the surrounding districts. The branch which had been established at Pinetown by an old Xhosa, James Mbete, when he was deported from Durban after the pass-burning, continued to flourish and was the centre from which propaganda was carried on. Groups were started in the reserves at Mlasa, Umgeni and Melevane. At these places, there were a number of fights with police over the confiscation of cattle. The depression was still on and the authorities were resorting to the seizure of cattle in areas where it was found impossible to collect money taxes in the usual way.

On Dingaan's Day, 1932, the communists were particularly active in the country districts near Durban. They issued a leaflet in Zulu calling for demonstrations and mass refusals to pay taxes. Two of the Pinetown members who distributed the leaflet were arrested and sentenced for "inciting to hostility." James Mbete was given six months and E. Dlamini three months. Mike Diamond, brother of Issy Diamond and also a barber, the only white communist in Durban who was not "underground," was arrested and charged before the magistrate with having printed the leaflet on a duplicator discovered by the police in his shop in Durban. Diamond in court made the following statement which was described by the magistrate as "serious": "The Communist Party organises the workers and peasants, black and white, in their struggles for an eight-hour day, higher wages and better conditions, against the rents and taxes, against the confiscation of the cattle from the peasants and the poor by the Government, and against all forms of national oppression. . . . The ultimate aims of the Party are to direct all these struggles of the workers, black and white, into a struggle against imperialist domination and a revolutionary overthrow of imperialism." This was the essence of what had appeared in the Zulu leaflet. Diamond was sentenced to six months' hard labour, but the verdict was quashed and the sentence set aside by the Supreme Court, which held among other things that Diamond could not be held responsible for printing the leaflet simply because a copy was found in his desk at home and a duplicator in his shop.

In August another Pinetown communist, James Ncwangu, was sentenced for "inciting to hostility" because he had urged Africans to refuse to pay taxes and "to refuse to sign themselves into slavery under the Native Service Contract Act." The sentence, twelve months' hard labour, was upheld by the Supreme Court at Maritzburg, which refused to be bound by decisions of the Supreme Court in the Cape Province and the Orange Free State that criticisms of the Government did not constitute an infringement of Clause 29 of the Native Administration Act. Unfortunately, through lack of funds and for want of a sympathetic advocate, it was not possible to lodge an appeal to the Appellate Division, which would almost certainly have set aside the Maritzburg decision.*

Another of Bach's efforts in Durban was his attempt to organise a Seamen and Harbour Workers' Union. This also was very difficult work, for the C.I.D. were always on the look-out to arrest and deport Native agitators. In *Umsebenzi* in January, 1933, it was claimed that the union had organised two successful "go slow" strikes against the "terrific speeding-up at the docks. They organised systematic delays in handling

---

* The decisions of the Natal divison of the Supreme Court are regarded as "bad" by many South African lawyers. On a number of occasions its interpretations have differed from those of the other divisions of the Supreme Court, at Cape Town, Grahamstown, Bloemfontein and Pretoria. Natal, the most English province of the Union of South Africa, has a record for being less liberal in its attitude to Africans than any of the other provinces.

cargo in the holds and on the docks. As a result each gang now performs less than one-third of the work it did previously without any reduction of pay."

Some of the African firemen on the whaling boats joined the Seamen and Harbour Workers' Union, as also did some of the white sailors. The white seamen were mostly Scandinavians and did not share the white South African's prejudices against people of colour. The union claimed to have secured certain improvements in the conditions of the workers on the whaling boats. But whales are hunted for only part of the year and it was found impossible to keep the members of the union together during the off season when the boats did not go out. After Bach's return to Johannesburg, most of the activity in Natal came to an end for the time being.

CHAPTER XXII

UNEMPLOYED AND PICK-UP VAN

THERE FOLLOWED DURING 1933 a sharp decline in communist activity. Two years of intensive bolshevisation had narrowed down party influence and membership almost to vanishing point. The direct interest of the Comintern and the enterprising labours of a handful of enthusiasts had kept things going for a time. But the Woltons, apparently feeling the strain of the constant bannings, prosecutions, imprisonments, left for England at the beginning of 1933, in flagrant defiance of that rigid discipline they had imposed on Party members. Branches continued to function at Johannesburg and Cape Town; subterranean activities continued in Natal; of country branches two only were at all active, at Cradock and Tarkastad in the Eastern Cape Province. It is probable that the total membership in the country was not more than 150 and of these the majority were Europeans.

On the Witwatersrand the only sustained activity was work among the African unemployed. Two new communist functionaries had recently come into the limelight. Both had come into the Party through the Pretoria Branch. Afterwards they were transferred to Johannesburg to fill vacancies in the Central Committee. They were rough and ready proletarians, not tribalists but location-born, and both were possessed of some gifts of speech and considerable enthusiasm and sincerity. Later enthusiasm for struggle and sacrifice declined and sincerity became corrupted while energies were bent to the difficult task of holding down a job in a party where factional struggle was becoming another symptom of decay. But in the time before they were overwhelmed by their new environment, Stephen Tefu and Peter Ramutla put up a good fight for the Bantu unemployed. Ramutla had himself suffered a year's confinement in a prison camp. Arrested while addressing a communist meeting in Pretoria and charged with vagrancy, he was unable to prove that he was working for a white *baas* or that he had a daily labourer's pass, and was accordingly sentenced to detention in a labour camp. The prisoners were set to road-making. The camp moved from place to place. When finally released, Ramutla walked forty miles back to Pretoria.

Unemployment had become very bad by the middle of 1933. Drought and the economic crisis had combined to drive thousands of Africans to the Witwatersrand. Even the labour market on the mines was glutted for the first time in history. The authorities admitted that at least 5,000 Natives were unemployed on the Rand. That is to say that 5,000 Natives were in receipt of "permits to seek work." Thousands were in gaol for breaches of the pass and poll tax regulations. Thousands more, illegally resident in town, led a precarious existence, trying as far as possible to keep out of the clutches of the police. A member of the Johannesburg City Council, A. Immink, declared that in October, 1937, there were "93,000 Natives in Johannesburg and on the Reef who live by their wits, sleep with their friends at night, and are not included in the census."*

So in 1933 it seemed good to the communists to start a soup kitchen in Ferreirastown. They raised enough money to pay the rent, but there was not enough to buy food. So the unemployed were organised to collect food and money from door to door. For a time the soup kitchen flourished. But in March, when a crowd of African unemployed were marching through the streets with their banner, collecting food, a number of them were arrested and charged with holding an illegal procession. Owing to some flaw in the Crown evidence, they

* Quoted by Ray Phillips in *The Bantu in the City*.

270

were discharged by the magistrate, who informed them that they must in future obtain a permit from the Johannesburg City Council if they wished to hold a procession. Accordingly, a week or so later, formal application was made for a permit. This was refused by the Town Clerk, no reason being given. On Saturday, April 15, they decided that, permit or no permit, they needed food, and a number of them went from door to door in President Street with a collecting box. They were soon spied by the police, who came and placed the man with the box under arrest. His comrades demanded his release, and, when this was refused, tried to rescue him. Police reinforcements came up and a general fight began, in which the unemployed defended themselves heroically. A number on both sides received severe injuries. Eventually the police got the upper hand and arrested a number of the unemployed. They then proceeded to raid the office of the Communist Party, where further arrests were made. During the fight a number of shots were fired by detectives "to frighten the crowd" as they said.*

Among those arrested was Stephen Tefu. Giving evidence at the trial, Tefu said: "These Natives were a few of the 5,000 workless Natives in Johannesburg who had been compelled by drought, the failure of harvests and the urgency of finding money for taxes, to leave their kraals, gradually drifting to the Witwatersrand in a vain hope of finding some work. The only alternative many Natives had to this drift to the towns was to be arrested for non-payment of taxes. . . . It was among these people that the Communist Party was active, and he . . . had interviewed deputations and many individuals all complaining about the prevalent distress.

"I was at the Communist Hall that day," he said, "when one of the accused told me that the leader of the procession had been arrested. That was the first I heard of the affair. With another communist I walked down to the scene of the conflict between the Natives and the police. I was on the opposite side of the street to the place where some of the accused were on a vacant stand. As I stood there, I saw a policeman shoot about three times and saw stones flying as the police advanced in great numbers on the crowd. As I stood there, a detective caught hold of me by the jacket and gave me a punch in the jaw. Five teeth were knocked out. I was knocked unconscious.

* *Umsebenzi,* May 1, 1933.

When I came to, my head, my arms and my ears were bleeding.

"We were handcuffed and marched to Marshall Square, where we were taken to the charge office. There was a Native police boy and he beat us all brutally with a stick. He did this in the presence of the sergeant in charge and several detectives and policemen. One of the sergeants told the boy not to be so harsh, but otherwise no one interfered. The boy said we were catching it for what we had done in the street."*

The prisoners were sentenced to six weeks' hard labour for public violence and to one week's hard labour for holding an illegal procession.

The activity of the police in stopping the collection of food and money from door to door finally put an end to the soup kitchen. An attempt was then made to persuade the authorities to provide food. Some hundreds of unemployed slept at the barracks at the Central Pass Office. It was comparatively easy to get them together. Big meetings were held in the streets outside the Chief Native Commissioner's Office. A deputation called upon that official and asked that food should be given to all the unemployed who needed it. Previously a small quantity of mealie meal had been given to a few specially needy or favoured persons. After the agitation, the authorities were for a time more generous and served a cup of dry meal per day to those living in the barracks. When urged by the deputation to supply soup as well, the Native Commissioner said that his department was not in favour of supplying appetising meals, as this might lead to a further influx of Natives into the towns.

In September, 1933, the communists again attempted to stage a joint demonstration of black and white unemployed. This affair is described in *Umsebenzi* (October 7, 1933) as "the most important event of its kind since May Day, 1931."† About 2,000 unemployed workers demonstrated, of whom about one-third were Europeans and the rest Africans. Communist influence over the white unemployed depended always upon their having some popular white leader. The great majority of the white unemployed being Dutch

* Report in Johannesburg *Star*, May 5, 1933.

† May Day, 1931, the occasion on which Diamond led a demonstration of black and white unemployed to the Carlton Hotel and the Rand Club, where they demanded food. A tussle with the police led to Diamond's arrest. Charged with incitement to violence, he was convicted and sentenced to one year's imprisonment.

Afrikaners, it was an advantage, though not always a necessity, for such a leader to be an Afrikaner and for him to address them in their own language. Almost all Afrikaners in the towns are quite capable of understanding an English speaker; but it is usually only an Afrikaner who can rouse them to action. Diamond was the exception in this respect.* Now, among white communists Afrikaners were not usually to be found, but in 1933 Gideon Botha arrived in Johannesburg.

Botha was an interesting character. In his young days he had travelled abroad. He had met Jack London when hobo-ing in America. Back in South Africa, he had worked on the Rand mines and taken part in the great strikes of 1913, 1914 and 1922. At the time of the Great War, he had joined the International Socialist League in Johannesburg and had figured on this platform as one of the few Afrikaner speakers. After this, he had disappeared from politics for some years, lived in the country, mixed a good deal with Africans and come to like them. Now in 1933 he returned to Johannesburg and approached the communists who were working among the African and European unemployed.

So in 1933, it was Gideon Botha who led the white unemployed. It had been announced in the Press that a number of Nationalist Cabinet Ministers, including Hertzog, Pirow, Grobler and Fourie, would be in Johannesburg on September 25, and that they would be staying at the Carlton Hotel. It was decided that the unemployed should call upon the Ministers to ask them to introduce relief measures. The whites assembled at the City Hall steps and began their meeting there. The Natives gathered at the Central Pass Office and from there marched to the City Hall. When they arrived there, they began a separate meeting some little distance away from the other one. There was a tense moment when "a racially minded white worker called upon the whites to attack the Native meeting. But Gideon Botha sprang to the front and, speaking in Afrikaans, pointed out that the Native meeting was not a hostile but a parallel one, that the starving Natives were also intent on seeing the Ministers and particularly the Minister of Native Affairs (Grobler), and that it was up to the whites to support the Natives in their struggle. This advice was received

* In spite of the initial handicap with Afrikaners of his being Jewish, Diamond's lively speeches and the rough and ready wit with which he disarmed hecklers never failed to carry the crowd, of whatever nationality.

with approval by the overwhelming majority of the white unemployed, and during the remainder of the morning there was the utmost solidarity and goodwill between the two sections."*

The two meetings then united their forces and marched to the Carlton Hotel. Failing to find the Ministers there, they proceeded to the offices of the Nationalist Party. At this point, the crowd in the street numbered over 3,000. Again it proved impossible to ascertain the whereabouts of the Ministers. The demonstration marched back to the City Hall steps, where a joint meeting was held. The chief speakers were Botha and Tefu on behalf of the white and black sections respectively. Tefu, speaking fluent English, received an ovation from the meeting, not only from the Natives, but also from the white unemployed. Before the meeting closed, it was decided to gather again on the same spot in the evening in order to go to Beckett's Building, where, it had been announced, the Ministers would be attending a meeting of the Nationalist Party.

But from the interracial point of view the evening meeting did not repeat the success of the morning one. The extreme anti-black section among the Afrikaners had evidently been taken off its guard by the events of the morning. During the afternoon it organised its forces so that in the evening the communists met with definite opposition from a section of the whites. It soon appeared that the police also had worked out a plan for putting a stop to such demonstrations of unity between black and white. When the meeting was opened, the anti-blacks, led by Mostert, then Editor of *Forward*, the only white labour paper, attempted to create a diversion, but without success, the majority continuing to listen to Botha. Suddenly a body of police appeared round the corner of the City Hall and without warning attacked the meeting with batons. In a few minutes the Native unemployed had been driven from the scene. The police had carefully singled out the Natives and had refrained from striking the whites. The police having thus cleared the ground for them, Mostert and his supporters captured the platform.

Under such conditions, with both police and white reactionaries against them, the communists now found that joint activity of black and white unemployed was practically impossible to organise.

* *Umsebenzi* report.

At the end of 1933, the communist paper, *Umsebenzi*, took on a new lease of life. Under Moscow tutelage, it had enjoyed since 1931 a hectic career, extra large special editions alternating with long periods when the paper, nominally a fortnightly, failed to appear at all. Its contents, formerly consisting mainly of news items from everywhere, had been under Wolton largely abstruse political essays. Now it was enlarged and converted into a weekly paper. At the same time, since the leading theoreticians had gone, it became more readable.

The expansion of *Umsebenzi* in 1933 and 1934 meant a great improvement in communist propaganda among the Bantu masses. During the interval since 1930, *Umsebenzi*, once the most widely-circulating of Bantu papers, had been eclipsed by other Bantu newspapers, notably by *Umteteli wa Bantu* (The Mouthpiece of the Bantu) and the *Bantu World*, both of which had built up considerable circulations. Now *Umsebenzi* forged ahead and soon claimed once more to be the most widely read of Bantu newspapers.

Hitherto not much attention had been paid to a most important section of the Africans, what has sometimes been called the Bantu intelligentsia. There are in South Africa some thousands of African teachers, clerks, minor officials and other *petit bourgeoisie*. It has been noted that the bulk of the African voters in the Transkei were of this class and how Bunting had tried and largely failed to win their support. The slogan of a "Native Republic" was supposed to be aimed at winning over these people. In practice, it failed to do so. The violent attacks made by communists upon all Native leaders and intellectuals, except the extreme leftists, attacks which dubbed them "reformists" and "good boys," had made it very difficult to get their sympathy and support. *Umsebenzi* too had failed to interest them.

New methods, however, brought about a change. A style more informative, less vituperative and less violently dogmatic, the revival of educational activities, the discussion of such problems as "the new Bantu orthography,"* "What should we call ourselves—Bantu, Africans or Natives?" health, and

---

* The various languages of the Bantu family had been first put into writing by missionaries of different nationalities, who compiled dictionaries and translated the Bible for their converts. In many cases different symbols had been used by the French, German, Swiss and English missionaries to represent the same sound. Attempts were now being made to introduce a new universal orthography.

so forth, attracted the interest of numbers of African teachers. The communists started a special magazine, cyclostyled, for Bantu teachers and students. Known as *Indlela Yenkululeko* (The Road to Freedom), the little magazine, written mostly in English, enjoyed a fair circulation among the Fort Hare students. *Umsebenzi* reports in August, 1933, that "white communists have visited Fort Hare in the Ciskei, the only Native university college in South Africa, and addressed meetings of the students." They were secret meetings, held in the bush, for the college authorities had gated the students to prevent them from attending a public meeting held in the village.

Numbers of African teachers now became subscribers to *Umsebenzi*. Others became agents for the sale of the paper. Some of the latter suffered victimisation. They were warned that they would be dismissed if they continued to circulate the paper. In October, 1934, N. J. M. Shoko, an African teacher at Plumtree in Southern Rhodesia, who sold copies of *Umsebenzi*, was deported by the Rhodesian authorities to Bechuanaland. The police confiscated all copies of the paper in his possession. He was taken to the Bechuanaland border and there released. Apart from teachers, other African intellectuals who became interested in *Umsebenzi* were to be found among the numerous class of independent ministers and religious leaders. Ministers of the African Methodist Episcopalian Church were prominent in this group. They were, of course, free from the supervision of white missionaries and supervisors and thus able to profess any political faith they pleased.

The communists found that anti-religious propaganda in the sense of attacks upon theological beliefs did not meet with any ready welcome among Africans. The belief in a supernatural world of spirits who interfere frequently in the affairs of mankind is, of course, universal among the tribal Bantu. The Christian God, the Devil and the angels are accepted by them usually without question as being in the nature of things, and take their place quite naturally among the hosts of the ancestral spirits, Tikoloshe, Mpundulu and other denizens of the spirit world. Communists who denied the existence of a god or gods caused amazement and simetimes fear. To behave thus was as if to invite a thunderbolt to strike one down. Nevertheless, rationalism has claimed some converts among the Bantu.

At the same time criticism of the missionary and of the average white Christian was readily understood and usually acceptable. It was plain for all to see that white Churches, even some of the most liberal among them, practised the colour bar. Here were Christians in name, but not in deed. "The missionaries told us to close our eyes and pray," Africans often say. "We did so. When we opened our eyes we found that the white man had taken away our land." The communists readily developed this form of propaganda, while at the same time trying to cast doubt on the missionary's theological beliefs as well.

But as time went on the communists began to realise that making war upon the missionaries, though many of them enjoyed it exceedingly, was not good tactics. The latter were in many ways the natural allies of the communists and the only other disinterested friends the Africans had in the country. Anti-religious propaganda had to be dropped, and the communists found that it was possible on certain issues to make a united front with some of the parsons. One of the first attempts at this form of co-operation occurred during the campaign against the pick-up van.

The pick-up was described in *Umsebenzi* in November, 1933, in the following terms: ". . . At any time of the day or night, but mostly during the week-ends, when people are not working and are visiting their friends in the locations, the police came out in a motor van. They proceed to any populous locality, jump out of the van and arrest anyone they can lay their hands on. The arrested persons (all Natives, of course) are bundled into the van, often seriously assaulted in the process, taken to the lock-up, and brought before the magistrate the next morning. There is no difficulty in laying charges—it is always possible to find that any African man or woman at any time falls foul of one or other of the thousand and one oppressive laws and regulations that constitute the glorious heritage of South African civilisation. Accordingly, the persons arrested are charged with contravening the pass laws, poll tax ordinance, liquor laws, urban areas act, location regulations, etc., etc. If the police are at a loss, they can always charge them with being drunk or noisy.

"The magistrate sentences them in batches of ten or twenty at a time. (A magistrate is considered efficient if he can polish off a couple of hundred cases in an hour or two!)

Usually fines are inflicted with alternative imprisonment, and every effort is made to get the prisoners to pay up. We even know of cases (and are prepared to substantiate them by witness) where people who had money in their possession when arrested preferred to go to gaol rather than pay fines, and where the police have practically forced the money from them and refused to allow them to serve sentences."

Umsebenzi goes on to allege that the chief motive of the pick-up van is an economic one, an attempt to swell the revenue brought in by the police department. Though it says that an additional motive is an idea that "the growing discontent and 'uppishness' of the Native population must be met by a policy of 'frightfulness.' " The paper advocated the formation of "defence committees" in the locations as a means of combating the activities of the pick-up van.

In December, 1933, the slogan, "To Hell with the Pick-up!" was devised. Large posters with these words were stuck up at night in prominent places in Johannesburg. A cartoon in *Umsebenzi* showed a motor van with the label "s.a. pick-up ltd. Coalition Van." In the van were a number of Africans, while members of the Cabinet were depicted as police in charge of the van. Dingaan's Day, December 16, was announced as a special day of protest against the pick-up and police brutality. Mass meetings were advertised to be held at the City Hall steps and in the locations. For speeches delivered at some of these meetings, Roux was arrested and charged with incitement to violence. In the course of the trial the communists tried to lead evidence with regard to the activities of the pick-up van, but such evidence was disallowed by the magistrate as having no bearing on the case. Roux admitted having said: "How can we fight against the pick-up? By organising a defence committee in every location throughout the country. These committees should be on a united front basis and should have representatives from all the different African organisations, including the Churches. Scouts should be sent out to report the approach of the vans. If the police commit assaults upon people, people should resist. I know that what I am saying may be interpreted as advocating defiance of the police, but in view of what I have told you about the pick-up I think the location people would be justified in defending themselves against these brutal attacks. . . . We are out to smash the pick-up, to put an end to the

278

brutal warfare the Government is making upon location inhabitants. The people must stand together and adopt a militant attitude." The accused was found guilty on two counts of incitement to violence and sentenced to four months' imprisonment with hard labour, with an alternative fine of £40. In the course of an address to the court, Roux drew attention to the reign of police terror to which the Native people of South Africa are subjected. He stated that "Bands of armed hooligans are terrorising the people in the locations. In the ordinary course of events, one would appeal to the police authorities for protection against hooligans, but in this case we cannot do that, as the hooligans are the police themselves. I have shown that the police authorities are fully aware of what is going on. It is significant that though many articles have appeared in the Press asking for a commission of inquiry into police brutality, the Government has done absolutely nothing about it. In the circumstances, I think we are justified in calling upon location inhabitants to organise to defend themselves against these assaults and even to arm themselves if necessary."

An unsuccessful appeal against the conviction was made to the Supreme Court, where it was argued by the appellant that the detectives who gave evidence at the trial had distorted much of what the speaker had said at the meeting. The court held, however, that there was even in the accused's report of his own speech sufficient evidence to convict him. And the "To Hell with the Pick-up!" poster was in itself considered an incitement to violence.

In the meantime the communists attempted to call a "united conference on Native disabilities, with special reference to assaults committed on Natives by the police." Invitations were sent to a number of organisations and prominent persons of liberal views, but few were prepared to associate publicly with the communists in this matter. Among those who responded were W. G. Ballinger and the Rev. Dexter Taylor, of the American Board of Missions. The conference decided that as the Government had plainly no intention of holding an official inquiry into the conduct of the police and the activities of the pick-up van, it would itself appoint a commission of inquiry. A committee was therefore set up and instructed to obtain the services of a number of prominent citizens who would be in sufficiently good standing with the white public to make the results of such an inquiry worth publishing. It would naturally have been easy enough to get a commission of communists and well-known nigrophiles, but the findings of such a commission would have carried little weight with the authorities. Various prominent persons were approached, including an ex-chief magistrate, but none was willing to serve. Finally, the project had to be abandoned.

The communists found it difficult to get authenticated reports of unlawful acts by the police. The general activities of the police were perfectly legal. If in the course of pass law, liquor and poll tax raids they displayed a certain animus against the Natives, that was only to be expected. It was the laws themselves which were at fault. Attempts to show that the police had exceeded their authority on a number of occasions really did not go to the root of the matter. In any case, it was very difficult to get African witnesses who could stand up to hostile cross-examination in court. African communists themselves would have made better witnesses than the average rank and filers who suffered at the hands of the police. The latter, however, showed an uncanny skill in avoiding overt acts of brutality in the presence of communists who might report them. Under the heading "Police Drop a Hot Potato," the following appeared in *Umsebenzi* on January 13, 1934: "On Monday, January 8, Johannes Molefe was in Jeppe Street, Johannesburg, looking for work, when he met a number of Native members of the C.I.D. led by a white detective, whose nickname is 'Sporting' (from his habit of wearing a sports coat when on duty). They demanded Molefe's pass. He produced a pass, but was declared under arrest and handcuffed. A large number of Natives had already been arrested by the patrol, and the lot were marched about the streets for many hours while further arrests were made. Molefe met a friend *en route*. To him he handed his *Ikaka* (Labour Defence*) membership card and asked him to take it to the *Ikaka* office, so that arrangements might be made for his legal defence. Molefe then began to write down on a piece of paper, a difficult job when handcuffed by one wrist to a fellow-prisoner, the names of all the streets through which they were being forced to march. The African detectives noticed this and informed 'Sporting' of the activities of this unusual prisoner. 'Sporting,' realising

* *Ikaka labaSebenzi*, branch of International Red Aid (a Communist Organisation) undertook the defence of arrested Africans.

that he had caught a tartar, said: 'He's a communist—we had better let him go.' Whereupon Molefe was released."

The Johannesburg Joint Council of Europeans and Africans, while not prepared to join with the "reds" in public meetings of protest, did try to draw public attention to the evils of the pick-up. Some of its members put forward the idea of a "public defender" for Africans. There was some talk of getting a panel of lawyers who would be prepared to give their services free in cases where it seemed that Africans were not likely to secure an adequate trial if not legally represented. But few of the liberal lawyers seemed to like the idea. If every Native case were argued fully, the whole system of "justice" would get clogged with prisoners awaiting trial. Instead of being able to polish off Native cases at the usual speed of a few dozen per hour, the magistrates would have to listen to arguments in each case; witnesses in numbers might be called. It would be doubtful whether they would be able to dispose of more than three or four cases in a day. The lawyers who conducted such cases gratis would be accused of sabotage, even treason. Besides, the law societies would object on trade union grounds if any of their members made a habit of working without pay. The panel of lawyers could not be obtained. The scheme fell through.*

One of the members of the Joint Council, a Mr. Ramsbottom, himself an advocate, did carry a particular case through to the Supreme Court. It was alleged that Ramsbottom's African servant Salatiel was standing on a street corner one Sunday evening when a pick-up van appeared on the scene. The police jumped out and bundled him into the van. At the charge office, he was accused of being drunk. Ramsbottom had been told of the arrest and hastened to the charge office. On learning the nature of the charge, he telephoned for a doctor, who certified that Salatiel was not drunk. The police argued with the doctor and maintained that the man was still under the influence of alcohol. In the magistrate's court, Ramsbottom, the doctor and the police all gave evidence. The magistrate, trying to please all parties, found Salatiel guilty, cautioned and discharged him. Ramsbottom took the case to the Supreme Court where he secured a verdict of "Not guilty."

* Some years later a Legal Aid Bureau was established in Johannesburg on the initiative of the Institute of Race Relations. This body has functioned on lines similar to those of the Poor Man's Lawyer in England. Its services are given mostly to Africans, though it helps Europeans also.

Commenting on the case, *Umsebenzi* remarked: "Every African who is wrongfully arrested by the pick-up on a trumped-up charge has not got a liberal lawyer for an employer. Nor is it possible to bring a doctor's evidence to prove the police are liars. Thousands, we believe, are arrested in this way. The magistrate believes the police evidence and they go to gaol or are fined. We can only fight the pick-up in an organised fashion." There followed further appeals to attend anti-pick-up conferences.

Nothing came of the conferences. Further communist agitation led to the arrest of Ramutla, Tefu and Chuenyane. They were charged with "promoting feelings of hostility," and Ramutla was sentenced to five months' imprisonment, two months being without the option of a fine. The others were discharged.

The communist agitation died down, but feeling against the police did not. Some years later an event took place which did at last cause the Government to sit up and take notice. On Sunday, September 19, 1937, the police made one of their usual raids on the location at Vereeniging. It seems that police raids had for some time been growing in frequency and the police were becoming more than usually brutal. On this occasion, they encountered what appears to have been organised resistance. The previous day police raiding the location for illicit beer had been stoned, two or three of them being hit. On the next morning, Sunday, the police again visited the location with a pick-up van "and it was at once apparent that the Natives were in defiant mood."* The police officer withdrew his men and asked for reinforcements from the neighbouring villages of Heidelberg and Evaton. When these arrived, the police entered the location for the third time. "Several thousand Natives," according to the newspaper report, attacked them with stones. The police were compelled to retire, but the pick-up van was cut off and surrounded. It was bombarded with stones, overturned and thrown against a fence. Two white constables and one African policeman were battered to death. The remaining police were eventually rescued by reinforcements armed with rifles and bayonets. A number of Africans, including women, were seriously wounded by rifle fire, but none was killed.

The reactions of the authorities to this practical protest

* *Star*, September 20, 1937.

against the pick-up raids were by no means so violent as some had expected. The local police immediately arrested 450 of the location inhabitants. Thousands of others left the location fearing that their turn would come next. Now, Vereeniging is a very important industrial centre. Its power station supplies electricity to the Witwatersrand gold mines. There is an important iron and steel works and there are other large factories. The flight of some thousand of workers had an immediate effect on these industrial plants, which found it impossible to carry on without labourers. A hasty telegram from the Government headquarters at Pretoria ordered the police to release the Natives, and the use of the pick-up van was thereafter discontinued. Almost unwittingly, the masses had demonstrated that strike action on a large scale at any time brings the Government to its senses.

Some of the local whites organised a demonstration in Vereeniging Market Square. Fascist Grey Shirts* roused the white farmers in the surrounding district and hundreds poured in on wagons and in motor cars. Grey Shirt speakers declared that the communists and the Jews were responsible for the riot. An unfortunate African who rode on to the square on a bicycle was pursued and attacked. He was later admitted to the hospital suffering from serious injuries. Wherever Africans appeared on the streets, they were assaulted. General Smuts was invited to attend the meeting, but he did not come. On the contrary, he gave orders to the police that assaults on Natives must stop. The reign of terror did not at that time suit the employers, who were trying to coax their workers back.

A number of Africans who had participated in the attack on the police were eventually placed on trial. A Jewish lawyer who was briefed to defend the prisoners was threatened by the fascists. The Law Society protested against this attempt to interfere with the right of every prisoner to legal representation. Three hundred farmers met in Vereeniging and decided to boycott the attorneys who were defending the prisoners. The attorneys had been warned, one speaker said, but they had not listened. I. Rautenbach, one of the fascist leaders, declared that he "had written to a firm of Vereeniging attorneys. He had not wanted them to defend the Natives, he

*The Grey Shirts were an openly pro-Hitler organisation, led by Weichardt, a South African of German descent. Weichardt was interned by the Government during the Second World War.

said, for everyone in the district wished to show sympathy towards the families of the murdered men—to deprecate the action of the Natives. And yet there were at least two offices in Vereeniging who were not prepared to carry out the wishes of the farmers." Another member of the "committee," K. Barnard, said "he did not wish to oppress the Natives, but it was the duty of every person, whether he was an Englishman, an Afrikaner or a Jew, to see that the Native lived to-day as he had lived in the time of Oom Paul [Kruger]. The Natives were satisfied in those days. When punishment was necessary, it was meted out adequately. 'We must consider this matter most seriously,' he said. 'We must make this country fit for our children to live in' " (*Rand Daily Mail*, October 14, 1937).

It is noteworthy that it was the farmers in the surrounding districts who made most of the rumpus. It was not only the traditional nigrophobia of the Dutch Afrikaner that was roused; there was also a strong feeling that the Africans had no right to be there in Vereeniging at all, earning the higher wages paid by industry. Their proper place was on the farms working for the Boers. The labour shortage in the country districts was a perennial source of annoyance to the farmers. By 1937 the depression of 1932-3 had given way to an unprecedented boom based on the enhanced price of gold.

The leading English newspapers deprecated the attempts to intimidate lawyers briefed for the defence. The court gave what may in the circumstances be considered very light sentences. It was anticipated by many that at least some of those who had attacked the police would hang for it. Of the fifty-four charged, only eleven were sentenced. The heaviest sentence was seven years' imprisonment for two of the convicted, another received four years and the rest lighter sentences.

The Secretary for Native Affairs reported for the Commission of Inquiry into the location disturbances. He found that there was no justification for the "brutal murder of the constables." But at the same time, the Government tacitly acknowledged that the police in the country as a whole were behaving with unnecessary violence in their treatment of Natives. A circular from the Minister of Justice instructed the police to exercise more restraint in handling Native offenders in future.

Liberals who had prophesied a general massacre of Africans

284

if the latter should take militant action were proved false prophets. The South African Youth movement, a Government sponsored organisation, appealed to whites not to show animus. Possibly the industrial boom and the shortage of Native labour helped to make people more tolerant. The Prime Minister, General Hertzog, made it clear that the riot had produced no fundamental change in the attitude of the authorities. "Those who delight in protecting the Native in his wrongdoing against the white man, as was apparent recently in connection with the Vereeniging crime, and encourage him by ridiculing the laws of the country and making accusations against the police while the latter are maintaining law and order, should be reminded that we are dealing here with the place of the Native, not in a Native territory, but in the land of the white man where the white man shall rule and shall have the right to live safely and peacefully. Nobody compels the Native to settle in this territory [the speaker had evidently forgotten the poll tax and other provisions which force the Native to leave the Native territories and come to work for the whites—E. R.] but if he does so it is demanded from him that he shall respect the white man and obey the laws of the country. . . . I would again like to assure the Native that the white man entertains for him the greatest goodwill and friendly feelings, and that the white man is quite determined to carry out faithfully that fatherly care which had been promised to the Native ever since the laying of the foundations of the white man's settlement in South Africa. . . . I would, however, warn him at the same time that the white man to-day is just as determined as in the days of the pioneers that the control of the country will be held by the European under the influence of European civilisation, and that, just as little as a father in his own home would allow a minor to rule the house, would the white man of the Union allow the government of the Union and its people to be held by the Native, or that the Native would be given any authority within or over the government of the country. Whatever may be said to the contrary by mischief-makers or by stupid white people, I wish to warn the Native that whoever is so presumptuous as to claim equal authority with the white man in the Union will experience the greatest measure of disappointment and failure."

It is interesting that, in spite of this warning and prophecy, the movement for the emancipation of the black man in South Africa still continues.

Interesting too to compare the whole Vereeniging affair, when white police were deliberately attacked and done to death, with the pass-burning on Cartwright's Flats at Durban in 1930. At Vereeniging the resistance was violent, the sentences comparatively mild. At Durban the police attacked a gathering of passive resisters, killed four of them and injured many, then brought charges of "incitement to violence" against others. What emerges from these considerations is that the situation is always complex. Success or failure, light sentences or heavy reprisals, these depend on the whole situation of the moment, on the need that the white man has of the African as a labourer in factory and farm.

CHAPTER XXIII

SOUTH AFRICA PUTS THE CLOCK BACK

GENERAL HERTZOG'S NATIVE BILLS, first formulated in 1925, were published in 1926 and in 1927 referred to a Select Committee. The Committee toured the country and collected evidence. It was more than a decade before the Bills were presented to Parliament, and in the interval they had undergone much chopping and changing. There were originally four Bills. The Representation of Natives Bill aimed at abolishing the Cape Native vote completely, and by way of "compensation" a second Bill promised to the Natives of the whole Union a degree of representation by white senators. The third Bill took the form of an amendment to the Native Land Act of 1913. In 1916 a commission had been appointed to delimit certain additional areas which were to be added to the Native reserves. For various reasons, the additional land was not forthcoming. Now it was proposed to carry out the promise made in 1916 and originally suggested in 1913. The Bill proposed also to set up a Union Native Council which the Government would be able to consult in connection with Native Affairs. The fourth Bill, known as the Coloured Persons Rights Bill, aimed at taking away the franchise from the Coloured people in the Cape and placing the

Coloured voters on a separate roll. This last Bill was subsequently dropped.

Evidence was given before the Select Committee by a large number of persons, representing all shades of political opinion. White liberal opinion was chiefly represented by the Joint Councils. Evidence was given on behalf of the Johannesburg Joint Council by Howard Pim and Professor Macmillan (whites) and by Selope Thema (African). African Churches, the African National Congress, the Cape Native Voters' Association and other African organisations also sent representatives to state their case. The most important African witnesses were Professor Jabavu, Dr. Rubusana and Rev. Mahabane. Their evidence, however, did not produce any marked effect on the Select Committee.

Finally, at the end of 1935, the Bills, now reduced to two, were presented to a joint sitting of both houses of Parliament. The Bills in their new form proposed that no more Natives were to be allowed to register as voters in the Cape Province. The 11,000 on the roll would be allowed to keep their vote, so that the Cape Native franchise would eventually disappear through natural causes. The Natives of the whole Union would be allowed to elect, by indirect means, four white members of the Senate. In the Cape Provincial elections the Natives would be placed on a separate roll and would be entitled to two representatives on the provincial council who must be Europeans. In addition, the Bill proposed to establish a Union Native Representative Council consisting of twenty-two members, including the Minister of Native Affairs as Chairman. Of the twenty-one, five would be (European) Native Commissioners. The remaining sixteen would be Natives, but only twelve would be elected, four being appointed by the Governor-General—that is, the Government. The election of the twelve would be vested in electoral colleges consisting of chiefs, headmen and members of district councils and location advisory boards. The Native rank and file would thus have no direct vote. This council would have the right to pass opinions on proposed legislation affecting Natives, but the Government would not be bound to conform to its decisions.

All the above proposals were contained in the first Bill, the Native Representation Bill. The second Bill, embodying modifications of the 1913 Land Act, was called the Native

Land and Trust Bill. It proposed to set up a board of trustees which would acquire for the Natives, with moneys voted from time to time by Parliament, some seven million morgen of land. When these were acquired, they would increase the existing Native Reserves by about 50 per cent., thus allowing the Natives a total of about 12 per cent. of the land of the Union. It was understood that the Natives would have to be content with this for all time. Simultaneously the right still possessed by Africans in the Cape Province to buy land outside the reserves was to be abolished.

At once African political organisations throughout the country prepared to fight the new measures. There was a remarkable degree of unanimity. Organisations which had previously opposed each other now agreed to work together. An All-African National Convention was announced for December 16 (Dingaan's Day), 1935, at Bloemfontein. Professor Jabavu, Kadalie and other Bantu leaders arrived in Johannesburg to organise a unity campaign. The Johannesburg office of the Communist Party became their headquarters. The lion and the lamb lay down together. Over 400 delegates gathered at Bloemfontein. There was only one outstanding traitor: the Rev. John Dube publicly declared himself in favour of the Bills. But who cared for Dube? He was known to be a Government man. The meeting passed resolutions rejecting the Bills. "The proposals for the establishment of the Union Native Representative Council are not acceptable to this Convention, for they are no substitute for the Cape Native franchise. . . . The Government already has the machinery provided by the Native Affairs Act (of 1920) through which it has power to consult the Native people on matters and legislation affecting their interests." There was equally unanimous opposition to the proposed changes in the Cape provincial system.

While welcoming an increase in the area of the reserves, the Convention pointed to "the gross inadequacy of the morgenage of seven millions which it is proposed to set out as a minimum amount of land to be acquired by the Native Land Trust to be established under the Bill. When it is further borne in mind that even if this morgenage were to be made available, it would secure to the Native population only about seventeen million morgen out of 143 million morgen in the Union, and would fail to take into account the needs of an increasing

Native population. . . . The fact that this aim is ignored . . . can only be interpreted by the African people as an attempt to force them into a position of economic dependency."

All this was very well. The Convention was able to put up excellent arguments against the Government's Bills. But it was clear, at least to the left wing, that something more than arguments would have to be put forward if the bills were not to become law. And here a tremendous contrast revealed itself. There were over 400 delegates present. But what did they represent in the way of effective organisation? The years of collapse and disintegration had played havoc with the once powerful organisations of the Congress and the I.C.U. The 400 delegates represented very little but themselves. Most of them had no idea of stirring up the countryside. In vain the communists and other radicals pleaded for militant action, for strikes, for passive resistance. They were cold-shouldered into silence. The "big guns" of the Convention were all for negotiation and moderation. The communists called mass meetings in different centres. There was a very poor response. Try as they might, they could not rouse the masses even to effective demonstrations, let alone to strikes and passive resistance. An Afrikaner paper proclaimed in newspaper placards: "*Naturelle bly stil*" (Natives remain quiet). It was only too true; the masses did not act.

At Cape Town there were deputations and lobbying. Rheinallt Jones and Sir James Rose Innes were there leading a group organised by the Institute of Race Relations and the Joint Councils. A "National Conference on the Native Bills" was held in Cape Town. The conference issued a pamphlet which asked whether the proposal to abolish the Cape Native franchise was wise. "Whether the proposal is wise or unwise depends, presumably, on whether it is likely to benefit present and future generations of South Africa. It would be proper to consider the matter from the standpoint of the interests of all sections of the community, but we propose to assume that the interests of the European section are of paramount importance, and to propound the question, 'How should a European of robust common sense, who is mindful only of his own interests and those of his descendants, decide whether the Cape Native Franchise should be abolished or not?' " There followed the usual arguments. "If it be accepted that the Natives must be given some political power [but it was not accepted. E. R.]

it is surely better from the European point of view that this should come by allowing individual Natives to exercise the vote as and when they reach a certain level of civilisation than that a separate organisation of solidly race-conscious Natives should be forced into being . . . But the hard-headed European whose point of view we are investigating would doubtless take account of the possibility that, on a common roll the white vote might some day be 'swamped' by the black vote. That is of course, proper matter for consideration, but it must be treated soberly and without panic. . . . Any system which makes for a higher standard of living tends towards a lower birth rate. . . . The method of raising the required qualification to prevent such 'swamping' has Cape precedent in its favour, and could be used again if required. The figures show beyond question that even on an admittedly low qualification basis, the idea of 'swamping' is a mere bogy. The Native vote in the Cape Province amounts to approximately 1 per cent. of the whole Union electorate. It would be simplicity itself to control the number of Native voters by relating the franchise to the attainment of recognised school standard with or without an income or property qualification."

It was clear that opposition of this type could rouse little enthusiasm among the Natives themselves. Nor did it provide an effective answer to the nigrophobes. Since the opposition had agreed that precautions should be taken against the Natives ever securing a majority or even a substantial minority of votes in the Cape, the best thing from the anti-swamping point of view was to abolish the Cape Native vote once and for all. Members of Parliament would thus not be bothered in the future with having to raise the qualification for Natives from time to time as necessity arose.*

The Joint Councils' point of view, as expressed in this document, was not based on the essential justice of the Natives' ultimate right to a majority in Parliament. It was simply the old Cape "liberalism" over again, the "liberalism" which was satisfied so long as there remained a "token" Native vote.†

* See Chapter VII, where this process is described as it occurred under the liberal constitution of the old Cape Colony in the nineteenth century.

† Commenting on this statement when it appeared in an article in *Trek* in 1943, the late Mrs. Rheinallt Jones wrote:

"You do some injustice to the attitude of the Conference and Continuation Committee. So far as I know, every member of that Committee from Sir James down was convinced of the rightness of the direct personal vote

There was at first some doubt as to whether Hertzog would be able to secure his two-thirds majority. The chief stumbling block appeared to be the English-speaking M.Ps. in the Cape. Many of these people were accustomed to relying on the support of the Native voters at election times. They could not very well support the Bills without losing face to some extent. The political wire-pullers sought a face-saving compromise. At last it was discovered. The Cape Native vote would not be abolished. The Native voters would simply be put on a separate register. They would vote independently for three white members of Parliament. The number would remain at three, however much the Native vote increased in the future. These "Native representatives" would not be allowed to vote in the House on any financial Bill or on any matter affecting the constitution of the country. Apart from that, they would be allowed the ordinary privileges of Members of Parliament. The Native "electoral colleges" would choose four senators to represent their interests. The Native Representative Council would be set up and the amendments to the Land Act passed.

This proposition was put to the Cape M.Ps. and was accepted by them. They agreed to support the Bills. The National Conference was asked to withdraw its opposition. Rumour had it that the "moderates," Rheinallt Jones and Professor Jabavu, were prepared to accept the compromise, but to their credit the Joint Councils and the African leaders associated with them finally rejected it.

The nigrophilists sought vainly to persuade the Cape members to continue their opposition. These gentlemen replied

for Africans and saw no reason whatsoever to fear the results of any 'swamping' where an educated and trained African electorate became in the majority. My own opinion as expressed often during those years of fight for the real franchise was: 'The vote is in any real democracy the right of all those capable of exercising it intelligently. I know of no reasons to suppose that the desires of the civilised African people are any different from those of any other democratic people. They would, under any progressive system receive the right to vote gradually as the numbers of those capable of exercising it increase. Africans would finally be in the majority and there would be nothing to fear in that.' I still hold those opinions though every year that passes under the present regime makes such ultimate racial co-operation for the good of all South Africa more difficult.

"But the Conference and Continuation Committee were not only concerned with the enunciation of principles—they were trying to persuade South Africa not to take so far-reaching a step in the wrong direction as the abolition of the common franchise. They had therefore to try to persuade politicians and the man in the street that the then system had no dangers and that further developments would be in the hands of future generations who would presumably be capable of judging for themselves."

that they would no longer oppose the Bills, since the Native vote was not going to be abolished! It was clear that Hertzog would get his majority.

Many looked to J. H. Hofmeyr to take a firm stand for the retention of the franchise. A descendant of "Onze Jan," he had publicly declared himself a liberal. Thus, speaking to the old students of the South African College in November, 1935, he had said: "When I speak of liberalism I think especially of the relations with the Native people of this land. I think 'Sacs' men can claim that our Alma Mater has been a foster-mother of liberalism in that sense. If we think of the great names in the history of liberalism we will find that they were 'Sacs' men—Solomon, Schreiner, Sauer, Rose-Innes, de Villiers, Onze Jan. Every one of them regarded the retention of the Cape Native franchise as the very Ark of the Covenant so far as the Cape was concerned. It would be wrong to deprive any citizen born in this country of the opportunity to aspire to the full rights of citizenship merely because of race or colour."

But Hofmeyr was a member of the Cabinet. He was silent when the Disfranchisement Bill passed its first reading. He made no overt attempt to organise opposition to the Bill. During the debate on the Second Reading, he was ill in bed, some said "conveniently ill." But he was present at the Third Reading and finally got up to speak. It was clear that the Third Reading would be carried by a large majority. What Hofmeyr did was to make a personal declaration of faith. It was a good speech, on liberal lines; but it was a belated effort. It did not affect the issue as it might have done had he made it when the Bill was first introduced.

The attitude of the Labour members was that the Bills did not go far enough. The Labour Party claimed that it really believed in segregation, unlike the other parties who merely wanted to herd the blacks in compounds whence they could be drawn out at need for cheap labour services. "Segregate the Natives completely," they said, "and let us run our industries with white labour only." They criticised the Government, but supported the Bill.

The Native Representation Bill was finally passed at a joint session of both houses of Parliament by 169 votes to eleven. The minority consisted of J. H. Hofmeyr, C. F. Stallard, J. S. Marwick, C. W. A. Coulter, J. G. Derbyshire,

J. Chalmers, A. J. McCallum, R. S. du Toit, R. M. Christopher, Senator F. S. Malan and M. Alexander. These were all members of the United and Dominion Parties.

A diversion was created by a Native communist, John G. Masiu. As one of those disfranchised by the new measure, he applied for an interdict in the Supreme Court declaring the Act illegal. When the sheriff attempted to serve notice of the application on Mr. Speaker, he was refused admission to the House. He then tied the notice on the door. The courts upheld the legality of the new measure.

The Bills were passed in April, 1936, and all eyes were now turned to Bloemfontein, where the National Convention was due to meet the following June. As the communist paper put it, "the Native organisations would now have to decide whether to follow a policy of abstention, i.e. have nothing to do with the working of the new law, or to use the Native Representative Council as a propagandist platform from which to demand the extension of the franchise and the vote for all South Africans, black and white, on the same basis."

It was hoped that the unity shown by African organisations in opposing the Bill would be maintained. In particular the suggestion was made that the All-African Convention would form unity committees all over the country and that these bodies would replace the various I.C.U. and African National Congress branches; that the way would be clear for the formation of a new Bantu mass organisation on a large scale. But splitting tendencies soon showed themselves. There were the usual personal jealousies between the leaders. Dr. Seme, who represented a section of the A.N.C., declared himself definitely opposed to the idea that the All-African Convention should form local branches. When the Convention met, Seme and his supporters were in a minority. But the majority wisely determined not to force the issue. It was decided that the All-African Convention should be a permanent body, meeting at regular intervals, that it should have provincial sections as well as local committees. But it would remain a federative body and would not attempt to recruit individual members.

Professor Jabavu gave the presidential address on what were for him radical lines. He quoted Jawaharlal Nehru, the leader of the Indian National Congress, who had emphasised the fact that the vital sections of the Indian people in their struggle for national liberation were the labouring classes and the peasantry and that Indian tactics were "applicable to us in South Africa. . . . The time is ripe for us, leaders, to rehabilitate and reconstruct all our mass organisations to fight starvation, poverty and debt."

On the question of whether Native organisations should participate in the forthcoming elections of members of the new Native Representative Council, of white senators, also (in the Cape) of white members of Parliament, the Convention decided in the affirmative. A left wing group, consisting mostly of Trotskyists,* declared itself in favour of boycott.

The first elections under the new dispensation were held in 1937. Nineteen "Native representatives" were to be elected as follows: twelve African members of the Native Representative Council; four white senators (one for the Transvaal and Orange Free State, one for Natal, two for the Cape Province); three white members of Parliament (the divisions were Cape Western, Cape Eastern and the Transkei).

The Communist Party decided to enter candidates for the elections. Here was an opportunity which had never presented itself before: a purley African electorate could be approached. Would it return the candidates of the revolutionary party? But the communists found that they had a dearth of suitable candidates, both black and white. Their most prominent African member was Edwin Mofutsanyana, but he was by no means a national figure. Honest Edwin was a loyal Party member. He always supported the Moscow line. Thoughtful and reserved, he was a poor public speaker and not popular with the masses. The C.P., however, put him forward as one of the candidates for the Transvaal. In the other three provinces there were no African communist candidates.

With regard to the elections for the senators and the Cape parliamentary contests, the communists were equally handicapped, this time by the lack of candidates well known to the Africans. Candidates for the Senate had to have fixed property worth £500, and how many white communists had that? However, H. M. Basner, the communist lawyer, contested the Transvaal and Orange Free State constituency. He was opposed by J. D. Rheinallt Jones of the Joint Councils, also by W. G. Ballinger.

A provision of the new law made it necessary for candidates for the three Cape parliamentary seats to have been resident

* For an account of the Trotskyists in South Africa, see Chapter XXIV.

in the Cape Province for at least two years. This effectively barred certain white communists from the Transvaal who might otherwise have stood, and it barred also W. G. Ballinger. It was for this reason that Ballinger now decided to contest the Transvaal and Orange Free State senate constituency, while his wife, Margaret Ballinger (Margaret Hodgson), stood for the parliamentary seat in the Cape Eastern districts, where she was born.

The elections for the Senate were held in two stages: first the nominations and then the elections proper. African members of location advisory boards (in the towns), members of district councils, chiefs and headmen (in the countryside) were the electors. Each advisory board, council or chief had as many votes as there were African adult males resident in the location or district. In the Transvaal-O.F.S. Senate nominations there were five candidates in all—Rheinallt Jones, Ballinger, Basner and two others. Heated exchanges between Ballinger and Basner took place at various public meetings prior to nomination. Ballinger maintained that radicals—and he counted himself and Basner as such—should not oppose each other, but should put up a united front against the "conservative" Rheinallt Jones, who was obviously a very strong candidate. Basner agreed and suggested that Ballinger should withdraw. Ballinger replied that he was better known to the Natives than Basner and it was up to the latter to withdraw. At the time it seemed to many that Ballinger was probably right in his contention. To these the results of the nominations came as a complete surprise. Rheinallt Jones scored 305,333 votes. Basner, to the joy of the communists, came second with 77,349. Ballinger came a poor fourth with only 4,757 votes. All the candidates except the first two then withdrew from the contest and left the field to Jones and Basner. Ballinger went off to the Cape to help his wife in her campaign.

The elections took place in June. Rheinallt Jones got 404,447 votes and Basner 66,234. The communist paper stated that the results by no means reflected the true position, as the voting was extremely close in almost all the electoral units. Thus in Pietersburg a block vote of 20,639 went to Jones by a majority of two on the district council and in Bloemfontein Jones obtained 4,773 votes as the result of a majority of one on the location advisory board. In many cases the block vote was decided by the casting vote of the chairman.

The communists considered that a more equitable system of voting would have given them 40 per cent. of the votes.

The reasons for Basner's comparative success are probably, firstly, that he was a lawyer with a Native practice and as such known to many of the chiefs and other Native leaders. The faith of the Bantu in lawyers has been mentioned more than once in this history. Basner had done much legal work for various African organisations. Clements Kadalie and other well-known leaders came out strongly in his support and against Ballinger. Also there can be no doubt that Basner's platform propaganda did appeal to the Native masses and, though the "good boys" voted for Rheinallt Jones, there was a strong popular feeling in favour of Basner and the communist policy.

The elections for the Senate in the other three electoral colleges were less exciting. In Natal Professor Edgar Brookes secured a majority. One of his opponents was G. D. Shepstone, a grandson of Sir Theophilus Shepstone. Brookes had formerly been a Professor of Native Law at Pretoria University. He had at one time publicly supported Hertzog's views on segregation, but had afterwards decided that such an attitude was inconsistent with the evangelistic doctrines he had always believed in. His position at Pretoria became untenable and he gave up his professorship to become head of the Adams Mission Native College at Amanzimtoti in Natal. He was a foundation member of the South African Institute of Race Relations. The Cape Eastern circle chose Welsh, the ex-chief magistrate of the Transkei (who had led the prosecutions against Bunting in 1929). The Cape Western circle elected Malcomess, about and from whom very little has been heard either before or since.

In the three Cape parliamentary contests the voting was direct. Mrs. Ballinger scored a notable victory in the Cape Eastern circle. In spite of the fact that she was a woman (it was held that this would count against her with the Bantu voters) and that her chief opponent was a well-known lawyer with an African clientele, she received an overwhelming majority. She was far and away the most capable and intelligent of the candidates and her platform manner stood her in good stead. She has become one of the most accomplished Members of Parliament. Before marrying W. G. Ballinger, she had been a lecturer in history at the University of the Witwatersrand. She had worked under W. M. Macmillan and had been a well-known member of the Johannesburg Joint Council of Africans and Europeans.

In the Cape Western circle, there was a three-cornered contest, the candidates being D. B. Molteno, M. Mauerberger and J. T. Thompson. Molteno, a member of the Molteno family which had played a big part in the early days of representative government in the Cape, represented the old Cape liberal tradition. Mauerberger was a big business man, a textile manufacturer. He put forward a policy of economic development for the Bantu, which in itself was excellent, though it came strangely from a man whose only interest in Africans hitherto had been to sell them blankets. The communists, who supported Molteno, pointed out that when they had attempted to organise the workers in Mauerberger's factories he, Mauerberger, had tried to play on the prejudices of the white workers and had warned them against joining the union, as the "reds" were trying to set up a single organisation for black, white and Coloured workers. In spite of Mauerberger's grandiose programme and the fact that some African leaders appeared on his platform and spoke for him, Molteno was returned with a small majority. The African electors showed a high degree of political consciousness. The third candidate, Thompson, at one time an agent of the United Party (Smuts Party) came at the bottom of the poll.

The Transkei returned a local lawyer, G. K. Hemming, man of moderate views, who had been one of Bunting's opponents in the Tembuland election of 1929.

Of the twelve Africans elected to the Native Representative Council, a number have already been mentioned in this history. They represented a good average cross-section of the new African middle class. The most capable of them was probably R. V. Selope Thema. He had been a radical in the early days and played a prominent part as an African National Congress leader in the anti-pass campaign of 1919. He afterwards accepted the post of Secretary to the Bantu Men's Social Centre in Johannesburg, an institution financed largely by the Chamber of Mines and founded with the object of exercising a moderating influence on African intellectuals. He quarrelled with the management, however, and became Editor of the *Bantu World*, a Bantu newspaper run on business lines by Europeans.

Also on the Council was A. M. Jabavu, son of John Tengo Jabavu, brother of Professor D. D. Jabavu, and Editor of *Imvo*.

B. B. Xiniwe, of Kingwilliamstown, was a lawyer employed by a white attorney. His father had the distinction of founding the first Native hotel in the district.

The most radical of the younger members of the Council was certainly R. H. Godlo of East London. He was known as a prominent Wesleyan and Chairman of the local Joint Council of Europeans and Africans.

Thomas Mapikela, of Bloemfontein, had been associated with the African National Congress since its foundation, and had been on a number of deputations to England. He was described as a successful carpenter, builder and contractor.

The Transkeian representative, Charles K. Sakwe, was a business man and a member of the United Transkeian General Council.

R. G. Baloyi, described as a Native capitalist, owned a fleet of buses which plied between Johannesburg and the Alexandra Native Township. He and Basner were prominently associated in the election campaign, but he has not proved a particularly vocal or leftist member of the Council.

The Rev. John Dube, who was returned as one of the Natal members, has been mentioned frequently in earlier chapters.

The proceedings of the Native Representative Council have been interesting enough to those concerned with Native affairs. Those who foretold that the Council would prove a mere talking shop and nothing more have been justified in their prophecy. It may be added, moreover, that the talking shop has not even been an effective one. The debates have not been entirely ignored by the Press, though in general the publicity given to the N.R.C. has been meagre. Everyone realises that the N.R.C. cannot *do* anything, however eloquent its members may be. One of the chief complaints of the Council is that the Government has not, as promised, consulted it before introducing laws affecting Africans, and certainly has seldom taken its advice about other non-legal matters.

In spite of the evident ineffectiveness of the N.R.C. the movement to boycott the elections of members has not gained ground. Everyone, except those on the extreme left, realises that an election boycott must be universal to be effective. If only 1 per cent. of the electorate vote, candidates will still be elected, and if radicals abstained from voting, the elected would be persons of the most milk-and-watery kind. The technique adopted by the Irish nationalists in the old British Parliament of voting in their own candidates, who subsequently refrained from taking their seats in the house, has never been copied in South Africa. If it were, it would mean that the members of the N.R.C., on being elected, would refuse to attend Council meetings. This would in fact be the most effective form of boycott.*

As for the Native representatives in Parliament, these are not entirely ineffective for they can and do vote on many issues affecting Africans and other non-Europeans. This is particularly the case in the Lower House, where occasionally their votes become important when the other parties are equally divided. It is unfortunate, however, that the House is seldom equally divided on matters affecting Africans.

Two of the Native representatives have made names for themselves, not only as gallant fighters for the rights of all non-Europeans (for they have taken up the cudgels with equal enthusiasm on behalf of Indians and Coloureds) but also as accomplished parliamentarians. These are Margaret Ballinger and D. B. Molteno. The former has said that only those Europeans who do not believe on principle in the Native Representation Act are capable of representing Africans, and there appears to be much truth in this saying.

The second election of Native representatives took place in 1942, during the Second World War. The Communists again failed to gain any seats on the Native Representative Council, though they did rather better than they had done five years earlier. The most important newcomers to the Council were Dr. J. Moroka, A. G. W. Champion, Professor Z. K. Matthews of Fort Hare College, and P. R. Mosaka. Champion, who has been described as "the most vehement and aggressive" of all the councillors, we have met before in this history. Matthews is probably one of the most sophisticated and Westernised of Africans. Mosaka is a graduate of Fort Hare College. He was famous as a radical when a student and later became a prominent business man and politician at Orlando Location, Johannesburg.

* Actually in 1946 the N.R.C. was driven to discontinue its meetings in protest against the Government's policy of ignoring its views. See Chapter XXVI. (See further note on p. 309.)

In the Cape elections of 1942, the three M.Ps. retained their seats. Margaret Ballinger was returned unopposed. Molteno faced opposition from U. P. Raubenheimer, a building contractor who was persuaded to stand by a small group of African politicians who were looking for employment as election agents and platform speakers. He had apparently shown no previous interest in politics or in Africans, and, quite innocently, made the damning mistake early in the campaign of referring to Africans as "Kafirs." "I believe in a square deal for the Kafirs," he remarked cheerfully when addressing an audience of Africans. In spite of this gaffe, he managed to poll 587 votes against Molteno's 2,164.

The election for the Transvaal-O.F.S. seat in the Senate was again to prove the most interesting of the election contests. It was known beforehand that this was going to be a fight between J. D. Rheinallt Jones, the previous choice of the electorate, and H. Basner, who had been the runner-up in 1937. Basner had broken with the communists in 1939 at the time when the Soviet Union made its pact with Hitler, but he was still considered a radical and a firebrand. Jones had done much patient, plodding work for Africans during his five years as senator. He had toured the country, listened to grievances, made representations on behalf of Africans to officials and Government departments. Negotiation and lobbying were his favourite methods. No one could describe him as a firebrand.

Basner too had been about the country a good deal during this period and in a much more spectacular way than Jones. A strike, a boycott, a clash between Africans and the police—where such a thing happened, there would Basner arrive at speed prepared to speak, and, as a lawyer, to defend the Africans in court.

Jones was unfortunate in that he had often toured the country in company with the Secretary for Native Affairs and other members of the Native Affairs Commission. It was convenient, because meetings called by chiefs and headmen to listen to the officials of the Government could afterwards be addressed by Jones. Inevitably Jones came to be associated in the minds of many of his constituents with the Department of Native Affairs. And that was a bad thing, for in the mind of the average African the Department of Native Affairs was their chief enemy.

On the other hand, though the rank and file might for

various reasons favour Basner, it must be remembered that these had no direct vote in this election. The vote was exercised on behalf of the people by the members of the electoral college —that is, by chiefs and headmen in the country districts, by the location advisory boards in the towns. Many of these would, if left to themselves, have continued to support Rheinallt Jones. All the masses could do was to exert popular pressure upon their leaders, and in fact this did happen to a large extent. When the various blocks of votes were added, Basner was declared the victor with 332,798 votes against 237,919 for Rheinallt Jones. A notable victory for Basner.

In the Senate, Basner has lived up to his reputation as an extremely forceful and candid speaker. In his election speeches, he had said: "I do not undertake to change the laws if you elect me. In fact there is little or nothing that the Native Representatives, that small minority in Parliament, can do to help the Africans. All that I can promise is to use my position as senator to help you to organise. The Africans must organise and become a pressure group. Unless they do that, they will always be exploited." Though he has not always succeeded, Basner has tried to live up to this promise. Inevitably he has been drawn into negotiations with the officials of the Government. Judging by his speeches, he seems on occasion to believe that it is possible to convert his fellow senators to his views. Nevertheless, it is Basner, more than any other Native representative, who is known as an agitator among the people who sent him to Parliament.

Rheinallt Jones, after his defeat in the 1942 elections, resumed his work, never completely abandoned, in the Institute of Race Relations. To many it has seemed a pity that both these men cannot be in Parliament at the same time. Basner's place is obviously in the Lower House, where his dynamic oratory could be more appropriately employed; and Jones could function equally well in the more staid Senate. Under existing laws, the two million Africans of the Transvaal and Orange Free State are allowed only one representative in Parliament, and Basner is the man of their choice.

[*Note:* In 1947 the African National Congress decided on a policy of boycotting the Native Representative Act.]

CHAPTER XXIV

AFRICANS AND THE SECOND WORLD WAR

The war in Ethiopia had a remarkable effect in South Africa. It was the only political event that had roused the Africans for many years. Many realised for the first time that there existed still in Africa an independent country where the black man was master and had his own king. They were inspired by the idea of black men defending their country against white aggressors. The Bantu newspapers published pictures of Ethiopian soldiers, black men with rifles and machine guns. Pictures of Haile Selassie were in great demand. All Bantu newspapers experienced an unprecedented boom in sales. *Umsebenzi's* circulation rose to 7,000 copies weekly, and *The African Defender*, a new monthly paper published by *Ikaka labaSebenzi* (Labour Defence), appeared in editions of 10,000 which were completely sold out. For the first time in history, a paper without advertisements paid for itself merely by its sales. At first the war appeared to be going well for the Ethiopians. Newspaper reports tended to exaggerate the difficulties of the Italians.

In Durban, the I.C.U. *yase* Natal did nothing about the war. But the Communists circulated their newspapers and appealed for action. By a manœuvre they obtained permission from the municipal authorities to hold a meeting.* Though the rain poured down, the meeting was a great success. When an Italian steamer called at Durban harbour to load meat, the dock workers went on strike and refused to load her. The usual trick of bringing in "raw Natives" from outside was tried and eventually the ship was loaded. A train carrying meat to Durban was derailed, but whether by accident or design was never discovered. African women at East London collected money for Ethiopia. A Natal chieftain declared that he wished to lead a band of his tribesmen to fight for Ethiopia, but, of course, the Government would not allow them to go.

The reaction, when it finally became clear that the Ethiopians were defeated, was terrible. Bantu newspaper sales

* All such public meetings having been banned for some years by the municipality.

sank not merely to the pre-war level, but far below it. The new *African Defender* dwindled and died.

The outbreak of the Second World War in September, 1939, produced a parliamentary crisis in South Africa. At this time there were four parties in Parliament. The United Party, which had come into being in 1932 when Hertzog and Smuts joined forces in face of the gold-standard crisis, was in power. The official opposition consisted of the die-hard Nationalists led by Dr. Malan. On the cross benches were two small groups: the Labour Party, led by Walter Madeley, and the Dominion Party, led by Colonel Stallard. The latter represented the extreme British jingo section, most of its few members coming from Durban or East London. In addition, there were the three Native Representatives, Margaret Ballinger, Molteno and Hemming.

While it had been possible for Hertzog and Smuts to co-operate for a time on domestic affairs, they could not agree on the question of South Africa's attitude to the war. Hertzog's "neutrality motion" split the United Party in two. The voting was extremely close. With the support of the Dominion Party, the Labour members and the three Native Representatives, the neutrality motion was defeated and Parliament decided to declare war upon Germany by a majority of only seven votes. Smuts immediately resumed the office of Prime Minister and took Madeley and Stallard into his Cabinet.

The decision of the Native Representatives to support the Government in the war crisis was defended by Molteno in an article published by the Left paper, the *Guardian*, on September 29, 1939. Hitherto, he argued, the Native Representatives had found themselves in a "somewhat anomalous position" in the House. The differences between three parties were based on issues which divided English and Afrikaners, and these parties in turn differed from the Labour Party on certain economic matters. But none of these parties was prepared to accept the principle of no discrimination between persons on the basis of colour. The Native Representatives had in fact no allies in the House. They were forced to take up an independent position. Now they had elected to vote with the Government on the war issue, thus committing themselves to support of the Government's war effort. This they had done for two reasons: Firstly, they believed that the war was being fought by the forces of liberty, international order and tolerance against the forces of dictatorship, aggression and racial discrimination. A world victory for Nazism would not help in the fight against the colour bar. Secondly, they had perceived that the new Government, with the new alignment of forces produced by the split on the war issue, was "the most liberal that can be hoped for at the present time."

It is perhaps too early to say definitely that the world conflict of 1939-45 was a war of ideologies whereas the First World War was not. Certainly during this Second World War its supporters in South Africa, in so far as they were interested in Native opinion, made the most of its anti-Nazi character, and in general had little difficulty in persuading the Africans that in fighting Hitler they were opposing something which menaced the future of the whole Negro race. Their task was rendered all the more easy by the fact that the pro-German group in South Africa consisted of some of the most vociferous advocates of keeping the black man down. Malan's "purified" Nationalists, the Grey Shirts and Pirow's New Order, were all committed to a policy of racial discrimination. So also, though less crudely, were the majority of Smuts' followers, the Dominionites and the Labour Party. But while liberals might be found among the members of all these latter parties, there were none on the other side.

The war raised an old grievance which had rankled in 1914-18. Africans were called upon to join up; but they were not to be armed; they must content themselves with driving lorries, digging trenches, fetching and carrying for the white armed forces. South Africa's laws did not allow black men to handle firearms and even in time of war this prohibition would not be relaxed.

The overwhelming majority of Africans were prepared to join up and fight the Nazis, provided they were given arms. But this was not to be. Would the Africans then refuse to support the Government which continued thus to discriminate against them even when it was fighting a war, as some of its spokesmen claimed, against the whole principle of racial discrimination?

At the African National Congress meeting in Durban in December, 1939, a resolution prepared by the Resolutions Committee offered to support the Government only on condition that African soldiers were armed. But this resolution was amended by the President-General, Dr. Xuma. The Congress finally declared that the decision by the Union Parliament in favour of a declaration of war on the side of Great Britain was correct; that the time had arrived for the Government to "consider the expediency" of admitting the African and other non-European races into full citizenship of the Union with all the rights, privileges, duties and responsibilities appertaining to that citizenship; and that the territorial integrity of the country could be effectively defended only if all sections of the population were included in the defence system on equal terms.

Thus the African National Congress, and with them many politically-minded Africans, forebore to embarrass the Government by making support of the war conditional on some local instalments of that "world freedom" for which the united nations were fighting. In fact, the Government would have been seriously embarrassed had there been at this time any large-scale movement on the part of Africans for non-co-operation in the war effort. It was not merely that Africans were needed to do spade work for the Army. They were needed too in the iron and steel works, in the munition factories and in all the other industries which were vital to the prosecution of the war. Smuts was in a difficult position. His pro-war motion had been carried by a narrow majority. He could not rely on a large section of the Afrikaner population. While the more moderate Nationalists were merely non-co-operative, others, such as the Ossewa-Brandwag members, were actively hostile. The Ossewa-Brandwag was a product of the Voortrekker Centenary of 1938. An organisation nominally deriving from the old Boer commandos, it yet bore a close resemblance to modern fascist organisations. The name Ossewa (wagon) and Brandwag (sentinel) is descriptive of what it stood for. Its members wore uniforms, drilled in commandos and were pledged to establish an Afrikaner Christian-Socialist republic in South Africa. Under the leadership of J. van Rensburg, formerly administrator of the Orange Free State, it gained rapidly a large following among Afrikaners. During the war the O.-B. was not actually banned, though the members were prohibited from wearing their uniforms and many of the members were interned. There is little doubt that much of the sabotage which occurred must be attributed, if not directly to the O.-B., at least to semi-secret societies which sprang up under its influence. In practice there was little to distinguish the members of the O.-B. from Weichardt's Grey Shirts or followers of Pirow's New Order. All were bitterly opposed to fighting "England's war." In the circumstances, it is plain that any organised opposition on the part of the Africans might well have had a crippling effect on South Africa's war effort.

Africans, however, as has been said, supported the Government, but, in view of the Government's decision that they were not to bear arms, there was only a poor response to the appeal to join up. Some thousands did in fact enlist during the early stages of the war, hoping that they would be given arms after all. But when it became clear that the Government was not going to give way on the arms question, recruiting slumped badly.

There seemed some possibility of a change of attitude on the part of the authorities at the beginning of 1942, after Singapore had fallen and the Japanese had reached the Indian Ocean. It seemed then possible that the Japanese might capture Madagascar and that South Africa itself would be attacked. The Cape Coloured people were not at all alarmed by this prospect. Indeed, they viewed the Japanese victories with almost open jubilation. Their sympathies and hopes were with the little yellow-skinned men who had proved too smart for the British and Americans. In these circumstances, Smuts, always the politician, made his famous "retreat from segregation" speech in the Cape Town City Hall. Speaking at a meeting called by the S.A. Institute of Race Relations, he condemned as "outrageous" the attitude of these people "who spoke of the population of South Africa as two million," for this implied that "the Africans did not count, or were not worth counting." He declared, "Isolation has gone and I am afraid segregation has fallen on evil days too."

Clutching at this straw, many liberals thought they spied the glimmerings of a new dawn for South Africa. A writer in a Left paper said: "To the Natives of the country segregation is a growing horror. They will welcome the Prime Minister's admission that it is impossible to enforce these measures, measures which General Hertzog struggled for decades to bring into logical pattern. For the Natives in their war-like simplicity will expect that it will not be long before Parliament wipes off the statute books the more onerous of these provisions and that, as further steps, it will gradually remove all these blots from the official records of the country."

If the Japanese had in fact conquered Madagascar and if Rommel had captured Suez, some of the dreams inspired by Smuts' speech might have been realised. But Rommel was beaten at Alemein and the tide of Japanese aggression dried up on the frontiers of India. South Africa reverted to its old ideas: its old ways had never been altered.

While no actual promises to provide them with arms were made to the African recruits in the Union, the same cannot be said of those who joined up from the British Protectorates of Basutoland and Bechuanaland. These, it is said, were told definitely that they were being recruited as fighting men. But the South African infection spread beyond its borders. When the Basuto and Bechuana arrived in the Western Desert, they found that the only arms given to them were knobkerries and assegais. The South African authorities in the Middle East had persuaded the British to adopt this policy. If the Natives from the Protectorates were armed, the Union Natives would become discontented! When the Bechuana chief Tshekedi returned from a visit to his men in the Middle East at the beginning of 1943 he was furious. He had persuaded many of his fellow tribesmen to join upon the understanding that they would be armed. When he went to Egypt, they showed him their assegais and asked whether those were the "arms" he had meant. Further, they declared that on occasions they were stationed at places in the desert where they might easily be attacked by the enemy. When they asked the British officer in charge what equipment they should take, he replied: "Assegais will be of no use. Better not take anything."*

At Sidi Rezegh, there was severe fighting in which South African soldiers were killed, among them a number of African stretcher-bearers. They were buried in a common grave. When South African Army Headquarters heard of this, an order was sent commanding the disinterment of the bodies and the burial of white and black in separate graves. Thus even in death they must be divided.

In Basutoland the League of the Poor (*Lekhotla la Bafo*) was active in demanding the arming of Basuto soldiers. The authorities took action against them, interning their leaders,

* Information supplied to the writer in January, 1943, by a missionary who had interviewed Chief Tshekedi on the previous day.

Josiel Lefela, Hlakane Mokhitli and Rapoho Nthayane, at the end of 1941. This failed to stop the activities of the League, and Rabase Sekike, its acting President, was similarly arrested and interned in July, 1942. These men were still in custody when the war ended.

The South African Communist Party had moved away from its ultra-left policy during the years immediately preceding the war. This was the time of the "popular front" when communists the world over sought by every means to create a united front of all democratic and liberal-minded people. Not only were the Nazis threatening a new war in Europe and an attack on the Soviet Union, but their followers in South Africa were rapidly gaining ground.

With the Hitler-Stalin agreement of 1939 there was a sudden swing back to the Left. The war against Hitler had at last materialised, but, since the U.S.S.R. was not yet involved, the communists now refused to support the war they had so long advocated. On the other hand, alliance with the O.-Bs. and the Nationalists was unthinkable. There remained only the Africans, who, themselves the victims of something very similar to Nazism, could not be expected to offer to die in defence of their bosses. The communists showed consequently a renewed interest in Native grievances and started a campaign against the military recruitment of non-Europeans, both African and Indian. A number of leading communists, both black and white, suffered prosecution and internment.

Among these was Y. M. Dadoo, an Indian doctor who had recently joined the communists. Dadoo became prominent as an Indian leader and also exerted considerable influence among Africans. In July, 1940, he was charged in Johannesburg under the war emergency regulations with publishing a leaflet addressed to all non-Europeans and stating: "You are being asked to support the war for freedom, justice and democracy. Do you enjoy the fruits of freedom, justice and democracy? What you do enjoy is pass and poll-tax laws, segregation, white labour policy, low wages, high rents, poverty, unemployment and vicious colour-bar laws." The leaflet drew attention to the great disparity in rates of pay offered to whites and non-whites in the Army.

The trial aroused much excitement and Africans and Indians demonstrated for Dadoo's release in both Johannesburg and Durban. Addressing the court, Dadoo declared that the war could only be transformed into a just war for the preservation of democracy and the defeat of fascism if full democratic rights were extended to the non-Europeans in South Africa and when India and the colonial countries were granted their freedom and independence.

Dadoo was sentenced to a fine of £25 or one month's imprisonment with hard labour, plus a further two months with hard labour suspended for two years. But in January, 1941, he was again before the courts on a charge of making at Benoni Location statements which were calculated to incite the public to oppose the Government. On this occasion the sentence was four months' imprisonment without the option of a fine.

There can be little doubt that Dadoo's speeches and writings expressed the views of large numbers of politically-minded non-Europeans of all races, who felt it was up to the Government to make some attempt to release them from the discriminatory laws of South Africa before demanding their support in a war against race discrimination. The sentence caused a stir among non-Europeans and feeling ran high. It was reported that there was hardly a street in Durban where one failed to find slogans chalked in bold letters and demanding the release of Dadoo. A protest meeting attended by many thousands was addressed by African, Indian and Coloured speakers.

It seemed that Dadoo was destined to become a new South African Gandhi and that pressure from the Left was going to force the Government to make at least some concessions to non-Europeans. But in June, 1941, the German army invaded the Soviet Union, and at once the Communist Party, as ever subordinating the South African struggle to the needs of the world situation, became committed to supporting the Government's war effort. The propaganda against non-European recruiting was dropped and replaced by the slogan, "Arm the non-European soldiers." The Africans were now told that it was not wrong to fight in the war, because, although they still suffered under the colour bar, Hitler, if he won, would still further enslave them. Moreover, fighting in Egypt meant fighting indirectly for Russia, and if Russia won it would be better for oppressed people throughout the world. There was much logic in this, though an oppressed African might have retorted, as many in fact did retort, "That is all very well, but why must I face the German tanks armed only with an assegai while the South African Government still treats us as the Nazis treat the Jews? Would it not be better to refuse to join unless and until the Government shows that it is prepared to give us something to fight for?"

Dadoo, who had remained a disciplined member of the Communist Party, accepted the new policy. Thus we find him in February, 1942, demanding arms for the non-Europeans. They had originally opposed the war, he said, but the Nazi attack upon the Soviet Union had altered the whole character of the war. It had become a war against world fascism in which South Africa must play its part. He urged that the Government be given unconditional support in the struggle against oppression. With the defeat of fascist aggression was linked the lifting of the oppression under which they suffered.

The Minister of Justice, Dr. Colin Steyn, responded suitably to this change-over on the part of the communists. Two white communists, Dr. Max Joffe and his brother Louis, who had spent many months in an internment camp, were released in September, 1941. The communists were able also to carry on their agitation for the repeal of the pass laws, since they always combined this with pro-war propaganda. Every now and again, some communist was arrested by the police, who found it difficult to change their habits, but the intervention of Colin Steyn usually secured his release. This was the experience of Moses Kotane, Secretary of the Communist Party. He had gone to Bloemfontein to support the candidates of the Party during the Native Representative Council election campaign in November, 1942. Communist protests against the arrest of "the leader of a party whose whole energies are bent towards the successful prosecution of the war against the Axis enemies" were successful and Kotane was released.

The communists met with a certain amount of Government interference with regard to their Press, not so much in the case of the *Guardian*, a weekly in English, published in Cape Town, as in the case of their vernacular organ, *Inkululeko*,* issued fortnightly and published in Johannesburg from December, 1940. In February, 1944, it was discovered that a secret postal ban had been operating against *Inkululeko*. The postal authorities

---

* *Inkululeko* (Freedom) replaced *Umsebenzi* (The Worker) as the official organ of the C.P.

accepted copies of the paper addressed to subscribers, but did not deliver them and did not inform the publishers of the fact. When it became clear that papers were being tampered with in some way, the communists approached the Deputy Chief Censor in Johannesburg. He admitted that there had been a postal ban which had now been lifted. He said that with regard to *Inkululeko* the censorship was not concerned with military considerations or the war effort, but with political opinions, particularly about overseas politics. It was made clear to the *Inkululeko* representatives that the censorship considered that there should be discrimination between what could be printed in an African paper and what Europeans were allowed to read.*

While the non-Europeans who followed the Communist Party kept more or less faithfully to the new line, there were others who were loth to abandon the policy of no support for the war unless some present concessions were made as an earnest of future improvements. D. A. Seedat, a Durban Indian, who had gone to prison in April, 1942, was released in July of that year after serving his sentence for offending against the Security Code. He was then told that he would be exempted from internment only on condition that he undertook not to engage in any subversive activities which would be in any way harmful to the Government or its allies. Among other things he was forbidden to attend the meetings of some half-dozen political organisations, ranging from the non-European United Front to the Left Book Club, or "any other political meetings of a similar nature." Seedat refused to agree to these restrictions on his liberty, and in September he was again sentenced to forty days' imprisonment for failing to report to the Alien Registration Officer in the forenoon on Saturday of each week, and for attending a meeting held under the auspices of the Library Study Group.

The only Left organisations which were at this time, in theory at any rate, unequivocally opposed to participation in the war effort were certain groups of Trotskyists. Ultra-left groups adhering to the "Communist Opposition," to Trotsky himself, or to the Fourth International, had been in existence in South Africa since the early 1930's. They were chiefly concerned to fight what they called "international Stalinism" and to keep pure the doctrines of Marxism and Leninism.

* Report in *Inkululeko*, March 4, 1944.

The purity of their political ideals made it extremely difficult for them to work with other Left groups, the members of which they steadily denounced as betrayers of the working class.

In Cape Town, Trotskyism had flourished among the European intellectuals during 1934 and 1935. Lectures and debates at the Lenin Club drew large audiences. Trotskyist organisations have in South Africa, as elsewhere, exhibited always a strong tendency to split, which might almost be regarded as inevitable in view of the tremendous importance they attach to nice distinctions in matters of doctrine. In 1934 the Cape Town Lenin Club split into two sections. One section, calling itself the Workers' Party of South Africa, formed a new club, the Spartacist Club. The others eventually became the Fourth International (Trotskyists) of South Africa. The nominal cause of the split was some difference of opinion on the significance of the Afrikaner Nationalist movement in South Africa (was it anti-imperialist, and, if so, to what extent), but in practice it was to be observed that most of the "intellectuals," university people and so on, went to the Spartacist Club, while the others who wanted to hold street-corner meetings stayed with the Lenin Club.

The Spartacists published a duplicated paper, *The Spark*. It was capably edited, and during its five years of life it published a number of interesting articles and contributed a searching analysis of South African conditions in terms of Bolshevik theory. The Spartacists also produced propagandist plays and discovered notable dramatic talent among some of their African members. The plays, which merited a wider public, never achieved publicity, being performed only before small and rather select audiences in Cape Town.

In its June number in 1939, three months before the outbreak of the Second World War, *The Spark* announced that it was ceasing publication. A new Press law had made it impossible, the paper said, for it to continue to exist as a legal publication. The new law in fact made little difference to the Left Press and both official communist and Trotskyist papers have continued to be published. Perhaps it was merely that the publishers of *The Spark* had grown weary. In its valedictory message, the paper said: "To-day darkness descends over the world, but the sun must rise and will rise, bringing liberty to the workers and the colonial slaves. The capitalists may run amuck, they may plunge the world into war, but they will perish. The victory of the world revolution is certain." That was the end of *The Spark* and the last word of the Workers' Party of South Africa.

The other section of Cape Town's Trotskyists carried on openly. They linked up with a Johannesburg group and published the *Workers' Voice*. This section of Trotskyists gained considerable influence among the younger generation of Coloured teachers and university students in the Cape. Dr. Goolam Gool and a number of students played a prominent part in propaganda. The organisation gained much prominence and support during the anti-C.A.C. agitation in 1943-4.*

The Johannesburg section of the Fourth Internationalists eventually quarrelled with the Cape Town group, and withdrew to form the Workers' International League, which published a paper called *Socialist Action*.

The various Trotskyist papers which were published between 1939 and 1945 adopted a critical attitude towards the war. It was, they maintained, essentially an imperialist war. When Soviet Russia became involved in 1941, the attitude remained unchanged. The Government did not ban any of the Trotskyist papers, apparently regarding the movement as too insignificant to be worth suppressing. No Trotskyists were ever arrested under the Emergency Regulations, as were Dadoo and other Stalinists prior to Russia's entry into the war.† There was one occasion, however, when the Trotskyists were able to score a victory against their foes, the Stalinists. In 1942 at a local conference of the Non-European United Front at Port Elizabeth, the communists moved a motion urging a second front in Europe. A Coloured follower of the Trotskyist organisation opposed the motion from the body of the hall and secured its rejection by the meeting, which then affirmed its belief that non-Europeans should not support an imperialist war.

The race riots and the slaughtering of Africans by police or soldiers which may be said to have punctuated South Africa's recent history did not cease during the war. Such periodic riots are symptomatic of the system of racial domination of whites over blacks which is, ultimately, based on force;

* See Chapter XXVIII.

† The internment of Max Gordon, nominally a Trotskyist, was due to other circumstances. See Chapter XXVI.

conditions arising out of the war itself seemed to stimulate them. In December, 1942, fourteen Africans and one European soldier died as a result of riots at the Marabastad municipal compound in Pretoria. The wounded numbered 111. Trouble began when the Pretoria municipality sought to gain exemption from a wage determination made by the Wage Board and raising the wages of African municipal workers as from the beginning of November, 1942. The municipality's application for exemption was rejected by the higher authorities concerned, but by the end of December the municipality had not yet raised the rates of pay. The workers were becoming restless in face of this delay of the promised higher wages. A meeting was called in the compound by the superintendent, who tried to explain the causes of the delay. He said that the new rates of pay would be introduced in due course and that workers would be paid retrospectively as from the beginning of November, 1942. Many of the 2,000 workers present misunderstood the superintendent's explanation and gathered that they would not be paid at the new rate until November of the following year. They shouted and threw stones, the police were summoned, and, as the crowd could not be controlled even with their aid, finally soldiers were called in. The soldiers arrived accompanied by armoured cars. As they were trying to disperse the crowd, a soldier was killed. The military then opened fire. The Africans were trapped in the yard of the compound and were by this time trying to escape through a narrow exit. But the firing continued.

General Smuts, in an official statement, expressed his deep sorrow at the tragic occurrence, and promised a commission of inquiry. The commission reported that the cause of the trouble was the failure of the Pretoria municipality to pay the higher wages granted the workers by law, as soon as the law came into effect. The firing was mainly unwarranted and unnecessary except for the shots fired when the European soldier was attacked and killed. "The situation," the report said, "did not warrant the interference of a body of seventy-eight soldiers with firearms." The commission considered that discontent among municipal workers could be allayed considerably if living conditions in the compound were improved, and further suggested that much of the trouble was caused by the fact that the Natives had no voice in the management of their own affairs. It suggested that Natives should be represented on the Municipal Council, and that the non-European trade unions should be recognised. It was clear that the misunderstanding in the compound would never have arisen if the municipal authorities had communicated with the workers through a trade union. The recommendations of this comparatively enlightened report on the shooting incident at Marabastad compound are interesting. They furnish an instance of the complete divergence of viewpoint which exists between educated and cultured persons, such as would be asked to serve on commissions of inquiry, and the uneducated police and other authorities, who normally deal with the Natives.

It was hoped by many friends of the African that the war would bring about better relations between black and white in South Africa. In particular, it was thought that a new comradeship between the races would grow up on the battlefields in northern Africa. Though the black man there had not been exactly a comrade in arms, he was at least a stretcher-bearer and as such had acquitted himself bravely. Many Africans had been awarded distinctions for bravery under fire, and no doubt many a wounded white man had cause to be grateful to them. Information officers with the Army came under the direction of two of South Africa's leading liberal educationists, E. G. Malherbe and L. Marquard, who were first and second-in-command of Army Educational Services. South African soldiers were thus given every opportunity of broadening their views on the colour question. Some of them no doubt have developed a greater friendship for and interest in the black man, but there is plenty of evidence that the rank and file* of South African soldiery has remained unregenerate in this respect.

One instance may be quoted. At Pietermaritzburg in November, 1943, a dance was held in the City Hall by the Coloured Welfare League. White soldiers entered the hall and broke up the dance. In the resulting tumult two European soldiers and three non-European civilians were injured. Military comment on the incident was that the City Council of Pietermaritzburg ought not to permit Coloured dances to be held in their City Hall. Mrs. Russell, the Mayor, replied

* An investigation into the question of colour prejudice among white Army recruits has shown that the degree of prejudice grows less according to the standard of education attained. Men who had passed standard VIII showed much less prejudice than those who had only reached standard VI.

to this that the civil authorities were running the town and that she was "not impressed by or interested in what the military thought."

The race riots which occurred in Johannesburg in November, 1944, bore no special relation to war conditions, though food shortages, rising prices and similar factors may have tended to increase the general feeling of tension which existed among the workers, both black and white, and may thus have been a contributory cause of the flare-up. Johannesburg's Western Native Township lies next to the white working-class suburbs of Martindale and Newclare, from which it is separated by the main tram and bus route. The white workers here are mostly Afrikaners of the poorest section of urban whites. Between them and their fellow black victims of misfortune little love is lost. The riots began on a Sunday afternoon when an African was knocked down and killed by a tramcar. It was a municipal tram for Natives only, but the driver was, as is always the case, a white man. A crowd collected after the accident and began to throw stones at the tram and later at passing motor cars containing Europeans. This led to general fighting between blacks and whites throughout the area. African buses arriving from town were stoned by Europeans, and tramcars carrying Europeans were similarly stoned by Africans. The police intervened and used tear gas, but failed to prevent whites from breaking into the premises of the *Bantu World* newspaper, destroying machinery and paper and setting fire to the building.

Commenting on the riot and its causes, the *Race Relations News* declared: "Apart from certain incidents connected with the accident which resulted in a young African being killed . . . and the natural resentment of the African people against rising prices and the lack of such staples as meat, there appear to be other forces at work disposing them to seek redress for grievance in organised direct action of various kinds, which may in time become uncontrolled violence. On the other hand, the means used in the destruction of the premises and printing plant of the *Bantu World* by Europeans after two previous attempts indicate organised use of violence by Europeans, of which the riot was not the cause but the opportunity."

The war in Europe ended in May, 1945, and 20,000 Africans marched in the "People's Day of Victory" celebration convened in Johannesburg by the Council of non-European

Trade Unions, the African National Congress and the Communist Party. By way of contrast, the Government published the cash and clothing allowances to be granted to Service men on their discharge from the Army which were as follows:

	Discharged with benefits		Discharged without benefits	
	Cash	Clothing	Cash	Clothing
Europeans	£5	£25	£5	£15
Cape Coloured	£3	£15	£3	£9
Native Military Corps	£2	Khaki suit (worth £2)	£4	Nil

Peace was made with Japan in August, 1945. In September General Smuts returned to South Africa from Europe. "Thank you General Smuts Day" drew enormous crowds to the City Hall steps in Johannesburg, among them numerous Africans who gathered to get a glimpse of the country's leader and to listen to what he had to say. Many of them had taken up their positions hours before. Shortly before the General was due to arrive the white military police present began to attack the Africans, driving them away with blows and kicks. Thus symbolically it was demonstrated that though the war for world freedom had been won, black men and women must not forget that they have to keep their place.

CHAPTER XXV

BUS STRIKE AND SHANTY TOWN

SINCE THE COLLAPSE of the I.C.U. and the failure of the pass-burning campaign of 1930, there have been few indications of an advance in African political consciousness. There were no large-scale political movements during the period of the Second World War. Here and there, however, groups of Africans did take action against particular grievances, and some of these local battles are well worth recording. The history of the Alexandra bus dispute may well become a classic instance of the use to which passive resistance may be put by those who are in the ordinary way denied any say whatever as to the conditions under which they shall live and work and travel.

The Alexandra bus strike should be studied against the background of segregation, low wages and social discrimination which are the common lot of urban Africans. Alexandra is not a typical location. It lies outside the Johannesburg city area. It is one of the few places where Africans may acquire landed property. Its population has grown enormously in recent years, being estimated at well over 60,000.

The buses which transported people the nine and a half miles between the township and Johannesburg were operated by private companies, which declared that they could no longer, under war conditions, run the service at 4*d.* for the single fare. In August, 1943, the companies, with the authority of the Transportation Board, raised the fare to 5*d.* The bus strike began immediately. Nobody used the buses and 15,000 people trudged the nine or more miles to work and back again for nine days. Some were given lifts in cars or lorries, but most of them walked. They blocked all other traffic for miles along Johannesburg's main northern highway. The bus owners gave in and reduced the fare to 4*d.* The Government appointed the Bus Commission, which took a long time to publish its report.

The Commission found that "transport charges, in relation to the workers' wages or even to the total family income, are beyond the capacity of the African workers to pay. Indeed, it may be said that they cannot afford to pay anything. They certainly cannot afford to pay anything more in any direction except by reducing still further their hunger diet." And it went on to declare: "The Europeans have forced a policy of segregation on the Africans. The transportation of the Africans is therefore very much a financial obligation of the Europeans."

Before the report was published, the bus companies put in further claims. An emergency regulation was framed raising the fare to 5*d.* and requiring the workers to collect the extra 2*d.* a day from their employers. The people of Alexandra rejected this, first, because it did not cover casual workers, washerwomen, children, visitors and people looking for work, and secondly, because it would certainly have resulted in many Alexandra workers losing their jobs to workers living nearer town. On November 14, 1944, the second bus strike commenced.

This second bus strike lasted seven weeks. A Johannesburg university lecturer has described the strike in the following terms: "The hastily improvised transport service, consisting of cars belonging to friendly Europeans, horses and mule-carts, cycles usually carrying two passengers, and a number of taxis and African-owned lorries—fifteen of these were later victimised for their solidarity with their own people by the withdrawal of their licenses—failed to satisfy the demand of what is virtually an African city. Alexandra walked alone, in straggling little groups of twenty; old men, tiny children, washerwomen loaded with their bundles, industrial workers doing a fifty-hour week twenty miles from home in war industries, walked through sun, wind and rain for seven weeks before the deadlock showed signs of breaking."

The marching was exhausting, but the people were determined and the people won. On December 29 the Johannesburg City Council proposed that books of twelve coupons should be offered at 4s. It undertook to erect and staff booths for the sale of coupons. The residents declared that many of them could not afford to buy a book at a time and there was some talk of continuing the strike, but in practice it was found that tickets could be bought in quantities of less than twelve. Early in 1945 the entire bus service was taken over by a so-called "utility company," which has reverted to the old fare of 4d. without coupons.

Like almost all recent African strikes or boycotts, the first Alexandra bus strike was a spontaneous mass movement, unprepared and owing little or nothing to political leadership. During the strike an "emergency committee" was set up, representing certain European sympathisers, the Communist Party, African trade unions and the recognised leaders of the African community in Alexandra. The leading figure on the committee was Gaur Radebe, himself a resident in the township. The second strike (in 1944) was well prepared and had the support of a large committee representing numerous African and pro-African organisations. Many European sympathisers helped by giving lifts to the walkers until they were stopped by officials of the Transportation Board.

Many different political currents revealed themselves during the strike. The success of the first march in August, 1943, had led to the formation of an African Democratic Party in Johannesburg. This was sponsored by Basner, who had previously placed his hopes in the rejuvenation of the African National Congress. He now declared that the A.N.C. was played out and that a new organisation led by younger men was needed. The young men who helped to found the African Democratic Party included the following: P. R. Mosake, of the Native Representative Council; D. Koza, a leading trade unionist; J. J. Lesolang, President of the Transvaal African Teachers' Association; and S. Mampuru, who was African consultant to the Friends of Africa.*

The African Democratic Party failed to become the large mass organisation that its founders had hoped. The communists continued to pin their faith to the African National Congress. At the end of 1943, the Congress declared that the pass law was "enemy number one." Local anti-pass committees, in which the communists and many trade unions participated, were set up and preparations were made to hold a great national anti-pass conference during Easter, 1944. Anti-pass law agitation in some form or other never completely dies down in South Africa, for the pass law is a perennial source of grievance and in recent years there has been a growing threat that municipal pass laws at least will be extended to the Cape. But though feeling against the passes is strong, it has become difficult to rouse any really large-scale mass enthusiasm for an anti-pass campaign, so often have these campaigns in the past ended in failure.

The anti-pass conference held in the Gandhi Hall, Johannesburg, on May 20 and 21, 1944, was on the face of it a rousing success. Five hundred and forty delegates were present claiming to represent 605,222 people. A demonstration of 20,000 marched through the city. The conference declared that the pass laws were in conflict with the high and progressive aims for which the country, together with the other united nations, was fighting; held the African people in conditions of abject poverty and subjection; retarded the economic and industrial development of the country; were the cause of sharp racial friction between the peoples of South Africa; upheld the cheap labour system which resulted in malnutrition, starvation and disease; and filled the gaols with innocent people, thus creating widespread crime.

* An organisation to promote the social, economic and political organisation of all races in Southern Africa. It owed its existence to Winifred Holtby and had a branch in London. The South African section was started by William and Margaret Ballinger.

The conference elected an Anti-Pass Council and Working Committee, with Dr. Xuma as Chairman, Dr. Dadoo as Deputy Chairman, and D. W. Bopape as Secretary. It was decided to launch a nationwide campaign to obtain a million signatures to an anti-pass petition to be presented to the Government by a deputation of African leaders in August, 1944, simultaneously with the holding of demonstrations against the pass laws throughout South Africa.

The only immediate result of the conference was an act of victimisation against its Secretary. D. W. Bopape was a teacher in the mission school in Brakpan location. As a result of a report on Bopape's political activities made by the municipal Manager for Native Affairs, the Brakpan Town Council asked the superintendent of the school, Dr. Taylor, to transfer Bopape to another district. The superintendent accordingly gave Bopape notice to go. This was followed first by a school strike. African parents raised the slogan "No Bopape, no school." As this produced no immediate effect on the Town Council, the residents decided on a general strike. On August 10, 1944, some 7,000 residents of the location failed to turn up to their jobs in Brakpan. In addition to the reinstatement of Bopape, they declared they had other demands, including the dismissal of the Manager for Native Affairs. At eleven o'clock that night, a representative of the Town Council informed the location residents that Bopape would be reinstated and that all other complaints would be investigated immediately. The people therefore returned to work the next morning. But, as happens so frequently in cases of this sort, the undertaking given was not carried out. Bopape was not reinstated and the Manager for Native Affairs was not dismissed. Further protests were unavailing and divided counsels among the political leaders of the location prevented another strike. Bopape, however, remained Secretary of the Anti-Pass Council.

The "million-signature petition" was a failure. Signatures were canvassed from whites as well as blacks, but people showed no enthusiasm over handing round the petition forms. August, 1944, passed and no attempt was made to present the petition. The date of presentation was postponed and then postponed again. In February, 1945, Josie Mpama complained in a letter to *Inkululeko* that the Transvaal had "gone to sleep over the anti-pass campaign." The petition was finally brought to Cape Town for presentation to the Government in June, 1945. It was said to contain some hundreds of thousands of signatures. A deputation from the Anti-Pass Council asked for an interview with the acting Prime Minister, J. H. Hofmeyr. Smuts was away in Europe at the time. Hofmeyr said he was too busy to see them and offered them the Minister of Native Affairs, Major van der Byl, in his stead. But this the deputation did not want. A meeting of 5,000 Africans and other non-Europeans on the Parade protested against Hofmeyr's "undemocratic refusal to meet the Anti-Pass Deputation representing some million Africans." They then demonstrated outside the Houses of Parliament. The leaders of the demonstration were arrested and fined for leading an unlawful procession. They included Dr. Dadoo, R. V. Selope Thema and S. Moema.

In spite of this rebuff, which was really no more than could have been expected, the Anti-Pass Council carried on. Their second anti-pass conference was held in Johannesburg in June, 1946. Dr. Xuma, the President, said, "We have been talking. We must now prepare for intensive organisation of the people to take action." The conference resolved "to commence a mass struggle within three months from this date, which mass struggle will culminate in the national stoppage of work and the burning of passes." What will come of that still remains to be seen.*

While the leaders of the anti-pass campaign during the war years refrained from any sort of direct action to secure their demands, the same cannot be said of the people of Orlando location who built "Shanty Town." The war industries had drawn large numbers of African workers into the urban areas. Since Native housing schemes automatically came to an end in 1940, the resulting congestion in the urban locations can be imagined. On the Witwatersrand there were literally thousands of people without homes. Things came to a head at Orlando in April, 1944. The location had become super-saturated with human beings: it could no longer hold all those who were trying to live there. Some thousands of men, women and children left the location and camped on vacant municipal ground nearby. They built themselves

* The 1946 anti-pass campaign has so far proved a failure. Little enthusiasm has been aroused and the leaders have had to postpone more or less indefinitely the "final day" on which there is to be a nation-wide burning of passes.

shelters of sticks, sacking, old tins, and maize stalks. Thousands of other homeless persons came to join them from other parts of the Reef. Thus was Shanty Town born.

This movement, like so many other apparently spontaneous movements of the African people, brought to light a "prophet." James Mpanza, a member of the Orlando Advisory Board, it was who led the people in this mass exodus and who became the uncrowned king of Shanty Town. This is part of the story of Mpanza, as told by himself:* "I, Sofazonke Mpanza, born May 15, 1889—only three weeks younger than Hitler—had many blows in my youthful days. At the age of eighteen in 1908 I started working as an interpreter and clerk in a solicitor's office at Camperdown in Natal. In 1912 I got into serious trouble and was imprisoned for fraud. In 1914, while under the influence of strong drink, I committed murder and was sentenced to death, but was reprieved.

"In 1918 I had a vision: was converted to the Lord in the Cinderella Prison, Transvaal, and was born again. I began to testify for the Lord. I was given permission to preach to the prisoners and to teach a class about the spirit of the New Birth and many prisoners were converted. After preaching thus for three years, a new Governor came to that prison and at his instance I was sent to Pretoria and, without any cause on my part, was put into solitary confinement for six months. It was there and then that a feeling of depression came upon me and I was convinced that I should make the Lord's message known to the world. I asked the Governor of the Gaol for writing materials and this was my prayer at the time, 'O God, if I am given permission to write this book I will understand that I am sent by you, Be with me Lord.'

"I was given materials to write and I sat down and wrote. In 1927, after thirteen years' imprisonment, I was released on parole and placed with a Swiss Mission in Pretoria as a teacher. I served for three years as an Evangelist in that congregation under a devoted white missionary, a great believer, the Rev. P. Dourquin. I had a happy life here. I preached with success at the Mental Hospital, Leper Hospital and many other places, such as the Railway Location, Pretoria, Lady Selbourne, etc. In 1930 I came to Bertrams and taught in Mr. Light's private school. I remained here until the place was demolished."

* In the *African Sunrise*, March, 1946.

Mpanza's followers at Shanty Town knew that they were trespassing and defying the authorities. They expected the authorities to take action to remove them from the land they had occupied. Some may have heard of Bulhoek and what happened there under somewhat similar circumstances. Their slogan was "Let us all die together." "*Sofazonke*" means in Zulu "We shall all die." Their leader, James Sofazonke Mpanza, called his movement the Sofazonke Party. His political rivals complained that he behaved as a dictator in Shanty Town, that he collected rents from the people and that he would allow no one to trade there but himself.

The Johannesburg municipality did not eject the Africans from Shanty Town. Instead, they began to tackle seriously the problem of providing some sort of housing for the homeless thousands. The Manager of the Non-European Affairs Department of Johannesburg was given authority to house all Shanty Town dwellers in weather-proof, breeze-block shelters. Building materials were released for the purpose and permission was obtained to use non-European labour for the work of construction.

That was not the end of housing troubles at Orlando nor of Mpanza's Sofazonke Party. There were further developments which led to clashes with the police and the deportation of Mpanza. But these happenings are so recent that they will have to be left to a future edition of this history.

More recently, in 1946, at the time when London's homeless have entered and occupied blocks of luxury flats and when the squatters' movement has spread to all the big centres of population in England, two more unofficial African towns have grown up alongside existing overcrowded locations. At Pimville and Albertynsville, locations lying within the Johannesburg municipal boundary, the acute housing shortage has brought about the growth of squatters' camps where over 25,000 Africans have built themselves shanty towns of some thousands of huts roughly made of hessian stretched over a framework of split poles. At Albertynsville a natural leader emerged in the person of E. Kumalo. Under his direction, the camp had broad streets flanked by neat rows of improvised dwellings. The committee, with Kumalo as chairman, saw to it that cleanliness and order were maintained. Military style latrines were erected. From these squatters' camps the Africans were ejected in September, 1946. Municipal police placed a

cordon round the camps and employes of the Johannesburg
Native Affairs Department, armed with axes and crowbars,
methodically demolished the wood-and-canvas dwellings.
The occupants gathered up their meagre belongings and
watched the destruction of their homes in silence. They had
nowhere to go. Kumulo and others were arrested and charged
with illegally occupying the land. The City Council's ejectment
order was upheld by the Supreme Court. In neighbouring
districts European landowners hastily sought, and obtained,
the protection of the law against the occupation of their land
by African squatters.

The squatting movement is so widespread and persistent,
and so spontaneous, that there can be no doubt that, at a
modest estimate, some 40,000 Africans in Johannesburg have
literally nowhere to live. Ill-clad and ill-nourished, they have
spent the bitter nights of the winter huddled together in groups
on the open veld.

Faced with this situation, the Johannesburg City Council
now proposes to spend £8,000,000 on building what will be
virtually a new African town, to house 43,000 Natives on
6,000 acres of land adjacent to Orlando. The projected town
"will bring all the amenities of civilisation to the native.
Provision is being made for a university, thirty Government
schools, three to five railway stations, cinemas, libraries,
communal halls, post offices, police stations, markets, clinics,
restaurants, food centres, laundries, a swimming bath and a
35-acre sports stadium. . . . It will be a model for local
authorities to follow. It will be an economic scheme and will
not be financed from the rates."*

Thus the squatters of Shanty Town have not suffered in
vain. In the meantime, the plan remains a plan for the future.
Even if building is commenced immediately, the new African
town cannot be ready for months or even years. The homeless
Africans must suffer the rigours of another winter before help
comes to them.

* *Cape Argus*, September 9, 1946.

CHAPTER XXVI

THE AFRICAN TRADE UNIONS

ONE OF THE MAIN PROBLEMS of the South African
Labour movement has been, and still is, the industrial
organisation of the main body of the workers. The traditional
South African trade union movement never interested itself
in the unskilled worker—partly because he was unskilled,
and partly because he was black. After the First World War,
with the rise of secondary industry, increasing numbers of
white workers of both sexes entered the factories as semi-
skilled or at least as comparatively lowly-paid operatives.
They were increasingly drawn into trade unions of a type
rather different from the old organisations dominated by
the aristocrats of labour. This process was facilitated by
the Industrial Conciliation Act—passed in 1924 by the Smuts
Government just before its defeat by the Nationalist-Labour
Pact. This law, though denounced by the left wing, actually
stimulated trade union development among whites. It has
made possible all sorts of stable jobs for rising trade union
leaders, agents of industrial councils and the like. Into this
occupational vacuum stepped large numbers of capable and
enthusiastic young men and women, and new trade unions
sprang up all over the country.

In many of these new secondary industries the line of
demarcation, so characteristic of the older industries, between
highly skilled white artisans on one hand and unskilled non-
Europeans on the other was blurred or non-existent. It therefore became increasingly possible or even essential to organise
both Europeans and non-Europeans in the same union. The
tendency towards joint organisation was offset to some extent
by the exclusion of "pass-bearing Natives" from the scope of
the Conciliation Act (which did not regard them as
"workers"). On the other hand, the Wage Act of 1925, which
laid down minimum wages irrespective of colour, definitely
stimulated the organisation of interracial unions in certain
industries.

The first African trade unions (apart from the I.C.U.,
which was an all-in association of Africans and was not

organised on trade union lines) were started by the communists on the Witwatersrand in 1927 and have been described in an earlier chapter of this history. By 1929 they claimed to have an aggregate membership of nearly 10,000. They fought a number of strikes, many of them to secure conditions which were already laid down by the Wage Board, but which the authorities seemed unwilling or unable to enforce against the opposition of the employers.

These various unions were united in a Non-European Trade Union Federation. This body disintegrated, as did also a number of its component unions during the period 1930-3, partly in consequence of the severe depression of those years and partly as a result of the unfortunate policy pursued by the Communist Party, which controlled them. The Native Clothing Workers' Union, having broken with the Communist Party, survived. Led by Gana Makabeni, himself an expelled communist and a man of some ability and high integrity, it became the nucleus of a new group of unions entirely under African leadership. The Native Laundry Workers' Union also broke away from the official communists, but dwindled away until it was taken in hand by Max Gordon, who reorganised it and then went ahead to organise other Native unions.

Gordon's contribution to African trade unions was considerable. Though adhering to a Trotskyist political group, he was nevertheless able to subordinate matters of doctrine to the practical necessities and compromises involved in organising African workers. He trained a number of African trade union leaders, among them D. Koza, a man of considerable organising ability and perspicacity. The most important and stable of the unions organised by Gordon was among the commercial employees, workers in the department stores, warehouses, etc. He also re-organised the African bakers and printing workers. By 1937 he was secretary to four African unions which were all in a flourishing condition. Inevitably a certain amount of jealousy began to show itself among the more ambitious African leaders in the different unions. They urged that the individual unions should have African secretaries. Gordon, realising that his leadership was the most important factor in the efficient functioning of the unions, was unwilling to agree immediately to this proposition, though he admitted that eventually it would be desirable for African secretaries to take over. In 1938, a Joint Committee was formed in Johannesburg, comprising representatives of the African laundry, commercial, baking and printing unions. Three new unions were formed later in the year and these too affiliated to the Joint Committee. They comprised the dairy, chemical and general workers' unions. The last grew to be an enormous body, claiming 10,000 members in 1941. D. Gosani became the paid organiser of this body.

In the meantime the other group of unions under the leadership of Makabeni was also making progress. In 1938 these unions and those controlled by the Joint Committee came together in a loose federation known as the Trade Union Co-ordinating Committee. This body received both moral and financial support from the South African Institute of Race Relations, but it did not endure. The two groups preferred to remain separate.

In 1939, the Joint Committee decided that all its affiliated unions should have their own secretaries and that Gordon should be the general secretary of the group as a whole. D. Gosani became Chairman of the Joint Committee, while Gordon remained Secretary of the Commercial Workers' Union, with Koza as Assistant Secretary. In May, 1940, Gordon was arrested and interned as a "safety measure" on the part of the Government. The leaders of the trade unions approached Madeley, the Minister of Labour in the War Government, and asked for an explanation as well as for Gordon's release. Madeley said he knew nothing about it: the Department of Justice were responsible. The Trades and Labour Council then took up the matter with the authorities, but received no satisfaction; nor would the Government reveal the nature of the charges against Gordon.

The Joint Committee now had to decide upon a new Secretary. The name of A. Lynn Saffery was put forward. Saffery, a member of the Race Relations Institute, had been largely responsible for that body's interest in African trade unions. There could be no doubt of his ability. The idea of having another white Secretary, however, met with strong opposition from most of the members of the Joint Committee. They chose Gosani instead.

Gordon tried from the Baviaanspoort internment camp to continue to advise the trade unions he had founded. In a letter dated May 8, 1940, he advised that Saffery be accepted as

Secretary and added: "thrash matters out in a comradely way. Some of the comrades have a tendency to impose their opinions on others." But in spite of his efforts, it proved impossible to influence matters by occasional letters.* The Joint Committee unions probably reached the zenith of their influence and membership in 1940, just prior to Gordon's internment, when a new determination made by the Wage Board for commercial employees brought a substantial increase in wages. The workers heard the news at a large and enthusiastic meeting on the Bantu Sports Ground. The Joint Committee had twenty-one unions, with 23,000 to 26,000 members. Thereafter some of the unions languished and some broke away from the Joint Committee. Koza, however, managed to maintain the Commercial and Distributive Workers' Union, if not on its former level, at least as an active and permanent body.

Before discussing later developments in the field of African trade unionism in the Transvaal, it may be well to return to events in the Cape. In that province the organisation of non-European workers, both African and Coloured, developed significantly after 1935. In that year there were three main groups of unions in the western Cape. The aristocratic unions, such as the Typographical and the Engineers' unions, were affiliated through their national organisations to the South African Trades and Labour Council. There was also an independent group of small unions led by A. G. Forsyth. But the main body of unions in the Cape were affiliated to the Cape Federation of Trades, a body largely dominated by Robert Stuart. The Cape Federation claimed to be free of colour prejudice, a large proportion of its members being Cape Coloured, and it persistently refused to join up with the S.A.T.L.C., though frequently invited to do so. In spite of its non-Eruopean membership, the Cape Federation was largely moribund. It was dominated by Europeans and it was making little or no attempt to organise the masses of unorganised non-Europeans in the Cape.

In 1936 Leftist organisers from the Rand irrupted into the Cape and began a movement which has changed the whole aspect of labour organisation in the Western Province. The

* Gordon was finally released in 1941. He returned to trade union work on the Rand for a time, assisting in the formation of various new unions. He was eventually compelled to leave Johannesburg to escape being interned again.

immediate cause of this new development was the attempt by the Transvaal Garment Workers' Union, led by E. S. Sachs, to expand and acquire national status. In both Durban and Cape Town, this move encountered immediate opposition on the part of the vested trade union interests, and in the Cape the opposition was serious. Sachs and his supporters started a second Garment Workers' Union in Cape Town and for a time there was a bitter struggle between the rival unions. The Transvaal attempt was unsuccessful and was finally abandoned, but it had the effect of stimulating the original Cape union to renewed activity and increased militancy. The Leftists were more successful in penetrating some of the other unions affiliated to the Cape Federation and they built up also a number of new unions. Finally, the Cape Federation was captured by the militants and Stuart broke away, taking with him a minority of the unions of which the most important was the Garment Workers' Union.

This breaking of new ground in the Cape was largely the work of a young girl communist, Ray Alexander, who was associated with the organisation of at least a dozen new unions. These new bodies were organised on an interracial basis and many of them consisted predominantly of non-Europeans. There was thus a complete breakaway from the old Cape policy, which allowed the non-Europeans in, only to relegate them to the back benches at branch meetings. These new unions boasted in many cases Coloured and African organisers, chairmen and secretaries. The non-European workers were definitely beginning to pull their weight.

One of the most outstanding achievements in the Cape was the organisation of the non-European Railway and Harbour Workers' Union. Founded in Cape Town in 1936, it has spread to all the other provinces and in 1943 claimed a membership of over 20,000.

In Natal similarly the communists were busy, organising Indians, Africans, and sometimes whites as well, into new industrial unions. Beginning with the strike of Indian and African workers in the Durban Falkirk Iron Factory in 1937, trade unionism spread rapidly in many industries. The most important among the unions formed was the Natal Sugar Industry Employees' Union, representing both Indian and African workers.

At the end of 1942 came an epidemic of strikes by African

workers, chiefly on the Witwatersrand, but also in Natal. Sweet workers, coal miners, dockers, dairy workers, brick workers, railway labourers and municipal employees were among those involved. Many of the strikes were led by trade unions, but some were spontaneous outbreaks by workers hitherto largely unorganised. The most important of these strikes was that of the African municipal workers in Johannesburg. The Wage Board had decided upon a wage of 24s. a week for unskilled workers. This represented an increase of 60 per cent. on the wage previously paid by the Johannesburg City Council to its African employees. The City Council pleaded its inability to pay the award and applied successfully to the Minister of Labour for exemption from the ruling of the Wage Board. The workers responded by a strike, which, though it lasted only one day, was completely effective. The Johannesburg Municipality agreed to pay the new wage. Other Witwatersrand municipalities, seeking exemption, had their applications turned down. The Minister was obviously not prepared to repeat his mistake.

The Government's reply to the strike wave was the promulgation of War Measure 145, which, as Margaret Ballinger summed it up, made "all strikes of all African workers in all circumstances illegal." At the same time, the Government continued in its refusal to recognise African trade unions. General Smuts had in fact declared in 1942 that he was considering an amendment of the Industrial Conciliation Act so as to include African workers in the scope of the machinery thereby created for the discussion and settlement of industrial disputes. In 1943, the Japanese military menace having receded, he not only forgot this half-promise, but now gave his consent to a measure which made it even more difficult for the African worker to give voice to his grievances through any legal channel. When African employees of the Victoria Falls Power Company struck in August, 1944, the Government's answer was the arrest of the strikers and the drafting of members of the Native Military Corps to perform their work. In spite of War Measure 145, some sixty illegal strikes of African workers occurred between its promulgation at the end of 1942 and December, 1944.*

Though the attitude of the authorities and of the white population in general towards African workers striking for

* *Race Relations News*, January, 1945.

increased wages in a period of rising living costs showed little improvement during the Second World War as compared with their attitude during the First World War, there had been a definite step forward in the attitude of organised white labour. Both the municipal Labour Party and the S.A. Trades and Labour Council supported the strike of municipal employees and certain other strikes of African workers.

The South African Trades and Labour Council (the descendant of the South African Trades Union Congress) had shown itself willing to admit to its ranks all *bona fide* trade unions irrespective of their racial composition. But there was no large influx of non-European unions, while those which did affiliate did so on a basis of representation very much smaller than their actual membership. In 1937, the S.A.T.L.C. had thirty-eight affiliated unions, including two small non-European unions, the Cape Stevedoring Union and the African Iron and Steel Workers' Union. In 1941, the number of affiliated unions was forty-six, of which eight were either non-European or mixed unions. But the eight unions represented only 400 in a total of 21,500 affiliated members. The non-European membership of the S.A.T.L.C. was therefore little more than a token of that body's theoretical break with the colour bar. More important than the admission of non-European unions to its ranks was the willingness of the S.A.T.L.C. to co-operate with the African organisations in various ways. This co-operation has taken various forms since the first joint discussions with the I.C.U. and the sponsoring of the I.C.U. approach to Madeley in 1928; it has not always been consistent (there have been occasions when the T.L.C. has done little or nothing to help African workers on strike); but on the whole it has increased during the past decade.

We have seen how in 1938 an attempt to amalgamate the two main groups of African trade unions on the Rand ended in failure. In 1942, a more successful attempt was made. In November of that year the first conference of the new Council of Non-European Trade Unions took place in Johannesburg. Eighty-seven delegates were present, representing twenty-nine affiliated unions. The conference was opened by the Minister of Labour, Walter Madeley, who disappointed the delegates by telling them that "many difficulties stood in the way of official recognition of African unions."

This new body had Makabeni for Chairman and Gosani for

Secretary. By 1945 the Non-European Trade Union Council claimed to represent over 150,000 organised African workers. The following approximate figures were supplied to the Institute of Race Relations and published in their bulletin for September, 1945:

				Number of Unions	Membership
Johannesburg	.	.	.	50	80,000
Pretoria	.	.	.	15	15,000
Bloemfontein	.	.	.	10	5,000
Kimberley	.	.	.	5	3,000
East London	.	.	.	10	15,000
Port Elizabeth	.	.	.	19	30,000
Cape Town	.	.	.	10	10,000
Total	.	.	.	119	158,000

Though it was able to produce these imposing figures, the Council had in 1945 still a long way to travel on the road to really effective trade union organisation of black workers in South Africa. While nominal unity had been achieved by the affiliation of unions to the Council, this did not mean the end of the different groups mentioned earlier in this chapter. Many of the unions had originated as the by-products of political activities on the part of Left organisations working among the Bantu. From time to time, unions severed their connections with particular political organisations which sought to "capture" them and "guide" them. To generalise about a situation which was and remains extremely unstable and fluid, we may say that in 1945 the fifty or so African unions which were centred on the Rand were grouped politically as follows:

(1) The communist-controlled unions.

(2) Unions controlled by the Workers' International League (Trotskyist).

(3) A group of originally independent unions, led by Gana Makabeni. Makabeni co-operated closely with the communists during most of the war years, but during 1945 he fell out of favour with them. Communist support led to the election of John Marks, Secretary of the African Mineworkers' Union, as Chairman of the Non-European Council of Trade Unions.

(4) A group of unions led by D. Koza, originally with Trotskyist affiliations, but claiming, in 1945, to be without political affiliation.

Apart from these groupings, there was the general influence of the African Democratic Party, with Senator Basner as the leading figure. Basner intervened dramatically and with great effect at the 1945 Non-European Trade Union Conference against the Workers' International League, which, it was said, was making a strong effort to capture the Council.

The two most obvious gaps in the African trade union movement are the absence of effective organisation of miners and farm labourers. The number of African miners rose steadily during the pre-war years, reaching over 400,000 by 1939. African farm labourers probably number nearly a million, but no serious attempt has even been made to enrol them in unions.

With regard to the African mine workers, the communists tried to organise them in 1931 and again in 1932. The most serious difficulties were encountered. The South African gold mines recruit their labour from the Natives Reserves as well as from beyond the Union's borders. The workers come for periods of eighteen months or so and then return home. During their period of work, they are segregated in compounds on the mine property and make little contact with the more sophisticated urban workers. They retain to a large extent their interest in cattle and land and do not consider work on the mines as anything more than a rather unpleasant interlude in their lives. The vast majority of them are illiterate. Tribal feelings are strong and intertribal fights in the compounds not infrequent.

Apart from these initial difficulties, the trade union organiser is faced with the impossibility of entering the compounds and speaking to the workers. The mine authorities keep a sharp look-out for the organiser or "agitator" and usually manage to nip in the bud any incipient attempt to unionise their African employees. Early attempts at organising the Native miners were not successful.

On August 3, 1941, a big conference was convened in Johannesburg for the purpose of inaugurating a trade union for African mine workers. The leading protagonist of the idea was Gaur Radebe, who had been appointed Secretary for Mines in the Transvaal African Congress. The conference

334

was attended by representatives of all the leading African trade unions, and in addition a number of white unions gave their moral support. Even the paramount chief of Zululand sent an encouraging telegram. The conference elected a committee of fifteen and instructed it to proceed by every means it thought fit "to build up an African Mine Workers' Union in order to raise the standards and guard the interests of all African mine workers." The work of organising was at once begun and at the beginning of 1943 strong demands by the new union led the Government to establish a Commission of Inquiry into the conditions of employment on the mines. Among the members of the Commission was A. A. Moore, President of the Trades and Labour Council. The African Mine Workers' Union presented the Commission with a memorandum which subsequently led to litigation. Certain newspapers which published the memorandum were sued for damages. Four mining companies sought to recover £40,000 from the *Guardian* on the grounds that some of the statements made in the memorandum were false and that the recruiting of African mine labourers would be hindered. The courts decided against the *Guardian* and awarded £750 damages to each of the four companies.* Senator Basner and W. G. Ballinger were involved in libel actions arising out of statements made by them when giving evidence before the Commission. Colonel A. E. Trigger, manager of the mines' police for New Consolidated Goldfields Ltd., claimed £1,000 for alleged defamation contained in Basner's statements to the Commission. In giving a decision against Basner in the Supreme Court, Mr. Justice Murray awarded £50 damages, but commented that "the method adopted by the plaintiff to safeguard the interests of the mining industry was to insinuate a spy into the councils of the Native Union . . . a method which . . . leaves behind an unpleasant taste." He added, "There is much to be said for the belief that Communistic doctrine and theory is too heady a wine for consumption with safety by the mass of the members of the Native Mine Workers' Union. Even so, Communism in theory is entirely legal and permissible according to the laws of this land, and the Native Mine Workers' Union on the evidence before me is a perfectly legitimate association, even if—which has not been proved—its leaders were Communist or inclined to

* The sum paid by the *Guardian* in damages and costs was over £6,000.

335

Communism." Basner won on appeal. The Ballinger case was withdrawn.

The report of the Commission appeared in April, 1944. It recommended an increase of 5*d*. per shift for surface workers and 6*d*. per shift for underground workers, on the basic rate of 1*s*. 10*d*. per shift which had obtained for nearly a generation. Other recommendations were: cost of living allowance of 3*d*. per shift, boot allowance of 3*s*. for thirty shifts, two weeks' paid leave per annum for permanent workers, and overtime wages at time and a half. Subsidised by the Government, the Chamber of Mines granted an increase of 4*d*. for surface and 5*d*. for underground workers. The cost of these increases was met by remission of taxation. The Chamber also agreed to overtime pay. But none of the other recommendations mentioned was carried out.

Meanwhile, the African Mine Workers' Union had succeeded in organising some thousands of mine employees. The Government intervened, however, and introduced War Measure No. 1,425, which prohibited meetings of more than twenty persons on mine property without a special permit. J. B. Marks, the Secretary of the Union, and two other officials were arrested in December, 1944, when they held a meeting at the Durban Deep Compound. A few days later, P. Vundi and W. Kamye were arrested on a similar charge at Springs. The arrested men were subsequently found not guilty on a technicality. The crime created by the new measure was that of being present at a gathering of more than twenty persons, whereas the accused had been charged with "holding a meeting." In future, the police were careful to frame their charge in correct legal phraseology and from that time all trade union meetings in or near compounds have ceased. Though the war ended, the proclamation was not withdrawn.

The African Mineworkers' Union had by the beginning of 1946 gained a fair following in numerous mines throughout the Witwatersrand. A problem now presented itself to the organisers of the Union, a problem inherent in the nature of the task they had set themselves. In certain other industries the building up of African trade unions from small beginnings had been comparatively easy, and subsequent *de facto* recognition of the unions by the employers or authorities concerned had usually been achieved. The organisers would approach the workers, hold meetings, set forth the advantages of trade union organisation and begin to recruit members. A small union, representing as yet only a minority of the African workers in a particular industry, could nevertheless begin to function. It could make representations to individual employers, give evidence before the Wages Board, draw the attention of labour inspectors to infringements of wage determinations. In this way it could secure benefits for its members and also for other African workers in the industry who had not yet joined the union, but who thus became convinced of the value of organisation. The growth of the union would thus be facilitated and it would in time become truly representative of the workers in the industry.

In the case of the African gold-miners, such a normal development of a union was ruled out by the circumstances. There were no channels through which representations could be made, no means of taking up the individual grievances of members. The mines were specifically excluded from the operation of the Wages Act. The new union tried to approach the Chamber of Mines directly, but was simply ignored. According to information obtained by the Union, the Chamber of Mines in 1944 issued a circular to all compound managers and other officials, instructing them under no circumstances to meet or negotiate with union officials.[1] Between 1941 and 1946 numerous letters were sent to the Chamber, but on one occasion only was any reply received by the Union, and that reply was merely a printed postcard saying that "the matter" was "receiving attention." This was apparently sent in error by a subordinate clerk.

Nor did appeals to the Government meet with any response. Thus in 1941 the Prime Minister was asked to extend cost-of-living allowances to African mine workers, such allowances having been granted to workers in other industries. The request was supported by the Trades and Labour Council, but was ignored by the Prime Minister. In 1945 an attempt to arrange an interview between representatives of the Union and certain Cabinet Ministers ended in failure. The acting Prime Minister and the Ministers of Justice and Labour all refused to meet the union.

During the war the leaders of the African Mineworkers' Union were reluctant to force the issue. Most of them shared the prevailing Left view that nothing should be done which might hinder the war effort. By 1946 this restraint no longer operated and it seemed clear that they had no alternative but to organise a general strike of African mine workers. The rank and file were clamouring for such action. At the annual conference of the union, held in April, 1946, it was resolved to demand 10s. a day for African miners, "in accordance with the new world principles for an improved standard of living subscribed to by our Government at U.N.O." This demand was criticised by friends of the union as being excessive, but the reply was that 10s. a day had been advocated for years by the white trade union movement as the minimum wage for unskilled work.

The April conference was followed by spontaneous strikes by Africans in a number of mines where demands for 10s. a day and better food were put forward. The union stated that, "despite the difficulties placed in our way by both employers and Government, our organisers succeeded in contacting these workers and impressing upon them the need for discipline and restraint."[1]

On Sunday, August 4, 1946, a public conference of the union, "attended by over 1,000 delegates," took place on the Newtown Market Square, Johannesburg, where the following resolution was carried unanimously: "Because of the intransigent attitude of the Transvaal Chamber of Mines towards the legitimate demands of the workers for a minimum wage of 10s. per day and better conditions of work, this meeting of African miners resolves to embark upon a general strike of all Africans employed on the gold mines, as from August 12, 1946."

After the decision was taken, the President, J. B. Marks, stressed the gravity of the strike decision and said that the workers must be prepared for repression by possible violence. "You are challenging the basis of the cheap labour system," he told them, "and must be ready to sacrifice in the struggle for the right to live as human beings." His speech was loudly cheered, as was also that of the Secretary, J. J. Majoro, who declared that their repeated efforts to secure improvements by negotiation had always ended in failure, owing to the refusal of the Chamber of Mines to recognise the existence of the union. There is little doubt that both leaders and rank and file were well aware that the Government would attempt to suppress the strike by brute force. But the meeting was in militant mood. An old miner shouted: "We on the mines are dead men already!" His view was apparently shared by most of his fellows.

The strike thus decided upon began on August 12. From the mass of conflicting reports, it is still impossible to know exactly what happened on every part of the Reef on that day and on the three days immediately following. The account given below is based mainly on reports in the daily Press.

Monday, August 12. Reports indicate that 50,000 of the Reef's 308,000 African mineworkers are on strike. Six large mines have been brought completely to a stop and several others are affected. Most of the mines concerned are on the East and Central Rand. "Generally the Natives [on strike] remain quietly in their compounds and listen to statements made by mine officials. The arrest of three of the alleged ring-leaders of the strike in the Benoni area resulted in a demonstration by several thousand Natives outside the Benoni police station at midday. These Natives, who had followed their compatriots to the Benoni police station, demanded their release, and police officers advised the crowd to disperse. Police reinforcements were hurried to Benoni from other centres."

Tuesday, August 13. Thirty-two of the Rand's forty-five mines are reported as affected. There is a total stoppage on eight mines and a partial stoppage on two. Strikers attacked police escorting scabs to work at the Sub-Nigel Mine. The police opened fire and six miners were wounded. A further six were "crushed to death" by the crowd as it dispersed in panic. The police have raided the offices of the African Mineworkers' Union in Johannesburg and are carrying out extensive searches. The Natal Indian Congress in Durban has voted £100 to assist the strikers. The news of the strike has come as a "shock to the market" in City circles in London, where the price of gold-mining shares has fallen. A sub-committee of the Cabinet, appointed by the Government to deal with the strike, has got to work.

Wednesday, August 14. Clashes between hundreds of police-men, armed with batons, and Native strikers are reported at the Robinson Deep, Nourse and Simmer and Jack mines. At noon total strikes on seven mines were reported, partial strikes on four. The strike leaders allege that police are being used to force the strikers back to work and that police armed with batons are entering the compounds for that purpose. The daily papers do not mention this directly, though the following report appears in the *Cape Argus*: "During the night the strikers at the Robinson Deep and Nourse mines were told that they were expected to go on shift. They refused and adopted so threatening an attitude that the police were called in. About 150 policemen were sent to the Nourse Mine. On entering the compound stones and other missiles were thrown at the police and a fight followed. . . . Later the police reported that about 90 per cent. of the strikers at the Nourse Mine had returned to work. A few Natives were injured in the clashes. No policemen were injured. Simultaneously 290 police, under the command of Captain J. Taillard, were sent to the Chris shaft of the Robinson Deep Mine, where they were involved in a fight with the strikers. A baton charge was made into the rooms in the compound and within a few minutes hundreds of Natives streamed out. They formed up, however, and stoned the police. The police charged again and scattered them. Many hid among the mine dumps."

Similar clashes between strikers and police are reported from many other areas. The Transvaal Council of Non-European Trade Unions decided: "Late yesterday afternoon to call a sympathetic general strike of members of affiliated unions on the Witwatersrand if the Chamber of Mines was not prepared to open negotiations with the Native mine strikers by to-morrow night."

Thursday, August 15. More than 41,000 strikers are reported back at work, while the strike continues on two mines, the Nigel and the Robinson Deep, where 9,000 are still out. There has been no response yet to the appeal to the Natives in Johannesburg to come out on strike in support of the Native mineworkers. A meeting called by Native industrial unions at Newtown Market Square is banned under the Riotous Assemblies Act. When the order is read the crowd disperses quietly. The Native Representative Council, in session at Pretoria, on a motion by R .V. Selope Thema, has decided to adjourn "as a protest against the Government's breach of faith towards the African people." General Smuts, speaking on the previous day at Pretoria, is reported as saying "that he was not unduly concerned over what was happening on the mines because the strike was not caused by legitimate grievances, but by agitators" (*Cape Argus*, August 15, 1946).

Friday, August 16. It is reported that 1,600 police are on duty and that the strike has ended. "No developments have been reported yet in the threatened general strike of Natives in Johannesburg." The office of the National Executive Committee of the Communist Party in Cape Town has been raided by the C.I.D., who have removed seventy files of documents. A similar raid has been made on the C.P. office in Johannesburg.

To do more than give this brief day-to-day summary of events is not possible. The causes of the strike will be clear in a general way to the reader who has persevered so far with this history. The detailed records of events during the historic four days are still being collected—largely from men in hospital, since it is virtually impossible to obtain any information directly from the compounds. According to estimates issued by the Chief Native Commissioner for the Witwatersrand, twenty-one mines were affected by the strike, eleven wholly and ten partially, and 73,557 workers were involved. The dead number nine, of whom four were trampled to death, three died in hospital, one was shot dead and one "killed himself by running into a dustbin."

It is interesting that a strike of white gold miners was in progress at Blyvooruitsig at the same time as the Native strike. The white miners, though their strike was illegal, were not batoned back to work, nor was any form of violence used against them. The Government entered into negotiations with these white strikers and with their union, and finally a peaceful settlement was reached.

The strike of the African miners was followed by what has been described as the biggest political trial in South African history. It opened in the magistrate's court in Johannesburg on August 26, 1946. Over fifty persons, including Africans, Indians and Europeans, were charged with conspiracy and infringement of War Measure 145 (the law which made all strikes by Africans illegal). The accused included the leaders of the African Mineworkers' Union and a number of leading members of the Communist Party. Among the latter were Moses Kotane, General Secretary of the Party: Danie du Plessis, an Afrikaner and district organiser of the Party; Dr. Yusuf Dadoo, an Indian: Hilda Watts, communist City Councillor of Johannesburg: also Brian Bunting, a son of S. P. Bunting.

The trial was interpreted as an attempt by the Government to substantiate Field-Marshal Smuts' claim that the strike was entirely due to agitators. But if this was true, it soon became clear that the prosecution, in spite of the police raids upon the offices of the Communist Party, the *Guardian*, the Springbok Legion and many trade unions, had inadequate evidence. The charges of conspiracy and other similar charges under the Riotous Assemblies Act were dropped and only the charges under War Measure 145 proceeded with. To these the majority of the accused pleaded guilty and were sentenced to various fines and imprisonments.

This, however, was not the end of the matter. In November, 1946, the authorities returned to the attack by arresting the whole of the National Executive Committee of the Communist Party, who were brought to Johannesburg to stand trial upon a charge of sedition.*

CHAPTER XXVII

BANTU PRESS AND NIGHT SCHOOL MOVEMENT

IT GOES WITHOUT SAYING that the struggle of the black man for freedom in South Africa is at the same time a struggle for education and knowledge. The first European governments in this country, both the old Dutch India Company and the British administration for the major part of the nineteenth century, did not consider it a State duty to provide educational facilities even for whites, and still less would they have envisaged educating blacks and Coloured. Hottentots, ex-slaves and Africans thus received their education entirely from Christian missionaries. It was not until comparatively recent times that Government began to share the cost of non-European education by paying the salaries of teachers, and only during the last decade or so were any Government schools established for the non-European sections of the population. The vast majority of those Africans who receive

* September, 1947. The trial is still proceeding.

any education to-day are taught in mission or Church schools.

There are no exact statistics dealing with the degree of literacy of the Bantu population of the Union. Official figures do reveal, however, the approximate numbers of Bantu children who are attending school. It is interesting to compare these figures with the numbers of European children at school and the sums spent by the Government in educating the two main sections of the population.* In 1938 there were 407,000 European children being educated at a cost of about £24 16s. per head and 428,000 African children scholars at a cost of £2 2s. 1d. per head. In the same year almost 20 per cent. of the total European population were of school-going age and attending school, primary education for whites being compulsory. The percentage of the African population attending school was 6·2. Thus less than one-third of the African children of school-going age were at school. Current expenditure on African education would have to be multiplied by thirty-six to place it on the same level as European education.†

It should be noted too that of the African children who do attend school very few complete the primary course: in point of fact, many never get further than the sub-standards. In 1939, of 450,000 African school children, 310,000 were below Standard II. In 1936, less than 2 per cent. were in schools other than primary. The standard required of an African schoolteacher is considerably lower than that of a European; many African teachers have not gone beyond Standard VI.‡ It has been estimated (in 1941) that approximately 85 per cent. of African scholars leave school before attaining Standard III. If literacy is fixed at Standard III level this means that only about 15 per cent. of those who attend school become literate, that is less than 5 per cent. of the African population. Of course, Africans do in fact learn to read to some extent in other ways than by attending schools when they are children. Some learn from their fellows and, as will be described later, there is a growing adult night school movement combating illiteracy in some of the larger centres. The report of the Adult Education Committee, published in 1946, states that 80 per cent. of the

* The Coloured fall between Black and White, both in respect of the proportion of children in school and the amount of State money expended per scholar.

† O. D. Wolheim, in an article in *Race Relations News*, No. 2, Vol. 10, 1943.

‡ The Coloured teacher is required to possess a Standard VIII certificate and a teacher's certificate awarded on a two-year training course.

African and 70 to 75 per cent. of the Coloured population are illiterate.

The writer's own experience, gained in Johannesburg and Durban, suggests that possibly more than half of the permanently urbanised African population have some knowledge of reading and writing their own language. The proportion who are literate in English is, of course, very much lower. The degree of literacy among African mine workers on the Witwatersrand is very low, probably less than 5 per cent.

African higher education is chiefly centred at Fort Hare College in the Eastern Cape. The founding of this college has been described in the chapter on Jabavu and the Cape Liberals. In 1946 Fort Hare had a roll of 238 students taking degree course, the vast majority being Africans, with a few Cape Coloured and Indians.

It is an interesting fact that non-Europeans are not barred from the universities at Cape Town, Johannesburg and the university colleges at Durban and Pietermaritzburg. Those universities have never recognised a colour bar in their constitutions, and when non-Europeans applied for admission they were accepted. Very few did apply in the early years, but from the 1930's onwards increasing numbers of non-Europeans were admitted. In 1946 there were 143 non-Europeans at the University of the Witwatersrand, of whom seventy-two were Africans. Cape Town had 107 non-European students, mostly Coloured; and Natal University College at Durban and Pietermaritzburg had 239, of whom the majority were Indians. Thus the total of African students taking degree courses was about 360.

The presence of these small non-European minorities in what are otherwise white universities has raised some interesting problems both for the students and for the university authorities. The white students, most of whom are inclined to share the ordinary colour prejudices of white South Africans, have tended to ostracise the non-Europeans, excluding them from the social and "sporting" life of the universities. On the other hand, a new generation of radical or liberal-minded students has now begun to make itself felt. Usually a minority, it has on occasion been able to rally the majority of students against some reactionary measure, as, for instance, when in 1945 at the University of Cape Town an unsuccessful attempt was made to prevent non-Europeans from being elected to the Students' Representative Council. In general, one may say that a friendly attitude to the black man among English-speaking university students has grown markedly in recent years.

This cannot be said of the Afrikaans-speaking universities of Stellenbosch and Pretoria. These have always rigidly excluded the non-European student. In fact, no non-European student would even think of applying to them for admission. The persistence of the colour bar in the field of sport at both Cape Town and Johannesburg is partly due to the attitude of Stellenbosch and Pretoria, for the most important inter-varsity matches are those between Cape Town and Stellenbosch in the south and between Witwatersrand and Pretoria in the north.

In the early 1920's the National Union of South African Students came into being. It was joined by the student bodies of all the South African universities, both English and Afrikaans, at a time when colour problems had not yet troubled the universities. The organisation split in 1933, partly over the colour question and partly over politics in general. At this time many of the Afrikaans-speaking students were going fascist. The colour issue came to the front in connection with the proposed admission of Fort Hare to N.U.S.A.S. The Afrikaans universities withdrew and formed the Afrikaner Nasionale Studentebond. The N.U.S.A.S. committee, however, did not in the event admit Fort Hare, but carried on with its old policy of white exclusiveness, hoping perhaps to mollify the Afrikaners and win them back. It did not work out this way, and when the Second World War broke out, relations between English and Afrikaner students became even more strained. Finally, in 1946 the radical students of Johannesburg and Cape Town secured a majority on the national committee of N.U.S.A.S. Fort Hare students were admitted forthwith.

While it is true that anti-colour feeling finds its strongest expression among Afrikaners and that the Afrikaans universities are hotbeds of racialism, it must not be imagined that all the descendants of the Hollanders and Huguenots who colonised the Cape in the seventeenth century are believers in racial intolerance and oppression. A. I. Klopper, who became Chairman of the N.U.S.A.S. committee which admitted Fort Hare, is an Afrikaner; and even in the Pretoria and

Stellenbosch Universities, N.U.S.A.S. has been able to establish (small and much persecuted) branches.

One of the most notable achievements of the radical student movement in South Africa has been its contribution to the African night school movement. The history of these night schools begins in 1925, when the Johannesburg communists founded their first night school in a Ferreirastown slum. They taught by candle-light, without blackboards or desks. The pupils sat on benches and struggled with complicated political doctrine at the same time as they learnt their letters. Later more suitable readers were provided. This school flourished for some years, but dwindled away at the period when the Communist Party leadership, purging the party of right deviationists, alienated most of the African trade unions and other organisations which had used the party offices and night school as an unofficial club-room. A small party night school was also started in Durban, but this was at the time of police persecution of communists there and for an African openly to attend this school was virtually to invite deportation.

In 1936 a school was started in Cape Town in rooms loaned by a Church of England school in District Six. This school occupied four class-rooms and took pupils from the stage of absolute illiteracy up to the Junior Certificate (Standard VIII). It lasted a few years, but was finally extinguished by war conditions, which made it impossible to get teachers in the evenings.

In 1939 a group of progressive people, mostly university students, founded the African College in Johannesburg. The venture flourished and the response from Africans was immediate. The teachers found they had to cope with nearly a hundred students nightly, dividing these into six classes and teaching all in one room. Equipment was lacking. Many pupils had to sit and work on the floor. But there was plenty of enthusiasm and the school struggled on.

At the end of 1941 the organisers found more suitable premises; they were allowed the use of a school building. They continued to acquire books and ran also a clinic for the pupils. But in December, 1945, the building was burnt down and books and medical equipment valued at over £200 were destroyed. The school is now carrying on in less suitable premises and is always in need of funds.

The Transvaal Teachers' Association also began a night

346

school in Johannesburg during the war and this too has been well supported. About twenty other night schools of various sizes also came into existence soon after and most of these are still flourishing. One is especially worthy of notice: the African night school run by the senior boys at King Edward VII High School in a Johannesburg suburb. It has about 150 pupils.

In the Army one of the first teachers at the African College started night classes for African soldiers. In different camps six such schools were started and the number of pupils was about 600 in all.

The schools and their difficulties have been described by Betty Lunn,* who says: "The schools all operate in the face of considerable difficulties. The teachers are usually untrained, and even if qualified, cannot always adapt themselves to the special problems involved in adult education. As they are not paid, they do not all attend regularly, and the pupils are subject to frequent changes of teachers and teaching methods. Even when teachers do come regularly, they teach one night a week only, so that the same class is taught the same subject by as many as four different teachers during the week. This difficulty has been partly overcome by planning the course so that each teacher deals with a specific portion of it. (Thus, one will always take reading, while another will always take dictation and grammar, etc.).

"In spite of the many difficulties, however, the pupils are pathetically anxious to learn, and teachers do not have any disciplinary problems nor do they have to complain of inattention. The sacrifice of leisure time on the part of teachers is occasionally rewarded by a flash of unconscious humour, such as the pupil, who when asked to write an essay on the newspaper, began thus: 'The newspaper is a very useful thing: to read, to wrap up parcels, and to light the fire.' "

One difficulty encountered by the teachers is the fluctuating attendance of the African workers who may be put on night shift and thus kept away from school, or may return to their homes in the country for a period. Another problem is that the students are always tired from long hours of work. To prescribe home-work is virtually impossible. An African describes his home conditions in these words: "The roof is full of holes,

* In the *South African Socialist Review*, January, 1946.

347

the walls and floors are wet from the rain. The windows are covered with old bags. If we want light we must have the door open and then the wind blows in. We shiver from cold."

But in spite of these and other handicaps, the progress made by the pupils is notable. Their rate of learning is probably the normal rate of children attending school.

In 1944, with the formation of a Federal Council for non-European Adult Education, the teachers and organisers were able to pool their experience and collaborate over their problems. It seems that this unpaid voluntary experiment in eduation is now well established and hopes are expressed that subsidies may soon be available from Government sources.

It should be mentioned also that in Durban and Pietermaritzburg municipal African night schools for adults were established in 1929. These schools teach reading, in Zulu, and elementary arithmetic. They are staffed by part-time African teachers who are paid for their work. The expenses of the schools are paid out of the profits made by the sale to Africans of municipal beer.

In Johannesburg during the war the Technical College initiated a non-European section giving education from the standard VII level up to matriculation. The fee for these classes, while less than that charged to Europeans, was considerably higher than the 1s. per month paid by Africans attending the unofficial night schools. In practice, these latter give education up to standard VI in English, arithmetic and general knowledge, passing their pupils on to the Technical College for work beyond standard VI.

An aspect of African adult education which has only recently been studied is the need for special literature for use in the night schools and for general reading. The Institute of Race Relations has published the Pim Pamphlets —"specially written and designed for African readers"— while the African Bookman, a publishing firm in Cape Town, commenced in 1944 to publish a series of books in simple English "aimed at opening up the big wide world to the African."

But the chief index of the increasing Westernisation of the black man in South Africa has been the growth of the Bantu

Press. A Bantu newspaper may be defined as one which caters primarily or exclusively for Africans. Such papers are not necessarily printed either wholly or partly in the vernacular. All of them contain some English and some have appeared exclusively in that language. But such unilingual papers have usually been produced for specially sophisticated groups of readers. Thus the *African Sunrise*, recently launched in Johannesburg and published exclusively in English, aims at becoming the newspaper of music fans, jazz enthusiasts and crooners, of whom there are now many among urban Africans.

The more general types of Bantu papers may roughly be classified, on a language basis, into two kinds: (1) national newspapers, circulating throughout the Union and beyond its borders; and (2) provincial papers. The national papers are multilingual: English predominates, but there are sections also in Xhosa, Zulu and Suto, and sometimes in Tswana or Venda or Shangaan as well. Afrikaans is not much used. Of the national papers, all published weekly, the two most important are the *Bantu World* and *Umteteli wa Bantu* (Mouthpiece of the Bantu).

Of provincial papers there are several. They are usually bilingual, employing English and some special vernacular, with the latter predominating. Thus *Imvo zabaNtsundu* (Native Opinion) appears in Xhosa and English and circulates chiefly in the Eastern Province; *Ilanga laseNatal* (Natal Sun), in Zulu and English, is read largely in Natal and Zululand; while *Mochochonono* (The Comet), in Suto and English, is published in Basutoland and read by Suto-speaking peoples in the Orange Free State and elsewhere.

The pioneer Bantu newspaper, apart from certain missionary papers which antedated it slightly, was *Imvo zabaNtsundu*, first published in Kingwilliamstown in 1884 and edited by the famous John Tengo Jabavu. The *Ilanga laseNatal* was founded in the early 1900's and edited by an almost equally famous African, Dr. John Dube. In his youth Dube was accounted a radical. He got into trouble in 1905-6 at the time of the Bambata rebellion for articles which offended the authorities. In his more staid old age, however, his paper became less radical and Dube himself received an honorary doctorate from the University of South Africa, granted him for his work in connection with African education.

349

Of all Bantu papers perhaps the most interesting was *Abantu-Batho*. Founded in 1912 as the organ of the Native National Congress, its first Editor was Dr. P. ka I. Seme, one of the first Africans to take a law degree. It played an important part in the unsuccessful struggle against the first Native Land Law in 1913, at a time when Jabavu's paper was supporting the law, and subsequently led the victorious fight against the women's pass law in the Orange Free State at the time of the First World War. It was *Abantu-Batho* which first popularised that rousing slogan, "*Mayibuy' i Afrika*" (Let Africa come back!)

One of the weaknesses of Bantu newspapers originally founded, owned and edited by Africans, has been their tendency to fall into the hands of European business firms. This is tragically exemplified by the history of *Abantu-Batho* itself. After flourishing for many years, the paper declined in content and appearance. It was still in the early 1930's being printed with what was apparently the original type purchased in 1912 and had become almost illegible. It was finally bought up by a firm of patent-medicine vendors, who used it mainly for advertising their wares. This did not save it and it finally died an ignominious death about 1935.*

Another Bantu paper of some promise which came to an untimely end was the *African Leader*. It incorporated one of Seme's papers, *Ikwezi* (Morning Star). Published in Johannesburg in 1933, it lasted only a short time. It was widely read and had an imposing list of subscribers, but collapsed through sheer bad business management.

Mention should also be made of another important but ephemeral African-owned and controlled paper. This was the *Workers' Herald*, organ of the I.C.U. and edited by Clements Kadalie and H. D. Tyamzashe. It slumped with the collapse of the I.C.U., was revived for a few issues by W. G. Ballinger, but finally ended about 1929.

In 1932 two enterprising Europeans, B. G. Paver and I. J. La Grange, founded a new national African newspaper,

---

* It is a blot on the South African archives that no file of this paper is to be found anywhere in the country. The Act of Union required that copies of all publications should be sent to the four state provincial libraries. Little or nothing was done, however, to preserve files of Bantu newspapers. Is this another manifestation of the racial attitude of South African officialdom? Cf. the recent objection of civil servants to addressing Africans as *sir* or *madam* in official correspondence.

The Bantu World. Paver sought to put the African Press upon a sound business basis. It was his ambition to see the existing papers gain strength by working in co-operation. He approached the owners of the long-established *Mochochonono, Ilanga laseNatal* and *Imvo Zabantsundu* to win their support for his scheme. Some months later *The Bantu World* made its first appearance. Associated with Paver and La Grange in the new venture was the African journalist, R. V. Selope Thema. The initial capital, £350, was lent by Howard Pim. The new paper forged rapidly ahead. With its modern set-up and lively presentation of news items it was easily the most sophisticated of Native newspapers. It was, moreover, competently managed and after a struggle of a year or two it had achieved a healthy circulation and secured the support of advertisers. Other Bantu newspapers, less well-managed and with inadequate funds and meagre advertisements, began to feel the competition of the newcomer. It was not long before they were being bought up by the Bantu Press, the new company which had been founded by Paver with the aim of giving to Bantu newspapers some measure of co-operative strength and stability.

In this company the largest shareholder is the National Trust* and 16 per cent. of the shares are owned by the Argus Company—that juggernaut of newspaper power in this country. No dividends are paid. Besides buying up South African Native newspapers, the Bantu Press has also founded or bought up Bantu papers in Rhodesia and beyond. The position to-day is that a large number of African papers are thus linked in co-operation. African editors, journalists, printers and so forth have benefited accordingly: where there were formerly three African editors, there are now twelve; and where not more than thirty Africans found employment on African newspapers, five times as many are now employed. On the face of it, African journalism flourishes. But the very facts of the success of these newspapers in getting the support of important advertising interests and the existence of the Bantu Press Company, in which the National Trust is the biggest shareholder, have their significant corollary which will be at once apparent to the thoughtful observer. It is clear that the ideal of co-operative strength has indeed been achieved, but

---

* I.e. The Government.

351

at the cost of independence.* Of independent Bantu newspapers, owned and edited by Africans, the only one of any importance at present is the *Inkundla* (Bantu Forum), published in Natal.

Among Bantu papers serving special interests or published mainly for propaganda purposes we may mention firstly the missionary journals. *Leselinyana* (The Little Light) is published by Morija Press in Suto. It contains a certain amount of general news, but is mainly concerned with religious instruction. *UmAfrika* (The African) is published in Zulu and English at Marianhill, Natal. Like all Roman Catholic papers (cf. *The Southern Cross*), it has a definite political outlook. In addition to papal encyclicals, its columns abound in polemics against communism, radicalism and free thought. There are not many African adherents of Rome in this country at present,† but those among them who read Zulu are kept well on the party line by this very carefully edited paper.

Of political papers the largest and most heavily subsidised was *Umteteli wa Bantu* (Mouthpiece of the Bantu), organ of the Native Recruiting Corporation [read Chamber of Mines]. Founded in 1921 immediately after the big African goldminers' strike in which 40,000 workers participated, it had as its original aim the guidance of "educated Bantu opinion" along the "right lines." It has included among its nominal editors various African political leaders and it has always opposed the colour bar in industry. Here perhaps we may find indications of a community of interest between mine-owner and mine labourer, at least in so far as both feel the social pressure of the organised white aristocracy of labour. *Umteteli's*

* It is the contention of certain supporters of the Bantu Press Company that the Bantu newspapers are still independent. A letter appearing in the *Guardian*, October 10, 1946, at the time of the prosecutions arising out of the African miners' strike, furnishes an apt comment on this from the African point of view. W. M. B. Nhlapo writes: "Recent events have brought home to the reasoning Bantu the realisation that they have not yet a real national Press and mouthpiece nor genuine responsibility in journalism. Everyone expected the Bantu newspapers to write scathingly about the African miners' strike. But sad to say the newspapers sat upon the stop valve. . . . The omittance of such very important news, the half-hearted measures displayed by one or two: lack of wide and personal diversity of treatment of subjects from European newspapers' editorials and reports, is a shameful issue smacking much on the journalism of the Bantu newspapers. . . . If our newspapers are not for the furtherance of vested interest of capitalists, let them . . . tell the whole . . . truth about the strike, as did the newspapers of the Left."

† 82,000 in 1938 (*South African Year Book*).

concern for the African people did not go so far as support for the African Mine Workers' Union.

With the appearance of the *Bantu World* in 1932, a period of intense competition began. The newcomer and *Umteteli* were the two giants of the Bantu Press. Behind each, in the last analysis, were the same political and economic forces. But rival professional interests were at stake. Each strove to become bigger and better than the other. From a purely journalistic aspect, this competition was a good thing, the African reader getting more and more value for his money. This rivalry has now ended and the two papers are linked.

Since 1928 the Communist Party has been prominent in the Bantu newspaper field. Its vernacular paper has changed its name a number of times and has varied a good deal in size and quality with the fortunes of the Party. Originally the *South African Worker*, it became *Umsebenzi* (The Worker) in 1930. *Umsebenzi* enjoyed peak periods in 1930 (Durban pass-burning) and in 1935 (the war in Ethiopia). During the latter period all existing Bantu newspapers achieved record sales, so keen were Africans to hear news of Ethiopian victories. With Mussolini's triumph, sales slumped badly.

The present vernacular organ of the Communist Party is *Inkululeko* (Freedom). From the African's point of view, it can be held against it that it is unduly, though not exclusively, concerned with putting over the Stalin line on world affairs. Thus it falls into the category of controlled papers, such as *UmAfrika* and *Umteteli*. However, with that the resemblance ceases, for in spite of political ups and downs it remains very much a militant organ of African liberation. Unfortunately, paper control and other factors have prevented its regular appearance in recent years.

Editors of Bantu journals share a common characteristic of editors in refusing to be frank about the circulation of the papers they run. One can therefore only guess at the total circulation of Bantu newspapers in South Africa. Before newsprint was rationed, it is probable that the total weekly circulation of all Bantu papers was between 50,000 and 100,000 copies.* Allowing that every paper sold was read by

* Mr. Paver, to whom I am much indebted for corrections of certain statements in this chapter, considers these figures to be an underestimate "by about 50 per cent." E. R.

three or four people, we may conclude that between 150,000 and 400,000 Bantu in South Africa have got the newspaper habit.

CHAPTER XXVIII

NON-EUROPEAN UNITY

SOUTH AFRICA HAS A TOTAL population of some eleven and a half million people. Of these approximately 65 per cent. are Africans (Bantu), 22 per cent. Europeans (of whom about two-thirds are Afrikaners), 10 per cent. Cape Coloured and 3 per cent. Indian. The non-Europeans thus form 78 per cent. of the total population. In spite of the numerical preponderance of the blacks, the government of the country rests with the white minority and, as has been shown in this book, this minority denies to the blacks equality of treatment in almost every sphere of life. The inability of the non-Europeans hitherto to assert themselves to secure more equitable treatment has been partly a result of their general backwardness, for it is inconceivable that the present forms of discrimination could continue once the non-European population became as sophisticated as the Europeans. Conversely, it is also true that inequality of treatment has the effect of keeping the non-European backward. As they tend inevitably to break through the barriers imposed on them so new laws are framed in an attempt to maintain the old restrictions. In the old Cape Province prior to the Act of Union in 1910, it was possible to imagine a steady upward movement of educated Bantu and other non-Europeans into positions of power and responsibility—a gradual broadening of the democratic basis of the State as more and more Africans qualified for the vote and as men of African race began to be elected to Parliament. The African voter was then a citizen sharing equal rights before the law with all other citizens.

The breakdown of the Cape liberal system has often been attributed to the Afrikaners, who imposed their racial ideas upon the territories of the Transvaal and Orange Free State and who, after 1910, became a majority of voters in the Union of South Africa. But it should be noted that the movement to limit the power of the African voter began in the old Cape

Province long before union, and that Natal, with a white population almost exclusively English, has never been prepared to grant equal rights to either the African or the Indian.

In 1936 the Cape liberal system was finally given the *coup de grâce*. The black man's voice in Parliament was limited to indirect representation through a very small number of Europeans.* From that date the African was expected to develop along his own lines in such restricted political, economic and territorial spheres as the white man might determine for him. Political developments since 1936 have now been broadly outlined.

In the meantime, what has happened to the Cape Coloured and Indians? These people are racial minorities in South Africa; but their geographical distribution is such as to make them important elements of the population in certain parts of the country. Thus in Natal the Indian population is now slightly in excess of the white population and is increasing more rapidly than the latter; while in the Cape the Coloured population is almost equal to the white.

Have these minorities sought to throw in their lot with the Africans and to struggle with them for a common solution of their difficulties in the abolition of the colour bar? The answer is that hitherto no such general movement has taken place. Each community has tried independently, and by its own special methods to obtain more rights for itself or, more often, merely to ward off various attempts to restrict its existing liberties.

The Coloured people, by virtue of their special position as persons of mixed blood, have been offered now and again the prospect of assimilation by the whites. This was particularly so in the early 1920's, when the Nationalist Party made assimilation a definite plank in its platform. The new Afrikaner Bond,† established by the Nationalists, was a Coloured organisation. Its members supported the Nationalist candidates in elections. Bruckner de Villiers, returned for Stellenbosch in 1924, was borne on the shoulders of a group of his Coloured constituents on the night the result of the poll was declared. It will be recalled that during the same period

* Three in the Lower House and four in the Senate.

† Not to be confused with the old Afrikander Bond led by Jan Hofmeyr during the nineteenth century. See Chapter on Jabavu and the Cape liberals.

the Nationalists made overtures to the Cape Native electors also.

The Nationalists, having got into power on the wave of anti-Smuts feeling in 1924, dropped their Coloured assimilation programme and at once began to introduce legislation against all non-Europeans. The Bond, having served its purpose, was allowed to collapse. Few Coloured votes have gone to the Nationalists since that time, though a few Cape Malays still vote Nationalist, believing that they will be specially favoured under a Nationalist government.

The chief political party of the Coloured people was until recently the African People's Organisation. This was founded by Dr. Abdurahman in 1905. It consistently supported the English Party in the Cape and the South African Party of Botha and Smuts after the amalgamation of the S.A.P. and Unionists in 1920. For many years Dr. Abdurahman represented the Salt River (Cape Town) constituency in the Provincial Council. Though he was not nominally a member of the S.A.P., that party refrained from putting up a candidate against him, and he returned the compliment during parliamentary elections by supporting the S.A.P.

Prior to 1930 the Coloured vote in the Cape Province was important. There were two or three constituencies in which the Coloured voters were in the majority; and these usually returned Coloured men to the Cape Provincial Council. In that year, however, Parliament passed a law enfranchising white women, who were granted adult suffrage throughout the Union. At the same time the electoral law in the Cape was altered. Previously the old Cape law had been in force allowing all men regardless of colour to register as voters provided they could sign their names and earned a minimum of £50 a year or possessed £75 worth of immovable property. The new law granted adult suffrage to all white men in the Cape, but retained the old restrictions on the enfranchisement of the Coloured. The Coloured women remained voteless. The net result of the measure was to double the white vote in the Cape. The Coloured vote lost much of its importance.

Coloured franchise privileges in the Cape included the right to become municipal voters. Comparatively few Coloured citizens are able to qualify, but in Cape Town and Port Elizabeth they are able to exert their influence in a few municipal wards. Dr. A. Abdurahman was for a considerable term of his long life a respected member of the Cape Town City Council. A master of political manœuvre, it has been said of him that he would eventually have been Mayor of the "Mother City" had he not been Coloured. He died in 1940.

For over thirty years the A.P.O. dominated Coloured politics and, except during the brief period when the Bond existed, it was the only political organisation of any importance among the Coloured people. It could be relied upon always to support the S.A.P. and was considered by its critics as little more than a Coloured branch of that organisation. The first serious challenge from the Left came in 1937 with the establishment of the National Liberation League in Cape Town. This new body, largely communist-inspired, was a reflection of the growth of radical ideas among the younger generation of the Cape Coloured people. Interestingly enough, the leading figure in the League was none other than Abdurahman's own daughter, Mrs. Z. (Cissie) Gool. Other Coloured leaders who were prominently associated with the League were Dr. Goolam Gool (brother-in-law of Cissie Gool), J. A. La Guma, E. W. Ernstzen and John Gomas. Various new segregation measures introduced in Parliament at this time were opposed by the League, which rapidly gained followers from the A.P.O. Cissie Gool was elected to the Cape Town City Council in 1938. The League figured prominently in a new united front organisation, the Non-European United Front of South Africa. In that year the Cape Provincial Council passed a measure granting to town councils in the Cape the right to introduce segregation in transport services and in the use of town halls. This threatened privileges which non-Europeans had always enjoyed in the Cape—they had never existed in the other provinces. The new measure resulted in huge meetings on the Parade in Cape Town and demonstrations outside the Houses of Parliament. For once non-European protests were effective and the hated new measure was vetoed by the Government. The threatened outbreak of the Second World War may have helped the Government to come to this decision, as it did not want domestic complications at this critical time. But in any case the segregation of non-Europeans on buses and tramcars in Cape Town is a thing which could only be put into practice after a long and bitter struggle. The matter has not been raised since.

The Liberation League languished during the war, as did

also the Non-European United Front. But in 1943 there was a dramatic revival of political feeling among the Coloured population of the Cape. The Government, in preparation for a general election, had passed various measures designed to raise its prestige with the electorate. Among other things, it had decided to set up a Coloured Advisory Department. This body was to care for the welfare of the Coloured people and a number of prominent Coloured leaders would be appointed on it. Immediately there arose a storm of protest. Instead of pleasing the Coloured people, the new measure had exactly the opposite effect. The new body bore too close a resemblance to the Native Affairs Department; its establishment meant another degree of differentiation from the Europeans, one more step on the road to segregation. The Coloured people declared that they wanted equal treatment with the Europeans.

It has been mentioned that the Trotskyist Fourth International had since 1939 been winning converts among the younger generation of the Coloured people in the Cape. Many of those who had taken a leading part in the African Liberation League and the Non-European United Front were in 1943 members of the Fourth International, and it was they who started and led the agitation against the C.A.D. The communists, much preoccupied with helping the Government to win the war, were caught napping. They too came into the fight against the new measure. But Goolam Gool and his fellow Trotskyists had already secured the leadership of the new "Anti-C.A.D." organisation, which rapidly gained adherents throughout the Cape.

Faced with an uproar such as had previously not been known among the Coloured people, the Government hastily changed the name of the C.A.D. to "Coloured Affairs Council." They persuaded Dr. H. Gow, a Coloured parson and music teacher in Cape Town, to accept the chairmanship of the Council. A number of less well-known Coloured leaders filled the other places. But Coloured leaders as a whole boycotted the new body and have continued to do so. Little has resulted from the labours of the Council thus inauspiciously founded, but it has continued to exist. The Government secured a handsome majority in the elections of 1943 and had the support of most of the Coloured voters, who indeed in most constituencies had no alternative but to vote Nationalist.

The Communist Party scored moderately well in some Cape areas, though badly in others, and failed to secure any seats.

Meanwhile, the Anti-C.A.C. has become to all intents and purposes a new Coloured political party. Goolam Gool and most of his followers have broken away from the Fourth International.

One of the chief results of the agitation against the C.A.C. has been the radicalisation of the old A.P.O. During the height of the agitation its members divided for and against the C.A.C. Finally, the "antis" won. At the moment, Coloured political affairs are rather complicated. All one can say with certainty is that there is a general movement to the Left. This movement has even influenced such traditionally conservative groups as the Coloured teachers. The new Teachers' League is a definitely radical body and has won many members from the older Coloured teachers' organisation.

While the Coloured people of the Cape have thus been moving to the Left during the war years, an equally important radical development has shown itself among the Indians in Natal and the Transvaal. The Communist Party in Durban gained its first Indian converts following a textile strike in 1935. Two young Indian workers, G. Ponen and H. A. Naidoo, joined the Party, which soon had an appreciable Indian following. A struggle began for control of the Natal Indian Congress, a body hitherto controlled by a group of Indian merchants who believed in a moderate policy and in any case did not wish to co-operate with Left organisations among other sections of non-Europeans. Communist permeation began with the formation of a "Nationalist *bloc*" within the Congress. Dr. Dadoo was the leader of the Nationalist *Bloc* in the Transvaal and Congress in that province was soon converted to new and more radical ideas. In Natal the Leftward move-movement met with more opposition, but further attempts by the provincial and municipal authorities in Natal to restrict the liberties of Indians led to the formation of an Anti-Segregation Council dominated by communists and other radicals. It was clear that the majority of the rank and file members of the Congress supported the Anti-Segregation Council. They demanded a re-election of Congress officials. The leaders of the Congress succeeded in postponing the election for a considerable time in defiance of a provision of the Congress constitution. The opposition went to law and eventually the meeting was held in October, 1945, following upon an order from the Supreme Court. At this meeting which was attended by 7,000 Indians, the forty-six nominees of the Anti-Segregation Council were all elected to the executive of the Natal Indian Congress. Among them were twelve communists.

The new President, Dr. G. M. Naiker, declared that the immediate aims of the new congress would be the repeal of the Pegging Act (which maintained the *status quo* regarding Indian ownership of property in Durban, pending further legislation), the vetoing of the Natal Housing and Expropriation Ordinance, the removal of provincial barriers to Indian migration, the granting of full franchise, and the obtaining of free compulsory education for Indians up to the Junior Certificate (standard VIII).*

Just as the South African Government in 1936 attempted to settle the Native question once and for all by passing the Hertzog Bills, so in 1946 it has tried finally to provide a solution of the Indian question by introducing the Asiatic Land Tenure and Indian Representation Bill. Firstly, the Bill proposed to prohibit entirely the further sale of fixed property to Indians in Natal. Thus the Pegging Act, which had been introduced temporarily for Durban, was to become permanent for the whole of the province. Exceptions were to be made in certain small urban areas considered to be predominantly Asiatic where Indians would be permitted to buy land. In effect, the Bill proposed to segregate Indians permanently in limited areas and to prevent them in future from extending beyond these. The Bill was correctly described by its opponents as the Indian Ghetto Bill. In compensation for this loss of rights suffered by the Indian community the Bill offered them a communal franchise. They would be allowed to elect three representatives, who must be Europeans, to the Lower House in Parliament. In addition, they were to have two European senators and two Indian members of the Natal ·Provincial Council. A body to adjudicate on land tenure disputes was to be set up, consisting of two Indians and two Europeans, under a European chairman.

Commenting on the provisions of the Bill, J. D. Rheinallt Jones wrote: "The Prime Minister [General Smuts] has

* *Cape Times*, October 22, 1945.

adopted the tactics which General Hertzog used so successfully with the Native Bills in 1936. By working together two
unrelated subjects, he hopes to hold his parliamentary majority
together sufficiently to carry two measures, either of which
alone will not be sure to have enough supporters in his own
party. Had he introduced the restriction on Asiatic land tenure
as a separate Bill, it is likely that the Prime Minister would
have had to rely upon Opposition support—which would be
only too eagerly given—to carry it. By offering Indians a
form of political representation on the same principle as the
representation given to Africans, he has placed his liberal-
minded supporters in a dilemma. They fear that, if this opportunity of establishing the citizenship* of Indians is not grasped
it may not recur, and the status of Indians in the Union will
continue to decline. So they have decided to vote for the
Bill.''

The adoption of the Bill was a foregone conclusion, but
during its passage through Parliament some interesting things
happened. The Nationalist opposition accepted the first part
of the Bill, embodying the restrictions on Indian land tenure,
with enthusiasm, but was violently opposed to the second portion, which granted the Indians even this limited representation in Parliament. The Dominion Party (except for one
member who, it was reported, "did not speak and seldom
voted") was equally keen on seeing that the Indians got
nothing in the way of parliamentary representation. As for
the Labour Party, the debate on the Bill produced a first-rate
crisis in its ranks.

The South African Labour Party has during the last ten
years been moving, haltingly and with many a twist and turn,
to a less prejudiced attitude on the subject of colour. In the six
years or so preceding the Second World War a number of
people holding leftist views joined the Labour Party with the
idea of converting it from within. Some of them had left the
Communist Party for various reasons. Among these newcomers
the most persistent were B. Weinbren and Richard Feldman
in Johannesburg and Alec Wanless in Durban. Other leftists
who joined declared after a year or two that the task of

* It is not clear how the presence of a handful of Indian representatives
in Parliament could succeed in establishing the citizenship of Indians, while
the presence of the Native representatives there since 1937 has failed to bring
the Africans any nearer to citizenship.

converting the Labour Party was more than they could manage. They left to form the Socialist Party, which, in spite of the leading part played in it by Senator Basner, does not seem to have any prospect of becoming much more than a propagandist group.

Richard Feldman and his associates tried, with a certain amount of success, to lead the Labour Party along lines reminiscent of Fabian policy in England. They formulated plans for the reorganisation of South African banking, industry, agriculture and health services on socialist lines. J. R. Sullivan, a new Labour M.P. from Natal, became famous for his advocacy of a comprehensive scheme of social security which would include all races. Richard Feldman, elected to the Transvaal Provincial Council, took up the cudgels there on behalf of ill-paid African teachers. In a manifesto published in 1945, the Labour Party gave the following explanation of its Native policy.

The "Native problem," the manifesto said, was merely one aspect of a general economic and social problem which faced all nations under the capitalist system. Capitalism in South Africa had failed to use to the full the human and material resources of the country to provide the essentials of life for all. Socialism would automatically solve this problem and with it the Native problem. Pending the achievement of socialism, however, the Labour Party was seeking the realisation of a number of short-term objectives. These included improved educational, occupational, health and housing facilities for Africans, increased land, higher wages and the right to organise trade unions. The Labour Party was in favour of the recognition of African trade unions: the African worker should be recognised as an employee under the Industrial Conciliation Act, with rights to participate, under the guidance of the established trade union movement, in the industrial legislation of the nation. Repressive legislation which was the cause of resentment and enmity, e.g. pass laws and Master and Servant Act, must be eliminated and give way to general legislation which would bring the non-European within the industrial and other legislation of the country. Instead of manufacturing criminals, they should be creating useful citizens.

This new attitude did not imply that the Labour Party would admit Africans into its ranks as the Communist Party had done. The Labour Party declared that it did not favour *segregation,* but was nevertheless in favour of *separation.* Sufficient good land should be set aside for the exclusive use of Africans where they would be able to develop scientific farming and set up industries with the active assistance of the State. Africans would not be forced to live in these areas, but if they elected to come to the predominantly white areas they would have to accept equal pay for equal work. Thus the white workers would be protected against undercutting by cheap Native labour. The policy of separation was contrasted with the "myth of segregation," which was based on the fantastic idea that all the Africans could be forcibly removed from industries, farms and domestic service in the white areas, leaving the small European population stranded without a labour supply.

The socialists in the Labour Party who drafted these proposals were well aware of the fact that their own views on the Native question were in advance of those held by the white workers and middle-class people whose votes they sought at election times. Separatism was in a sense an attempt to mollify the electorate. Dr. T. Osborne expressed the views of many other socialists in the Labour Party when he tackled the communists more or less on the following lines. "You people," he said, "are always talking about social equality. Forget about it. That only makes the white voters angry. Without the white voters you can do nothing. Help us to control the banks and to establish a socialist government. Socialism will provide work and a rising standard of living for all. When people are economically secure, racial hatreds will die away."

Left critics of the Labour Party answered this by pointing out that the racial issue could not be by-passed in this easy way. Socialism would not come in a day. In the words of Margaret Ballinger, "All South African politics are Native affairs." The racial issue would continue to obtrude itself, and unless both the members of the Labour Party and their working-class supporters began to lose their racial prejudices that Party could not follow a consistent progressive policy.

Having considered this brief account of recent developments in the Labour Party, we may now return to the situation in Parliament at the time of the passing of the Asiatic Land Tenure and Indian Representation Bill. The ten Labour Party members in the Lower House found themselves unable to agree about the Bill. They decided to adopt the democratic procedure of allowing everyone to vote and speak according to his own views. Walter Madeley, the veteran leader of the party, moved an amendment to omit Clause 40—which provided a communal franchise for Indians. He was seconded by M. J. van der Berg and supported by H. C. Cilliers, fellow Labour members. The Nationalists were overjoyed. They and the members of the Dominion Party happily supported Madeley's amendment. The following members of the Labour Party refused to follow their leader and voted with the Government and the Native representatives against the amendment: A. Latimer, A. Wanless, A. C. Payne and J. R. Sullivan. Two of these, Wanless and Sullivan, represented Natal constituencies, and it is particularly to their credit that they took the line they did. The amendment was lost and the Bill carried.

General Smuts, so often accused by the Labour members of illiberalism, was able on this occasion to get a bit of his own back. Speaking in favour of rejecting Madeley's amendment, he said: "Nothing exposes the nakedness of the Labour Party more than this position—that they have proved untrue to a fundamental tenet of their creed, and that the best they can do is to give their members a free hand to vote as they like . . . that will not be lost on the country. A party of the Left that stands for human rights, that poses as bearing the torch of human advance, should not behave in that way. I think that part of South Africa which has looked to them for guidance will not easily forgive them the step they have taken now and the confusion that reigns in their ranks."

Since this crisis, with its revealing lesson that racial issues cannot be ignored, there has been much speculation as to the future of the South African Labour Party. Press statements that the Labour Party was "split from top to bottom" have been indignantly denied by the official organ of the Party, the *Labour-Arbeids Bulletin*, but it is clear that the organisation is facing a severe crisis. In the height of the flare-up, van der Berg resigned and joined the Nationalist Party. Madeley went back to his constituency of Benoni in the Transvaal and asked for a vote of confidence at a meeting of his branch. The latest news is that Madeley has resigned from the Labour Party. Whether this portends the emergence of a new liberalised Labour Party, purged of its extreme racialists, remains to be seen. There is little doubt that if Madeley fought a by-election at Benoni he would still be returned.*

Meanwhile, the Indian community in South Africa has begun a campaign of passive resistance against the Ghetto Act. Indian resisters, men and women, pitched their tents on a plot of municipal land in Durban. Beaten up by the white mob, their tents burnt and torn, the passive resisters still refused to go when ordered by the police to vacate the plot. Protests throughout the country have forced the authorities to restrain the mob, but all Indians who camp on the plot are arrested. The struggle goes on. Almost every day one hears that a new group of resisters has been arrested and imprisoned for trespass. Others continue to take their places on the municipal plot. Some hundreds are already in gaol, including Dadoo, Naicker, a number of Indain women, and Michael Scott, an Anglican parson who has identified himself with the resistance movement. Resistance volunteers have come from Johannesburg, including a number of Indian students who are sacrificing their academic careers by taking this action. At the time of writing, Cissie Gool is on her way from Cape Town leading another group of volunteers. The Government of India has severed relations with the Union of South Africa. A South African Indian delegation has gone to the U.S.A. to state its case before the United Nations' Organisation.

It is too early to foresee the outcome of this new struggle of the Indian people in South Africa, or to judge how far it will stimulate the other non-European groups to offer similar resistance to the colour bar laws. Efforts to unite Africans, Coloured and Indians through the Non-European Congress in 1937 came to nothing. Similar attempts through the All-African Convention or more lately through the Unity Movement (inspired by the Fourth Internationalists and the Anti-C.A.C. movement) have proved equally ineffective. Perhaps unity will come in the course of the actual struggle rather than through committees and "united front" organisations conceived by Left theoreticians. The *Guardian* reports† that large

---

* At a meeting in Benoni in December, 1946, Madeley inaugurated a new Labour Party. The general tone of the meeting was distinctly anti-Indian.

† July 27, 1946.

anti-pass meetings have ben held by Africans on the Witwatersrand, at Germiston, Springs, Boksburg, Benoni, Orlando,
Randfontein and Roodepoort. At Germiston resolutions were
passed supporting the anti-pass campaign, and the meeting
pledged themselves to organise Germiston to come out
in full force. Support was promised for the Indian passive
resistance campaign.

It is possible that resistance against the Ghetto Act and
against the passes will merge into a single campaign against
the discriminatory laws. If this happens, it will be a new thing
in the history of this country.

CHAPTER XXIX

THE TRIUMPH OF APARTHEID

THE COMING TO POWER of the Nationalist Government in
1948 was the most significant event in South African history
in recent times. All previous Nationalist Governments had
been compromises involving the sharing of power with other
parties. The "purified" Nationalists, who had broken away
under D. F. Malan during the gold-standard crisis of 1931,
were returned in 1948 with a majority over all other parties.

There began for South Africa a period of racial legislation
more thoroughgoing, more grotesque perhaps, than anything
the country or the world had yet seen. The new laws were
described by their supporters as legislation for *apartheid*, a
term which replaced the old *segregation* and achieved international coinage almost overnight.* A number of writers have
described this legislation and have sought to analyse the
motives that gave rise to it. In this book, which is concerned
in the first place with the Africans and their organisations,
it has been found impossible to discuss this huge body of law,
regulation and administrative enactment in all its ramifica-
tions and implications. However it is against these laws and
practices that Africans and their supporters have been reacting
since 1948, as many of them had reacted to the laws imposed
by previous governments. Racial laws and segregation there

*Apartheid, a-part'hāt, n. segregation (of races). Afrikaans.
Chambers's Twentieth Century Dictionary (1952).

had always been, but after 1948 racism became a political creed or ideology transcending all other creeds and providing the motive for a sustained program of legislation by the party in power. In this chapter therefore an attempt will be made to describe the genesis of the ideology of *apartheid* and how this has found expression in the actions of the Nationalist Government.

Race relations have been enormously complicated, not merely by the presence of various groups of non-whites (Africans, Coloured, Asians), but also by the division of the whites into Afrikaners and English. Much of the written history of the country has been devoted to the clash of Boer and Briton. Political conflict between the ruling groups of whites still continues and the rise of black African nationalism has created a triangular conflict in which each group appears to have interests opposed to the other two. It has been said that the basic cleavage is between a privileged white minority and a suppressed non-white majority. While this is so, it is clear that there are significant differences, if not of principle at least in methods, between the English United Party and the Afrikaner Nationalists.

The former has been described as a conservative party. Its financial support comes mainly from mineowners, financiers and industrialists who feel that "ideological legislation" on colour lines is interfering with the free flow of labour and with the rise in productivity, standard of living and purchasing power of the vast mass of non-white labourers. The majority of its supporters in the electorate are members of the middle and upper classes. The gulf between them and the Africans who labour in their factories and mines or act as their domestic servants is wide and they do not feel that their security is immediately threatened by African economic and social progress. The colour bar for them seems to be a conse-quence of their class position: it does not require to be bolstered by fresh legislation. They have, in fact, the attitude of an aristocracy.

The Nationalists on the other hand owe their political power in the main to white voters whose financial position and sense of security are by no means comparable to those possessed by the supporters of the United Party. The Nationalists get their votes from numbers of rich farmers, from a small but increasing class of business men and from civil servants (the civil service being almost exclusively staffed by government supporters). But their main electoral support comes from comparatively poor people—the vast mass of only moderately well-to-do farmers, artisans and factory workers. These poorer sections of the white population, almost entirely Afrikaans speaking, form a sort of lower middle class, economically not very far removed from the better-off non-Europeans. Even in purely white communities members of the lower middle classes are known to be sensitive regarding their position vis-a-vis the "lower" classes. In other words they are said to exhibit an inferiority complex. Inevitably in South Africa lower middle class snobbery becomes colour snobbery. This is one reason why the Nationalist Party, much more than the United Party, has found it profitable to exploit colour issues. The Afrikaans workers are Nationalist almost to a man. They regard the Government as their protector against exploitation by their employers on one hand and competition from non-European labour on the other. The once powerful white and predominantly English Labour Party has completely disappeared.

These, however, are not the only reasons for the strength of the Nationalist Party, which is the product of more than a century of struggle by the Afrikaans people for cultural and economic independence.

The Afrikaner nationalist is himself a member of a group that has rebelled against colonial subjection in the past and still feels the weight of that subjection, even though its major burdens have long since been removed. Skin colour does not enter directly into the patterns of Briton-Boer relations, but many of the elements of the colonial problem are still there, especially on the emotional side. White Afrikaner nationalists control the government and the organs of state power: the police, the armed forces and the civil service. But in the field of economics and culture it is different. We have already explained how the Afrikaners are in general the poorest section of the whites. In the field of language and culture also they are conscious of disabilities.

In the period immediately following the Boer War a conscious attempt was made by Milner and his followers to assimilate the Afrikaners politically and linguistically. The conquered people were to become loyal supporters of the British Empire. With the help of outstanding Boer leaders like Botha and Smuts, this attempt very nearly succeded. It was foiled partly by the excesses and faulty tactics of the English administrators, partly by the jingoism of the English colonials, particularly those of Natal who became known as "little Englanders," but mainly by the rise of a Nationalist Party founded by J. B. Hertzog and Tielman Roos.

Inevitably the Nationalists made the survival and extension of the Afrikaans language a major issue. Bilingualism was conceded by the English in theory, but in fact it was resisted for years and this added fuel to the flames.

It is possible, in terms of Toynbee's theory of "challenge and response," to explain the continued growth of Afrikaner nationalism and its present vigour. For every advance towards what they considered their national rights or aspirations the Afrikaner Nationalists have had to fight: for their language, for their parliamentary majority, for freedom from being involved in England's wars, for a national flag instead of the Union Jack, for "Die Stem van Suid-Afrika" instead of "God save the King," and more recently for their republic. The emotional energy generated by each struggle was heightened by each success and then mobilised for the next campaign. With nothing remaining to be achieved on the home front except economic advance of the Afrikaner to equality with the English (a process facilitated by the use of state power), it would have seemed that the struggle would become less bitter, emotions would die down and the Afrikaner would lose his sense of frustration and inferiority.

However the facile utilization of anti-black feeling for political ends, which seemed to yield such high political dividends, is now bearing bitter fruit. There was a brief period when leading Nationalists were prepared, as was shown in Chapter XVI, to make common cause with African and Coloured organisations for the defeat of Smuts, and, as Hertzog said, for the "prosperity of the nation." But this "true patriotism," as D. F. Malan described it, was still-born and the Nationalists became committed to a policy of racial discrimination. To-day Afrikaner nationalism is confronted with another nationalism, the nationalism of the blacks, a force which their own policy has strengthened. It has so happened that the movement for racial freedom in South Africa is now part of a world movement against the remnants of colonialism, and this has the support not only of the new states of Africa and Asia but of the former imperialist powers

369

as well.

Faced with opposition within and without their borders, the Afrikaner nationalists now cultivate a back-to-the-wall or *laager* mentality, and they seek to involve the whole country in a campaign of defence against agression from without. If *apartheid* is subjected to criticism in the United Nations then this is an "attack on South Africa," and if South Africans join in this criticism they are "betraying their country."

The Nationalists are now so strongly entrenched within the electoral system and they have so firm a hold on the state machinery that probably only a major economic crisis could shake them. But South African industry continues to expand. The economy is in fact so buoyant that the country can, as it were, afford the luxury of *apartheid* with its numerous duplications and inefficiencies. And while the blacks in South Africa suffer from inferior wages, malnutrition, poor housing, inferior social services, inferior education and inferior opportunities, their position in absolute terms is not markedly worse and in some respects is distinctly better than that of blacks in other parts of the continent. The Nationalists therefore hope that they are strong enough to withstand the revolt from within and defy the pressure from without. However with regard to neither of these threats have they become complacent. On the home front they continue to develop the autocratic and military power of the state, while their representatives abroad try by all means to mollify criticism.

The desire to make a good case for *apartheid* and win friends overseas has led to the creation of so-called "Bantustans" or "Bantu homelands" within the Republic's borders. These are the old "Native Reserves" now dressed in new garb. They will offer "positive *apartheid*" or extension of rights, in return for "negative *apartheid*," or deprivation of rights, which is to continue within the Republic itself. Since at the most optimistic estimate the Bantustans will house only about a third of the country's African population, while the remaining two-thirds will continue to suffer under negative *apartheid*, it seems that overseas' opinion, well informed of these facts, is unlikely to be mollified.

Before we describe the reactions of the Africans and other non-whites and of their white supporters to the programme of *apartheid* as it developed after 1948, we shall give an outline of the various laws and enactments in which the programme has been enshrined.

It is an interesting fact that in 1948 the Nationalist majority in Parliament represented a minority of voters. This happened again in 1953, though on this occasion the excess of opposition voters must have been very small. A major objective of the Nationalists was therefore to make themselves secure in the legislature. The South West Africa Affairs Amendment Act of 1949 added six members to the Legislative Assembly and four to the Senate. The enfranchised whites of this mandated territory were expected to return Nationalist members and in fact they did. Equally useful to the Nationalist hold on Parliament was the removal of the Cape Coloured voters from the common roll. This was finally achieved, after a long parliamentary and legal struggle, in 1956. It meant also a further advance in negative *apartheid*.

While consolidating its control over Parliament, the Government has taken drastic measures to suppress extra-parliamentary opposition to *apartheid*. It has given to its Minister of Justice, and his special police, powers of suppression and banishment of organisations and individuals without reference to the courts. Arbitrary powers invested in the administration already existed prior to 1948, as this history has shown. Since then these powers have been increased to an alarming extent. Some have seen in this a movement towards the final suppression of the rule of law and the creation of a police state. It is interesting to recall that with the introduction of each new bill proposing further drastic curtailment of liberty, liberals have said: "This is our last chance to protest: after this, protest will be impossible." And yet further legislation or administrative enactments of a repressive kind were still to come and protests were still made. It seems that the road to totalitarianism is a long one and that while the white parliamentary franchise remains, there will still be some semblance of a democracy very much curtailed and limited to whites only. In this connection it should be noted that while numerous leftist newspapers have been suppressed, and the Government has given itself powers to suppress any journal, certain widely-read newspapers, such as the *Rand Daily Mail*, still voice strong opposition.

Legislation for negative *apartheid* has affected rights of residence, of movement, of employment, of trade, of appeal to the courts, of education and of sexual relations.

The Group Areas Act of 1950 and the Group Areas Consolidation Act of 1957 were aimed at the complete separation of the various races, African, Coloured and Asian from each other and from the whites, in separate residential areas in all urban areas throughout the country. This legislation was also directed to the elimination of so-called "black spots" within or next to white areas. The few remaining places where Africans owned free-hold property, such as Sophiatown (suburb of Johannesburg) were cleared of their former inhabitants who were moved to locations ("Bantu townships"). Within the locations again, special areas were set aside for different ethnic or tribal groups. An attempt was thus made to reverse the process of tribal mixing which had been going on for years in urban areas. Since the overwhelming majority of location residents worked in towns and since the new townships were often many miles away, Africans were faced with additional hardships, such as finding money for transport, early-morning queuing, and absence from home for many hours a day.

A group that has suffered severely under the Group Areas Act is the Indian community. In the Transvaal these people were often traders and their removal to special residential areas meant economic ruin. "Of the total Indian population of 48,892 in the Transvaal, 38,367 face eviction from their premises. . . . In Johannesburg 1,200 Indian traders are to be moved and 22,167 Indians are to be moved to the new group area at Lenasia (nearly 20 miles away). A total sum of R41,166,000 is involved in stocks and property. . . . The Transvaal Indian Congress alleges a process of 'attrition' of the Indian Community, which is intended to reduce the Indian to the level of a manual worker " (Stanley Uys, in *The Sunday Times*, 10 March 1963).

The Urban Areas Act applies equally to the Coloured people, but here the Government faced difficulties, particularly in places like Cape Town where certain white and Coloured areas had for centuries been inextricably mixed. *Apartheid* also implies separation of races on beaches. The solution of this "problem" was transferred to the municipality of Cape Town and the Cape Divisional Council. Port Elizabeth proclaimed separate beaches for whites, Coloured and Malays, Asians, Bantu and Chinese.

Laws relating to movement have been in existence since the

promulgation of the first pass laws. In 1952 the Nationalists introduced the Natives (Abolition of Passes and Co-ordination of Documents) Act. Far from abolishing the hated passes this law in fact consolidated the pass law for the whole country. It did however reduce the number of pieces of paper an African must carry on his person if he wished to avoid arrest and imprisonment. The various documents, including tax receipts, were incorporated in a single "reference book." This book must be carried at all times and the African who is found at any time or place without his book commits a criminal offence. The carrying of reference books is now (1963) made compulsory for African women, and thus the long struggle against passes for women, which began in 1919 (see Chapter XI) ended in defeat.

The Government (with an eye on overseas and liberal criticism) said that passes should apply also to whites. In 1950 the Population Registration Act declared that Europeans, Asians, Indians and Coloured must possess registration cards, with photograph and registration number (but without thumbprint). At the time of writing (July 1963) this legislation has not yet been fully implemented and some thousands of whites have not yet taken out cards. In any case, the law does not envisage that whites will be compelled to carry their cards with them on pain of arrest and imprisonment, as Africans must. As in the case of motor-driven licences, the police may be empowered to call upon a white citizen to produce his card within a specified time.

The pass laws as now enforced make residence of Africans in towns more and more precarious. Any African working in a town for less than 10 years but not born there, may, if he loses his job, be compelled to return to the place where he was born. He must then apply for permission if he wishes to seek work in any urban area. An African may not sleep with his wife, supposing she is a domestic servant and resides on her employer's premises. If he does he commits a criminal offence; and so does the householder who permits him to sleep there. The householder would be contravening "C/Sec. 9 (5) Act 25/1945," a law passed, be it noted, not by the Nationalists but by the Smuts Government.

"Foreign Bantus," i.e., immigrants from beyond the Republic's borders, have been removed from urban and peri-urban areas and told to leave the country on pain of imprisonment, unless they are indentured mine labourers. Foreign Africans employed in rural areas will similarly have to leave if they lose their present jobs.

The industrial colour bar, which received legal sanction in the Mines and Works Act of 1926 (a product of Labour-Nationalist cooperation) has been extended in various ways and notably by ministerial enactment known as "job-reservation." One effect of the country's industrial revolution, which has proceeded apace under all governmental regimes since 1933 has been the absorption into industry of many thousands of Africans and other non-Europeans. A report of the Department of Labour, covering the period 1937–56, stated that of a total 304,000 persons judged to be semi-skilled (and presumably employed in 1956) some 27.7 per cent were whites, the remainder being non-whites. Job reservation did not aim at excluding non-whites from skilled or semi-skilled occupations in general, but at giving the authorities power to reserve certain favoured jobs or a certain proportion of jobs for whites. There has been relaxation of the occupational colour bar, as enforced by the white trade unions, so as to allow Africans to become skilled workers provided they are employed only in Bantu areas. This relaxation has enabled municipalities to employ Africans on housing schemes in the new urban locations.

Among the various forms of negative *apartheid* which Africans have endured is the steady deprivation of opportunities for economic advancement. During the period of contact prior to 1948, Africans had made some slight but significant advance in the field of business and trade, and this in spite of legal restrictions and lack of capital and experience. We have indicated in early parts of this history that there were African traders, cafe proprietors, owners of buses, small-scale furniture workshops and the like (p. 298).

The *apartheid* policy of the Nationalists after 1948 involved the complete removal of African business, trade and professions from all white areas. The exclusion of African traders from all areas other than their own townships and locations was confirmed in 1956 by the Secretary of Native Affairs, who declared, however, that they would obtain an exclusive monopoly in urban African residential areas.* The Secretary said:

*See an article by Jonathan Love, *Rand Daily Mail*, 12 April 1963.

"I submit that this has opened up to them a field of unlimited opportunity, very much more valuable than the few isolated opportunities which they may ultimately lose as the result of the curtailment of their activities in areas set aside for other racial groups." In other words, in return for negative *apartheid* outside the urban locations there was to be an instalment of positive *apartheid* within the locations. Since the majority of Africans work in white areas and merely live in locations, they would continue to spend a good deal of their income in the shops of white traders. They would also continue to patronise white shops situated just outside the locations. But within the location gates, only African traders and businesses would be permitted. This would give African business and trade opportunities of expansion. Thus African capital would have a limited but exclusive field for expansion.

However, such is the fanaticism of the apostles of *apartheid*, that even this concession was withdrawn. In 1958 a statement by the Minister of Bantu Affairs made it quite clear that facilities for African traders in urban areas was temporary "and only to give them an opportunity to build up capital and gain experience for use in their home areas," namely the Native Reserves. Even during this temporary period African trading in the locations was to be restricted to "daily domestic necessities." The lucrative African urban market in everything else was to remain the monopoly of white trading concerns.*

The colour bar in educational institutions was very general before 1948 and was based both on law and custom. It has in fact been complete in primary and secondary schools, both public and private, except that a very small number of favoured Chinese were able to attend private secondary schools. Prior to the middle 1920's there was only one university college for non-Europeans, namely Fort Hare (see Chapter VII). But in the period between the world wars the "liberal" universities of Cape Town and the Witwatersrand began to accept a few non-European students, giving them academic, but not social, equality with other students. They were allowed for instance to join cultural societies, such as the debating society, but not to attend student dances or join other students in sport. These newcomers were chiefly Coloured at Cape Town and African and Indian at the Witwatersrand.

*Jonathan Love, *Rand Daily Mail* 12 April 1963.

Natal University set up parallel classes for non-Europeans, chiefly Indians.

This significant, though limited, advance of non-whites into the field of university education led to the introduction by the Nationalists of the Separate Universities Education Bill in 1957. This proposed to exclude non-white students from the so-called "open" universities which had admitted them. There was strenuous opposition from both staff and students, including academic processions of protest, but the bill became law. Non-European students already attending were allowed to complete their studies. A few others were subsequently admitted, by special permission of the Minister of Education, on the grounds that no non-white college could provide them with the course they wished to take. In effect all Africans are now excluded from the universities of Cape Town and the Witwatersrand, while a few Indians and Coloured still attend.

The Act made provision for the setting up of Bantu Colleges on tribal lines. Fort Hare became a Xhosa college. A college for the Zulus was started in Natal and one for the Sotho in the Northern Transvaal. Further developments led to the founding of a college for the Coloured near Cape Town and one for Indians near Durban. These new institutions are not independent universities: they are administered directly by government departments and their professors and lecturers are civil servants, subject to appointment and dismissal by the Minister. Grounds of dismissal include "any act commenting adversely upon any department of the government or any province." The students similarly are subject to isolation and to disciplinary rules quite unknown in any ordinary university.

The Nationalist Government had already in 1953, with its Bantu Education Act, removed the control of African primary and secondary education from the provincial councils and vested it in the Bantu Affairs Department. Further administrative enactments have largely displaced the missionaries as purveyors of education to the non-Europeans. At the same time the education provided is being "slanted" more and more to conform to the ideology of *apartheid*. Compulsory mother-tongue education has been introduced in the lower grades, and English, once the common medium of instruction, is being steadily eliminated in the middle and high schools. The government claims that more African children are being educated than ever before. This has been achieved by reducing the hours of schooling and making the teachers work double shifts. The overwhelming majority of African students leave school with only two or three years of instruction behind them. Education is still not compulsory for non-Europeans. The disparity between the amounts spent on white and non-white children remains gross, as the following figures for 1959–60 show:

	Number in schools	Amount spent per head
Whites	640,000	R125
Coloured and Indian	412,000	70
African	1,608,000	14

The white children in school constitute 21 per cent of the white population. The corresponding figure for Africans is 14 per cent.

Legislation affecting sexual relations between the races was first introduced in Tielman Roos's Immorality Act of 1927, which made extra-marital sexual relations between Europeans and Africans an offence. It did not prohibit marriage between the races (this being in any case extremely rare) and it did not affect illicit sexual relations between Coloured and Europeans. In 1949 Parliament passed the Prohibition of Mixed Marriages Act and in 1950 the Immorality Amendment Act which prohibited all carnal intercourse between a European and a non-European. This Act has caused numerous tragedies which have had considerable publicity both in South Africa and overseas. Men and women who had lived together for years and had reared families, suddenly found themselves arrested and imprisoned for breaking the law. In the eleven years up to 1960, 3,890 persons were convicted for offence under the "immorality" laws (*Rand Daily Mail*, 7 February 1962).

Viewed against the vast mass of colour-bar legislation, the "compensatory" concessions of positive *apartheid* appear singularly unimpressive. The Bantu Authorities Act of 1951 abolished the Native Representative Council which had not been called since 1948. The new law allowed for the establishment of "Bantu Authorities," tribal, regional or territorial. Little was done to establish such bodies until 1959 when the Promotion of Bantu Self-Government Act was passed. In June 1960 white "commissioners general" were appointed for the different tribal areas, and the Transkei was chosen for the establishment

of the first Bantu Territorial Authority. Apart from the
Transkei no other area has been favoured in this at the time
of writing (March 1963), while in the Transkei itself the
establishment of the Authority was marked by revolt and
political turmoil, as we shall describe later.

CHAPTER XXX

SUPPRESSION OF THE COMMUNISTS

WHEN THE NATIONALIST Government came into power
in 1948 it was faced with active opposition from many quarters,
not least from the Communist Party, which had grown considerably in strength and influence during and since the war.
The party had trained an appreciable number of African,
Coloured and Indian members and exerted considerable
influence in both the African National Congress and the
South African Indian Congress. It had also managed to
secure a direct voice in Parliament itself.

At the elections for Native representatives in 1947, D. B.
Molteno had not offered himself for re-election for Cape
Western. His place had been taken by the Communist, Sam
Kahn, who was returned with a large majority. Kahn did not
confine his propaganda activities to his own constituency.
When he visited Johannesburg in March 1949, a magisterial
order was issued forbidding him to address certain meetings.
He was prevented from entering Benoni location. He was
again on the Rand two months later. The *Rand Daily Mail*
reported that "mounted police and a flying squad car were
stoned, batons were drawn and two crowds were dispersed
when police carried out a ban on meetings which were to be
addressed by Mr. Sam Kahn, South Africa's only communist
M.P., in Rand Native townships." It was reported later that
he had "outwitted" the Minister of Justice and had managed
to hold a meeting at Newclare. The Minister then issued a
general ban preventing Kahn from attending for a year any
public meetings on the Witwatersrand.

Another method of restricting the movement of agitators or
critics of the Government was the withholding of passports to

travel overseas. A ding-dong battle on this issue went on for some years, with frequent appeals to the courts by those whose passports were seized. In May 1949, E. S. Sachs, the militant secretary of the Garment Workers Union, had his passport withdrawn. He had intended to attend a clothing and textile union conference in France. In June the Appellate Division of the Supreme Court upheld the decision of a lower court that Dr. Yusef Dadoo, the Indian leader, had been unlawfully deprived of his passport, and the ruling calling upon the Minister to return the passport was upheld. The Government's prerogative in issuing or refusing to issue passports was not affected by this decision. In February 1954, Sam Kahn and family were reported to have sailed for Britain with "Sam Kahn passports." These were identity documents with which Kahn had provided himself and his family. They apparently had no difficulty in entering Britain and they returned to South Africa in due course. This led to the Departure from the Union Regulation Act of 1955, which made it a crime visited with severe penalties for any South African to leave the Union without a passport.

The ability of the Communist Party, the African National Congress, and their supporting organisations to organise demonstrations against the government was shown on May Day 1950. On 26 April the Minister of Justice, C. R. Swart, told Parliament that strong measures would be taken to counter "freedom day" demonstrations which non-Europeans were planning to hold the following week. All meetings would be banned. The press reported 13 Africans killed and more than 24 wounded in May Day rioting on the Rand when the ban on meetings was defied at Benoni, Sophiatown and Orlando. Three days later Margaret Ballinger moved in Parliament for a debate on the Rand riots as a "definite matter of urgent public importance." The motion was defeated. The United Party refused its support and only the 3 Natives' representatives and the 6 Labour members supported the motion.

On 6 May, Swart announced that he would seek wide powers to outlaw communists. The Suppression of Communism Bill then passed its first reading. A communist was defined as "a person who professes to be a communist or who, after having been given a reasonable opportunity of making such representations as he considers necessary, is deemed by the

Governor-General . . . to be a communist on the ground that he is advocating . . . any of the objects of communism." Communism was defined in very broad terms. Among other things, the law could regard as a communist a person who "aimed at bringing about any political, industrial, social or economic change in the country by unlawful acts." It must be noted that it would be an unlawful act to urge mine-workers to strike for higher wages and thus bring about an "industrial change." The definition of communism also included encouraging feelings of hostility between black and white. The Act further made provision for the compilation of a list of persons who had at any time been associated with the Communist Party. Once on the list any such person might, without further formality, be proscribed by the Minister. He could be ordered to resign from any organisation to which he belonged or by which he was employed. Among other provisions of the Bill was one stating that "if the Governor-General is satisfied that any periodical or other publication serves inter alia as a means for expressing views or conveying information, the publication of which is calculated to further the achievement of any of the objects of communism, he may, without notice to any person concerned, by proclamation in the *Gazette* prohibit the printing, publication or dissemination of such publication."

The press reported, on 14 June, that a baton charge by police dispersed a crowd of several hundred people, mostly Coloureds, who demonstrated outside the House of Parliament in protest against the Suppression of Communism Bill.

The communists did not wait for the Bill to be passed before dissolving their party. Its dissolution was announced in Parliament by Sam Kahn before the completion of the third reading. The national chairman of the party, I. Horvich, issued a statement: "Recognising that the day the Suppression of Communism Bill becomes law every one of our members, merely by virtue of their membership, may be liable to be imprisoned without the option of a fine for a maximum period of ten years, the central committee of the Communist Party has decided to dissolve the party as from today." It was said that the decision to dissolve was not unanimous, and that W. H. Andrews and a number of others recorded their vote against it.

The Bill passed the Senate on 22 June 1950, by the chairman's casting vote. It had been opposed by the United Party in both houses. That party, though approving of the need for anti-communist legislation, considered that the Bill was too great an interference with civil liberty. It considered that persons charged with communist activity should have the right of appeal to the courts.

In August it was announced that J. de Villiers Louw, assistant magistrate of Johannesburg, had been appointed liquidator in terms of the Suppression of Communism Act. His first duty was to compile a list of former supporters of the Communist Party of South Africa. Among the first to be "named" was E. S. Sachs. The fact that he had been expelled from the C.P. nineteen years before did not avail him. In May 1952, he was ordered to resign from the Garment Workers Union. The same order forbade him to attend gatherings "except church, recreational and social gatherings" The Garment Workers Union called a mass meeting of protest on the Johannesburg city hall steps. A large crowd of garment workers assembled. They were mostly women, and whites and non-whites were about equally represented. Sachs addressed the meeting. While he was speaking a small group of police moved forward from the city hall to arrest him. As they made their way through the throng, small bannerettes, which many of the crowd had been carrying were thrown at them. After a slight scuffle Sachs was taken in charge and removed amid the jeers of the crowd. Other police then emerged from the city hall, some with staves, others with chairs which they had picked up in the foyer. With these assorted weapons they attacked the crowd. Women were hit and chased by the police who apparently had got out of hand. The writer of this history, who was present, can recall similar acts on the part of the police, but none in which so many women were involved and which occurred in such a public place.*

In July Sachs was found guilty in the magistrate's court of addressing meetings and was sentenced to six months imprisonment on each of two charges. In December his appeal against this conviction was dismissed by the Appeal Court. The sentence was, however, suspended for three years, con-

*In February 1959 the police attacked a crowd of some hundreds of women assembled in a hall in Lady Selbourne, Pretoria, to protest against the issue of passes. Entering the hall they ordered the meeting to disperse and then drove the women out with batons.

ditional on his not being convicted of any offence under the Riotous Assemblies Act and the Suppression of Communism Act during this period. Forced to leave the organisation he had built and which he had led for twenty-four years, and finding all forms of trade union and political activity closed to him, Sachs eventually left for England, where he joined the Labour Party.

Proceeding against other opponents, the Government banned the Cape Town newspaper, the *Guardian* in May 1952. This paper, founded shortly before the war, had functioned as a mouthpiece of communists and fellow-travellers. It had given uncritical support to the Soviet Union on nearly all occasions and had seemed to follow the communist line fairly closely. The suppression of the *Guardian* was followed immediately by the appearance of another weekly, the *Clarion*, edited by approximately the same staff as the *Guardian*. For technical reasons *Clarion* became the *People's World*. This was proscribed by the Government and a new paper, *Advance*, appeared. This carried on till October 1954, when it in turn was banned. Apparently quite unperturbed the publishers formed a new company and brought out the *New Age*, which was not finally suppressed till 1962. Even then the indomitable editor of the *New Age*, Brian Bunting, and his associates, managed to produce a new paper, *The Spark*. Publication of this became impossible however when the producers were forbidden on pain of imprisonment to take any part in editing, writing or publishing any journal whatsoever.

Legislation against ex-communists in elected bodies proved more effective. In May 1952, Sam Kahn was expelled from his seat as Native representative in the House of Assembly. At the same time his colleague, Fred Carneson, was removed from the Cape Provincial Council. In July of the same year Kahn was ordered by the Government to resign from the Cape Town city council. He did so, saying "I am one of many victims of terrorist assault on civil liberties." In August by-elections were gazetted to take place in the vacant seats. Both Kahn and Carneson were nominated by their supporters, but the legislation stood the test and their nominations were refused. But Brian Bunting, editor of *Advance*, apparently discovered a loophole in the Act. He was nominated, and though the Government invoked its legal machinery, it could not prevent his nomination being accepted by the electoral officer. Accordingly the by-election was held and Bunting was returned by a large majority. "He won't be M.P. for long," said the Prime Minister, Dr. Malan. The procedure used against Kahn was now employed against Bunting. He was expelled from the House of Assembly—but not until he had received at least one payment of his salary as an M.P.

In spite of official discouragement, the voters of Cape Western continued in their attachment to Leftist candidates. In 1954 came a general election for Native representatives. In the meantime Parliament had passed the Anti-Communism Act in an endeavour to close some of the gaps in the original Act. The ex-communist, Ray Alexander, stood for Cape Western, though she was informed that she would be expelled from Parliament if she were returned. She polled 3,525 votes against the Liberal R. Gibson's 998 and the Independent J. Jonker-Fiske's 657. When she attempted to enter the Houses of Parliament she was barred by detectives.

The police paid her damages when she threatened legal action proceedings over this incident.

In January 1955 Lee Warden was elected. The government could not unseat him because it had no legal machinery for doing so, as he had not been named as an ex-communist. Warden was a printer and publisher who had established a well-deserved reputation in liberal circles for his willingness to print radical journals which the ordinary printer would not dare to handle. He retained his seat in Parliament as a representative of Cape Western until the final removal of the Cape Native Representatives from parliament in 1960. With him went also Margaret Ballinger, who had represented Cape Eastern since this type of representation was first established in 1936.

CHAPTER XXXI

DEFIANCE CAMPAIGN

THE SUPPRESSION OF THE Communist Party did not mean that those who had previously adhered to Marxist doctrines automatically ceased to take part in political activities. Since the war the communists had established intimate links with organisations such as the African National and Indian Congresses. These organisations had not become completely communist bodies, but they had become permeated with many of the ideas of militancy and direct action which had characterised the C.P. In its inability to distinguish what was communist and what was not communist, the government tended to equate all forms of anti-*apartheid* activity as practised by non-white or mixed organisations as communistic until finally avowedly anti-communist liberals were prosecuted for forwarding the "aims of communism." More than a decade was to go by before the special police secured powers of arrest and imprisonment without trial of all whom they suspected of "subversive activity" and before the last allegedly "communistic" organisation was finally driven underground.

In the 1950's above-ground political opposition was still possible on a large scale, as the government discovered when it sought to consolidate its powers by limiting the voting right still possessed by some non-Europeans in the Cape. In February 1951, a measure was introduced which aimed at removing the Cape Coloured voters from the common roll and placing them on a separate roll with the right to return four representatives, who must be whites, to Parliament. A leading motive was to prevent the participation of Coloured voters in ordinary parliamentary elections where they almost always voted against the government and sometimes held the balance of power as between government and opposition candidates. It will be recalled that the Native (African) voters in the Cape had been similarly treated by the Hertzog legislation of 1936. On that occasion the majority of the United Party, led by Smuts, had supported the legislation, but now the United Party was not prepared to accept the change. Consequently a long legal battle started, because in terms of the Act of Union the rights of voters could not be altered without the consent of a two-thirds majority of both Houses of Parliament voting together in a joint sitting.

The opposition to the new Coloured Franchise Bill was far-reaching, for it comprised not merely the politically-minded non-Europeans but also that large section of anti-Nationalist white opinion which supported the United Party. U.P. politicians were thinking of the electoral implications of the new measure and were tired of making concessions to the Nationalists. For many U.P. supporters, however, the vital issue was the attempt of the government to "tamper with the constitution," for when the Nationalists failed to secure their two-thirds majority they resorted to various expedients of doubtful legality. When the Supreme Court ruled that a two-thirds majority was necessary, the government passed the High Court of Parliament Act which gave Parliament the right to decide any constitutional question by a simple majority. The Supreme Court ruled that this was illegal. The Nationalists, since they were determined to push the measure through, were finally forced to adopt the expedient of altering the structure of the Senate. This was finally achieved in 1955 in the passing of the Senate Act. The total number of senators was approximately doubled and proportional representation of provincial appointees to the Senate was abolished. Since the Nationalists had majorities in three out of four provincial councils, they were able to secure an overwhelming majority in the Senate, and to swamp the United Party completely in a joint sitting. In 1956 the South Africa Act Amendment Bill was passed at a meeting of both Houses sitting together. This finally removed the Cape Coloured voters from the common roll and allowed them to elect four representatives who must be Europeans.

This gerrymandering of the constitution roused the opposition, as we have said, of both Europeans and non-Europeans. In April 1951, a call for a one-day protest strike, made by the radical Franchise Action Committee, received strong support in Cape Town and Port Elizabeth. Almost all factories were affected and many thousands of African and Coloured workers stayed away from work.

Among whites the chief opposition was centred in the

385

activities of a new organisation which sprang into existence almost overnight. It was called the Torch Commando and its organisers were ex-servicemen who felt that the democratic rights for which they had fought in the war against Hitler were now being filched from them. The Torch Commando displayed great militancy and roused great enthusiasm. On 7 April a torchlight procession in Johannesburg brought about 20,000 white people, largely ex-servicemen, out on the streets. Speakers emphasised the "rape of the constitution." Some went so far as to speak of the rights of the Cape Coloured man threatened by the new law. A similar mass demonstration occurred in Cape Town. There was fighting at Vrededorp, a National Party stronghold in Johannesburg, when a Torch Commando meeting was broken up by pro-government supporters. Some 32 persons went to hospital. In the general election which took place in April 1953, the Torch Commando played a leading role in supporting opposition candidates. In spite of this help and though the opposition parties still had a majority of votes, the United Party was severely defeated and the National Party increased its majority to 29. The Torch Commando did not survive this defeat. Though urged from time to time by its more militant members to make common cause with the non-Europeans in an attempt to unseat the government by extra-parliamentary mass pressure, it had confined itself to more orthodox methods. Some of its members subsequently helped to form the new interracial party, the Liberal Party.

The "defiance campaign"* of 1952–53 coincided in time with the activities of the Torch Commando. The two movements, though directed against the government, had little organisationally or ideologically in common. There were however some whites who participated in both.

In April 1952 the African National Congress announced that it was planning, in conjunction with the South African Indian Congress, a campaign of passive resistance against unjust laws. This announcement had been preceded in January 1952, by a letter sent to the Prime Minister, Dr. D. F. Malan, by Dr. J. S. Moroka, the President-General of the A.N.C. Dr.

---

*For an account of the defiance campaign, written largely from the Natal angle, see Leo Kuper, *Passive Resistance in South Africa*, Yale University Press, 1956.

Moroka had asked the Prime Minister and his government to abolish certain laws which the people felt were oppressive and unjust, failing which a campaign in defiance of these laws would begin. Dr. Malan had refused the request.

On 2 June, Moroka declared at Port Elizabeth that the campaign would start on the 26th of the month, but before that date certain leaders of the African and Indian people would defy the unjust laws. Dr. J. L. Z. Njongwe, the Port Elizabeth leader, declared: "The defiance of unjust laws begins on 26 June. This is the commencement of the struggle for the ultimate liberation of the oppressed and exploited millions, both black and white of South Africa. It is against certain specified unjust laws whose continued operation, enforcement and observance is both humiliating and degrading to the non-Europeans of South Africa." He stated that the struggle would unfold itself quietly and non-violently. Organised, disciplined and trained groups of volunteers would defy the laws. The non-European public was asked not to act independently. Such action would embarrass the volunteers. The unjust laws to be defied included the pass and curfew laws, most of which had been in operation for more than half a century, the Group Areas Act and the Suppression of Communism Act (both of 1950), the Bantu Authorities Act of 1951, stock limitation regulations, and the Separate Representation of Voters Act of 1951.

A few days later it was reported that Dr. Yusef Dadoo, president of the S. A. Indian Congress, and David Bopape, secretary of the Transvaal branch of the A.N.C. had been arrested in Johannesburg when they had spoken at a meeting in defiance of a ban imposed on them by the Minister of Justice. Demonstrations occurred when the arrested men appeared in the magistrate's court. Crowds gave the clenched fist, thumb up, sign of Congress and shouted "Afrika! Afrika!"

On 26 June the mass campaign started according to plan. There were 103 arrests on the Witwatersrand, 30 in Port Elizabeth and 3 in Durban. The law-breakers had defied curfew regulations and had entered locations without permits. On 7 July, Y. A. Cachalia, secretary of the Indian Congress, was reported arrested at Evaton, Transvaal, together with five other non-European leaders. A week or so later, Moses Kotane, former secretary of the Communist Party, was sentenced in Johannesburg to four months' imprisonment for speaking at a public meeting. He had been prohibited from addressing meetings in terms of the Suppression of Communism Act.

For some months the newspapers continued to report instances of defiance which were occurring on an ever-increasing scale. It was interesting to see how certain defiers, offending as they thought against long-established laws, discovered that their actions were not in fact illegal. They had simply broken common customs which they and the police thought had the force of law. Thus 19 non-Europeans, who had been arrested in the European section of the North End post office at Port Elizabeth on 5 July, were acquitted in the magistrate's court of a charge of obstructing the business of the post office. The magistrate said that there was no evidence to support the charge. The accused had apparently lined up quite peacefully in the white queues in an attempt to buy postage stamps. The public prosecutor said that the charge had been put that way because there were no specific regulations relating to post-office segregation. The magistrate held that although segregation had been introduced by the erection of partitions and notices, and the setting aside of separate telephone booths for Europeans and non-Europeans, there was nothing in the postal regulations to enforce this.

Some magistrates went even further. When (Coloured) Goodwood town councillor, Hendrik Bestenbier, demanded to be served at the Elsie's River post office in November, it was admitted that he created a disturbance. He held up business for about twenty minutes. But he was acquitted because the magistrate held that facilities for non-Europeans were so hopelessly inadequate at the Elsie's River post office that there was no equality of treatment as between Europeans and non-Europeans. In these circumstances, said the magistrate, the post office regulations had no validity.

It is a tribute to the sense of justice of many magistrates and of the Supreme Court that equality of treatment was declared to be an essential feature of segregation if it was to have the force of law.

In March 1953, the Appeal Court at Bloemfontein upheld the acquittal of George Lush on a charge of refusing to leave a European waiting room on Cape Town railway station when asked to do so by a constable. The defence had shown that the facilities provided for non-Europeans on the station were grossly inferior to those provided for Europeans, and the court held: "It was unlikely that the legislature intended that users of the railways should have partial or unequal treatment meted out to them."

Whenever loopholes in the *apartheid* laws were thus discovered by liberal lawyers or by judges, the Government hastened to close them. Thus we find Parliament in 1953 passing the Reservation of Separate Amenities Act which laid it down that separate amenities need not be "substantially similar to or of the same character, standard, extent or quality" as "those set aside for the other race."

There were other examples of resisters escaping from the clutches of the law through the leniency or good humour of magistrates or because of legal flaws in police procedure. Michael Harmel, a European, had defied an order under the Suppression of Communism Act by addressing a meeting in the Selbourne Hall, Johannesburg, in August 1952. The meeting had been convened by the Peace Council, but Harmel was acquitted by the Supreme Court because the Crown had failed to show "that the meeting was not of a social or recreational nature."

In July 1952, defiance men were acquitted by the Johannesburg magistrate. They had been arrested in the street after their leader, Boshielo, had told the police, "We are defying unjust laws." It was twenty-five minutes after the curfew hour. The magistrate in releasing them, said: "The accused should have been asked individually for their passes, and this was clearly not done."

In October the Mafeking magistrate freed twenty resisters, including the Congress leader, Dr. S. S. Molema, who had been found guilty of defying the curfew regulations. He said that as the gaol was overcrowded he would not punish the resisters. They filed out of court giving the "Afrika" salute.

However, these cases were the exception rather than the rule. Most magistrates imposed comparatively heavy sentences and, as the campaign developed, punishment became increasingly severe.

The defiers intended in all cases to refuse to pay fines and to go to prison. In some instances they were prevented from doing this. A news report on 25 July, after stating that 32 defiance women had been sentenced for using the European entrance at New Brighton (Port Elizabeth) station, went on to declare: "Non-European defiers of unjust laws are being turned out of gaol, against their will, by the prison authorities. Money found on them at the time of their conviction has been seized and is being used to pay their fines, although they refused the option of a fine when sentenced."

In August 1952, the government announced that new laws would be passed to deal with the defiance campaign and a week later the press reported new developments in the form of raids by detectives carrying search warrants and seeking evidence of treason, sedition and other offences. On 14 August, Dr. Moroka was reported arrested at Thaba 'Nchu, Orange Free State, and charged under the Suppression of Communism Act. In Port Elizabeth Dr. Njongwe had been similarly charged and had been sentenced with 15 others, to nine months' imprisonment.

In November Moroka was brought to Johannesburg to stand trial with 20 others for "advocating or encouraging the achievement of an object of communism." Crowds of non-Europeans besieged the court with cries of "Afrika." Moroka was greeted with applause when he came out accompanied by his lawyer. After the Crown case had closed, the defence, who had pleaded "not guilty" announced that they were calling no witnesses.

At the end of August 1952, a political correspondent of the Johannesburg *Star* attempted a summary of the defiance campaign at that stage. He said that the campaign had reached a critical point. It was planned in three phases and the organisation was superior to anything the non-Europeans of the country had ever yet achieved. The first stage had been propaganda. The second, then in progress, was selective defiance not involving stoppage or work. A total of 3,198 arrests had been made to date. The third stage would be mass defiance when the present series of court cases was complete. This stage was intended to be passive also, but it might become indistinguishable from a general strike. The leaders of the movement were said to be in doubt whether they would be able to control the movement and keep it passive. The writer considered that factors playing into the hands of the extremists among the non-Europeans included the government's refusal to consult with non-Europeans or give them a voice in their country's affairs, the imposition of whippings on resisters introducing an element of violence which helped to breed violence in return.

The reference to whippings is substantiated by a report in the *Rand Daily Mail* (29 August 1952) which recorded that young Africans who had entered the Johannesburg station through the white entrance had received cuts at the order of a magistrate.

By this time the defiance campaign was attracting considerable publicity overseas, and particularly in Great Britain and the United States. Canon John Collins, of St. Paul's Cathedral, had given it his moral support. The Secretary for Native Affairs, Dr. W. M. Eiselen, attempted to counter unfavorable reactions overseas. He declared that "many resisters don't understand 'unjust laws.' The term is a complete mis-nomer. These laws are vital to our common existence in this country."

By the middle of October the number of arrests had passed the 5,000 mark. Violence had been avoided except on the part of the authorities, but at the end of the month events occurred at Port Elizabeth which gave the movement its first real setback. At New Brighton location, which had been the scene of many acts of defiance, a fierce racial riot broke out. Rioters attacked whites and killed the European proprietor of the local cinema. They set fire to buildings and wrecked the post office and a number of shops. In suppressing the riot, the police shot dead a number of Africans and wounded many more. The A.N.C. and the Indian Congress issued a joint statement denying the accusation of the Minister of Justice that the disturbance was a direct result of the defiance campaign. They asked the government to set up a judicial commission of enquiry and Dr · Njongwe asserted that the rioting began when the railway police fired at and seriously injured an African at New Brighton station.

The Port Elizabeth riot was followed by an even more serious one at East London about two weeks later. The immediate cause of this riot is definitely known. The authorities had placed a ban on meetings in the locations. At West Bank the Africans had met in defiance of the ban and had refused to disperse when ordered to do so by the police. The police then opened fire on the meeting. In the rioting that followed three whites were killed, including a Catholic nun and a doctor. The white town councillors of East London blamed the Government for what had occurred, saying that the town had been peaceful until the ban on meetings was imposed.

While the Congress was able to assert with some truth that the immediate cause of the riots in Port Elizabeth and East London could not be laid at their door, it could be argued that the defiance campaign had somehow helped to create an atmosphere of excitement and resentment against authority which was liable to blaze up when provocation was offered. It was also a serious matter that Africans could be quite indiscriminate in their attacks on whites. It had become clear that, while the Congresses were able to discipline their own members in the practice of passive resistance and non-violence, they had little control or authority over the masses of non-Europeans, especially the *tsotsi* or delinquent youth element in the locations.

Nevertheless the defiance campaign went on to achieve new records in numbers arrested as well as in the participation of members of other racial groups. On 27 November it was reported that the first Chinese resister, Keem Lau-Kee, a shop-keeper, had entered a Pretoria location without a permit. He was alone when arrested. He said he was protesting against the wrongs suffered by South African Chinese under the Group Areas Act. He was reprimanded and discharged.

At the end of November new orders were issued by the Government "to control meetings and curb excitement." Regulations gazetted provided penalties of £300 fines and imprisonment up to 3 years. The same newspaper issues that announced these penalties carried a news item to the effect that Patrick Duncan was joining the resisters. Duncan was the son of Sir Patrick Duncan, one of Milner's "young men," who had been a minister in the Smuts' Government in 1921–24 and 1937–39, and subsequently Governor-General of the Union of South Africa.

Duncan, with six other Europeans and a group of non-Europeans including the Indian leader Manilal Gandhi (second son of Mahatma Gandhi), entered the Germiston location on the evening of 8 December 1952. The *Rand Daily Mail* reported: "Mrs. Cynthia Duncan watched her husband as he entered the location. To his crutches—he broke his leg in a motor accident recently—Duncan had tied the yellow, green and black colours of the movement. Gandhi walked at his side. Within a few minutes a crowd of a thousand singing Natives were following the group. Radio police cars with uniformed policemen and members of the Special Branch followed the procession. Mr. Duncan stopped the crowd in a side street. Using both English and Sotho he said: 'To-day South African people of all kinds have come among you. They have come with love for you and with peace. I ask you to do what you have to do without making trouble but in a spirit of love. Mayibuy'i Afrika!' When the procession reformed the police arrested 38 persons."

In February 1953, the accused were placed on trial. Duncan said he was born in Johannesburg. He had been a judicial commissioner in Basutoland but had left the service to do what he could in the political sphere in South Africa. Asked why he joined the defiance campaign, he replied: "I wished to show that there were at least some whites who were prepared to co-operate on a basis of loyalty with the two congresses." He and the others were charged with "behavior in a manner calculated to cause Natives to resist and contravene a law, or to prevail upon them to obstruct the administration of any law by leading a procession or group of Natives into the Germiston location."

The regulations under which the Germiston defiers were convicted put an end for all practical purposes to the defiance campaign. They were virtually the last defiers. The Criminal Law Amendment Act was rushed through Parliament early in 1953 with little ceremony. It made it a criminal offence to break a law by way of protest against that or any other law and it provided the severest penalties. Thus a person sitting on a railway bench designed for one of another colour might be fined a few pounds or sentenced to a few days' imprisonment for the offence itself. But if it could be shown that he had acted in protest against colour discrimination in stations, he would be liable to be fined up to £500, imprisoned for five years and perhaps in addition be given a whipping of ten strokes.

The same session of Parliament, with the consent of the United Party, had passed another law even more drastic. The Public Safety Act of 1953 was described by a group of liberals who protested against it, as giving the Government power "at its unfettered discretion to decide when to declare that a state of emergency existed; deal with any aspect of the life of individuals by over-riding existing laws and imposing any type of penalty, without limit; empower any person to impose such penalties, thus excluding the courts of the land; and make such regulations and penalties retrospective for four days."

The government did not find it necessary to invoke the second of these laws until 1960. It remained in the armoury for further use. The penalties threatened under the Criminal Law Amendment Act were enough to cow and overawe the resisters.

The Congresses had by the end of 1952 mobilised some 8,000 resisters to defy the unjust laws. People had been prepared to suffer imprisonment for weeks and in some cases for months. But they were not willing to risk imprisonment for years, with floggings in addition. The defiance campaign had shown the strength of Congress; it had also revealed its weakness. Its loyal followers had responded to the call but it could not swing the millions into a passive resistance campaign.

CHAPTER XXXII

"ASIKWELWA"
AND TREASON TRIAL

THE CRIMINAL LAW AMENDMENT Act of 1953 had aimed at rendering various forms of passive resistance illegal. It was a useless weapon however against some forms of passive action which did not involve the breaking of laws. It was not illegal to walk to work rather than ride; and, in the absence of compulsory education for non-Europeans, you were not breaking the law if you did not send your child to school.

In 1953 the government introduced another of its many *apartheid* measures, the Bantu Education Act. This placed control of Native education, formerly administered by the Department of Education and the different provincial councils, in the hands of the Department of Native Affairs. This was no mere technical change. It meant a revolution in the nature of the education to be given to Africans. This was henceforth to be "Bantu education" and its motif was defined by Dr. Verwoerd, the Minister of Native Affairs, when he declared: "My department's policy is that education should stand with both feet in the Reserves and have its roots in the spirit and being of Bantu society . . . . There is no place for him (the Bantu) in the European community above the level of certain forms of labour." (Speech to Senate, June, 1954.)

The Act made the maintenance of any unregistered Bantu school (including night schools) or the conducting of any unregistered class for Africans, an offence punishable by fine or imprisonment, and it aimed at the eventual elimination of the mission schools.

Politically conscious Africans reacted against "Bantu education" in typical fashion. Anything specially designed for Africans could only be inferior and Dr. Verwoerd had practically said as much. Congress sent out a call for the boycott of Native schools. Parents were asked to withdraw their children. Would the children then be left with no education whatever? Not at all, the enthusiasts replied: Congress would organise special schools where real education, not Bantu education, would be given.

The boycott began in April 1954, and had some initial success, particularly on the Witwatersrand. On 16 April it was reported that 5,500 children were "out" on the East Rand. On the same day the police dispersed anti-Verwoerd demonstrators at Brakpan. On 21 April over 10,000 children in different Rand centres were said to be absent from school Verwoerd then declared a lock-out and announced that all children who did not return within a specified period would be struck off the rolls. Many thousands did not go back and were accordingly expelled. However in July he declared that the 7,000 thus expelled would be allowed to go back. "But," he added, "there must be no further boycott."

The attempt of Congress, with the help of a number of white supporters, to set up independent schools was frustrated by police action. Since such schools had no hope of securing government recognition, they were unlawful. The organisers tried to avoid the law by calling them "cultural clubs." The police proceeded to raid the clubs. If the children were discovered reading or writing, or if blackboards and chalk were found, the teachers were arrested and charged with infringing the law. Attempts to provide education without the usual technical aids were not very successful. Bantu education triumphed, at least in the primary schools. For secondary schools a special "Bantu matriculation" was instituted, but it was some years before this was enforced. The Africans had lost the day, but they remained bitterly resentful of "Bantu education" and all that it implied.*

The most amazing example of African use of the boycott weapon was seen in the Alexandra bus passenger strike of 1957. This was the third bus boycott centred on Alexandra. The earlier ones were described in Chapter XXV. It will be recalled that in 1945 the bus service had been taken over by a "utility company" which maintained the old single-journey fare of 4d. During the first week of 1957 this Public Utility Transport Corporation (Putco) announced that the fare would be raised to 5d. Costs had so increased, they declared, that they could not continue unless income was raised. The local residents called a meeting and announced a boycott. An "Alexandra People's Transport Action Committee" was set up. The dispute was not confined to Alexandra, for Putco buses also served Johannesburg's western locations and the Pretoria location. The boycott was extended to these areas but its main centre remained at Alexandra.

The boycott was noted, as the previous ones had been, for the persistence of the marchers, who trudged the long distances day after day with undiminished fortitude, for the sympathy it aroused among many whites who casually or in an organised way gave lifts in their cars to the marchers, for the action of the police in attempting to break the boycott, and for the intervention of the Johannesburg Chamber of Commerce in an effort to settle the dispute.

On 1 February the newspapers reported that the boycott was still on. "As the thousands of African boycotters walked their 360th mile last night, the police applied a new policy of firmness towards the marchers and to motorists who gave them lifts. At about six check points along the route they stopped all vehicles in which Natives were travelling, questioned the drivers, searched the passengers for passes, took some passengers to police stations, took the names of all drivers and passengers, and arrested many passengers." (*Rand Daily Mail*, 1 February 1957.)

*The "Extension of Universities Education Act" (so called) of 1959, which was adopted in spite of sustained protests from the "open" universities of Cape Town and the Witwatersrand and achieved world-wide notoriety, in effect merely extends the principles of "Bantu education" to a higher sphere.

On 6 February it was reported that cyclists giving lifts were stopped by the police who removed the valves from the tyres to deflate them. It was not illegal for the people to walk rather than ride, but every possible by-law, regulation and form of intimidation was used by the Government to break the boycott. European members of the Liberal Party, the Congress of Democrats* and the Black Sash† who offered lifts were prepared to face the police and so were a number. of others who sympathised strongly with the marchers. Others were frightened and stopped giving lifts. But the people kept on walking. "Asikwelwa!" they said, "we will not ride!"

Towards the end of February the Johannesburg Chamber of Commerce suggested that employers should pay their African workers an extra "transport allowance" of one shilling a week. The Government declared that it was unshaken in its determination that the boycott must be ended "before the Cabinet would co-operate in any investigation of the poverty of Natives on the Rand." Putco stated that its buses would be withdrawn completely if the boycott did not end by 1 March. Some 4,000 residents of Alexandra met and decided to continue the boycott. Putco gave its staff a week's notice. The police arrested 100 marchers for crossing a street against a traffic light at five o' clock in the morning. The press reported that 1,200 criminal summonses had been issued by the Johannesburg magistrate's court for traffic offences alleged to have been committed by bus boycotters since the boycott began.

On 2 March the Chamber of Commerce made a last-minute effort to end the dispute. It proposed to subsidise the buses if users would pay the extra penny and then queue up and have it repaid. When an attempt was being made to read the terms to a meeting of 5,000 at Alexandra, a boycott leader jumped on the platform and set fire to a paper on which they were written. The crowd shouted "Asikwelwa."

Many thought that the boycott would fizzle out. The intransigents had virtually won their victory; the fare was back at 4d. But they would not agree to queue. Strangely enough the

*See page 398.
†An organisation of European women, the Black Sash, had been started in 1955. Its members, wearing black sashes, held silent public demonstrations against the passing of the Senate Bill. The organisation has continued its activities in defence of democratic freedoms in South Africa.

boycott continued. At the end of March, after nearly three months of walking, a settlement was finally negotiated by a "liaison committee." The Bishop of Johannesburg, Ambrose Reeves, and members of the Liberal Party had been working behind the scenes. The Chamber of Commerce and the Johannesburg Municipality were willing to make good the losses of the transport company for a limited period of three to six months. The fare would be 4d.

There were some boycott leaders who were still dissatisfied: they wanted a permanent settlement. But the people were now willing to ride and ride they did. Putco brought back its buses from Pretoria where they had been sent for safety.

In June the Minister of Transport, B. J. Schoeman, introduced his Native Services Transport Bill in Parliament. This empowered him to increase the levy paid by employers for the transport of their African workers. Thus one of the most dramatic feats of passive resistance ended in the complete victory of the resisters.

Though the defiance campaign of 1952 had failed to secure the abolition of unjust laws, it had resulted in an increased degree of cooperation and unity among non-European organisations. The African National Congress and the South African Indian Congress had learned to work together, and their association continued. Following the proscription of the Communist Party, a new leftist organisation, the Congress of Democrats, came into being in 1952. It was a white organisation pledged to work for equal rights for non-Europeans, and it formed a close alliance with the other two congresses. In September a similar body catering for the Coloured people was formed in Cape Town. These four organisations together formed the Congress Alliance and in March 1954, they decided to call a "Congress of the People" to frame a "freedom Charter."

The proposed congress met in Kliptown, near Johannesburg, on 26 June 1955. There had been extensive preparation for months ahead and thousands of delegates and supporters attended—as well as a considerable body of police who proceeded to search the persons and take the names of 3,000 of those present.

The charter was a lengthy document. The following is a

summary of its main demands and aspirations:

> "The people shall govern. Every man and women shall have the vote and the right to stand for election to all bodies which make laws. All national groups shall have equal rights. The people shall share in the country's wealth. The land shall be shared among those who work it. All shall have equal rights before the law. All shall enjoy equal human rights. There shall be work and security. The doors of learning and culture shall be opened. There shall be houses, security and comfort. There shall be peace and friendship."

The charter concluded with the words: " . . . let all who love their people and their country now say as we say here, 'These freedoms we shall fight for side by side, throughout our lives, until we have won our liberty.' "

The 26th of June, the day on which the Congress of the People had met, became for the Congress Alliance an anniversary to be celebrated by demonstrations and protests. Thus on 26 June 1957, the A.N.C. and its associated organisations called for a one-day stoppage of work as a protest against *apartheid* and the pass laws and in favour of a minimum wage of one pound a day. There were responses in various centres, particularly on the Witwatersrand, where many thousands stayed away from work. That the pass laws were still a burning grievance after nearly half a century of protest against them was emphasised two days later when the newspapers published the annual report of the Department of Justice for 1956. It appeared that during that year some 600,000 Africans had been gaoled for offences under these laws.

In the meantime the Special Branch of the police had been preparing to act against those who continually raised their voices against the pass laws. On 17 September 1955, raids were made on the homes and premises of some 400 persons and organisations suspected of engaging in treasonable activity. Nothing was heard for some time. Presumably the Special Branch was busy sorting out the vast quantity of books, pamphlets, documents and other items collected. Over one year later, on 5 December 1956, 156 persons were arrested and brought to Johannesburg for trial. They comprised people of every racial group and from every province, men and women. Nearly all the prominent leaders of Congress were there, including the President General, Chief Luthuli, and Professor Z. K. Matthews of the Cape section. In fact almost the whole of the *avant garde* of South Africa's liberation movement was crowded into the cells of the Johannesburg Fort.

The story of the trial has become well known in South Africa and overseas. Its first sessions in the Drill Hall in Johannesburg were attended by mass demonstrations. Crowds swarming round the Drill Hall were fired on by the police. The Bishop of Johannesburg, Ambrose Reeves, became chairman of a defence committee which collected large funds in South Africa and abroad for the payment of lawyers and for the sustenance of the accused during the months and years that the trial lasted. Judicial organisations in Europe sent representatives to watch and report. The preliminary examination, conducted by a magistrate, lasted the best part of two years. The record ran into thousands of pages and vast numbers of documents were handed in as evidence.

A witness of whom the prosecution hoped much during the early stage of the trial was Professor Andrew Murray of the University of Cape Town. He was brought in as an expert on Marxism and communism. He pointed out to the Court that the phraseology used in captured A.N.C. documents, of which hundreds were available, was similar to that found in avowedly communist publications from Lenin to Stalin and onwards. Defending counsel included many able lawyers who had little difficulty in making Murray look foolish. At one stage he was asked to pronounce on certain passages produced by the defence. He declared that these were in communist phraseology. It was then revealed that they were extracts from his own writings.

However there was some truth in Murray's contention: the language of the African liberatory movement for a generation had been permeated with Marxist words and phrases. The reason for this was quite clear. It was the Marxists who first introduced South African black men to political theory. The first constitution of the I.C.U. was written for Kadalie by a Cape Marxist and modelled on the constitution of the Industrial Workers of the World. Young African radicals engaging in political discussion inevitably used terms like "proletariat," "imperialism," "oppressed colonial masses," "comrade" and so forth, even when they were engaging in polemics against the Communist Party. They knew no other language.

Following the preliminary examination, lasting over a year, the accused were committed for trial. Subsequently the majority were discharged but the trial continued against 30 of the original accused of whom only two were whites. These were Helen Joseph and Leon Levy. The prominent heads of the A.N.C. such as Albert Luthuli and Professor Z. K. Matthews were among those released. The final judgment by Mr. Justice Rumpff (Mr. Justice Bekker and Mr. Justice Kennedy concurring) was pronounced in March 1961. In his judgment Rumpff found that there was no evidence of communistic infiltration into the African National Congress. It was not proved that the A.N.C. had become a communist organisation. "On all the evidence presented to this court and on our findings of fact," the judge said, "it is impossible for this court to come to the conclusion that the A.N.C. had acquired or adopted a policy to overthrow the state by violence." The court found all the accused not guilty and they were discharged.

A staff reporter of the *Rand Daily Mail* wrote on the day after the acquittal: "Orlando sang last night as the acquitted African treason trial accused were feted from house to house through the sprawling township in a marathon celebration party which started at dusk and ended only at dawn. The usual tense stillness of the township was shattered by singing and dancing. 'Nkosi sikelele Afrika,' the African national anthem, reverberated between the long rows of houses flanking the narrow streets. 'Man, this is a night we won't forget in a hurry,' a beaming Mr. Duma Nokwe, former secretary general of the banned African National Congress, said."

But the Special Branch of the Police, who had been responsible since 1956 for the collection of material and witnesses for the prosecution, celebrated the occasion in a different way. When acquitted treason trialists assembled at the home of Joseph and Ruth Slovo for a party, they were raided by the Special Branch who turned the house upside down in a search for alcohol. Under the laws of the country it was an offence for Europeans to offer non-Europeans wine and brandy.

Because of the Congress Alliance, the A.N.C. now formed part of a movement with clear and consistent aims and with a centralized leadership. At least, so it appeared on the surface. The Treason Trial, by bringing together leftist leaders from all over the country and keeping them in close association for years, helped to consolidate the movement. Feelings of political solidarity were reinforced by friendship and common suffering.

The ideology of the Congress movement was said to be communist and this was what the prosecution during the five years of the trial sought in vain to prove. However it was certain that many of the members of the Congress Alliance and possibly the majority of its most active leaders had been avowed communists prior to the proscription of the Communist Party in 1950. It was equally certain that such leaders as Chief Luthuli, Oliver Tambo and Prof. Z. K. Matthews were not communists. The assertion that these men were woolly-minded stooges exploited by scheming Reds seemed very far from the truth. What then was the political philosophy which bound these people together in common struggle? It must have been the feeling that the struggle for racial equality in South Africa transcends all other loyalties. When condemned for associating with communists, Luthuli would reply that the A.N.C. was working for the emancipation of the black man and would co-operate with all individuals or parties that had similar aims.

Foremost among the principles which the Congress stood for was that of non-racialism. The Congress was not hostile to the white man. This point of view was shared by Luthuli and the communists and it was perhaps the chief reason why the A.N.C. was not captured by the Pan-Africanists when the attempt was made in 1959.

CHAPTER XXXIII

PAN-AFRICANISM AND THE SHARPEVILLE CRISIS

In seeking the origins of the Pan-African movement in South Africa we shall have to retrace our steps for a good many years. Pan-Africanism, with its policy of "Africa for the Africans," has always been endemic in African emancipatory movements. It has taken moderate as well as extreme forms. The Ethiopians of the 1890's merely withdrew from the white-led mission churches and appointed their own priests and parsons. They did not in general contemplate driving the white men into the sea. What saved African national movements for many years from avowed anti-white racialism was the fact that whites always were to be found who for religious, political or sentimental reasons, were prepared to identify themselves in one way or another with the aspirations of the blacks. This identification however has not always been disinterested. It has often taken the form of proselytisation: the enrolment of Africans in churches or parties or the attempt to control and direct African movements which had arisen spontaneously. This history has provided many examples.

If a particular event is to be sought for the beginnings of a conscious and organised pan-Africanism in the ranks of the A.N.C. it may be found in the formation of the Youth League in 1944.

This body seems to have been active in Johannesburg's Orlando location and also at Fort Hare. Prominent among the young radicals associated with the League were A. P. Mda, D. Mji, Oliver Tambo, Nelson Mandela, Walter Sisulu, J. Ngubane, Robert Resha, Godfrey Pitje and R. M. Sobukwe. Their leader was Anton Lembede who preached what he called "the ideology of African nationalism." Lembede died in 1946 only two years after the formation of the League, but his ideas lived on. Significantly enough, these young men were not Marxists, though no doubt some of them had been influenced by Marxist ideas.

The Youth League members were able to dominate the A.N.C. annual conference of 1949, not by virtue of their numbers but because of the fact that they were a coherent group with a definite programme. They proposed a "total and complete boycott of all the elections under the Native Representation Act of 1936, the bungas, local and district councils, advisory boards and similar institutions." They wanted a council of action appointed to "act vigorously" and a "national fund to finance the struggle for national liberation," the strengthening of the African trade unions and the establishment of schools for training African youths. Finally they succeeded in getting the conference to adopt "the creed of African nationalism as a basis for the fight for national liberation."

The youth group carried the conference with them, and when the president general, Dr. Xuma, objected to himself and the executive being bound to a definite program, he was displaced by Dr. Moroka.

The 1949 victory of the "African nationalists" was short lived. Its much vaunted programme was not carried out. In particular there was no boycott of elections. After 1953 the Congress Alliance became well established and the followers of Lembede found that they exerted little influence in the leadership. Some of the young men of 1949, like Tambo, Sisulu and Mandela, became orthodox Congressites; others like Ngubane, became Liberals.

However, as we have said, Africanism must always be endemic in any African liberation movement and by 1958 its adherents had become sufficiently strong to make another attempt to secure the leadership of the A.N.C. At the provincial conferences held at the end of that year the "old guard" triumphed and the Africanists were decisively defeated. Only the Eastern Cape section gave them its support, and in this area the central leadership had already built a conformist branch. In the Western Cape, Natal and the Orange Free State whatever Africanists there were remained in Congress "to work from within," but those in the Transvaal withdrew as a body.

Their first conference, held in Orlando in April 1959, drew about 300 delegates from all parts of the country. The two main figures were Robert Sobukwe who was at this time a lecturer in Bantu languages at the University of the Witwatersrand, and Josias Madzunya, who had become prominent during the Alexandra bus boycott. The conference decided to establish a new body, the Pan-African Congress. It pledged itself to support the United Nations Charter of equal rights, but declared the salvation of the Africans must be the work of the Africans themselves. Other races, whites, Indians or Coloured, would be granted the franchise in a free Africa, but they must not claim for themselves any special privileges as racial groups. In fact they would have to consider themselves as Africans like everybody else.

The conference was a triumph for Sobukwe who had organised it for months. He and the other "intellectuals" were elected to the leadership. The *World* (formerly *Bantu World*) reported, "Although Josias Madzunya, father of the Africanist movement, saw years of work end in triumph with the founding of the Pan-Africanist Congress . . . he has not got a seat on the P.A.C. cabinet." But black-bearded Madzunya and his Alexandra followers did not walk out. They stayed to a man. And Madzunya pledged himself to obey the new president, Robert Sobukwe.*

Among students of politics who read the reports of the Orlando conference were many cynics who prophesied a short and ineffectual life for the new body. They recalled extremist groups in the past that had shouted much and done nothing, notably the so-called Unity Movement, a body with Trotskyist leanings which was formed in 1943 by the amalgamation of the Anti-C.A.D. and the All African Convention. African intellectuals, particularly teachers, found that their profession made it impossible for them to participate in mass movements involving physical danger or imprisonment. At the same time they were more politically conscious than the masses and realised the enormity of the colour-bar. They therefore sought psychological compensation in extremist programs which in fact were never implemented. Boycotts were called for but the only boycott practised was the boycott of the A.N.C. which persistently called for strikes, stay-at-homes and days of protest.

However the cynics who were thus prepared to write off the Pan-Africanist Congress as yet another talking body had underestimated Sobukwe. He meant business, as events were to prove.

Again it was resentment of the pass laws which roused Africans to new heights of protest and plunged South Africa into the Sharpeville crisis, so that the name "Sharpeville" has become, like "Amritsar," "Saint Bartholomew" or "Peterloo," a symbol of massacre. More prosaically, the word is now used by South African stockbrokers to refer to industrial and gold-mining share prices as "pre-Sharpeville" and "post-Sharpeville."

Sobukwe's programme was a simple one. The Pan-Africanist Congress was not worried, he said, by the fact that the A.N.C. had been so long established and seemed so much more powerful than the P.A.C. The vast mass of Africans had never in fact been in the A.N.C. and they were ripe for the taking by any organisation which would arouse their racial consciousness. The A.N.C., he alleged, had too long been controlled by whites. The masses would follow a pure African leadership if that leadership was prepared to lead them in struggle against

*Madzunya, however, was subsequently expelled.

the racial laws. On a given day the P.A.C. would call on the people to disobey the pass laws and that would be the beginning of the end of white domination. The campaign, Sobukwe declared in a press interview, would operate under the slogan "No bail, no defence, no fine," and the leaders of the P.A.C. would be the first to take part.

The date eventually fixed for the show-down was Monday, March 21, 1960. The P.A.C. called on Africans on that day to leave their passes at home and to surrender to the police.

In fact there were two places where the P.A.C. had a considerable following. These were Langa, at Cape Town, and Sharpeville and neighbouring locations at Vereeniging in the Transvaal. They were the only two centres where any sort of mass action occurred on March the 21st. Had the police not lost their nerve and opened fire at Sharpeville it seems probable that the campaign would have fizzled out, as so many had done before, and there would have been no crisis.

It was estimated that about 10,000 people, including many women and children, surrounded the Sharpeville police station. They demanded to be arrested for not having passes. The police barred the gates, some of the crowd began to throw stones. "The police opened fire," said a newspaper report. "Volley after volley of .303 bullets and sten gun bursts" tore into the crowd. "The hordes began to waver—as scores of people fell before the hail of bullets. Soon, they were routed. They fled so quickly that hundreds of shoes, trousers, jackets— and even chairs—were left behind. The police came out from behind the wire in front of the police station. Bodies lay scattered about. The wounded fled into back yards and side streets. Bodies lay in grotesque positions on the pavement. Then came ambulances—11 of them. Two truckloads of bodies were taken to the mortuary." (*Rand Daily Mail*, 22 March 1960.) Some 67 persons were killed and 186 injured.

Humphrey Tyler, editor of *Drum*, gave an eyewitness report as follows:

> "The crowd seemed to be loosely gathered around the Saracens (armoured cars) and on the fringes people were walking in and out. The kids were playing. In all there were about 3,000 people. They seemed amiable. Suddenly there was a sharp report from the direction of the police station. There were shrill cries of 'Izwe lethu' (our land)— women's voices, I thought. The cries came from the police

station and I could see a small section of the crowd swirl around the Saracens. Hands went up in the Africanist salute. Then the shooting started. We heard the chatter of a machine gun, then another, then another. There were hundreds of women, some of them laughing. They must have thought the police were firing blanks. One woman was hit about ten yards from our car. Her companion, a young man, went back when she fell. He thought she had stumbled. Then he turned her over and saw that her chest had been shot away. He looked at the blood on his hand and said: 'My God, she's gone!'

"Hundreds of kids were running, too. One little boy had on an old blanket coat, which he held up behind his head, thinking, perhaps, that it might save him from the bullets. Some of the children, hardly as tall as the grass, were leaping like rabbits. Some were shot, too. Still the shooting went on. One of the policemen was standing on top of a Saracen, and it looked as though he was firing his sten gun into the crowd. He was swinging it around in a wide arc from his hip as though he were panning a movie camera. Two other police officers were on the track with him, and it looked as if they were firing pistols.

"Most of the bodies were strewn on the road running through the field in which we were. One man who had been lying still, dazedly got to his feet, staggered a few yards, then fell in a heap. A woman sat with her head cupped in her hands. One by one the guns stopped. Before the shooting, I heard no warning to the crowd to disperse. There was no warning volley. When the shooting started it did not stop until there was no living thing in the huge compound in front of the police station. The police have claimed they were in desperate danger because the crowd was stoning them. Yet only three policemen were reported to have been hit by stones—and more than 200 Africans were shot down. The police also have said that the crowd was armed with 'ferocious weapons' which littered the compound after they fled.

"I saw no weapons, although I looked very carefully, and afterwards studied the photographs of the death scene. While I was there I saw only shoes, hats and a few bicycles left among the bodies. The crowd gave me no reason to feel scared, though I moved among them without any distinguishing mark to protect me, quite obvious with my white skin. I think the police were scared though, and I think the crowd knew it." (*Africa Today*, May, 1960.)

In the subsequent official inquiry into the shooting "Captain van der Bergh said he had tried without success to find out who fired first. Nobody had admitted to being the first to shoot. He also tried unsuccessfully to find out who shouted 'Shoot.' " (*Rand Daily Mail*, 25 May 1960.) In the report of the one-man commission of inquiry into the disturbances at Sharpeville, Mr. Justice P. J. Wessels gave his general view that there was no organised attempt by the crowd to attack the police on the day of the shooting. Referring to evidence that the crowd was at no time hostile and to police evidence that they were forced to ward off an attack, Mr. Wessels' report stated: "The two lines of evidence were in direct conflict and could not in the whole be reconciled with each other. It was impossible to ascertain with any measure of accuracy when the order to fire at Sharpeville was given. The commission was of the opinion that almost immediately after the first shots were fired Lieutenant-Colonel Pienaar and other police officers took steps to stop the firing. It was clear that some time elapsed between the giving of the order to cease fire and the actual stopping thereof." (*Rand Daily Mail*, January 1961.)

It was possible that some of the police were conscious of what had happened at Cato Manor, near Durban, only two months previously. Africans gathered in this shanty-town suburb on Sunday afternoons for beer-drinking and were constantly raided by the police. On January 24 they had turned on the police, killing nine of them—4 whites and 5 Africans.

Events at Langa followed a very similar pattern to those at Sharpeville. According to a report made by Mr. Justice Diemont, released in January 1961, the Pan-African Congress had called a meeting in Langa on March 21. The people would not carry passes and would march to the police station and demand to be arrested. The first meeting was a failure, the report said, "because the district commandant of police declined to arrest the leaders for failing to carry their reference books, and the march on the Langa police station was effectively stopped. The leaders reacted to this failure by calling a meeting for the same evening and represented that the purpose

408

of this meeting was to receive an official answer to grievances, which, it was stated, the police had undertaken to give." The police had in fact, the report said, not given any such undertaking.

A huge crowd began to gather at the meeting place at 5 P.M. and "when the district commandant observed the mounting tension . . . he decided that the public peace would be seriously endangered and asked the magistrate of Wynberg to ban the meeting under the Riotous Assemblies Act. This banning order was broadcast in Langa and, although it must have been heard by many people, it did not deter them from flocking to the meeting. . . . The commanding officer did not know that the meeting was expecting an official answer to grievances and this information should have been given to him by the Security Branch. Had he known the full facts he would have been less handicapped in the decisions he had to make."

In the event, the police ordered the crowd to disperse and, when it failed to do so, charged with batons. The report said that a number of policemen "acted in an undisciplined manner. They struck people who were running away, they struck people lying on the ground, and in several cases they struck people on the head in breach of the rule to strike on arms and legs." The report went on to say that the crowd then started to attack the police who were in constant danger, so that the commanding officer was justified in ordering his men to open fire. The firing was controlled and was not carried on for very long. Two men were killed and 49 injured.

One of the results of the clashes at Sharpeville and Langa was the temporary suspension of the pass laws, announced by the commissioner of police on March 26. The Transvaal Division of the Liberal Party, meeting in conference in Johannesburg expressed the hope that this was a prelude to the immediate and final abolition of the pass laws. The suspension in fact did not last for more than three weeks.

The effect of the events at Sharpeville and Langa was to rouse politically-minded non-Europeans and their white supporters throughout the country to carry out demonstrations and protests. In Cape Town thousands of Africans stopped work and stevedores in the docks walked off the ships. A "day of mourning" was called for March 28 and this resulted in riots and shooting in the Johannesburg locations. Tear gas and baton charges were used by the police to break up a large meeting of Africans and Coloured on the Grand Parade in Cape Town. On March 30 the Government declared a "state of emergency." In a swoop by the police over one hundred persons of all races considered to be radicals or liberals were arrested and detained in prison. There were hundreds of other arrests of Africans who had defied the pass laws or taken part in the demonstrations.

On March 31 a dramatic demonstration by some 25,000 Africans occurred in Cape Town. It was reported that crowds started gathering in the locations when it became known that the police had made mass arrests throughout the country. A column more than a mile long started marching from Langa and other points to converge on the Caledon Square police station to demand the release of their leaders. They were led by Philip Kgosana, the regional secretary of the Pan-Africanist Congress, a young student who had suddenly found leadership thrust upon him. The huge crowd blocked the main roads leading to the centre of Cape Town and by mid-day the streets about Caledon Square were a seething mass of black humanity. The huge crowd was within a few hundred yards of the Houses of Parliament where the members were in session. The officer in command, Colonel Terblanche ordered all business in the vicinity to close down. He seemed at a loss as to how to handle the situation. Patrick Duncan, editor of the liberal paper *Contact* happened to be standing nearby. He said to Terblanche, "Why not get in touch with the leaders?" The policeman replied: "I do not know who the leaders are." "I will put you in touch with them," said Duncan.

Kgosana was then called. According to statements subsequently published Kgosana agreed to ask the crowd to disperse quietly provided Terblanche would promise to arrange a meeting between the leaders of the P.A.C. and the Minister of Justice, Erasmus. He also said he would be unable to control the crowd if any arrests were made by the police. Terblance gave him this assurance and Kgosana then addressed the crowd through a loud-speaker. By 4 P.M. the vast crowds were on their way back to Langa. The demonstration had been peaceful from beginning to end.

A day or two later Kgosana was arrested. His promised interview with the Minister never took place.

On March 31 and April 1 there were demonstrations by

non-whites in many centres, at Simonstown and Stellenbosch in the Cape, at Pretoria in the Transvaal and at Durban in Natal where three Africans were killed. Passes were burnt at Bloemfontein.

On April 3 came the police "day of reckoning" in Cape Town. The *Rand Daily Mail* reported (4 April 1960). "Shortly after dawn detachments of troops moved in to guard all key points in Cape Town. . . . While the troops stood by, armed with rifles and machine guns and supported by armoured cars, groups of policemen scoured the streets. They stopped and checked hundreds of Natives and ordered those standing around to move on. They beat up some with their truncheons and sjamboks. Some they put into pick-up vans and took away." The newspaper *Contact* subsequently published grim details of some of the beatings-up that had occurred.

Sporadic demonstrations, riots and arrests occurred for the next week or so. On April 8 the P.A.C. and the A.N.C. were banned under the newly-passed Unlawful Organizations Act. To add to the excitement an attempt was made on the Prime Minister's life.

The David Pratt affair will probably remain one of the mysteries of South African history. On Saturday, 9 April, when Dr. Verwoerd was addressing a crowd at the opening of the Union Exposition at the Showground in Johannesburg a man stepped forward and, at very close range, fired a shot at him. The bullet passed through the Prime Minister's face and many thought he would die. He did not, however, as a result of what some described as a miracle. The bullet did not touch the brain. *Die Burger* wrote (11 April 1960): "In this miraculous escape all the faithful will see the hand of God and thank him that our country, which is already passing through troubled times, has been spared the greater horror of assassination of its head of state." David Pratt, who had wielded the revolver was a wealthy farmer, a man who had hitherto taken no part in politics. He was neither a communist, a leftist nor a liberal. When he was tried for attempted murder the court found that he was of unsound mind and he was confined in a mental hospital. Some months later he committed suicide.

The "state of emergency," proclaimed on March 30, continued for some months. The detainees languished in prison.

Their experience in some ways resembled that of the treason trialists: men, or women, of different degrees of radical opinion were flung together. But there could be no mingling of the races or of the sexes. White, black, Coloured and Indian were, following South African custom, kept in separate prisons. Speculation as to why particular Europeans were detained failed to produce any consistent theory. Individuals who had taken no part in active politics for decades were clapped behind the bars. Others who were thought to be more active figures escaped. Quite a number who expected to be arrested fled beyond the Union's borders, chiefly to Swaziland. A fair proportion of these political refugees decided not to return to South Africa. Among those who came back was Ambrose Reeves, Bishop of Johannesburg. He was immediately deported.

Among the detainees were members of all the parties and groups to the left of the Progressives, as well as some who belonged to no party but had merely at some time or other shown sympathy with Africans. The majority of white detainees were members of the C.O.D. Some members of the Liberal Party were there too, among them one of its founders, Jock Isacowitz, Ernest Wentzel, a young Afrikaner lawyer, Peter Brown, the Natal provincial chairman, and Dr. Hans Meidner a lecturer in the University of Natal.

While over 100 whites were detained, the number of non-whites summarily detained was nearly 2,000. In addition some 20,000 were arrested for demonstrating or defying the pass laws. In August the authorities began to release the detainees in batches and the last of them gained their freedom in August 1960, when the "emergency" ended. In the meantime leaders of the P.A.C. and A.N.C. and many rank-and-filers who had taken part in the anti-pass campaign were sentenced to imprisonment and fines. Robert Sobukwe was sentenced to three years' imprisonment for incitement. Albert Luthuli was fined £100 for burning his pass.

In some ways the Sharpeville affair seemed to have more profound effects beyond the country's borders than in South Africa itself. Already the target of European and American liberal criticism and of the Afro-Asian block, on account of its policy of *apartheid*, the South African government now found itself even more unpopular. Following Sharpeville there were repercussions on the stock exchanges of the world and for a time overseas investments in South African practically ceased.

However, many complacent white South Africans were stirred into thinking new thoughts on the subject of race relations. The Nationalist *Die Burger* in Cape Town produced at the height of the crisis a number of articles of a character unusual for this paper. On the day after the Langa and Sharpeville shooting, the editor in a leading article appealed to the government to win and mobilize the moderate and law-abiding Bantu in the interests of law and order. It emphasized that the A.N.C. and its leader Luthuli had not taken part in the previous day's demonstrations. For a week or two articles asking for a new approach to racial problems appeared in *Die Burger's* leader and correspondence columns. It seemed that that newspaper for the first time had discovered the existence of the urban African, for a reporter was sent into the streets to interview some of these strange people and ask them for their life-histories.

The most prominent soul-searcher among Nationalists at this time was none other than P. O. Sauer, Minister of Lands, chairman of the Cabinet, and acting Prime Minister during the absence of Dr. Verwoerd, who was in hospital recovering from the gunshot wound inflicted by David Pratt. Speaking at Humansdorp in the Cape, he said on May 20: "The old book of South African history was closed a month ago and, for the immediate future, South Africa would reconsider in earnest and honesty her whole approach to the Native question. We must create a new spirit which must restore overseas faith—both white and non-white in South Africa." Pinpricks, he said, which had ripened the Natives for propaganda by the African National Congress and the Pan Africanist Congress would have to be removed. The Native must be given hope for a happy existence. "We must alter the conception of 'baasskap' in the areas which will be made available by the government to the Bantus—there should be absolutely no reference to baasskap." However these deviations from the party-line became less frequent as the crisis subsided. The leading paper of Afrikaner nationalism gradually reassumed its former role of defender of *apartheid*, and Mr. Sauer did not make any more Humansdorp speeches.

The government did however learn some wisdom from the Sharpeville events. The beer raids on African townships gradually ceased, and in 1962 legislation was introduced abolishing the discriminatory liquor laws. Africans were allowed to buy European liquor. The change was partly motivated by the interests of Western Province wine farmers (mostly Nationalists) who for years had pleaded for an extension of the market to Africans, but it did in fact remove a constant source of friction between Africans and the police and a practice which had filled the gaols annually with hundreds of thousands of prisoners.

The Sharpeville crisis, as observed by readers of the press or by observers overseas, might have given the impression that the racialist regime in South Africa had been shaken to its foundations. In fact the Nationalist Government's hold on the country was as powerful as ever. There was no question of its having lost the confidence of the exclusively white electorate and that was all that really mattered as far as domestic politics were concerned. Liberalists might demonstrate on Trafalgar Square in London, or resolutions of condemnation might be carried by overwhelming majorities in the United Nations. Some of the top Nationalist leaders might have felt uneasy in the face of world opinion, but looking round at the serried ranks of their followers they felt a renewed confidence. This became the basis of the "laager"* mentality: embattled Afrikanerdom had its back to the wall and it would triumph in the end.

*When the voortrekkers during the Great Trek were faced with large numbers of armed Africans who barred their way they formed their wagons into a circle, the laager. The Americans used a similar device against the Red Indians.

CHAPTER XXXIV

LIBERALS AND PROGRESSIVES

THE PROSCRIPTION OF THE Communist Party created a political vacuum on the Left. For a time there were no political parties apart from the parliamentary white parties—the Nationalist Party (government), the United Party (opposition), and the rump of the South African Labour Party, which secured a few seats in the 1948 and 1953 elections with the support of the United Party, but lost all its seats in 1958 when that support was withdrawn.

In 1953 two new organisations came into existence. One of these was the Congress of Democrats, whose genesis we have already described. The other was the Liberal Party.

The Liberal Party was formed by individuals exhibiting various degrees of radical thought, such as D. B. Molteno, the Ballingers and the writer Alan Paton. A prominent member, who joined later, was Patrick Duncan, one of the European passive resisters in the Defiance Campaign. It recruited a few thousand white members and an almost equal number of Africans, as well as a number of Indians and Coloureds. As was the case with the Communist Party in its early days (see Chapter VII) its African recruits, who were mainly workers or rural tribesmen, were attracted to some extent by the hope that the party would be able to help them in various ways (for example providing legal assistance in their daily struggle with pass laws, location regulations and the like) and not because they had become convinced liberals. However the party was joined by a few outstanding Africans, among them its vice-president, Jordan K. Ngubane, of Natal, who had become well known as a journalist of independent views. In 1959 four of the seven (white) Natives' representatives in Parliament and Senate were members of the Liberal Party.[*]

The Liberal Party in its early years concentrated its energies largely on the fighting of elections, municipal, provincial and parliamentary, considering that one of its main tasks was the

*This form of representation was abolished by legislation in 1960.

education of the white voters and their conversion to the ideals of a common society. It found the most fruitful field for this propaganda in the ranks of the English-speaking upper-middle and professional classes. Thus in Johannesburg the liberal "strongholds" were in the northern suburbs. In no case did the party win a seat, and in many cases deposits* were lost.

In its early years the Liberal Party suffered a serious and protracted crisis over its franchise policy. The old Cape liberals (see Chapter VII) had placed their liberal faith, such as it was, in a qualified franchise which gave the vote, regardless of colour, to persons having certain property, salary and educational qualifications. A qualified franchise was at first adopted as the aim of the new party, but considerable opposition to this soon developed among its more radical members. The party had set out not merely to influence white voters and recruit them in its ranks but also to win support and membership of non-whites and particularly Africans. It was found that, on the whole, African intellectuals regarded advocacy of a qualified franchise as evidence of insincerity, of an unwillingness to concede to the non-whites the exercise of their majority rights in an emancipated South Africa. They felt that a token representation of Africans in the legislature would be a mere salve to the white liberal conscience and that even this could be abolished at the whim of the white voters, as had happened in the Cape. The liberals of the mid-twentieth century, therefore, found both tactical and fundamental reasons for proclaiming their belief in universal adult suffrage, and this became their avowed policy after 1960.

For a time it seemed that the Liberal Party had a place as the only non-racial and constitutional group to the left of the United Party; slow but steady progress was made and Liberal candidates retained their deposits in a number of election contests. It was hoped that the continual challenge of liberalism would eventually produce some sort of split in the United Party. It was known that many in the United Party were dissatisfied with the official line of the opposition which seemed to be merely a moderate version of the Nationalist

*The sum of money deposited by a candidate in an election is lost if he fails to get a minimum of one-fifth of the votes secured by the winning candidate.

Government's racial policy. The split came in August 1959, much sooner than the Liberals had anticipated. It did not result in the strengthening of the Liberal Party, rather the reverse, for a new political organisation, the Progressive Party, came into being. Eleven members of parliament resigned from the United Party to form the nucleus of the new group. They were led by Jan Steytler, M.P. for Queenstown, and Harry Lawrence, M.P. for Salt River. They were supported by the millionaire mine-owner Harry Oppenheimer, who had resigned his seat in Parliament two years before.

The Progressive M.P.'s, while leaving the United Party, did not give up their seats, and for two years—until the general election in October 1961—formed a small but active and eloquent third party in parliament.

The policy adopted by the new party bore some resemblance to the early policy of the Liberals. At their first national congress in November 1959, the Progressives declared in favour of a qualified but non-racial franchise, the exact terms of which were to be worked out later. Membership of the party would be open to all, irrespective of colour, who could qualify as voters on these terms. Eventually it was decided that this meant that the franchise on the ordinary roll would be granted without further qualifications to adults who had passed Standard VIII, or were literate and earned £500 per year or owned property worth £500. Adults who had passed Standard VI could qualify if in addition they earned £300 per year or had property worth £500. Further, there would be a special roll for literate persons who could not qualify in other ways. These would be allowed to elect 10 per cent. of the members of parliament. It was interesting that the Progressive Party declared against the granting of free trade unions to unskilled African workers.

The resources of the Progressive Party in men and money, vastly exceeded anything the Liberals had ever been able to muster. These resources were tested in the general election of 1961 when the country waited to see how many Progressives would retain their seats in what were in most cases straight contests against United Party candidates. In fact only one Progressive was returned (Helen Suzman in the Johannesburg constituency of Houghton). John Cope of Parktown was defeated by only 85 votes. The eleven Progressive candidates secured a total of 69,000 votes. In subsequent by-elections and in the provincial elections a few months later they did not do quite so well. With the disappearance of the Cape Native representatives, the voice of inter-racialism in parliament was reduced to that of a single woman. Helen Suzman had replaced Margaret Ballinger.

The formation of the Progressive Party caused the defection of a number of white members from the Liberal Party. A number of them joined the Progressives, among them Donald Molteno. Others despaired of South Africa and left the country. The Liberals continued to work actively among non-Europeans. They had the support of *Contact*, a fortnightly paper published in Cape Town by Patrick Duncan. In 1962 Duncan, under a ministerial order, was confined to the Cape Peninsula and forbidden to attent any meetings or public gatherings. He bore this for some months but eventually escaped to Basutoland. Always an intransigent member, he left the Liberal Party in March 1963, saying that he had abandoned his belief in non-violence, which he had previously held so strongly. He subsequently announced his support of the Pan-African Congress and his intention to raise funds for this organisation overseas. A small group of enthusiasts in Cape Town attempted to continue the publication of *Contact*, but without Duncan's active support this effort has proved difficult.

At the time of writing the Liberal Party has not been proscribed and it retains a precarious foothold in that small area of legality still available to it in a South Africa which is not quite a totalitarian state.

In the early years of their rule, after 1948, the Nationalists seemed quite prepared to ignore any criticism of their policy of *apartheid* both at home and abroad. But as world opinion became increasingly hostile and threats of boycott and intervention mounted, attempts were made to meet overseas criticism, by pointing to certain rights and benefits Africans would gain once *apartheid* had been perfected.

In theory, at any rate, the spokesmen, if not the rank and file, of the ruling party admitted one thing. It was wrong, they said, that the African should remain permanently without rights of self-determination. As such rights could not be tolerated within the framework of the South African state, the Africans must be segregated into separate states or

418

"Bantustans." The Native Reserves would in fact become these new states. Already in 1956 a blueprint describing the development and consolidation of the "Bantu areas" had been produced in the famous Tomlinson Report. In these Bantu states the Africans would have whatever form of government they desired. One difficulty about the proposed scheme was that, in spite of the vastly increased degree of segregation envisaged, there would still be, according to the Report, a vast mass of Africans, amounting to two-thirds of the population, living within the white areas. This practical difficulty Government supporters have never been able to resolve.

It was always said that the Bantustan policy was devised for overseas consumption (the Government was granting "self government" to the indigenous peoples) and for internal election purposes (the Government was once more "solving the Native question" and securing the future of White South Africa). A writer in the Progressive Party's monthly paper said: "Anyone with experience of grass-roots campaigning in South African politics knows that the vast majority of Nationalist voters do not vote for Bantu homelands. They vote, simply, to 'keep the kaffir in his place.' "* In another sense, however, the policy formed part of a very definite programme aimed at maintaining or restoring that tribalism which had been eroding under the impact of economic and social forces.

The urban African who wished to make representations to the government must do so through his tribal "Bantu authority." The existence of second and third generation urban Africans who have no tribal connections was completely ignored. "Ethnic grouping" in the locations would attempt to separate out the tribal elements which had been fusing for half a century.

One effect of the Sharpeville crisis was to accelerate the government's desire to do something concrete about the Bantustans. The Promotion of Bantu Self-Government Act had been passed in 1959. In June 1960, "Commissioners General" (white) were appointed for the different Bantu areas. The Transkei was chosen for the establishment of the first Bantu "territorial authority."

Unfortunately for the government, the first task of the commissioner general for this area was to handle a large scale

*Zach de Beer in *Forum*, October, 1962.

revolt which broke out among the Pondo, one of the major tribes in the Transkei. It appeared that the people had many grievances against the Government and against some of the Government-appointed chiefs. There was fighting and hut-burning and armed forces had to be sent to suppress a serious revolt. A number of Pondo were killed and there were many arrests. Severe emergency laws were hastily imposed, and these remained in force throughout all the subsequent negotiations and lobbying leading to the establishment of the new "Bantu State." It meant that no public meetings could be held and members of the different tribes were not allowed to gather together to voice their opinions on the "new deal" with which they would be intimately concerned.

The Transkeian chiefs were eventually summoned in January 1962 to draw up a "self-rule constitution." The conference appeared to have been carefully stage-managed. The Tembu Chief Sabata Dalindyebo was known to be uncooperative. He had come to the conference with a mandate from his people objecting to certain features of the proposed constitution. When he rose to state these objections he was told that they could not be raised at that particular place on the agenda. Apparently he never succeeded in finding where they could be raised and at the end of the conference they were still unstated.

Chief Sabata's opposition must have caused the government considerable trouble. His people, the Tembu, was the largest Transkeian tribe, numbering about half a million. Sabata was a young man with some missionary education, but in many ways an "old-style" chief. It was reported that his English, though good, was not perfect. (*Race Relations News*, April, 1963.)

His close collaborator was Randolph Vigne, a journalist and leader of the Liberal Party in Cape Town. Sabata's declared policy was one of equal rights for Africans within the Republic of South Africa. He did not regard the proposed Transkeian state as an instalment of freedom, and he was aware that a vast number of Africans including his own Tembu would have to continue to live and work outside the Transkei, and would thus continue to suffer the tribulations of *apartheid*.

The government had the power to depose Sabata, as they had the power to remove any recalcitrant chief, and as they had done with Albert Luthuli. However, a chief was found, equally young and capable and seemingly more pliant than Sabata, who was willing to support the government. This was Kaiser Matanzima, described as "the most capable man in the territory." He was destined, it was said, to be the first prime-minister of the Transkeian Bantustan.

CHAPTER XXXV

THE UNDERGROUND

THE INFERIOR STATUS TO which Africans were relegated within the South African state was not something they could be expected to accept indefinitely. This history is a record of the non-acquiescence which grew from early beginnings in Ethiopianism, through political and industrial organisation, and led to the growth of the Congress and Pan-Africanist movements. These various organs of protest were frowned on by authority and many stumbling blocks were placed in their way. But until the coming to power of the Afrikaner Nationalists in 1948 no political body or other organisation of the non-whites was ever proscribed. Their political activities were subject to legal restraint, and laws were made to circumscribe these activities. Individuals went to prison, prohibitions and banishments were imposed. But the bare right of political parties to exist was not questioned. Under these circumstances there were no secret organisations, no "underground."

The illegalization of African nationalism and its allies by Afrikaner nationalism was a process that took time. It proceeded in stages over more than a decade. The banning of the Communist Party in 1950 established a precedent for the banning of other organisations, but a full ten years elapsed before the African National Congress and with it the newly-formed Pan-African Congress were banned. And this only came after the events at Sharpeville. Why did the Government so long tolerate the existence of the Congress movement? One reason appears to be that the Government, acting through its special police, had developed a technique for dealing with the liberatory movement which did not involve complete illegalization. In fact it seemed that the continued "open" character of Congress and its associated organisations was essential to the efficient functioning of this technique.

During the years between 1950 and 1960 the Special Branch developed a method, if not highly efficient at least extremely elaborate, of keeping the Congress movement under control. Since the organisations concerned functioned in the open, all their public meetings could be subject to the surveillance of the Special Branch. It is probable that not a single open meeting, demonstration or conference took place during the whole of this period without police or detectives being present to record speeches and make lists of those who attended. On occasion the police demanded of everyone present that he should supply his name and address. When group meetings or parties were held in private houses, the police were normally outside, busy taking down the numbers of parked motor cars. It seemed that even the most casual attenders at meetings had their names recorded in the dossiers of the Special Branch.*

The other aspect of the Special Branch's technique could be described as the "cutting off of heads." As soon as a leader became prominent, or if the police considered that his or her activity was vital to the organisation, a restraining order was issued by the Minister of Justice. These orders took different forms. The individual could be prohibited from attending meetings, told to resign from particular organisations, confined to a given magisterial district in which he was already resident or banished to some particular area and forbidden to leave it. Other more drastic measures were subsequently taken, but these came after 1960, as we shall see.

With Sharpeville, the period of legal toleration of what the Government considered to be subversive organisations came to an end. In 1960 the African National Congress and the P.A.C. were declared illegal. It became illegal also for any individual or group to "further the aims of a banned organisation."

In the face of these restrictions it would have seemed that any further open activity on the part of those who had previously supported Congress had become impossible. But this was not so. An attempt was made to carry on the open struggle, though already this had begun to acquire certain "underground" features.

*It can be assumed also that the police had their informers or endeavoured to place their informers within the various organisations. How far they succeeded in getting their representatives into the inner circles of the leadership is difficult to judge. From their very nature such facts are not readily divulged.

The first attempt was made in connection with the proclamation of the Republic. For years the Nationalists had wanted to break the last nominal ties with Britain. The movement started by Hertzog and Roos in 1912 achieved its major aim in 1960. The republican referendum was held in October of that year. Coloured voters, by this time on a separate roll, were not consulted, but white voters in South West Africa participated. It was interesting to see how close the voting was in spite of the National Party's huge majority in Parliament: 849,958 voted for a republic and 775,978 against. In March 1961, Dr. Verwoerd attended the Commonwealth prime-ministers' conference in London and there announced South Africa's withdrawal.

The proclamation of the republic was postponed till May 31, 1961, the 51st anniversary of the Union of South Africa. This was called "Republic Day." In spite of the suppression of their major political organisations and the operation of so many new and drastic laws, there were still leaders to be found prepared to call for a stay-at-home on "Republic Day." An "All-in African Council" met in Orlando and then at Pietermaritzburg. The latter meeting was attended by a large number of delegates. The leading figure on this occasion was Nelson Mandela. He had taken a prominent part in the Defiance Campaign and had then been placed under a series of bans which prevented him from attending meetings. His latest ban had ended a few days before the Pietermaritzburg meeting and, by some oversight on the part of the police, had not been renewed. A leader of his calibre and prestige had been lacking hitherto. His dramatic appearance roused the enthusiasm of the delegates and he had little difficulty in persuading the All-in Council to call for a three-day stay-at-home starting on "Republic Day." Following the meeting he "went underground" and organised the stay-at-home in Johannesburg. For a further fifteen months he played hide-and-seek with the police and became known as the "Black Pimpernel." He was finally captured in August 1962. It was rumoured that during the interval he had managed to slip overseas and back again at least once.

The stay-at-home was not an unqualified success. The government too had made its preparations by calling out 5,000 troops and making numerous arrests. The only centre that responded at all well was Port Elizabeth. In Johannesburg a number of Africans stayed away from work on the first day but by the end of the day everyone assumed that the protest had ended.

The government proceeded against those who had attempted to organise the stay-at-home in attending the Orlando and Pietermaritzburg All-in Council conferences. Eleven of the leaders were charged with disseminating documents "to further the aims of a banned organisation," namely, the African National Congress. The persons charged included Duma Nokwe, an African lawyer who had previously been a member of the A.N.C. and three members of the Liberal Party (Jordan Ngubane, H. Bhengu and Julius Mali). Ngubane and Bhengu had resigned from the All-in Council conference, alleging that it was being manipulated by extremists, while Mali declared that he was attending in his personal capacity and not as a member of the Liberal Party. This did not prevent these three from being charged together with the others. The eleven were found guilty by a Johannesburg magistrate and sentenced to a year's imprisonment each. They appealed against the sentences, and in April 1962 Mr. Justice Trollip in the Supreme Court in Pretoria reversed the magistrate's decision. The judge said that the provisions relied on by the State were designed to end the activities of the A.N.C. but nothing in the statute penalised a person or a body for trying, in its own way, to achieve the same objects or aims as those of the African National Congress. The court ordered the convictions and sentences of all the accused to be set aside.

We have seen how, again and again, the government has found that laws aimed at suppressing the activities of liberatory movements have somehow failed to achieve their expected effect when tested in the Supreme Court. The result has always been fresh legislation even more comprehensive and Draconian in scope. The General Law Amendment (Sabotage) Act which followed this decision in June 1962, appeared to be a reply to various acts of sabotage which had occurred during the previous year. These had evidently been the work of two secret organisations—the National Committee for Liberation and Umkonto we Sizwe (the "spear of the Nation"). Attempts had been made to bomb pylons and to set fire to pass and post offices. Incidents had occurred in Johannesburg, Port Elizabeth and Cape Town. One of the would-be bomb throwers had blown himself up. It appeared that the saboteurs were amateurish to a degree. George Peake, a Coloured city councillor of Cape Town was charged with placing a home-made bomb at the back door of Roeland Street Prison. He was caught by two police officers before the bomb went off. In sentencing Peake to two years' imprisonment, the judge said he accepted the prisoner's statement that the bomb was intended as a demonstration and not aimed at injuring anyone.

In Johannesburg, Ben Turok, a leading member of the Congress of Democrats, was sentenced to three years' imprisonment for attempted sabotage. The court found that his fingerprints were found on a package containing a bomb.

The new law provided an extremely wide definition of sabotage and made it a capital offence. It provided for the house-arrest of banned persons to be implemented, if he should deem it fit, by the Minister of Justice. A list of 102 banned persons was published in the Government Gazette. Newspapers were forbidden under the law to publish any statement made by such persons and it was provided that any new newspaper could be made to deposit up to R20,000 (£10,000) before starting, this sum to be forfeit in the case of a breach of the law.

Simultaneously with the publication of the Sabotage Act, the Congress of Democrats was banned under the Unlawful Organisations Act (September, 1962).

The trial of Nelson Mandela which took place in October and November was the occasion for further attempts by former Congress supporters to stage public protests. A "Free Mandela" committee came into being. The government reacted by serving "house arrest" orders on Helen Joseph (previously of the Congress of Democrats), and on Ahmed Kathrada, general secretary of the Transvaal Indian Congress and secretary of the "Free Mandela" committee. A ministerial order banned all meetings in connection with the trial. The trial itself was hastily switched from Johannesburg to Pretoria, where it was thought demonstrations would be less likely to occur. In the course of his trial, Mandela, who conducted his own defence, made a famous speech which South African newspapers were not allowed to publish. It did however appear in the London *Observer* (14 November 1962).

Mandela challenged the right of the Court to hear his case. He considered that he would not be given a fair and proper trial, and that he was neither morally nor legally obliged to obey laws made by a parliament in which he as a black man was not represented. The court could not be regarded as an impartial tribunal where an African stood as an accused. He regarded it as his duty not only to his people but to his profession (he being himself a lawyer) to protest against racial discrimination. He ended by saying:

> "Nothing that this Court can do to me will change in any way that hatred (of the practice of racial discrimination) in me, which can only be removed by the removal of the injustice and the inhumanity which I have sought to remove from the political, social and economic life of this country.
>
> "Whatever sentence Your Worship sees fit to impose upon me for the crime for which I have been convicted before this Court, may it rest assured that when my sentence has been completed I will still be moved, as men are always moved, by their consciences; I will still be moved to dislike of the race discrimination against my people when I come out from serving my sentence, to take up again, as best I can, the struggle for the removal of those injustices until they are finally abolished once and for all."

Mandela was sentenced to three years for incitement and two for leaving the country without a passport. The large crowd of Africans in the court filed slowly out to join hundreds more in the street. Singing "Nkosi sikalela" they were dispersed by the police—without incident.

In the course of his address to the court, Mandela had said: "Already there are indications in this country that people, my people, Africans, are turning to deliberate acts of violence and of force against the government, in order to persuade the government in the only language which this government shows, by its own behaviour, that it understands." A fortnight later, as if to emphasise these words, violence broke out in Paarl.

The town of Paarl lies thirty miles from Cape Town in a valley famous for its vineyards. A large wine and fruit-canning industry had developed in this region and numerous factories exist there. The factories relied mainly on African labour and a typical African location was built at Mbekweni some little distance from the centre of Paarl. The labourers were mostly Xhosas from the Transkei.

The Food and Canning Workers Union had established a branch in Paarl. An African woman, Mrs. Elizabeth Mafekeng had become leader of the local branch of the union. She proved an apt pupil of the Left and visited Bulgaria, Poland and China as a workers' delegate. Following its policy of removing prominent leaders, the government in November 1959 decided to remove her to the Vryburg district in the northern Cape. She was to join the ranks of some eighty African leaders who had been deported from various industrial centres to remote parts of the country. This sparked off riots in the Paarl township of Huguenot. Thousands of Africans and Coloureds demonstrated in protest. Bands of children marched along the streets carrying sticks and shouting "Afrika." The police, wielding batons and lengths of rubber hose, attacked the crowds which had refused to disperse. Shots were fired, not by the police, it was said, but by white civilians. The riot was finally suppressed with the use of armoured cars, but not until a number of shops had been gutted and set on fire.

Elizabeth Mafekeng did not go into exile at Vryburg. She escaped in a car and sought refuge in Basutoland.

Unrest continued in Paarl and throughout the Western Cape. It was accentuated as the government began to implement its policy of removing Africans from that area. The industries in Paarl and throughout the western region had become highly dependent on African labour, and the Government proceeded slowly. African workers who relinquished their jobs had to return to the Transkei and then re-apply for admission to the Western Cape, which was generally refused. According to government statements there were present in 1960 some 150,000 Africans in the Western Cape. These comprised about 65,000 men, 35,000 women and 40,000 children. Between 1959 and 1962 some 26,000 were "endorsed out." Others wishing to visit their Transkeian homes on holiday had difficulty in getting back. The government began deporting the Xhosa women, the wives and consorts, of the location residents. This added fuel to the flames, for it meant that the African men who remained lived more and more a sort of barrack life of frustration and resentment.

The situation was highlighted by the case of Mrs. Mapheele. Her husband worked in a textile factory in Paarl and married her in 1957. He continued to live in the bachelor quarters at Mbekweni but slipped out at night to visit her in the "refugee camp" nearby. In 1962 the authorities discovered that she was illegally resident in the Western Cape and she was ordered to leave. She appealed to the High Court. The judge said he hoped she would be allowed to stay, but the order was perfectly legal. She was deported. The Mapheeles were among many who suffered in this way.

We have already described the Sharpeville emergency of 1960 and the important events which happened in Cape Town and its neighbourhood at that time. It was clear that the Pan-African Congress had gained a considerable following in the area. Following the proscription of the P.A.C. a secret organisation gained members in the various locations and, it seemed, particularly at Mbekweni. The organisation, as subsequently transpired was named Poqo and its aims were frankly terrorist. The word *poqo*, as given in Kropf's *Kaffir English Dictionary* is an adverb meaning *completely*. In the nineteenth century the term *uPoqo* had been used for a "Religious denomination that refused to have anything to do with the white man." The word became popular in underground circles after May 1961 when the Port Elizabeth branch of the Pan-African Congress issued a leaflet opposing the stay-at-home called by the All-in African Council, led by Nelson Mandela. The slogan "Poqo! Poqo! Poqo" was written at the head of the mimeographed leaflet.*

What the relations were between Poqo and the underground P.A.C. was not clear. It seems certain that the two organisations, if not identical, were linked in many ways.

According to an article in *Drum* (February 1963), there was at first no close link between the different Poqo organisations in the Western Cape, but gradually links were formed. A type of "cell" organisation came into being. Members of the individual cells were pledged to secrecy and were not supposed to know the members of other cells. Certain organisers were said to be acquainted with the different cells. Members who gave information to the police were threatened with death. It was said that at least eight people were killed for this reason. Arrests followed the murders and this led to the events of November 1962.

In the early hours of the morning of 21 November 1962, a group of about 100 Africans left the Mbekweni location and advanced on the Paarl police station. They were armed with sticks, spears and pieces of iron. Their intention was to overwhelm the police station and rescue seven of their comrades who were under arrest. The police were advised of their coming, for they had made considerable noise as they marched through

*See an account in *Drum*, February 1963, p. 37.

the town. The police dispersed the attack with rifle-fire, wounding one at least of the attackers and killing two. The band then rampaged through the town, breaking shop windows and setting fire to buildings. Two Europeans, a man and a young woman, who had been aroused and had come out of their houses, were murdered.

Some three hundred and fifty Africans were arrested in connection with the riot. Of the first twenty-one brought to trial, three who were identified as leaders of the Poqo organisation, were sentenced to death. Five were sentenced to 18 years' imprisonment and eight to 12 years'. Those who suffered the extreme penalty were Vezile Jaxa, Lennox Madikane and Mxolosi Damane. A further thirteen who were proved to be members of Poqo were sentenced (22 June 1963) to three years each. For this the State had relied on twenty-one witnesses who had also been members but had elected to give State evidence. When the sentences were pronounced there was a scene in court. The condemned men declared they did not know why they had been sentenced and they refused to leave the court. They were finally dragged from the dock by the police.

Followng the Paarl events the authorities carred out arrests all over the country in an attempt to liquidate the whole Poqo organisation. A statement by one of its leaders, Potlako Leballo, who had escaped to Basutoland after serving a two-year sentence for his part in the Sharpeville events, indicated that the movement was very widespread and had grandiose aims. Speaking to journalists in Maseru in March, 1963, he claimed to be a leader of the banned P.A.C. which had, he claimed, more than 150,000 members. He said: "An uprising will be launched this year. Our revolutionary council is discussing the time and manner in which positive action will be launched It is imminent." Mr. Justice Synman (the Paarl riots commissioner) was correct in finding that the P.A.C. and Poqo were synonymous. Sobukwe was in jail and knew nothing about their plans and activities. The P.A.C.-Poqo organisation was strongest in the Cape with 64,000 members. The Free State was the smallest with 12,000. The organisation was divided into 1,000 strong cells split up into smaller groups. The killings at Paarl and at Bashee (in the Transkei) were carried out by "angry and provoked" cell groups—in the face of opposition from P.A.C. leaders. He had prevented similar outbreaks in

Welkom (O.F.S.) and at Kentani (Transkei). He would give the signal for the revolt. All groups would be told at the same hour to attain certain objectives by violence. But until then political killings would not be approved by the P.A.C. leadership. (Johannesburg *Star*, 25 March 1963.)

How much of this amazing statement by Leballo was truth and how much was fantasy it is impossible to say. In any case, it showed the most naive behaviour on the part of a would-be revolutionary. It was not surprising that rumours began to circulate that members of the P.A.C. were out to "get" him for his betrayal and that he had gone into hiding. No news of his whereabouts has subsequently appeared.

Of the many thousands of alleged members of Poqo scattered throughout the four provinces of South Africa some 3,246 were subsequently arrested,* though not all were brought to trial. Most of them appeared to be young men and their local leaders as unsophisticated as the loquacious Leballo.

CHAPTER XXXVI

TIME LONGER THAN ROPE

VIEWING SOUTH AFRICA in the middle of 1963 one observes a pre-revolutionary situation almost classical in many of its features. There are close parallels, for instance, in the Europe of 1848 where the rule of feudal autocracy was ending and liberalist-nationalist-bourgeois revolutions were the order of the day. Verwoerd appears like some twentieth-century Metternich attempting by force and diplomacy to maintain the old order whose fabric has been strained to breaking point by the march of events.

One after another the states of Africa have achieved political independence. The tide of African nationalism has flowed south to the Zambesi. The Portuguese colonies of Angola and Mozambique and the still nominally British Southern Rhodesia act as buffers to the north. Within South Africa the emancipatory movement has become frankly insurrectionist, all hope of passive resistance and of reform having been abandoned. Its organisations, such as they are, are illegal and must function

---

*According to a statement by the Minister of Justice, in June 1963.

underground. Almost all its prominent leaders are in prison or have fled the country. Abroad they plan intervention and continue their sectional disputes; the A.N.C. versus P.A.C. controversy is transferred to London, Addis Ababa, Dar-es-Salaam.

The South African Government applies ever stronger measures: house arrest, imprisonment without trial under the "ninety-day law," continued incarceration for political prisoners who have served their sentences, the death penalty for sabotage. Albert Luthuli, still nominally leader of the A.N.C., is confined to his home village in Natal. Robert Sobukwe, having served a three-year sentence for leading the anti-pass campaign of 1960, is now a prisoner on Robben Island, to be kept there indefinitely at the Government's pleasure. The possibility of escape from the country has been considerably reduced. Passports are now required for entry to Swaziland, Basutoland and Bechuanaland, and it is reported that the police have considerably strengthened their border patrols.

Since the dramatic arrests of July 1963, when seventeen members of an "executive" (presumably of the Congress Movement) were arrested in a house in the northern suburbs of Johannesburg, it appears that the "nerve centre" of underground resistance has been destroyed. The arrested persons included an Indian, six whites and ten Africans. Among them was Walter Sisulu who had gone into hiding while awaiting an appeal against a six-year sentence for inciting Africans to strike and for being a member of a banned organisation. Govan Mbeki, also arrested, had "gone underground" following the Sharpeville crisis. Ahmed Kathrada, the Indian, was under house arrest when he disappeared some weeks before. The whites included Bob Heppel, son of a former Labour M.P., and Lionel Bernstein and Denis Goldberg, previously members of the banned C.O.D. In December 1963 the accused were on trial on a charge of high treason. Bob Hepple, who was released when he offered to give evidence for the state, fled the country.

But South Africa, though presenting many of the features of a country on the verge of revolution, is not likely to achieve *uhuru* in the immediate future. The pressure for change at the moment is stronger from without than from within. As we have tried to show, the Afrikaner Nationalist Government has great reserves of strength. Price indices of South African industrial shares fell to a low level after Sharpeville (1960). In 1961 they fell again. Since that all-time low they have risen steadily to well above the level of 1959. The Nationalist Party's parliamentary majority gives it complete control of the government, civil service, police and army. So secure does the Government feel that it now encourages immigration of whites from overseas. The official opposition, the United Party, does not offer a serious challenge. It supported the "No-Trial" Bill. The only real opposition in Parliament comes from the single Progressive Party member, Helen Suzman.

South Africa has many characteristics of a totalitarian state. It has acquired these features piecemeal as Parliament legislated to extend *apartheid* and to suppress the revolutionary movement. The Nationalist dictatorship was not established by a revolution or a *coup-d'etat*. It therefore preserves many of the features of democracy (as far as the whites are concerned) and some elements of the rule of law. This latter is now suffering severe erosion, especially since the passing of the "No-Trial" Act,* but in practice the courts still have rights of decision in many matters. Individuals have no power to resist the Minister of Justice when, for instance, he condemns them to house arrest; but should anyone so condemned leave his house he is brought before a magistrate for sentence. Furthermore he has the right of appeal to a higher court. Such rights may seem of dubious value, but these procedures mean that the special police do not operate in complete secrecy. The names of confined persons have hitherto been known to the public, and newspapers can report and comment on arrests and imprisonments. A recent official announcement however may be noted to the effect that the police do not propose to announce the names of persons arrested under the ninety-day law.

As for the newspapers, they are muzzled, but not completely. The Government is still the object of bitter attack by certain papers, and criticism of the state and its policy is not a criminal offence.† Outstanding in its opposition to the Government is the *Rand Daily Mail* edited by Lawrence Gandar. This paper now openly supports the Progressive Party and gives much publicity to the propaganda of the Liberal Party, which it treats as news. The Progressives and Liberals still carry on and

*General Law Amendment Act, 37, of 1963.
†Though persons named under the Suppression of Communism Act may not belong to any organisation which discusses or criticises any form of state.

work among whites and (with difficulty) among blacks. The authorities have the legal power to suppress them. They have refrained from doing so. African newspapers* circulate in increasing numbers in the locations and Reserves. They must be careful about openly attacking the Government, but they give political news of events in South Africa and abroad. Readers know what is happening at UNO, in Kenya, Rhodesia, Ghana.

These vestiges of legality and free speech are considerable, and they exist perhaps for two main reasons: firstly because the Nationalists still have a strong feeling of internal security, and secondly because they have become sensitive to some extent to overseas criticism. A generalisation which would apply here is that freedom of speech is a luxury which a state can afford so long as it does not immediately threaten its existence. Such luxuries are likely to be scrapped at time of serious crisis. That crisis is not yet.

It may be asked what has been the result of the century or more of struggle of the black man for freedom in South Africa which has been described in this book. Organisationally, it seems very little is left, and what little there is must, in the main, function secretly or abroad. Techniques of underground organisation are difficult to learn and the penalties of being found out are considerable. One may suppose however that underground activity will continue. Ideas themselves are difficult to suppress. The liberatory movement has been long at work: its message has penetrated deeply into the minds of hundreds of thousands, perhaps millions of people. While racial discrimination remains, the movement cannot die. There can be no going back to the old system of slavery and rural serfdom.

The most potent factor for change is the industrialisation of the country. This must continue and it must lead (in spite of the Bantustan policy) to increasing economic integration of all races. In spite of legal restrictions the African must become industrialized, westernized, more sophisticated. His unwillingness to accept inferior status based on colour must grow. Ultimately internal pressure for change must rise. If external pressure continues, a change will then be inevitable.

That history has lessons to teach no one will deny. Whether any ruling class has ever taken such lessons seriously is not so certain.

*See Chapter XXVII for an account of the "Bantu" press.

CHRONOLOGICAL SUMMARY OF
CHIEF EVENTS

B.C.

? 5000 Approximate date of earliest Negro skull, found in Fayyum Depression, Egypt.

? 3000-2000. Bantu peoples originate in commingling of Hamites and Negroes.

A.D.

? 1100. Earliest date of building of Zimbabwe.

1486. Discovery of the Cape by Portuguese under Bartolomeo Diaz; first contacts between Europeans and Hottentots.

1497. Vasco da Gama visits East Coast; first contact between Bantu and Europeans at Delagoa Bay.

? 1600. Bantu in what is now Natal.

1652. Dutch settlement at Cape under Jan van Riebeeck.

1658. First slaves imported.

1673. War with Hottentot chief Gonnema.

1688. Arrival of the Huguenots.

1737. George Schmidt, first missionary to Hottentots, founds Moravian mission station at Genadendal.

1770. Gamtoos River the eastern boundary of the Cape; sporadic contacts between Bantu and the settlers.

1779. First Xhosa War.

1780. Great Fish River declared boundary of the Cape.

1792. Genadendal mission station opened for second time.

1793. The amaXhosa occupy the Zuurveld.

1795. First British occupation of the Cape.

1799. Hottentot rebellion. London Missionary Society send first missionaries to the Cape.

1803. Cape returned to the Dutch; Jansens and de Mist sent out by the Batavian Republic.

1806. Second British occupation of the Cape.

1807. Transoceanic slave trade abolished.

1808. Slave rebellion at the Cape; Hooper and Louis hanged.

1809. Hottentot pass law introduced.

1811. The amaXhosa expelled from the Zuurveld.

1818. Makane and Ndlambe defeat Gaika.

1819. Arrival of Dr. John Philip at the Cape. In April Makana leads attack upon Grahamstown; in December the death of Makana.

1822. Beginning of Zulu wars of conquest under Tshaka.

1824. Edwards and Cook expose "prize Negro" racket.

1828. Ordinance 50 grants citizen rights to Hottentots and "all free persons of colour." Death of Tshaka; Dingane king of the Zulu nation.

1834. Emancipation of slaves at the Cape. War with Hintsa.

1835. Lord Glenelg returns the Ciskei to the amaXhosa.

1836. Beginning of the Great Trek.

1837. Voortrekkers enter Natal.

1838. Voortrekkers cross the Vaal River. Battle of Blood River; defeat of Dingane.

1839. Proclamation of the Boer Republic of Natalia.

1842. All non-Europeans in Cape Colony enjoy same rights before the law as white persons.

1843. British annexe Natal.

1846-7. War of the Axe.

1848. British annexe Orange River Territory.

1850-2. War of Umlanjeni.

1854. Orange Free State returned to the Boers. Representative government in the Cape Colony.

1856. Orange Free State makes war upon the Basuto under Moshoeshoe.

1856-7. Cattle-killing among the amaXhosa.

1859. Birth of John Tengo Jabavu.

1860. First Indian indentured labour brought to Natal.

1867. Discovery of diamonds; beginnings of Kimberley.

1868. Basutoland a British protectorate.

1872. Responsible government in Cape Colony; J. C. Molteno first Prime Minister.

1877. Transvaal annexed by British. Gordon Sprigg Prime Minister of Cape.

1878. British war against the Zulus under Cetywayo.

1880. Defeat of Cetywayo. Basuto resist the Disarmament Act. Beginning of First Boer War.

1881. Restoration of South African Republic (Transvaal) to Boers after British defeat at Majuba in 1880.

1882. Paul Kruger President of Transvaal Republic.

1884. *Imvo zabaNtsundu* (Bantu newspaper) established. Nehemiah Tile founds first Bantu Church.

1886. Beginnings of Johannesburg, following upon discovery of gold on the Witwatersrand.

1887. Native Disabilities Removal Act in Cape. Zululand declared British territory.

1890. Cecil Rhodes Prime Minister of the Cape.

1892. Mokone founds Ethiopian Church.

1893. Gandhi arrives in Natal.

1894. Glen Grey Act. Pondoland annexed.

1895. Jameson Raid.

1899. W. P. Schreiner Prime Minister of Cape Colony. Order of Ethiopia formed within the Anglican Church.

1899-1902. Second Boer War; Transvaal and Orange Free State annexed by Great Britain.

1904. Chinese labourers imported to Rand mines.

1905. African People's Organisation founded by Dr. Abdurahman in the Cape.

1906. Indian pass law in Transvaal; passive resistance campaign led by Gandhi. Bambata Rebellion. Founding of *Ilanga lase Natal* by Rev. John Dube.

1907. Transvaal and Orange Free State receive responsible government. Dinizulu imprisoned. Miners strike on Rand. End of Chinese labour plan.

1909. Founding of national South African Labour Party.

1910. Union of the four colonies.

1912. First meeting of South African Native National Congress (later African National Congress); founding of *Abantu-Batho*.

1913. Native Land Act. White miners strike on Rand.

1914. White miners strike on Rand. First World War begins.

1915. Union conquest of South-West Africa. Left socialists break away from Labour Party and form International Socialist League.

1916. Founding of South African Native College at Fort Hare.

1917. Industrial Workers of Africa founded by I.S.L.

1918. "Bucket Strike" in Johannesburg.

1919. A.N.C. leads pass-burning campaign on Rand. Industrial and Commercial Union founded at Cape Town. Shooting at Port Elizabeth (the Masabalala affair).

1920. African miners strike on Rand.

1921. Founding of *Umteteli wa Bantu*. Massacre of Israelites at Bulhoek. Formation of the Communist Party of South Africa.

1922. Massacre of the Bondelswarts. White miners' strike and Rand Revolt; death of Spendiff and Fisher.

1924. Industrial Conciliation Act passed by Smuts Government. Labour-Nationalist Pact electoral victory; white labour policy. Formation of the South African Association of Employees' Organisations. Founding of I.C.U. branch in Johannesburg.

1925. Growth of I.C.U. supported by C.P. S.A.A.E.O. becomes South African Trade Union Congress. First Native night school founded by communists in Ferreirastown, Johannesburg. The Wage Act. Native pass law extended to African women, but A.N.C. win test case against the law.

1926. Kadalie, banned from Natal, defies ban; arrested. Easter congress of the S.A.T.U.C. supports African wage demands at Bloemfontein and protests against ban on Kadalie. Colour Bar Act. Communists expelled from the I.C.U.

1927. S.A. represented at Brussels Conference of League against Imperialism by Gumede, LaGuma, Dan Colraine. I.C.U. at its zenith; Kadalie's visit to Europe. Pact Government's Native Administration Act with "hostility" clause. First African trade unions formed (by communists) on Rand.

1928. S.A.T.U.C. rejects I.C.U.'s application for affiliation. Secession of Natal branch of I.C.U.—to become I.C.U. *yase* Natal. Formation of Non-European Trade Union Federation. Strike of 30,000 African labourers on Lichtenburg diamond diggings. Arrival of W. G. Ballinger as adviser to the I.C.U. Onderstepoort strike; Madeley receives Kadalie and Ballinger with W. H. Andrews, on behalf of I.C.U. *S.A. Worker* appears in English and vernacular. First prosecutions under Native Administration Act.

1929. Nationalist victory in General Election; Pirow Minister of Justice. Kadalie leaves I.C.U., forms Independent I.C.U. Riotous Assemblies Act amended to give deportation powers to Minister of Justice. Beer Riots in Natal; Pirow attacks Africans at Durban with tear gas. S. P. Bunting's Tembuland campaign. C.P. forms League of African Rights and dissolves it immediately upon orders from Comintern.

1930. Enfranchisement of European women renders Cape Coloured vote ineffective. Communists and A.N.C. co-operation in Cape. *S.A. Worker* becomes *Umsebenzi*. Communist pass-burning campaign. Champion banned from Natal. Death of Nkosi on Dingaan's Day.

1931. C.P. driven underground in Natal. Riotous Assemblies Act used against revolutionary leaders. Joint demonstration of black and white unemployed in Johannesburg attacked by police. Diamond imprisoned. Wolton leadership in C.P. expels Bunting, Andrews, Sachs, Weinbren, etc.

1932. Bolshevisation of C.P. under Comintern; influence of Party among Africans declines; Native trade unions antagonised; expulsion of Gana Makabeni; decline of *Umsebenzi*. Communist Native "demonstration candidate" in Germiston by-election; fight against Lodger's Tax; four Party leaders and E. S. Sachs banned from Rand.

1933. Agitation on Rand among African unemployed. Police arrest African leaders. Joint demonstration of black and white unemployed in Johannesburg. C.P. issues *Indlela Yenkuleko* for African intellectuals; contact with Fort Hare students.

1934. C.P. campaign against Grey Shirts. Anti-Pick-up campaign in Johannesburg; *Umsebenzi* popular once more.

1935. C.P. leaders expel more members. Italy's war upon Ethiopia leads to temporary revival of Native movements. *Umvikeli-Thebe* founded; circulation 10,000 but collapses with the defeat of Ethiopia.

1936. Hertzog's Native Representation Act and Land Act passed. First elections under new Act: Basner contests seat in Senate for Transvaal and O.F.S. but is defeated by Rheinallt Jones. Margaret Ballinger and D. B. Molteno elected as Native representatives in Lower House. C.P. attempts to form united front with Labour Party. Collapse of *Umsebenzi*. Founding of Non-European Railway and Harbour Workers' Union.

1937. National Liberation League formed in Cape Town. Africans in Vereeniging location defy Pick-up van.

1938. African trade unions formed by communists. Voortrekker Centenary celebration; formation of the Ossewa-Brandwag.

1939. Soviet-Nazi Pact. Beginning of Second World War. A.N.C. support Government war effort.

1940. First printed issue of *Inkululeko*. Max Gordon interned.

1941. Dadoo in gaol for anti-war speeches; fifty-nine arrested after C.P. meeting in Vereeniging. Arrest of leaders of *Lekhotla la Bafo* for urging arming of Basuto soldiers. Founding of African Mine Workers' Union.

1942. Basutoland leaders of *Lekhotla la Bafo* interned. Seventeen killed, over 100 wounded in shooting at Pretoria municipal compound. War Measure 145. Successful strike of Johannesburg municipal African employees. Basner defeats Rheinallt Jones in election for Senate. Formation of Council of Non-European Trade Unions.

1943. Madeley, Minister of Labour, refuses recognition to African trade unions. Mass police and civic guard raids on Rand, 12,000 arrested in ten days. Commission of Inquiry into African miners' wages. Alexandra Bus Strike. Coloured Advisory Department set up in Cape. Anti-C.A.D. campaign.

1944. Native Mine Wages Commission recommends increase of 5*d.* per shift for underground workers. Shanty Town begins at Orlando. Native Laws Amendment Act. Strike at Brakpan against dismissal of teacher Bopape. Strike of 2,000 milling workers in Johannesburg. Riots at Sophiatown; offices of *Bantu World* burnt out by white mob. Second Alexandra March. *Guardian* sued by mining companies. Anti-Pass Conference in May. War Measure 1,425 prohibits meetings on mine property.

1945. Unity Movement Conference in Cape Town. Anti-C.A.C. campaign continues. Radicals capture Natal Indian Congress.

1946. Asiatic Land Tenure and Indian Representation Act; passive resistance in Natal. Growth of Squatters Movement on the Rand; ejection of squatters from Land near Pimville and Albertynsville. Strike of 60,000 African miners on Rand. Police attack strikers' demonstration march, five killed, many injured. 52 leaders (mostly communists) arrested and charged with conspiracy and promoting an illegal strike. Native Representation Council adjourns as protest against Government's "breach of faith." Xuma, Naidoo and Basner represent South African non-Europeans unofficially at U.N.O. U.N.O. rejects Smuts' plea for incorporation of South-West Africa.

1947. Arising out of miners' strike in previous year, executive committee of Communist Party charged with high treason; after trials lasting nine months, charge withdrawn. Indian passive resistance in Natal against segregation laws. Rev. Michael Scott exposes conditions of near slavery on farms at Bethal, Transvaal. Shanty-town crisis in Johannesburg; squatters clash with police.

1948. Indian passive resisters cross Natal border; Indian leaders, Dadoo and Naicker, imprisoned for defying Immigration Regulation Act of 1913. United Party defeated in general election; D. F. Malan, Nationalist prime minister. Railway *apartheid* introduced in Cape Town. Sam Kahn (Communist) returned as Native representative for Cape Western. Government rejects United Nations' Declaration of Human Rights.

1949. Zulu-Indian riots in Natal. Youth League dominates A.N.C. conference at Bloemfontein; Dr. Moroka replaces Dr. Xuma as president.

1950. Suppression of Communism Act. Communist Party dissolved. Registration Act aims at classifying all South Africans into the separate categories of White, Coloured, Bantu and African to prevent all "crossing the colour line."

1951. Beginning of constitutional struggle to remove Cape Coloured voters from the common role. Torch Commando formed.

1952. Tricentenary celebrations of the landing of van Riebeeck at the Cape. E. S. Sachs ordered to resign from Garment Workers Union; police disperse meeting in Johannesburg. *Guardian* newspaper banned. Kahn expelled from Parliament. Commencement of Defiance Campaign. Anti-white riots at Port Elizabeth and East London.

1953. Criminal Law Amendment and Public Safety Acts. General election: National Party returned with increased majority. Liberal Party and Congress of Democrats formed. Bantu Education Act.

1954. Strike of African school children on Witwatersrand. Ray Alexander returned for Cape Western, but refused admission to Parliament. Malan retires; Strydom prime minister.

1955. Departure from Union Regulation Act. Congress of the People at Kliptown adopts "Freedom Charter."

1956. S. Africa Act Amendment passed at joint sitting of Assembly and enlarged Senate: Cape Coloured voters removed from common role. Commencement of "Treason Trial."

1957. Third Alexandra bus boycott. June 26: stoppage of work in many centres. Immorality Act forbids all forms of sexual relationship between whites and non-whites under severe penalties.

1958. General election: Nationalist Government returned for third term of office. Death of Strydom: Verwoerd prime minister.

1959. University Apartheid Act. Ex-chief Albert Luthuli, President of A.N.C. banished to Groutville, Natal. Bantustan Act passed. Eleven United Party members resign: Progressive Party formed. Many white and black lecturers dismissed from Fort Hare. First Pan-African Congress meets at Orlando: Robert Sobukwe, president. Patrick van Rensburg in London, leads boycott of S. African goods. 300 prosecutions under 1957 Immorality Act, probably only a small proportion of actual offenders.

1960. Abolition of Cape Native representation. Rioting at Cato Manor, Durban; 9 policemen (4 white) killed. Anti-pass demonstrations at Sharpeville (Vereeniging) and Langa (Cape Town), led by Pan-African Congress; many Africans killed and wounded; "state of emergency" declared: hundreds arrested and detained in prison. David Pratt attempts to assassinate the prime minister. Sobukwe sentenced to three year's imprisonment. A.N.C. and P.A.C. banned. Clash between police and tribesmen in Pondoland. Government announces passes for African women. South African voters in referendum decide for a republic: 849,958 for, 775,978 against.

1961. S. Africa leaves Commonwealth. Treason trial ends with acquittal of all accused. Patrick Duncan, Liberal Party leader, banned from attending all meetings. General Law Amendment Act gives authorities sweeping powers to deal with agitators. Riots in Windhoek, South West Africa. All-in African National Council calls for stay-at-home on "Republic Day" (May 31); Government replies by calling up 5000 troops and making numerous arrests; stay-at-home meets with poor response in most centres; ex A.N.C. leader, Nelson Mandela, "goes underground." General election: Nationalists win 105 seats, United Party 49, Progressive Party 1, National Union 1.

1962. Following a number of unsuccessful attempts to blow up post offices and pass-offices, Parliament passes the Sabotage Act, making sabotage a capital offence and providing for house arrest of banned persons; a list of 102 banned persons is published in the Government Gazette. Mandela arrested. Congress of Democrats proscribed. Helen Joseph under house-arrest. Nelson Mandela and Walter Sisulu on trial. Bomb explodes in government office in Pretoria. Paarl riots; two whites killed; over 300 arrests.

1963. Nokwe and Kotane escape to Bechuanaland; subsequently many others follow the same route. Liberal leaders in the Cape, Vigne and Hjul, banned. Leftist newspaper "New Age" suppressed; its successor "Spark" forced to cease publication through banning of editor and staff. Duncan leaves Liberal Party, joins P.A.C. Ninety-Day Law (jail without trial) passed; in September Johannesburg newspaper *Forward* publishes list of 209 "ninety-day" detainees. Arrest of 17 members of alleged "underground executive" at Rivonia, Johannesburg. Four arrested persons, Goldreich, Wolpe, Moolla and Jassat escape from Marshall Square (police headquarters); the first two reach Bechuanaland.

1964. Many members of Umkonto, Poqo, African Resistance Movement arrested on charges of sabotage. Tom Harris convicted of murder for "station bombing." Rivonia trial—Mandela, Sizulu, Goldberg, Mbeki, Mhlaba, Matsoaledi, Mhlangene, Kathrada sentenced to life imprisonment. Eastern Cape A.N.C. and Poqo trials begin. Under 90-day law, 857 Africans, 102 whites, 78 Indians, 58 Coloured held; of these, 272 subsequently convicted and 210 discharged; 241 become state witnesses. Altogether in 1964, 1,604 persons convicted of offences relating to safety of the state. Escapes across the border, chiefly into Bechuanaland, continue. Hostel for refugees in Francistown blown up.

First Transkeian Legislative Assembly begins functioning under Matanzima. Odendaal Commission report on future of South-West Africa. South African representatives remain unpopular at U.N.O. and on associated committees.

1965. Ninety-day law suspended, but new provision made for detention of state witnesses up to 180 days. Heymann and about 13 others detained and Heymann later

443

gaoled as a recalcitrant witness. Numerous further trials for alleged sabotage or membership of A.N.C. or P.A.C. Twelve convicted in Johannesburg Communist trial and sentenced to 1–5 years.

Trialist Bram Fischer goes into hiding 25 January; recaptured 11 November. Authorities attempt complete liquidation of underground A.N.C. in Eastern Cape; of 918 arrested in this area in 1963–4, 514 convicted and sentenced (by Nov. 1965) to total of about 2,580 years. Banning orders extended, particularly against members of Liberal Party and Defence and Aid Fund. Mounting attacks on liberal organizations by S.A. Broadcasting Corp., now openly partizan. Cancellation of visit by U.S.S. *Independence*. Verwoerd states Maoris unacceptable in visiting rugby teams.

Growing evidence of breakdown of industrial colour bar. Many white trade unions abandon "equal pay for equal work."

NOTES

CHAPTER II

1. *A Kafir-English Dictionary*, by A. Kropf.
2. Note though that J. S. Marais, in *Maynier and the First Boer Republic* (1944) brings evidence to show that Ndlambe some years earlier had played just such a role as Gaika played later. In 1793 he had allied himself with certain Boer commandos and had been given a half share in the looted cattle.
3. *Makana's Gathering*, by Thomas Pringle.
4. The passage is quoted in Thomas Pringle's *African Sketches*, published in 1834.
5. Quoted by W. M. Macmillan in *Bantu, Boer and Briton—The Making of the South African Native Problem*. 1929.

CHAPTER III

1. *History of South Africa from 1795 to 1872*, by G. M. Theal.
2. *The Rise of South Africa*, by G. E. Cory.
3. *The Cape Coloured People*, by J. S. Marais. 1939.
4. *Miscegenation*, by George Findlay.

CHAPTER IV

1. *The Cape Coloured People*, by J. S. Marais. 1939.
2. *History of Christian Missions in South Africa*, by J. du Plessis. Longmans, Green and Co., 1911.
3. *The Cape Colour Question*. 1927. *Bantu, Boer and Briton—The Making of the South African Native Problem*, by W. M. Macmillan. 1929.

CHAPTER V

1. *Stories from South African History for Standards IV and V*, by Lancelot M. Foggin, Director of Education, Southern Rhodesia.
2. *Bantu, Boer and Briton*, by W. M. Macmillan. 1929.
3. *History of South Africa from 1795 to 1872*, by J. M. Theal.
4. *Ibid*.
5. This is an example of the use of the word "Bantu" in circumstances where "African" would not do, since Hottentots are clearly Africans.
6. *History of South Africa from 1795 to 1872*, by J. M. Theal.
7. *The Rise of South Africa*, by Sir J. Cory.
8. *The Grahamstown Journal*, volumes for 1856 and 1857.
9. *King William's Town Gazette*, August 14, 1856.
10. *History of South Africa from 1795 to 1872*, by J. M. Theal.

CHAPTER VI
1. *History of South Africa from 1795 to 1872*, by J. M. Theal.
2. *The Native Policy of Sir Theophilus Shepstone*, by J. R. Sullivan, Walker and Snashall, Ltd., Johannesburg.
3. *The Imperial Factor in South Africa*, by C. W. de Kiewiet.

CHAPTER VII
1. *The Life of John Tengo Jabavu*, by his son, Professor D. D. T. Jabavu, Lovedale Press.
2. *The Life of Jan Hendrik Hofmeyr*, by J. H. Hofmeyr. 1913.
3. *Cecil Rhodes*, by William Plomer. 1933.
4. *The Life of John Xavier Merriman*, by Sir Percival Laurence. 1930.
5. *Africa's Peril*, by H. R. Abercrombie.
6. *The Cape Native Franchise*, by E. A. Walker. Cape Town, 1936.

CHAPTER VIII
1. *The African Yearly Register and Black Folks' Who's Who*, edited by T. D. Mweli Skota. R. L. Esson & Co., Johannesburg.
2. *The Seething African Pot, a Study of Black Nationalism, 1882–1935*, by Daniel Thwaite. Constable & Co., 1936.
3. *Historical Records of the Church of the Province of South Africa*, by Cecil Lewis and G. E. Edwards.
4. *Imvo.*

CHAPTER IX
1. *A History of the Zulu Rebellion, 1906*, by J. Stuart. Macmillan & Co., 1913.
2. *Natal Mercury*, February, 1906.
3. *Ibid.*, March, 1906.

CHAPTER X
1. *South and East African Year Book*, published by the Union-Castle Mail Steamship Company, Ltd.
2. *The Tragedy of Gandhi*, by G. Bolton. 1934.

CHAPTER XI
1. *Imvo*, July 19, 1910.
2. *History of Native Policy in South Africa*, by E. H. Brooks. 1924.
3. Johannesburg *Star*, April 4, 1919.

CHAPTER XII
1. *The Transvaal Leader*, January 30, 1911.
2. *Comrade Bill*, by R. K. Cope.
3. *The Inside Story of South African Labour*, by B. Weinbren, a series of articles in *Forward*, 1944.
4. *Cape Argus*, June 11, 1918.

CHAPTER XIII
1. *Reaction to Conquest—Effects of Contact with Europeans on the Pondo of South Africa*, by Monica Hunter. Published by the International

Institute of African Languages and Cultures, Oxford. 1936.
2. *The Operation of the Mandate System in Africa, 1919–27*, by Rayford W. Logan. Washington, 1942.

CHAPTER XIV
1. *The Anatomy of African Misery*, by Lord Oliver. 1927.
2. Report in the *International*.
3. *Cape Times*, March 13, 1922.

CHAPTER XV
1. "The Masabalala Bloody Upheaval," an article by Captain S. Henry Kemp in the *Illustrated Bulletin*, May, 1946.
2. Johannesburg *Star*.
3. *The Truth about the I.C.U.* 1927.

CHAPTER XVI
1. *The Star*, November 15, 1928.
2. *Ibid.*, November 3, 1928.
3. *Ibid.*, November 2, 1928.
4. *The Times*, London, December 27, 1928.
5. *Reaction to Conquest—Effects of Contact with Europeans on the Pondo of South Africa*, by Monica Hunter. Published by the International Institute of African Languages and Cultures, Oxford. 1936.

CHAPTER XXVI
1. *The Impending Strike of African Mineworkers*. A statement by the African Mineworkers' Union, August 7, 1946.

SUGGESTIONS FOR FURTHER READING

Brookes, E. H. and J. B. Macaulay. *Civil Liberty in South Africa.* 1958.
Carter, Gwendolen. *Politics of Inequality in South Africa.* 1958.
Doxey, G. V. *Industrial Colour Bar in South Africa.* 1961.
Feit, Edward. *South Africa: Dynamics of the African National Congress.* 1962.
Hooper, Charles. *Brief Authority.* 1959.
Horrell, Muriel. *South African Trade Unionism.* 1961.
Kuper, Leo. *Passive Resistance in South Africa.* 1956.
Lewin, Julius. *Politics and Law in South Africa.* 1963.
Luthuli, Albert. *Let my People Go.* 1962.
Palmer, Mabel. *History of the Indians in Natal.* 1957.
Patterson, Sheila. *Colour and Culture in South Africa* (about the Cape Coloured People). 1953.
———. *Last Trek* (about the Afrikaners). 1957.
Roberts, Margaret. *Labour in the Farm Economy.* 1958.
Sachs, E. S. *Choice before South Africa.* 1952.
Sampson, Anthony. *Treason Cage.* 1958.
Shepperson, George and Thomas Price. *Independent African.* 1958.
United Nations: *Reports on the Racial Situation in South Africa.* 1953–1955.
Van Rensburg, Patrick. *Guilty Land.* 1962.

INDEX

449

451

455

457

National Convention (1908), 70
Nationalism (black, African),
367, 369, 403, 404, 421.
See also Pan-Africanism
Nationalist Government
(1948—), 366 *et seq.*, 378 *et
seq.*, 384 *et seq.*, 397, 412-4,
415, 418-20, 421-4, 426-7,
431-2
Nationalists (Afrikaner, Party),
111, 125, 128, 152, 159, 179,
183, 184, 193, 198, 199, 223,
224, 259, 260, 282-3, 303,
304, 307, 308, 314, 355, 356,
359, 361, 364, 414
National Liberation League, 357
National Trust, 351-2
National Union of Railway and
Harbour Servants
(N.U.R.A.H.S.), 155
National Union of South African
Students, 345-6
"Native," xiii, 8
Native Administration Act, 159,
165, 175, 203, 212, 213 *et
seq.*, 229. *See also* Hostility
Laws
Native Affairs Act (1920), 288
Native Affairs Department, 136,
193, 238, 247, 250, 266, 300,
358, 394. *See also* Bantu
Affairs Department
Native Bakers' Union, 207
Native Bills (Hertzog's),
286-301 *passim*
Native Christians, 80 *et seq.*,
86, 109
Native Clothing Workers'
Union, 207, 209 *et seq.*, 327
Native Convention, 108-9
Native Disabilities Removal Act,
59 *et seq.*

Native electorate (1882–1886),
58
Native Franchise Act (1892), 64
Native Labour Corps, 113
Native labour recruitment, 123
Native Land Act (1913), 74-6,
108, 110, 224, 286, 287, 350
Native Land and Trust Act,
286, 287 *et seq.*
Native Land Trust, 288
Native Laundry Workers'
Union, 207, 327
Native Laws Amendment Act
(1937), 60
Native Liquor Clause, 59
Native Location Act, 59
Native Mattress and Furniture
Workers' Union, 207
Native Mine Clerks' Association,
159
Native Mine Workers Union, 335
Native Representation Act,
286-7, 292, 293, 298
Native Representative Council,
286-8, 294, 297-9, 310, 320,
340, 377
Native Representatives, 379,
382, 383, 415, 418
Native Reserves, 52, 87 *et seq.*,
375. *See also* Bantustans
Natives (Abolition of Passes and
Co-ordination of Documents)
Act (1952), 373
Native Service Contract Act, 268
Native Services Transport Act,
398
Native Urban Areas Act, 244,
249, 252, 260-2
Natotsibeni, Queen Regent, 111
Ncwana, Bennet, 199
Ncwangu, James, 268

461

467